# Presumption of Guilt: The Global Overuse of Pretrial Detention

Copyright © 2014 Open Society Foundations.

This publication is available as a pdf on the Open Society Foundations website under a Creative Commons license that allows copying and distributing the publication, only in its entirety, as long as it is attributed to the Open Society Foundations and used for noncommercial educational or public policy purposes. Photographs may not be used separately from the publication.

ISBN: 978-1-936133-84-0

PUBLISHED BY:
Open Society Foundations
224 West 57th Street
New York, New York 10019 USA
www.OpenSocietyFoundations.org

FOR MORE INFORMATION CONTACT:
Martin Schönteich
Senior Legal Officer
Criminal Justice Program
Martin.Schoenteich@OpenSocietyFoundations.org

Design and layout by John Emerson, backspace.com
and Heather Van De Mark, heathervandemark.com

Printed by GHP Media, Inc.

Cover photo © Benedicte Kurzen/NOOR for the Open Society Foundations

# Table of Contents

| | |
|---|---|
| Acknowledgments | i |
| Executive Summary & Recommendations | 1 |
| Introduction | 7 |
| **The Scope of Pretrial Detention Around the World: Its Extent and Cost** | **11** |
| Introduction | 11 |
| The Extent of Pretrial Detention | 15 |
| The Cost of Pretrial Detention | 28 |
| Conclusion | 31 |
| **Who Are the World's Pretrial Detainees?** | **33** |
| Introduction | 33 |
| The Poor | 33 |
| Marginalized Minorities and Non-Citizens | 49 |
| The Mentally Ill and Intellectually Disabled | 51 |
| Low-Risk Defendants, Persons Accused of Minor Offenses, and the Innocent | 53 |
| Conclusion | 55 |
| **Circumstances of Detention and Impact on Detainees and their Communities** | **57** |
| Introduction | 57 |
| Worse off than Convicted Prisoners | 57 |
| Circumstances of Detention | 61 |
| Health Consequences of Detention for Detainees and their Communities | 76 |

| | |
|---|---|
| Economic Impact on Detainees and their Families | 81 |
| Criminogenic Impact of Detention | 91 |
| Conclusion | 93 |

## The Causes of Arbitrary and Excessive Use of Pretrial Detention — 95

| | |
|---|---|
| Introduction | 95 |
| The Presumption of Innocence: An Elusive Aspiration | 96 |
| Imprecise Laws Lead to Arbitrary Application | 98 |
| Restrictive Laws Promote Pretrial Detention | 100 |
| Flouting Limits on Detention | 101 |
| Public Pressure and Populist Policy Responses | 101 |
| Dearth of Political Will | 103 |
| Police and Prosecutorial Influence | 104 |
| Corruption | 106 |
| Procedural Factors | 108 |
| Lack of Coordination between Criminal Justice Agencies | 109 |
| The Role of Limited Resources | 111 |
| Inadequate Legal Representation and Assistance | 113 |
| Conclusion | 115 |

## The Implications for the Rule of Law — 117

| | |
|---|---|
| Introduction | 117 |
| Arbitrary Arrest and Detention | 118 |
| Restricted Access to Legal Counsel | 121 |
| Duration of Detention | 123 |
| Lack of Redress and Accountability | 125 |

| | |
|---|---|
| Mass Releases Due to Overcrowding | 126 |
| Impact on Public Confidence | 127 |
| Conclusion | 129 |

## Reducing the Arbitrary and Excessive Use of Pretrial Detention — **130**

| | |
|---|---|
| Introduction | 130 |
| Political Conditions that Support Pretrial Detention Reform | 130 |
| Laws and Policies to Reduce Pretrial Detention | 133 |
| The Role of Data in Assessing the Problem | 137 |
| Coordination between Criminal Justice Agencies | 140 |
| Reducing the Number of People Who Come into Conflict with the Law | 142 |
| The Role of Lawyers and Paralegals | 148 |
| Government Programs that Reduce Pretrial Detention | 159 |
| Conclusion | 172 |

## Conclusion — **174**

## Appendix: International and Regional Standards, Norms, and Jurisprudence — **175**

## Bibliography — **182**

## Endnotes — **203**

## ACKNOWLEDGMENTS

This report was written by Martin Schönteich, senior legal officer for the Open Society Justice Initiative's Criminal Justice program. Chapter Five, Implications for the Rule of Law, was contributed by Robert O. Varenik, program director for the Justice Initiative. The book was edited by David Berry, with the assistance of Kate Epstein. The author wishes to acknowledge the valuable contributions of many Open Society Foundations colleagues, including Denise Tomasini-Joshi, Ina Zoon, Jonathan Birchall, Kersty McCourt, Madeleine Crohn, Robert O. Varenik, Stanley Ibe, Edit Turcsan Bain, Marina Ilminska, Borislav Petranov, Louise Ehlers, and Mary Miller Flowers. Invaluable research was provided by Anna Husarska, Alina Finkelshteyn, Ari Brochin, Elena Kravtsoff, Steven Primeaux, and Iya Megre. Special thanks are due to the Open Society Foundations Human Rights Initiative for providing support for the research and publication of this report.

The Open Society Justice Initiative bears sole responsibility for any errors.

# Executive Summary & Recommendations

The arbitrary and excessive use of pretrial detention around the world is a massive form of human rights abuse that affects in excess of 14 million people a year. The right to be presumed innocent until proven guilty is well established. Yet this right is violated widely and often—in the developed and developing world alike—and the violation goes largely unnoticed. Few rights are so broadly accepted in theory, but so commonly abused in practice. It is fair to say that the global overuse of pretrial detention is one of the most overlooked human rights crises of our time.

Given that the presumption of innocence is universal, detaining arrestees pending trial should be rare. However, many jurisdictions around the world violate the principle that pretrial detention should be used sparingly, as a last resort. Instead, it has become the default setting of criminal justice systems.

One out of three people behind bars has not been found guilty of a crime. In some parts of the globe, pretrial detainees outnumber convicted prisoners. At this moment, 3.3 million people are in pretrial detention worldwide. And that is a conservative estimate, because official data ignore the tens of thousands of people detained in police stations. Cutting the number of pretrial detainees could resolve prison overcrowding, limit the spread of disease, reduce poverty, and spur development.

During the course of an average year, approximately 15 million people are admitted into pretrial detention. Some of them are detained for a few days or weeks, but many will spend months and even years waiting for their day in court. Council of Europe countries have some of the most developed criminal justice systems in the world, yet their average period of pretrial detention is almost half a year. The present global cohort of 3.3 million pretrial detainees will collectively spend an estimated 660 million days in detention—a terrible waste of human potential that comes at a considerable cost to states, taxpayers, families, and communities.

Most pretrial detainees are poor, and economically and politically marginalized. The poor and powerless lack the money to hire a lawyer, procure bail (or bond), or pay a bribe—all tools to secure pretrial release in many jurisdictions. Poor and marginalized people also lack the social and political connections and influence that can facilitate pretrial release in many places.

Ethnic and religious minorities and foreigners are significantly overrepresented in pretrial detention systems. Dalits in South Asia, indigenous people in Australia and Canada, and ethnic minorities in Israel and the United States are grossly overrepresented in pretrial detention. Mentally ill and intellectually challenged persons also face disproportionate risk of being held in pretrial detention.

Many pretrial detainees will eventually be released without trial, or tried and acquitted. Many others will be found guilty but ultimately receive a non-custodial sentence for a minor offense, or be sentenced to less time than they have already served. In England and Wales—a jurisdiction that uses pretrial detention relatively sparingly—over half of all pretrial detainees ultimately are acquitted or receive a non-custodial sentence. Among juvenile pretrial detainees the proportion receiving a non-custodial sentence or an acquittal is even higher. In Bolivia and Liberia, where between 80 and 90 percent of all prisoners are pretrial detainees, few detainees will ever be convicted of a crime that carries a prison sentence.

There are situations under which pretrial detention is warranted. When there is good reason to think an arrestee—if released—will commit a crime, threaten a witness, or abscond, he should be held pending trial. But these conditions do not apply to most pretrial detainees. The vast majority of pretrial detainees pose no threat to society and can be safely released pending trial. Simply put, they should not be in pretrial detention.

It is a cruel irony that many jurisdictions treat pretrial detainees worse than they treat convicted prisoners. Pretrial detainees are often held in police lockups—facilities not designed for long-term occupancy, where conditions can be particularly crowded and harsh—for extended periods of time. Prison systems treat pretrial detainees as temporary and incidental and therefore devote fewer resources to them. Compared to sentenced prisoners, pretrial detainees have less access to food, beds, health care, and exercise.

While convicted prisoners are often segregated into low-, medium-, and high-security facilities, a pretrial detainee charged with minor theft will be confined in the same facilities as someone charged with a serious violent crime. Pretrial detainees are at greater risk of not being separated according to age and gender. Many jurisdictions confine juvenile pretrial detainees with adults, especially in police lockups, and in some places women are confined with men.

Especially in resource-poor countries, pretrial detainees are likely to be confined with convicted prisoners. This exposes pretrial detainees to a hardened offender subculture, where violence, abuse, and criminal gangs dominate daily life. In such places, pretrial detainees suffer the most and are often denied food, a bed, blankets, clothing, and other necessities.

The particularly poor conditions afforded pretrial detainees serve an instrumental purpose. In numerous jurisdictions, police and prosecutors seek to use the pretrial detention period as an opportunity to obtain confessions that will lead to a conviction. Many authorities condone deplorable pretrial detention conditions as a tool to induce arrestees to incriminate themselves in order to achieve a non-custodial sentence or transfer to a prison with better conditions. In some places, pretrial detainees are routinely assaulted and tortured to get them to confess to the charges against them. Assistance from international donors, intended to enhance the capacity of law enforcement, may be accelerating global detention without addressing its excesses.

## Sample Timeline of Pretrial Detention and Its Consequences

Arrest — Police Station — Bribes expected — Interrogation — Risk of torture — Booking — Inadequate legal assistance — Detention — Economic hardship on family — Exposure to violent detainees

Miserable conditions, the heightened risk of torture and abuse, and uncertainty about the outcome of their impending trials all contribute to a high incidence of mental health problems among pretrial detainees. According to the World Health Organization, suicide rates among pretrial detainees are three times higher than those of convicted prisoners.

It is not only detainees who are harmed by the arbitrary and excessive use of pretrial detention—the damage spreads outward to their families, communities, and the state. The overuse of pretrial detention threatens public health, feeds corruption, undermines the rule of law, and stunts socioeconomic development.

Prisons serve as vectors for the spread of communicable diseases and aggravate existing health problems for pretrial detainees and those they come into contact with after their release. Infectious diseases, including HIV/AIDS, hepatitis, and tuberculosis, are common in pretrial detention facilities, while proper health care services are not. For this reason, pretrial detention has been described by one expert as "a death sentence."

In addition to spreading disease, pretrial detention spreads corruption—in fact, excessive pretrial detention and corruption are mutually-reinforcing. The pretrial phase receives less scrutiny than subsequent stages of the criminal justice process, giving discretion to the lowest paid and most junior actors in the system. Unhindered by accountability, the police, prosecutors, and judges may arrest, detain, and release individuals based on their ability to pay bribes. This arbitrary abuse of power destroys the justice system's credibility and undermines the rule of law in general, which can weaken governance overall.

Pretrial detention also critically undermines socioeconomic development, and is especially harmful to the poor. Not only does pretrial detention disproportionately affect individuals and families living in poverty, but the financial impact is greater. The detainee, of course, cannot earn income, and may lose his job. His family faces economic hardship due to lost income and the cost of visiting and maintaining the detainee, which can include medical expenses and bribes. And the state not only bears the direct costs (such as prison construction and guards) of jailing someone who should be presumed innocent, but it also loses out on the economic contributions (such as taxes paid) that the detainee could have made if he were released pending trial.

Virtually every country in the world could materially benefit from reducing its pretrial detention population. European taxpayers spend some $18 billion annually on incarcerating and managing the pretrial detainees in their jurisdictions. In the United States, the average annual cost to the state of detaining a juvenile is higher than the annual tuition at Harvard University. A reduction in the pretrial detention population could generate significant savings which governments could use to prevent crime through investment in education and social services, or, where

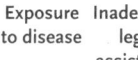

Investigation | Incarceration with hardened criminals | Loss of livelihood | Hearing | Exposure to disease | Inadequate legal assistance | Inability to afford bail | Harm to mental health | Loss of housing | Trial

needed, to combat crime directly through recruiting more police officers or improving their equipment.

The societal costs of excessive pretrial detention even extend into the future. Most prison environments are criminogenic; that is, prisons serve as breeding grounds for crime. Prisons psychologically harm incarcerated people, making it more difficult for them to live normal, productive lives, and more likely that they may take up crime. Being incarcerated once increases the chances that a person will be incarcerated again. And the harms reach into the next generation: Detention of parents is associated with negative outcomes for their children, including increased propensity for violence and other antisocial behaviors, increased likelihood of suffering anxiety and depression, decreased school attendance, and increased likelihood that they will also be incarcerated one day.

The manifold harms associated with the overuse of pretrial detention suggest the urgent need for remedy. But first it is necessary to understand the causes of the arbitrary and excessive use of pretrial detention. Why are so many theoretically-innocent people behind bars? Clearly, the gap between rights (the presumption of innocence) and reality (massive and arbitrary detention of people who have not been found guilty) is considerable. Many states have vague laws governing the application of pretrial detention, which fail to protect the presumption of innocence. Others have bad laws that directly flout it. Some jurisdictions lack the resources to operate a fair and efficient criminal justice system, while others may be warped by corruption or fears of being soft on crime.

Fortunately, positive reforms are possible. Both Finland and Singapore, for example, have shown that proactive and coherent policies can limit the unnecessary use of pretrial detention. In New Zealand and South Africa, the use of diversion and community-based conflict resolution mechanisms has limited the number of arrestees. In Malawi and Sierra Leone—among the poorest countries in the world—paralegal-based interventions have demonstrated how pretrial detainees can be released expeditiously in places with few lawyers. In Nigeria and the United Kingdom, duty solicitors at police stations are getting arrestees released pretrial. Australia and Mexico have seen results from pretrial evaluation services, which identify arrestees unlikely to abscond or commit a violent crime if released pending trial. In Chile and Germany, new laws have increased the use of alternatives to pretrial detention. In Liberia and India, "camp courts"—prison-based courts that hear bail applications—are succeeding in fast-tracking the release of defendants who have been remanded to detention by their countries' overburdened regular courts. Measures like these can be extended to other jurisdictions, and thereby lessen the problem of arbitrary and excessive pretrial detention around the world.

The global overuse of pretrial detention is a widespread, deeply harmful, yet frequently overlooked, human rights violation. The following recommendations are offered toward redress.

## Recommendations

To international and regional institutions and bodies:

- ▸ Call upon national governments to uphold and respect international and regional standards and norms regarding the use and conditions of pretrial detention—in particular, to focus their technical assistance and monitoring

- Support the gathering of accurate statistics on pretrial detention practices by jurisdictions worldwide. This should include data on the exceptionality or frequency of use of pretrial detention, the number of pretrial detainees held in police cells or lockups, the duration of pretrial detention, and accused persons' compliance with the conditions of pretrial release.

- Document and disseminate good practices that reduce the arbitrary and excessive use of pretrial detention. Such knowledge sharing should be complemented by context-specific national-level assistance, monitoring, and documentation so that country-level learning strengthens both ongoing efforts at improving pretrial justice delivery nationally and similar interventions elsewhere.

- Promote criminal justice reform models that pay due attention to the pretrial stage of the criminal justice process. This should include, at a minimum, crime prevention and diversionary schemes which reduce the number of arrestees entering the criminal justice system; mechanisms which provide legal aid or assistance for accused persons expeditiously after their arrest; legally mandated and adequately resourced alternatives to pretrial detention; full judicial discretion to release accused persons awaiting trial irrespective of the charge(s) against them; and, regular judicial review of prior pretrial detention decisions.

- United Nations Security Council resolutions should provide mandates to its field operations, thereby authorizing the latter to undertake—or support government efforts to undertake—assessments of the pretrial detention situation in their countries of operation.

- The United Nations General Assembly's Social, Humanitarian and Cultural Committee and/or Legal Committee should mandate a report and thematic debate on the global overuse of pretrial detention and remedial interventions to address the problem.

- The Office of the High Commissioner for Human Rights should ensure that reports, views, and recommendations from UN Special Procedures and Treaty Bodies relating to pretrial detention and related problems are excerpted for each country within the Universal Periodic Review process.

To donors and development agencies:

- Include pretrial justice reform in the planning of any criminal justice reform strategy supported through donor funds. This should include funding for assessments to identify the underlying drivers of the excessive and arbitrary use of pretrial detention, and to identify intervention points for improving day-to-day pretrial detention practices.

- Invest in pretrial detention reforms in a holistic and sustainable manner. Long-term interventions that address simultaneously the multiple challenges affecting pretrial justice systems have the greatest chance of success. Such investments should include monitoring and documentation efforts to improve learning from past interventions and promote the long-term and sustainable national-level political and operational commitment to improve pretrial justice practices.

- Leverage increased funding and development aid for pretrial detention reform by linking improved pretrial justice practices to protecting not only the rights and wellbeing of detainees themselves, but also wider societal benefits such as reduced torture and corruption, improved public health, and better performance of criminal justice systems.

To national governments:

- Modernize the legal framework and associated institutional practices governing pretrial detention to bring them in line with applicable law. This may include repealing laws and practices which make pretrial detention mandatory for persons charged with certain offenses; establishing and funding the provision of quality legal aid and assistance and providing them as soon as possible after arrest; requiring prosecutors who are requesting pretrial detention to demonstrate before a court that pretrial detention is an option of last resort; and promulgating statutory alternatives to pretrial detention.

- Invest strategically in the "front end"—or pretrial phase—of the criminal justice process, in order to generate improvements and savings throughout the system. Ensure that sufficient resources are allocated to avoid delays and excessive detention—for example, by supporting mechanisms to alert courts when detainees have been held for excessively long periods. Provide support for practical alternatives to pretrial detention.

- Develop a sustained national strategy to limit the use of pretrial detention and encode it as an exceptional measure only. Such a strategy should involve the collaboration of all criminal justice agencies, including the judiciary and the legal profession, as well as relevant civil society organizations.

To criminal justice practitioners and officials:

- Develop coordinated inter-agency efforts to regularly review weaknesses and related challenges in the pretrial justice process. These should be jointly identified and then addressed collectively at the national, regional, and local level.

- Develop data collection capacities which can consistently gather information on the performance of the criminal justice system during the pretrial phase, both for day-to-day operational purposes and strategic planning and evaluation purposes.

- Collaborate with civil society organizations to improve the delivery of pretrial services—both to pretrial detainees directly and to criminal justice agencies in cases where the state is unable to do so or has elected not to provide such services.

# Introduction

Detaining a person before he is found guilty of a crime is a particularly draconian decision for the state to make. Pretrial detention is one of the most severe things that can happen to a person: the detainee immediately loses his freedom, and can also lose his family, health, home, job, and community ties. As a senior British probation officer put it:

> When a person is remanded in custody, they can lose their accommodation, their job, be locked away for 23 hours each day, and endure the pressures, hazards and indignities of prison life. Remand prisoners have inadequate access to legal representation, their prison conditions whilst on remand are poorer than their sentenced counterparts, and the suicide rate amongst remandees is very high. Such defendants suffer regular invasions of privacy each time they are searched and often fear danger from those incarcerated with them.[1]

Persons in pretrial detention have not been convicted of a crime.[2] They should be considered innocent and as far as practicable be treated as such. Pretrial detainees become convicts only once their guilt has been proven in front of an impartial tribunal. Many pretrial detainees around the world are arrested and detained on flimsy evidence. A significant number of pretrial detainees eventually have the charges against them withdrawn, or are acquitted of their charges. Other pretrial detainees receive a noncustodial sentence upon their conviction because of the relatively trifling nature of their crimes, or receive a sentence that is actually less than the amount of time they have been in pretrial detention.

On an average day, some 3.3 million people are in pretrial detention worldwide, according to information provided by national prison systems. The real figure is likely to be higher, since official data rarely count those confined in police stations, for example. Pretrial detainees await trial in confinement by the state; they have not been convicted of the charge(s) for which they have been detained and are therefore legally innocent under international law and many national laws. Pretrial detainees the world over are disproportionately likely to be poor and marginalized individuals—those unable to afford the "three B's" crucial for pretrial release: bail, bribe, or barrister.

Although they should be presumed innocent, pretrial detainees are often held in conditions worse than those of sentenced prisoners. Torture, overcrowding, and disease are rampant. Even in developed countries, so few resources are dedicated to pretrial detention that access to food, healthcare, a bed, or exercise is severely constrained.

Collectively, today's cohort of 3.3 million pretrial detainees will spend some 660 million person days in pretrial detention.[3] These numbers serve as a glaring indictment of governments' cavalier attitude to the presumption of innocence, a cornerstone of any criminal justice system based on the rule of law.

This report does not advocate for the abolition of pretrial detention. Unlike, for example, cruel and unusual punishment or torture, pretrial detention does not, per se, constitute a human rights violation. International human rights norms recognize the need for pretrial detention provided it is applied fairly, rationally, and sparingly.

In rare cases, pretrial detention serves important functions: namely, to ensure that arrestees who pose a risk of absconding stand trial; that arrestees who present a violent danger to the community do not commit serious crimes pending trial; and that unscrupulous arrestees do not intimidate witnesses or otherwise interfere with the lawful collection of incriminating evidence. The right to personal liberty and the presumption of innocence require, however, that strict and carefully circumscribed criteria be met before the imposition of pretrial detention.

As this report documents, the majority of the world's pretrial detainees should not be in detention. Many pretrial detainees were arrested on minor charges. A significant number of pretrial detainees, even in countries with well-resourced and professionally staffed criminal justice agencies, will not be convicted of the charges that led to their arrest and detention. Many others will receive a noncustodial sentence for a minor offense. The majority of such arrestees would likely pose no risk to public security or the administration of justice if they awaited trial at liberty rather than in detention. Moreover, the design of the pretrial detention facility makes it likely that police will pressure them for false confessions. Violence, torture, and related physical and psychological abuses of prisoners are particularly concentrated during the pretrial stage of the criminal justice process, not least because police and others use these means to extract confessions from detainees.

Little public sympathy exists for pretrial detainees and their plight. Many people mistakenly believe that detainees should be presumed guilty by virtue of their detention status. Yet, the devastating societal impacts of the excessive and arbitrary use of pretrial detention should generate opposition to this practice.

Lack of awareness about the overuse of pretrial detention and its pernicious effects may be one reason why there is not more opposition to it. There is no extant resource that catalogues the extent of the arbitrary and excessive use of pretrial detention, its causes, or the many problems attendant to it. This report is the first attempt to comprehensively document the global overuse of pretrial detention and the damage it does.

This report begins by examining the extent of pretrial detention and its costs. It then looks at who is in pretrial detention, and the circumstances of their confinement. It considers the many causes of the excessive and arbitrary use of pretrial detention and implications for the rule of law. Finally, it looks at ways the problem can be addressed, including successful models from around the world.

A rational and effective pretrial justice system needs to balance two potentially competing rights: the right of arrestees to personal liberty and to be presumed innocent until convicted, versus the right of the community to live in safety and see arrestees stand trial and, if the evidence so indicates, convicted and punished. To achieve this balance in compliance with internationally accepted norms and standards is no easy task.

Although the problem of excessive pretrial detention is widespread and the harms stemming from it are severe, it is possible to reduce its overuse. This report explores changes made in a broad diversity of places and contexts, including

Argentina and Australia, India and Ireland, Malawi and Mexico, Sierra Leone and Singapore, Uganda and Ukraine. In all of these places, innovative interventions and reforms have succeeded in rationalizing and improving pretrial detention regimes, often under difficult circumstances. Positive, rights-based change is possible.

We are only beginning to understand the scale and consequences of pretrial detention around the world, and what can be done to improve pretrial practices in a variety of settings. Even though almost every third prisoner worldwide is a pretrial detainee, very little has been written on the topic of pretrial detention. This report seeks to fill that gap.

This report draws from an extensive global review of existing information, including reports by regional and international organizations and entities, national human rights commissions, ombudsman offices, governmental and non-governmental organizations, academia, and the media. The report includes the findings of numerous country-specific investigations undertaken by the Open Society Justice Initiative and its partners, and Open Society Foundations' grantees; much of which was not previously available. Interviews with criminal justice officials, lawyers, academics, experts from the non-governmental sector, and pretrial detainees and their families have provided a rich and nuanced source of information which is incorporated into the report.

Although this report attempts to be as comprehensive as possible, it should be viewed as an initial exploration of the global overuse of pretrial detention, rather than the last word on the subject. It is hoped that this report will serve as a springboard for further research and reform.

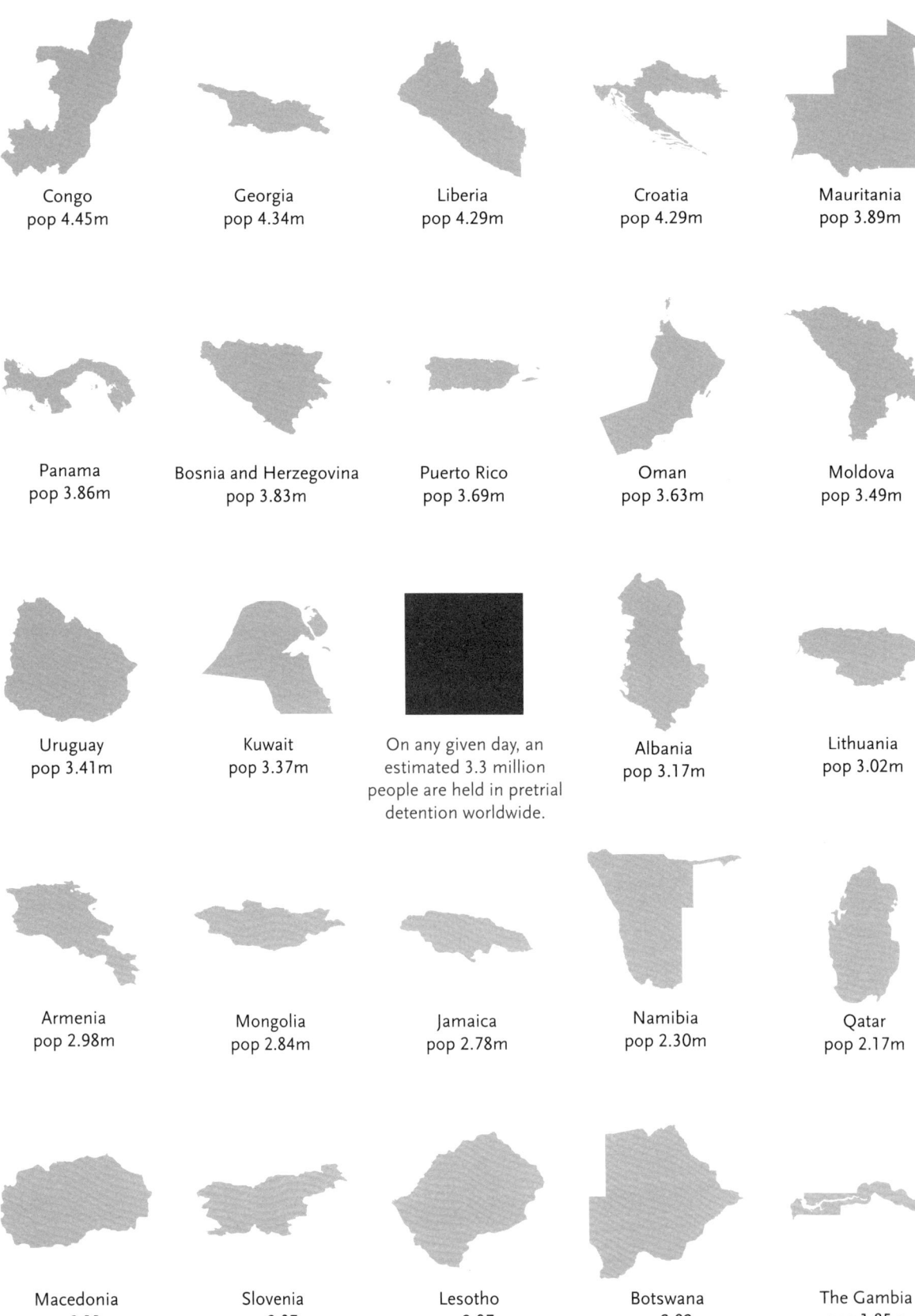

# The Scope of Pretrial Detention Around the World: Its Extent and Cost

## INTRODUCTION

At this moment, an estimated 3.3 million people are in pretrial detention worldwide, according to information provided by national prison systems.[1] Because of systematic undercounting, the real figure is likely to be higher: for example, pretrial detainees confined in police stations are typically not included in the official data.

Worldwide, almost every third prisoner is a pretrial detainee. In parts of the globe—including Central and West Africa and South Asia—the majority of prisoners are pretrial detainees. In some countries such as Bangladesh, India, Nigeria, and Paraguay, pretrial detainees comprise over two-thirds of all prisoners. These are persons who have not been convicted of the crimes they have been charged with and who should be presumed innocent. In numerous jurisdictions, a significant proportion of pretrial detainees are never convicted.

Collectively, the roughly 3.3 million persons in pretrial detention today will spend 660 million days in pretrial detention. Some will only spend a few days in detention, but many will languish for weeks, months, and even years before their trials are completed or charges dismissed. Even among Council of Europe countries, whose criminal justice systems are relatively well resourced and efficient, the average length of pretrial detention is almost half a year.

The sheer number of pretrial detainees and the amount of time they are held belie states' professed commitment to the presumption of innocence and starkly illustrate the extent to which excessive pretrial detention undermines human potential. The overuse of pretrial detention inflicts enormous costs on detainees, their families, and communities. Most pretrial detainees are young men in what should be their prime earning years. Many are productive members of society who are generating an income at the time of their arrest, often providing material support to their families and households.

Most pretrial detainees are suspected of relatively minor, non-violent offenses, and are unlikely to receive a custodial sentence if convicted.[2] A significant number of pretrial detainees are also never convicted of the charges which led to their detention in the first place.[3] This is because many are innocent and are acquitted after trial, or because the state is, for a variety of reasons, unable or unwilling to proceed with a trial.

Pretrial detention not only prevents millions of people from earning a living, it costs states—and by implication, taxpayers—billions every year. Council of Europe countries spent US$18 billion in 2010 incarcerating some 370,000 pretrial detainees.[4] Almost half the world's countries had a Gross Domestic Product (GDP) lower than this in 2010.[5] In a number of countries, the annual cost to the state of incarcerating a pretrial detainee is considerably higher than the tuition and related fees of attending the world's best universities.

This chapter, after offering a definition of pretrial detention and noting the limits of the available data on pretrial detention, will look at the number of people in pretrial detention and then examine the costs of its overuse.

## Defining Pretrial Detention

Agreeing on a definition of pretrial detention is not as easy as it might seem. In English-speaking countries alone, people in pretrial detention are referred to variously as "remand prisoners," "remandees," "awaiting trial detainees," "untried prisoners," "unconvicted prisoners," and "unsentenced prisoners." In countries with other languages and different legal traditions and cultures, the terms for detention vary, too. Indeed, one can get lost in the varied nomenclature used around the world to classify pretrial detainees, but establishing a common definition is essential to gaining an accurate estimate of their number.

All criminal justice systems appear to differentiate between sentenced and unsentenced prisoners, and most afford individuals in the latter category a different legal status.[6] Unsentenced prisoners include not only persons who are awaiting trial (i.e. "pretrial" in the literal meaning of the word), but also prisoners whose trials are underway or who have been convicted but not yet sentenced. In some countries, notably those with a civil law tradition, persons sentenced, but who have yet to appeal their sentence, are typically also classified as pretrial detainees.[7]

Persons popularly understood to be pretrial detainees can fall into one of four categories. In chronological order, according to the flow of the criminal justice process, the categories are: (i) detainees who have been formally charged and are awaiting the commencement of their trial; (ii) detainees whose trial has begun but has yet to conclude with a finding of guilt or innocence; (iii) detainees who have been convicted but not sentenced; and (iv) detainees who have been sentenced by a court of first instance but who have appealed against their sentence or are within the statutory time limit for doing so.[8] In some countries, notably in common law jurisdictions, persons falling in the last category are not classified as pretrial detainees. Individual criminal justice systems or jurisdictions thus have some flexibility when defining who should be counted as a pretrial detainee.[9]

Generally not included in the definition of pretrial detention are arrested persons or suspects who have not yet appeared in front of a judicial officer for a determination whether they should be released or detained awaiting trial (also known as "remanded in custody").[10] Also excluded from most countries' count of the pretrial detention population are asylum seekers, undocumented migrants, and others held administratively.[11] While these categories of people are usually not considered to be pretrial detainees, the problems they face as a result of their detention and the impact thereof on wider society is very similar to that of pretrial detainees generally.[12]

### What Is Administrative Detention?

While there is no comprehensive international definition of administrative detention,[13] one generally accepted description provides that, "[d]etention is considered administrative detention if, *de jure* and/or *de facto*, it has been ordered by the executive and the power of the decision rests solely with the administrative or ministerial authority, even if a remedy *a posteriori* (after the event) does exist in the courts against such a decision. The courts are responsible only for considering the lawfulness of this decision and/or its proper enforcement and not for taking the decision itself."[14]

According to the International Commission of Jurists, administrative detention may encompass several phenomena, including administrative detention and/or detention of illegal immigrants or asylum-seekers to be deported for public order or state security reasons; administrative detention of persons with mental illness; administrative detention or confinement for public health reasons; administrative detention in the context of extradition; administrative detention related to the status of aliens and asylum-seekers (deportation or *refoulement*); administrative detention aiming at social control and /or "rehabilitation"; administrative detention related to juveniles; and confinement during armed conflicts.[15] According to the UN Centre for Human Rights, "administrative detention applies to a broad range of situations outside the process of police arresting suspects and bringing them to the criminal system."[16] This report does not consider administrative detention in its examination of pretrial detention.

## Limits of Pretrial Detention Data[17]

The pretrial detention statistics discussed below must be treated with caution. Unless indicated otherwise, the pretrial detention data come from the International Centre for Prison Studies (ICPS) which maintains a global database of prison-related statistics.[18] It is the most comprehensive global database on pretrial numbers available, covering some 220 countries and jurisdictions. While extensive, the ICPS pretrial detention dataset does not cover some countries, including, at the time of writing, the Central African Republic, China, the Democratic Republic of the Congo, Eritrea, Iraq, North Korea, and Somalia (see endnote for discussion about China).[19]

While the ICPS database is regularly updated, the information is typically sourced from national prison authorities. This implies that the data are only as reliable as the people who collect them and as accurate as the systems that generate them. Some countries manually collate data on prisoner numbers and related information from every prison into one central database. Others collect data at irregular intervals, while some do not consistently gather any quantitative data at all. Thus, while the information for some countries is updated annually on the ICPS database, this is not the case for some jurisdictions where updates occur more infrequently.

As discussed above, individual jurisdictions' definitions of pretrial detention influence the data provided to the ICPS. For example, according to the ICPS data, 32 percent of prisoners in Belgium were pretrial detainees in 2012. In England and Wales, some 15 percent of prisoners were pretrial detainees at that time. The much higher proportion of pretrial detainees in Belgium compared to England and Wales is at least partly a product of the way pretrial detainees are counted: in Belgium, persons engaged in appeals procedures are included in the count of pretrial detainees, while in England and Wales they are not. Excluding persons who are appealing their conviction or sentence from the count would reduce the proportion of pretrial detainees in Belgium from 32 percent to about 26 percent.[20]

Most of the ICPS statistics cover only persons who are under the control of the various prison services that provide data to the ICPS. Generally excluded are persons held in police cells or lockups. Criminal suspects are usually held in police cells for not more than 48 or 72 hours until their first court appearance and thereafter transferred to a prison or pretrial detention center. However, some—mainly developing—countries hold a considerable number of pretrial detainees in police cells, often because of a lack of prison space, or because the nearest prison is too far removed from the courthouse to justify transporting pretrial detainees between prison and court until the trials have come to an end. (Detention in police lockups is examined in detail in Chapter Three, which looks at the circumstances of pretrial detention.) Consequently, only counting pretrial detainees held within a prison system substantially undercounts their real number in certain places.

The ICPS data for Brazil are unusual as they contain both the number of pretrial detainees held in facilities administered by the prison administration and those in police facilities. The Brazilian data are useful, however, as they provide a sense of the extent to which pretrial detainees are kept in police lockups in some places. Thus, according to the ICPS data, pretrial detainees held in police lockups comprise almost 10 percent of the pretrial detainee population in Brazil. Others put the proportion of pretrial detainees held in police lockups in Brazil at a bit over 13 percent.[21]

We also know from an investigation by the Inter-American Commission's Rapporteur on the Rights of Persons Deprived of Liberty that in early 2010 the Argentine province of Buenos Aires had a prison population of 30,132 inmates, of which 4,040 were held in police detention centers. According to official statistics, 61 percent of the province's prisoners were pretrial detainees; however, the Rapporteur noted that this does not include those detained in police station facilities.[22] On the presumption that all, or most, of the persons kept in police detention centers were pretrial detainees, this implies that around 22 percent of Buenos Aires' pretrial detainees were incarcerated in police facilities.

As pointed out above, not included in the definition of pretrial detention and in the ICPS data, are arrested persons or suspects who have not been remanded to detention.[23] Some such arrestees will appear in court, typically within 24-72 hours (although in many jurisdictions this can take much longer), where some will be remanded to detention. Many, however, will not end up in court at all. The reasons for this are varied. Some arrestees, after spending a few hours or days at the police station, will be released on police bail or a summons (citation). Others will be released because the police decide not to continue with their investigation, such as where a complainant asks that charges be withdrawn, or where someone arrested for public drunkenness sobers up and is simply released to go home. Yet others successfully bribe the police to let them go.

A case can be made that anyone arrested, who is no longer at liberty to walk away from the arresting officer, is *de facto* in pretrial detention.[24] In other words, even arrestees who are subsequently not remanded to detention could be counted as pretrial detainees. However, data on this population is virtually impossible to get, and this report does not include them in its calculations regarding the number of pretrial detainees.

National arrest data are difficult to obtain for most jurisdictions. Where available, the numbers can be considerable, and certainly higher than the number of pretrial detainees reflected in the ICPS database. For example, in the United States, law enforcement agencies undertake some 13-14 million arrests annually.[25] This figure stands in stark contrast to the roughly 490,000 persons in pretrial detention in the U.S. at any point in time.[26] In England and Wales, police arrested 1.4 million people over a 12-month period in 2009-10 (versus approximately 11,500 pretrial detainees at any point in time during this period).[27] In France, the police arrested 1.2 million people in 2010 (versus 15,400 pretrial detainees),[28] and in Portugal some 49,000 arrests were recorded in 2006 (compared to 2,300 pretrial detainees).[29] In South Africa, the police arrested 1.5 million people over a 12-month period in 2010-11 (compared to 49,000 pretrial detainees),[30] and the Indian Police Service arrested 2.9 million people in 2010 (compared to 245,000 pretrial detainees).[31]

The above discussion allows us to conclude that the ICPS data present a somewhat imprecise and certainly conservative figure of the number of people in pretrial detention around the world. Clearly, it is essential that all criminal justice systems increase the thoroughness and accuracy of the statistics they collect on pretrial detention, including the number of pretrial detainees, the duration of pretrial detention, the percentage of all detainees who are pretrial, and the number of pretrial detainees held in police lockups.

If arrestees who are not remanded to pretrial detention were to be counted, then the number of pretrial detainees worldwide would be considerably higher than the ICPS data reflects. Even the inclusion of all remandees who are kept in police lockups worldwide would likely increase the ICPS's numbers by between 5–20 percent globally. Thus, the analysis which follows presents a conservative picture of the use and extent of pretrial detention.

## THE EXTENT OF PRETRIAL DETENTION

The extent of pretrial detention can be measured in different ways. The following section will analyze and review the global pretrial detention population from a variety of perspectives: first, the number of pretrial detainees as a proportion of all prisoners; second, the number of pretrial detainees expressed as a rate or proportion of the general population; third, the total number of individuals in pretrial detention at a specific point in time; fourth, the cumulative number of persons admitted to pretrial detention over a year; and finally, the average duration of pretrial detention. These diverse yet complementary measures provide different lenses through which the overuse of pretrial detention can be viewed.

### Pretrial Detainees as a Proportion of All Prisoners

A common way to express the extent of pretrial detention (and the manner in which pretrial detention data are reflected on the ICPS database) is the number of pretrial detainees as a proportion of all prisoners. For example, in a prison system where every fourth prisoner is a pretrial detainee, the proportion of all prisoners who are pretrial detainees would be 25 percent.

A weakness of this measure is that it is directly influenced by the number of sentenced prisoners. Thus, hypothetically, if the number of sentenced prisoners increases from 100 to 200 and the number of pretrial detainees remains the same at 50, then the number of pretrial detainees as a proportion of all prisoners declines from 50 to 25 percent—notwithstanding that the actual number of pretrial detainees remained unchanged.

In Chile, for example, the number of pretrial detainees as a proportion of all prisoners declined from 48.5 percent in 2000 to 21.9 percent in 2012. While this decline was partly the result of a real reduction in the number of pretrial detainees, from 16,030 to 11,267 (a 30 percent decline) over this period, the main reason for the decline was a significant increase in the number of sentenced prisoners, from 17,017 in 2000 to 40,180 in 2012—a massive 136 percent increase (Figure 1).

FIGURE 1:

**Changes in the number of pretrial detainees and sentenced prisoners, and the proportion of pretrial detainees in Chile, 2000-2012**

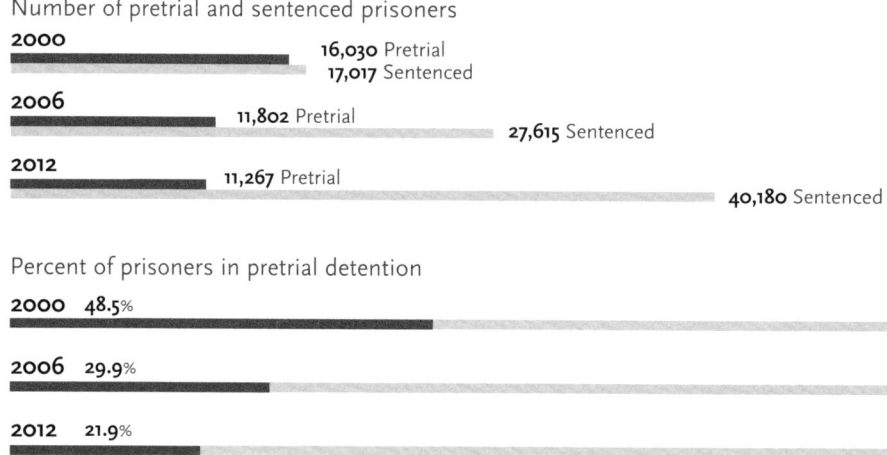

On its own, the proportion measure is not well suited to illuminating changes in the use of pretrial detention over time. It is, however, helpful in indicating the extent to which a prison system is burdened by pretrial detainees. After all, the ostensible purposes of prison is to punish convicted offenders, protect the public from them, serve as a warning to potential offenders, and to rehabilitate prisoners so they do not reoffend upon their release (i.e., retribution, incapacitation, deterrence, and rehabilitation). The greater the proportion of pretrial detainees in a prison system, the more difficult it is for prisons to serve these purposes.

Globally, almost one-third (32 percent) of the world's 10 million incarcerated persons was in pretrial detention in 2012.[32] This proportion varies considerably by region. The region with the highest proportion of pretrial detainees was Asia (40.6 percent) followed by Africa (34.7 percent). In the Americas somewhat over a quarter, and in Europe about one in five, of all prisoners were pretrial detainees in 2012 (Table 1).

TABLE 1:

**Pretrial detainees as a proportion of the total prison population, by region, 2012**

| Europe | Oceania | Americas | World | Africa | Asia |
|---|---|---|---|---|---|
| 18.8% | 22.3% | 27.9% | 32.0% | 34.7% | 40.6% |

Sources: World Prison Brief, International Centre for Prison Studies.

Within Africa, the sub-region with the highest proportion of prisoners who were pretrial detainees in 2012 was Central Africa (59.0 percent), followed by West Africa with 55.6 percent. East and Southern Africa's proportion of pretrial detainees—at a third of all prisoners—roughly reflected the global average (Table 2).

TABLE 2:

**Pretrial detainees as a proportion of the total prison population, by African sub-region, 2012**

| North Africa | Southern Africa | East Africa | West Africa | Central Africa |
|---|---|---|---|---|
| 26.2% | 31.7% | 32.8% | 55.6% | 59.0% |

Source: World Prison Brief, International Centre for Prison Studies.

In the Americas, the sub-region with the highest number of pretrial detainees as a proportion of all prisoners was the Caribbean (44.9 percent), followed by South America (41.1 percent), and Central America at 40.7 percent (Table 3).

TABLE 3:

**Pretrial detainees as a proportion of the total prison population, by American sub-region, 2012**

| North America | Central America | South America | Caribbean |
|---|---|---|---|
| 20.2% | 40.7% | 41.1% | 44.9% |

Source: World Prison Brief, International Centre for Prison Studies.

Within Asia, South Asia (Bangladesh, India, Nepal, Pakistan, and Sri Lanka) had the highest number of pretrial detainees as a proportion of all prisoners (65.5 percent), followed by East Asia at 37.9 percent (Table 4).

TABLE 4:

**Pretrial detainees as a proportion of the total prison population, by Asian sub-region, 2012**

| Central Asia | Middle East / West Asia | East Asia | South Asia |
|---|---|---|---|
| 13.6% | 32.4% | 37.9% | 65.5% |

Source: World Prison Brief, International Centre for Prison Studies.

In Europe, the number of pretrial detainees as a proportion of all prisoners varied from a high of 26.2 percent in the Nordic countries, to a low of 11.9 percent in Central Europe (Table 5).

TABLE 5:

**Pretrial detainees as a proportion of the total prison population, by European sub-region, 2012**

| Central Europe | Eastern Europe | Balkan countries | Western Europe | Nordic countries |
|---|---|---|---|---|
| 11.9% | 17.9% | 20.2% | 21.9% | 26.2% |

Sources: World Prison Brief, International Centre for Prison Studies.

The number of pretrial detainees as a proportion of all prisoners varies significantly within regions and countries. Using South America as an example, the number of pretrial detainees as a proportion of all prisoners ranged from a low of 23.5 percent in Chile to a high of 83.3 percent in Bolivia in 2012. In South America's largest country, Brazil, the discrepancy in the proportion of pretrial detainees is similarly broad. In the Brazilian state of Piauí, the number of pretrial detainees as a proportion of all prisoners was 74 percent in 2010; in the Federal District and the state of Rio Grande do Sul, respectively, the proportions were only 20 percent and 24 percent.

Excluding countries with a population of around one million people or less to avoid statistical aberrations,[33] the 20 countries with the *highest* number of pretrial detainees as a proportion of all prisoners are primarily located in Sub-Saharan Africa (8), Latin America (5), and South Asia (3). Four of the five countries with the highest proportion of pretrial detainees—75 percent and higher—are in Africa (Table 6).

All but one of these 20 countries are classified as developing economies by the World Bank, with nine classified as "low-income" economies, seven as "lower-middle income" economies, and three as "upper-middle income" economies (Libya, Panama, and Peru), and one as a "high-income" economy (Uruguay).[34] With the exception of Libya (arguably a special case given the collapse of its criminal justice administration after the recent war), the remaining upper-middle and high-income countries all fall on the lower side of the table, with none having pretrial detainee populations exceeding two-thirds of the overall prison population.

Excluding countries with a population of around one million people or less to avoid statistical aberrations,[35] the 20 countries with the *lowest* number of pretrial detainees as a proportion of all prisoners (Table 7) are primarily located in Europe (9), Central Asia (3), and East and South-East Asia (3 each).

Eight of the 20 countries are classified as "high-income" countries by the World Bank, six as "upper-middle" income countries, six as "lower-middle" income, and none as "low-income."[36]

The myriad factors that lead some countries to have much higher proportions of pretrial detainees than other countries are explored in Chapter Four: The Causes of Arbitrary and Excessive Use of Pretrial Detention.

TABLE 6:
Countries with the highest number of pretrial detainees as a proportion of the total prison population, 2012*

| % | Country |
|---|---|
| 89.4% | Libya |
| 83.3% | Bolivia |
| 82.0% | Democratic Republic of Congo |
| 78.0% | Liberia |
| 75.0% | Congo (Brazzaville) |
| 74.9% | Benin |
| 73.2% | Paraguay |
| 70.6% | Haiti |
| 70.2% | Central African Republic |
| 70.1% | Yemen |
| 69.5% | Nigeria |
| 68.3% | Bangladesh |
| 67.2% | Republic of Guinea |
| 66.2% | India |
| 66.2% | Pakistan |
| 65.0% | Togo |
| 64.1% | Venezuela |
| 63.8% | Panama |
| 63.7% | Uruguay |
| 63.4% | Chad |

TABLE 7:
Countries with the lowest number of pretrial detainees as a proportion of the total prison population, 2012*

| % | Country |
|---|---|
| 6.3% | Taiwan |
| 8.1% | Poland |
| 8.8% | Singapore |
| 9.0% | Kosovo |
| 10.0% | Kuwait |
| 10.0% | Georgia |
| 10.0% | Algeria |
| 10.5% | Bosnia and Herzegovina |
| 10.7% | Japan |
| 10.9% | Romania |
| 11.5% | Uzbekistan |
| 11.6% | Vietnam |
| 12.1% | Sudan |
| 12.1% | Lithuania |
| 12.3% | Nicaragua |
| 12.4% | Turkmenistan |
| 12.7% | Slovakia |
| 12.8% | Macedonia |
| 12.9% | England and Wales |
| 13.6% | Kazakhstan |

* Excluding jurisdictions with a population of roughly a million people or less.
Source: World Prison Brief, International Centre for Prison Studies.

## The Rate of Pretrial Detention

Another measure of the extent of pretrial detention is the number of pretrial detainees expressed as a proportion of the general population. This pretrial detention "rate" is unaffected by changes in the actual number of sentenced prisoners and thus may be a better guide to assessing the scale of pretrial detention around the world. It also makes it easy to compare the extent to which pretrial detention is used between countries with different sized populations.

Out of every 100,000 people on earth, 50.4 were in pretrial detention in 2013. The region with the highest pretrial detention rate—at more than twice the global average—is the Americas (107.4 pretrial detainees per 100,000 people in the general population), followed by Asia (43.1), Europe, Africa, and Oceania (Table 8).

TABLE 8:

**Number of pretrial detainees per 100,000 of the general population, by region, 2012**

| Oceania | Africa | Europe | Asia | World | Americas |
|---------|--------|--------|------|-------|----------|
| 28.0 | 33.7 | 38.6 | 43.1 | 50.4 | 107.4 |

Sources: World Prison Brief, International Centre for Prison Studies.

In Africa, the rate of pretrial detention was highest in Southern Africa at 48.4 per 100,000 of the general population, followed by East Africa at 44.2 per 100,000, and Central Africa at 43.5 per 100,000 (Table 9).

TABLE 9:

**Number of pretrial detainees per 100,000 of the general population, by African sub-region, 2012**

| West Africa | North Africa | Central Africa | East Africa | Southern Africa |
|-------------|--------------|----------------|-------------|-----------------|
| 20.8 | 30.8 | 43.5 | 44.2 | 48.4 |

Sources: World Prison Brief, International Centre for Prison Studies.

In the Americas, North America had the highest rate of pretrial detention at 130.0 per 100,000 of the general population. This was followed by South America at 96.0 per 100,000, and the Caribbean and Central America with both at around 90 per 100,000 (Table 10).

TABLE 10:

**Number of pretrial detainees per 100,000 of the general population, by American sub-region, 2012**

| Central America | Caribbean | South America | North America |
|-----------------|-----------|---------------|---------------|
| 87.3 | 92.1 | 96.0 | 130.9 |

Sources: World Prison Brief, International Centre for Prison Studies.

In Asia, the Middle East / West Asia had the highest rate of pretrial detention at 75.0 per 100,000 of the population. Significantly lower were East Asia at 57.7 per 100,000, and Central and South Asia which both had rates below 30 per 100,000 (Table 11).

TABLE 11:

**Number of pretrial detainees per 100,000 of the general population, by Asian sub-region, 2012**

| South Asia | Central Asia | East Asia | Middle East / West Asia |
|---|---|---|---|
| 23.1 | 25.7 | 57.7 | 75.0 |

Sources: World Prison Brief, International Centre for Prison Studies.

In Europe, it was Eastern Europe which recorded the highest rate of pretrial detention at 74.2 per 100,000 of the general population. Lower were the Balkans at 31.0 per 100,000, and Western and Central Europe with both at around 24 per 100,000. In the Nordic countries the rate was 18.2 per 100,000 (Table 12).

TABLE 12:

**Number of pretrial detainees per 100,000 of the general population, by European sub-region, 2012**

| Nordic | Central Europe | Western Europe | Balkans | Eastern Europe |
|---|---|---|---|---|
| 18.2 | 23.4 | 24.4 | 31.0 | 74.2 |

Sources: World Prison Brief, International Centre for Prison Studies.

As with the data on pretrial detainees as a proportion of the total prison population (discussed above), the rate of pretrial detention varies considerably between and within countries. For example, in South America, Ecuador's pretrial detention rate of 50.5 per 100,000 of the general population was less than a third of the Uruguayan rate of 182.5 per 100,000. In Brazil, the rate of pretrial detention varied from a low of 45.8 per 100,000 of the general population in the state of Alagoas to, at almost four times that rate, 180.2 per 100,000 in the state of Roraima.

The 20 countries with the highest rate of pretrial detainees present a different geographic pattern than the 20 with the highest pretrial detainee proportion (Tables 6 and 13). Ten of the 20 countries with the highest rate of pretrial detainees are in Latin America, but only one is in Sub-Saharan Africa (and two in North Africa). Three are in the Middle East, two in Asia, and one each in Europe and North America (again excluding countries with a population of around one million people or less to avoid statistical aberrations).[37]

According to the World Bank's classification, six of the 20 countries with the highest rate of pretrial detainees are "high-income" (one in Table 6); ten are "upper-middle" (three in Table 6); four are "lower-middle" and none are "low-income" (respectively, seven and nine in Table 6).[38] Jurisdictions with high rates of pretrial detainees thus have significantly higher average income levels compared to places where the number of pretrial detainees as a proportion of all prisoners is high.

When focusing on the 20 countries with the lowest rate of pretrial detainees per 100,000 of the general population (again excluding countries with a population of around one million people or less to avoid statistical aberrations), the picture is quite eclectic. Nine countries are located in Sub-Saharan Africa and six in Europe.

"High-income" countries comprise seven, and "lower-middle" countries six out of the 20 countries, (Table 14), followed by low- income countries (5), and upper-middle income (2) countries.

TABLE 13:
Countries with the highest rate of pretrial detainees per 100,000 of the general population, 2012 *

|  |  |
| --- | --- |
| 271.1 | Panama |
| 182.5 | Uruguay |
| 176.3 | Azerbaijan |
| 140.7 | USA |
| 127.6 | Dominican Republic |
| 120.3 | Peru |
| 117.6 | Bolivia |
| 110.4 | Thailand |
| 108.7 | Venezuela |
| 107.4 | El Salvador |
| 103.6 | Brazil |
| 102.4 | Saudi Arabia |
| 102.2 | Tunisia |
| 101.9 | Morocco |
| 93.9 | United Arab Emirates |
| 90.4 | South Africa |
| 89.2 | Mexico |
| 88.2 | Latvia |
| 87.3 | Paraguay |
| 80.3 | Israel |

TABLE 14:
Countries with the lowest rate of pretrial detainees per 100,000 of the general population, 2012 *

|  |  |
| --- | --- |
| 5.5 | Japan |
| 6.9 | Sudan |
| 7.7 | Egypt |
| 10.3 | Burkina Faso |
| 11 | Slovenia |
| 11.1 | Côte d'Ivoire |
| 11.5 | Finland |
| 11.6 | Malawi |
| 11.8 | Ghana |
| 12.2 | Ireland |
| 13.7 | Germany |
| 14.3 | Gambia |
| 15.5 | Kuwait |
| 15.6 | Guinea |
| 15.8 | Algeria |
| 15.8 | Mali |
| 16.5 | Romania |
| 16.6 | Sweden |
| 16.9 | Uzbekistan |
| 17.7 | Mauritania |

* Excluding jurisdictions with a population of roughly a million people or less.

Source: World Prison Brief, International Centre for Prison Studies.

There is a marked inverse relationship between countries' levels of economic development and their likelihood of either having a very high or very low number of pretrial detainees as a proportion of all prisoners. Thus, of the 20 countries with the highest proportion of pretrial detainees, 16 are classified as either "low-income" or "lower-middle" income economies and four as either "upper-middle" or "high-income" economies; while almost the reverse is the case in respect of the 20 countries with the lowest proportion of pretrial detainees (Figure 2).

This trend is also present, albeit less dramatically, when measuring the number of pretrial detainees as a rate or proportion of the general population. Thus, of the 20 countries with the highest rate of pretrial detainees per 100,000 of the general population, 16 are classified as either "upper-middle" or "high-income" economies and four as "low-income" or "lower-middle" income economies; while the majorities are reversed in respect of the 20 countries with the lowest rate of pretrial detainees.

FIGURE 2:

**Countries with extremely high and low proportions and rates of pretrial detainees and their levels of economic development, 2012**

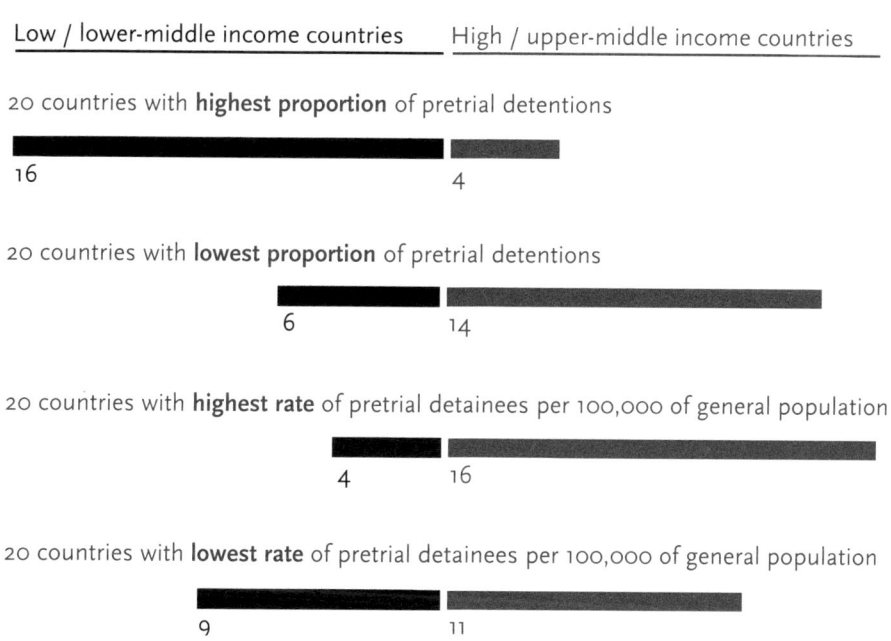

In low-income and lower-middle income countries, where state capacity is weak and the criminal justice infrastructure is limited, the rate of pretrial detention (i.e. the number of detainees per 100,000 of the population) is low. The dearth of police officers and forensic capacity means that relatively few persons suspected of having committed serious offenses are arrested. Those who are arrested can often use bribery to avoid pretrial detention. On the other hand, the number of pretrial detainees as a proportion of all incarcerated persons tends to be high in low-income and lower-middle income countries. This is because relatively few arrestees are convicted, due to the lack of courts, judges, prosecutors and investigators, and very limited forensic capacity to undertake complex investigations. In these countries, corruption is also a factor in the low number of convictions. But these same factors mean that periods of pretrial detention tend to be long in low-income and lower-middle income countries, as discussed further below.

In middle-income countries, rising levels of prosperity (and inequality) often coincide with increases in both crime and public concern about crime. The increase in state capacity, especially increased investment in policing, that often accompanies rising prosperity means that the rate of pretrial detention tends to be fairly high (and often rising) in middle-income countries. The number of pretrial detainees as a proportion of all incarcerated persons is typically more modest than in low-income countries, because the greater investigative and prosecutorial capacity in middle-income countries means that more cases go to trial. However, because of the increase in the number of suspects entering the criminal justice system, delays are common and the average duration of pretrial detention is often long.

In high-income countries, the rate of pretrial detention tends to be fairly high, as such states have the capacity to arrest and detain a relatively large proportion of persons suspected of having committed serious crimes. However, the number of pretrial detainees as a proportion of all incarcerated persons is low because there are sufficient court rooms, judges, prosecutors, and police investigators to ensure that trials are finalized relatively expeditiously. The average duration of pretrial detention therefore also tends to be short.

## Number of Pretrial Detainees at a Given Point in Time

Yet another, and perhaps more evocative, measure of the extent of pretrial detention around the world is the total number of individuals in pretrial detention at any given moment. While accurate and up-to-date data are not available for all countries, we know that on an average day in 2012, some 3.3 million people were in pretrial detention.[39] It is useful to place this large number into perspective. Some 44 percent (106 out of 242) of the world's sovereign states and dependent territories have national populations below 3.3 million people.[40] If the world's 3.3 million pretrial detainees were to stand in a straight line with arms outstretched and touching, they could form a continuous line stretching from London through New York City, and on to Washington D.C.[41]

Still, the figure of 3.3 million does not adequately convey the real extent of the use of pretrial detention around the world. This figure represents a snapshot in time, and only captures the number of persons in pretrial detention on a *specific day*—the last day of the year, for example. But in any prison system a significantly higher number of people are placed in pretrial detention over the course of a year than can be found in detention on a particular day.

## Number of Persons Admitted to Pretrial Detention

The number of individuals directly affected by a country's pretrial detention practices is considerably higher than the data at first glance suggest. For example, 10,864 persons were held in pretrial detention in Germany on September 1, 2010. Over the course of 2010, however, 50,704 pretrial admissions were recorded in Germany. In other words, while the conventional way of presenting the data indicates a pretrial population of just over 10,800 for Germany in 2010, close to five times that many individuals were detained during the course of that year. Scotland presents an even starker example of this disparity: the total number of pretrial admissions in 2010 was almost thirteen times as high as the count of pretrial detainees on September 1 of that year (Table 15).[42]

TABLE 15:

**Number of pretrial detainees on September 1, 2010 and number of pretrial admissions during 2010, selected European jurisdictions**

| Country / jurisdiction | No. of pretrial detainees on September 1, 2010[43] | Flow of entries to pretrial detention during 2010[44] |
| --- | --- | --- |
| Denmark | 1,381 | 9,770 |
| England & Wales | 12,464 | 91,436 |
| France | 16,457 | 47,405 |
| Germany | 10,864 | 50,704 |
| Italy | 27,873 | 74,586 |
| Lithuania | 1,541 | 6,380 |
| Netherlands | 5,690 | 17,677 |
| Poland | 8,159 | 21,624 |
| Scotland | 1,601 | 20,398 |
| Spain | 10,960 | 27,488 |

Sources: Council of Europe Annual Penal Statistics, Survey 2011.

According to the Council of Europe, the 39 European prison systems for which admissions data are available held 201,378 pretrial detainees on September 1, 2011. Over the course of that year the same prison systems processed 574,608 pretrial admissions—a ratio of almost 1:3. Non-European data are very hard to come by. We know, however, that in South Africa the comparable ratio for 2006 was 1:6.3.[45] In the United States, where 15 percent of the world's pretrial detainees are incarcerated at any one time, the ratio was about 1:16 in 2011.[46]

Using a relatively conservative ratio of 1:4.5 and extrapolating to the world as a whole, we can estimate that the world's penal systems processed at least some 14.9 million pretrial admissions during 2012. If we assume that the bulk of these admissions, say 80 percent, involved unique individuals, then 11.9 million persons spent some period of time in pretrial detention in 2010.[47] This is a large number of people. Most countries and territories (169 out of 242) have national populations below 11.9 million people. Moreover, our hypothetical line of 11.9 million pretrial detainees would now have to start at the southern tip of Africa in Cape Town, South Africa, to form one uninterrupted line going through the length of Africa to reach London, then cross the Atlantic to reach New York City, and then continue to Los Angeles and Vancouver in Canada.[48]

## The Duration of Pretrial Detention

Another way of assessing the amount of pretrial detention is to measure the number of days people spend behind bars. In 2010, in the 27 Council of Europe countries for which data are available, the average length of pretrial detention was 4.8 months or some 146 days.[49] There is scant equivalent data for most other countries.

In England and Wales (which is not included in the aforementioned Council of Europe data) the average length of time spent on remand in 2009 was 105 days.[50] In Ukraine (which is also not included in the Council of Europe data), the average length of pretrial detention was six months, although many defendants are detained for one or two years longer than this.[51] In the U.S. federal criminal justice system, defendants not released awaiting trial spent an average of 108 days in pretrial detention in 2003-04. For defendants charged with violent offenses the average detention period was 156 days.[52] In South Africa, the average length of pretrial detention in 2012 was estimated at 177 days.[53]

Both England and Wales and the U.S. have adequately resourced criminal justice systems, with enough police investigators, prosecutors, lawyers, judges, and courtrooms to ensure that criminal investigations and trials can be completed relatively expeditiously. Even Ukraine and South Africa, as middle-income countries, have reasonably well resourced criminal justice sectors. This is less likely to be the case in much of the developing world and low-income countries.

In Nigeria, the average length of pretrial detention nationally has been reported at 3.7 years.[54] In 2010, half of Nigeria's pretrial detainees had been detained for between 5 and 17 years, according to the country's National Prison Service,[55] with cases having been reported of detainees awaiting trial for up to 20 years.[56] Prisoners being held in pretrial detention for between seven and 17 years have also been documented in Benin.[57] In Malawi, concern has been raised about periods of pretrial detention lasting between four and ten years.[58] In Haiti, the average length of pretrial detention was 408 days (a bit over 13 months) in 2006, with 15 percent of detainees spending at least 1,000 days in pretrial detention.[59] In Pakistan, many defendants "spend more time behind bars awaiting trial than the maximum sentence they would receive if eventually convicted."[60] According to Human Rights Watch, pretrial detainees "in numerous countries ... make up the majority of the prison population. Such detainees may in many instances be held for years before being judged not guilty of the crime with which they were charged."[61]

> In 2010, in the 27 Council of Europe countries for which data are available, the average length of pretrial detention was 4.8 months or some
>
> **146 days**.

> In Nigeria, the average length of pretrial detention nationally has been reported at
>
> **3.7 years**.[54]
>
> In 2010, half of Nigeria's pretrial detainees had been detained for
>
> **between 5 and 17 years**.[55]

### India: 38 Years in Pretrial Detention[62]

In 1968, Jagjivan Ram Yadav was arrested for allegedly murdering his neighbor's wife. His trial never began because police records were lost. As a result, the trial court could neither grant him bail nor examine the charges.

In January 2005, Jagjivan's case resurfaced after prison authorities asked the court to rule on his status as a pretrial detainee. The district court asked the police to provide records and received the same reply as three decades earlier. Following a vigorous campaign by civil society and the media, Jagjivan was released in early 2006 after a Supreme Court directive ordering his release. Jagjivan turned 72 that year.

Ram Raj Yadav, Jagjivan's brother-in-law, who lives in the same village, has vivid memories of Jagjivan as a vibrant young man. He has a succinct, almost brutal, explanation for Jagjivan's introverted state today. "The jail finished him off," he says.

Keshav Ram, Jagjivan's 43-year-old son, comes home every two months to meet the man who is a virtual stranger. Keshav was barely a year old when his father was arrested. While growing up, his father's absence was an eternal mystery. "My mother refused to tell me about it," he remembers. "Everyone wore a shroud of silence."

Jagjivan's case is not unique in India. Boka Thakur and Rudal Shah spent, respectively, 25 years and 30 years awaiting trial without having their trials completed. Each would have received a maximum prison sentence of 14 years had they been convicted of the murder charges against him.[63]

In conservatively estimating that the global average period of pretrial detention is 200 days (6.5 months), then the estimated 3.3 million persons in pretrial detention at any time will spend a combined total of 660 million days in detention. In other words, the people in pretrial detention at this moment will cumulatively spend more than half a billion days in pretrial detention. To put that figure into perspective: it is estimated that the manpower required to build the Great Pyramid of Khufu (Cheops), the largest pyramid in Egypt, was 52 million man-days.[64] The Empire State Building took 875,000 man-days to build.[65] In theory, therefore, the total time the present cohort of pretrial detainees will spend in detention equals the man-days necessary to build an Empire State Building in every country of the world, plus a pyramid the size of the Pyramid of Khufu on all seven continents, and still have about a hundred million man-days to spare.

Measuring the length of a human chain of the world's pretrial detainees or the size of a potential labor force embodied in the pretrial detainees incarcerated today may seem frivolous. It does, however, allow us to better visualize the true extent of pretrial detention in the world today. In a crude way these accounts and the associated statistical information permit us to discern one important consequence of the widespread use of pretrial detention: the loss of liberty for a large number of people over huge periods of time.

# THE COST OF PRETRIAL DETENTION

Detaining people is an expensive undertaking for most states, especially for developing countries. For poor countries, where state budgets are rarely balanced and state funding to meet even the basic needs of all citizens is inadequate, expenditure on incarcerating pretrial detainees represents a stark opportunity cost. Every bit of state revenue spent on pretrial detention results in potentially less money for crucial social services, health, housing, and education. Moreover, states that spend large sums on pretrial detention in an effort to promote public security could arguably use some of that money for economic development, education, and other activities that prevent crime.[66] Alternatively, money spent on pretrial detention could be redirected to state functions which directly promote public security, such as employing more police officers or purchasing equipment which allows the police to function more effectively, such as vehicles or automated fingerprint identification systems. (The costs of pretrial detention to individual detainees, their families, and communities, is explored in Chapter Three, which considers the circumstances of detention and their impact—including financial impact—on detainees.)

The total budget of the South African Department of Correctional Services for the 2011-12 financial year amounts to R16.7 billion (approximately US$2 billion), and is estimated to be at around R20 billion by 2014-15.[67] Even for a relatively prosperous African country such as South Africa, this entails a significant opportunity cost in terms of state spending foregone elsewhere. For example, just half of the Department of Correctional Services' budget—R8 billion—could increase the country's national budget on basic education by almost 60 percent, or national health-related expenditure by a third, or triple the budget of the South African prosecution service. In South Africa, the annual cost to the state per average detainee was R88,700 in 2010-11.[68]

In the U.S. as a whole, taxpayers spend about $9 billion per annum for the incarceration of pretrial detainees.[69] In the U.S., the cost of incarcerating a pretrial detainee for a year can be up to $45,000.[70] For juveniles the costs are even higher. According to the American Correctional Association, the average annual cost nationwide to incarcerate one juvenile was $88,000 in 2008.[71]

In the state of Victoria, Australia, the annual cost of housing a prisoner was AUS$108,500 (approximately US$ 85,000 in 2009) in 2008-09. This is the average cost per prisoner and probably underestimates the cost of incarcerating pretrial detainees for at least two reasons. First, pretrial detainees require more intensive assessment and monitoring than longer-term convicted prisoners. Second, pretrial detainees are rarely housed in relatively inexpensive minimum security facilities.[72]

In Council of Europe countries for which data are available, the average annual cost of keeping a person in pretrial detention in 2010 was €34,310 (approximately

TABLE 16:

**Average amount (in Euros) spent by states on incarcerating one pretrial detainee per year in 2010, selected Council of Europe countries**

| Country | Average amount spent (€) |
|---|---|
| Netherlands | 73,402 |
| Ireland | 70,445 |
| Finland | 58,035 |
| Denmark | 50,735 |
| France | 31,135 |
| Portugal | 19,601 |
| Hungary | 10,038 |
| Turkey | 6,935 |
| Serbia | 5,475 |
| Lithuania | 5,220 |
| Croatia | 1,802 |
| Ukraine | 1,132 |

Source: Council of Europe Annual Penal Statistics, Survey 2011.

US$ 48,400). This cost varied significantly between countries, from over €70,000 in the Netherlands and Ireland to around €1,000 in the Ukraine (Table 16).[73] The roughly 370,000 pretrial detainees of the 47 Council of Europe Member States would have cost those states about €12.7 billion in 2010.[74] This is a significant amount of money; worldwide there were 91 countries with a Gross Domestic Product (GDP) less than this in 2010, according to the World Bank.[75]

The estimated 2010 expenditure on pretrial detention by European states is the same as the combined cost of the 2009 UN core budget,[76] the Global Fund's 2009 disbursements,[77] the biennial 2008-09 budget of the World Health Organization (WHO),[78] and the cost of feeding 23 million people for a year[79]—roughly the population of Afghanistan or Mozambique (Figure 3).

The cost of pretrial detention in developing and middle-income economies is often considerably less than the costs to wealthy, developed economies (see, for example, the relatively low annual cost of detention in Croatia and Ukraine at Table 16). But even in such places, the relative cost of detention can be painfully high. For example, in the Philippines, in 2011 the state spent P63,620 (approximately US$ 1,475) per annum to feed, guard, and house the average prisoner. By comparison, the state's allocation per elementary school student was about P8,600 per year.[80] In Zimbabwe, the annual cost of feeding a prisoner was US$ 1,457 in 2011.[81] In Nigeria, it cost the federal government an average of N73,600 or US$ 475 in 2011 to feed a pretrial detainee.[82] While these may appear to be low amounts, in both Nigeria and Zimbabwe an estimated one-third of the population survive on less than US$ 2 a day (or US$ 730 a year).[83]

All governments have limited resources, and all policy decisions have costs. Every amount a government spends on incarceration is money that cannot be spent on healthcare or policing or education. Moreover, and as discussed in greater detail in Chapter Three, the true cost of pretrial detention is often hidden, because the state counts only the direct costs of housing and feeding pretrial detainees. Largely overlooked are indirect costs such as the lost productivity and reduced tax payments of pretrial detainees who could have continued working if they were released before trial, or diseases transmitted from prison to the community when detainees are eventually released, to name just a few examples. The

FIGURE 3:
European expenditure on pretrial detention compared to selected global humanitarian, health and governance expenditures (US$)

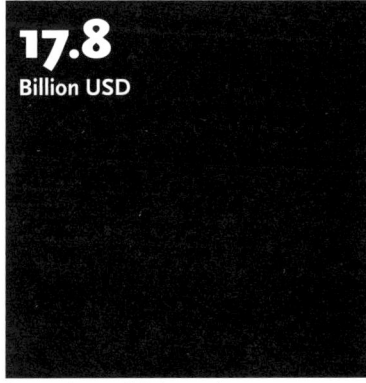

**Annual pretrial detention costs to European states** 2010

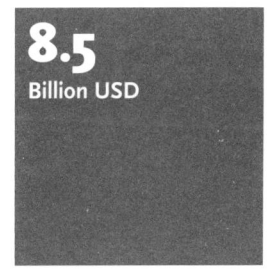

**Cost of feeding 23m people for one year**
roughly the population of Afghanistan or Mozambique

**World Health Organization biennial budget**
2008-2009

**Global Fund disbursement**
2009

**United Nations core budget**
2008-2009

Sources: UNICEF; WHO; Global Fund to Fight AIDS, Tuberculosis and Malaria; Worldwatch Institute.

traditional state-centric approach to calculating the costs of pretrial detention is thus both short-sighted and misleading.

In a 2008 study, the Open Society Justice Initiative sought to calculate both the direct and indirect (or "hidden") costs of pretrial detention in Mexico as borne by the state, detainees and their families, and the general public. The study found that the cost of pretrial detention to the state is almost matched by the cost to detainees, their families, and communities.[84]

## Overcrowding

Prisons are primarily designed for incarcerating convicted offenders and to serve as instruments of punishment, public security (by keeping dangerous offenders away from the public), and rehabilitation. These objectives of prison are regularly undermined by the excessive use of pretrial detention.

Pretrial detention significantly exacerbates overcrowding in prison systems around the world. An empirical analysis of the causes of overcrowding found only a weak correlation between countries' rates of imprisonment and overcrowding, but "a strong and significant correlation between pretrial detention and the extent of overcrowding."[85] While this does not hold for all countries or regions, it goes without saying that a reduction in the use of pretrial detention would reduce prison crowding.

According to the International Centre for Prison Studies, in 2012 there were approximately 10.3 million prisoners occupying some 8.7 million prison spaces—or 1.6 million more prisoners than the available prison accommodations. Expressed another way, prisons worldwide had an occupancy rate of 118 percent.

Also in 2012, there were roughly 3.3 million pretrial detainees accommodated in prison systems worldwide. Reducing the number of pretrial detainees by half would, in theory, solve the world's prison crowding crisis (Table 17).

TABLE 17:

Regional changes in prison occupancy rates by reducing the number of pretrial detainees by half

| Region | No. of prisoners in excess of prison capacity | Occupancy rate (%) | No. of pretrial detainees | Occupancy rate (%) with pretrial detainees reduced by a half |
|---|---|---|---|---|
| Global | 1,577,800 | 118% | 3,309,500 | 99.1% |
| Africa | 230,300 | 144% | 311,100 | 114% |
| Americas | 560,200 | 119% | 975,100 | 103% |
| Asia | 1,099,000 | 139% | 1,487,600 | 113% |
| Europe | -18,800 | 99% | 376,700 | 89% |
| Oceania | 900 | 102% | 11,000 | 86% |

Source: World Prison Brief, International Centre for Prison Studies.

In practice this would be more challenging to achieve because prisoners are often distributed unevenly among prisons. In many countries, some prisons—typically those in major urban centers—are heavily overcrowded while others have more modest occupancy levels. Moreover, exceptionally overcrowded prisons are often disproportionately filled with pretrial detainees.[86] Reducing pretrial detention numbers would alleviate crowding and many of the negative consequences that result from it, as discussed further in Chapter Three, which looks at pretrial detention conditions.

Prison overcrowding is often worse in developing nations than in the developed world. This is partly because of more rapid population growth in such countries and the lack of resources for prison construction, but also because governments in such states typically feel less compelled to limit crowding levels to avoid legal action or international opprobrium.

In such settings, crowding can reach levels where prisons cease to function: the limited number of guards are unable to even rudimentarily monitor and control the prisoners in their care. This leads to the unofficial "appointment" of prison inmates to act as supervisors and disciplinarians of other prisoners. The day-to-day functioning of prison life is left largely at the mercy of prisoners themselves. As prison crowding levels rise further, the risk of gang warfare or riots among prisoners increases and mass breakouts become more frequent.

Some governments seeking to avert reaching this stage often undertake periodic mass releases of sentenced prisoners—in the form of collective pardons and amnesties—typically on symbolic national celebratory days or the birthday of the country's leader.[87] Others provide remissions on sentences, such as reducing every prisoner's custodial sentence by a certain period of time.[88]

Such mass releases can have serious public security consequences. Criminal justice systems spend considerable resources to apprehend and convict criminal offenders, succeeding in only a small minority of cases. Criminal justice systems' ability to serve a deterrent function and to dispel the popular notion that "crime pays" is undermined if the few, often serious offenders who are convicted and incarcerated are released before the expiration of their judicially imposed sentences for the simple reasons that prisons have reached unmanageable levels of crowding. This situation is exacerbated when convicted prisoners are released but unconvicted pretrial detainees are not.

The mass and/or early release of sentenced prisoners also undermines public confidence in the justice system. In criminal justice systems operating within the confines of the rule of law, independent courts pass down sentences on those who have been convicted after a fair trial and a fair process leading up to the trial. Public confidence in the justice process is undermined when convicted and incarcerated prisoners are released before the expiration of their sentence because the prison system is overcrowded.[89] This can lead to a decline in the reporting of crime and public cooperation with the police or, in more extreme cases, popular vigilantism. Chapter Five looks in greater detail at the effect excessive pretrial detention can have on the rule of law.

## CONCLUSION

The overuse of pretrial detention is a global phenomenon that affects approximately 15 million people per year and costs scores of billions of dollars. As noted, the exact worldwide extent of pretrial detention is impossible to assess, given the uneven quality of national data; all countries must be more accurate in measuring their use of pretrial detention.

Although one can argue over the best way to measure the scope of pretrial detention and its costs (including direct costs to the state and indirect costs to the detainees, their families, and communities), it is inarguable that excessive pretrial detention represents a colossal waste of resources in order to jail people who should be presumed innocent. Exactly who those people are and why they end up in pretrial detention is examined in the next chapter.

# Who are the World's Pretrial Detainees?

## INTRODUCTION

Most people in pretrial detention are poor—often desperately so—by the standards of the society in which they live. The poor are more likely to come into conflict with the law, more likely to be detained pending trial, and less able to afford the three B's of pretrial release: bribe, bail, or barrister. Furthermore, given the link between poverty and marginalization, a disproportionate number of pretrial detainees belong to groups that are socially, economically, and politically discriminated against, including ethnic minority groups and castes, religious minorities, immigrants and non-citizens, and the mentally ill.

This chapter looks at who is in pretrial detention and seeks to explain why certain groups and individuals are overrepresented among the world's pretrial detainees. It shows how multiple factors, including a lack of access to bail funds, bribe money, and legal representation, combine with limited formal sector employment or haphazard housing patterns to diminish detainees' chances of securing their release awaiting trial.

Some defenders of strict detention policies argue that poor people and members of marginalized groups commit more crimes and are therefore appropriately overrepresented in pretrial detention. Even if the pool of persons selected for prosecution was a perfect demographic reflection of who committed crimes—an unlikely proposition which is beyond the scope of this report—and was decidedly weighted toward those who are poor and/or members of minority groups, this would not explain why such people are in pretrial detention in far greater numbers than individuals of greater means or status. Around the world, decisions about who is incarcerated pending trial and who is released are based on wealth: the wealthy and middle class are released, while the poor are detained. Most pretrial detainees are not likely to abscond, reoffend, or threaten witnesses—all reasonable grounds for pretrial detention. Rather, they are held in pretrial detention because they are guilty of being poor and/or from marginalized groups. Many of those persons should simply not be consigned to detention.

## THE POOR

Around the world, pretrial detainee populations consist disproportionately of the poor. This holds true for both developed and developing countries. There are a host of reasons why the poor are less likely to avoid pretrial detention, a measure which is supposed to be a last resort and a distinct exception to a bedrock international principle, the presumption of innocence.

As one expert report on pretrial detention noted:

> People having stable residence, stable employment and financial situation, or being able to make a cash deposit or post a bond as guarantee for appearance at trial are considered as well-rooted. These criteria of course are often difficult to meet for the homeless, drug users, substance abusers, alcoholics, the chronically unemployed and persons suffering from mental disability, who thus find themselves in detention before and pending trial when less socially disadvantaged persons can prepare their defence at liberty.[1]

The number of studies documenting the socioeconomic background of pretrial detainees is limited. However, where such information is available it consistently shows that pretrial detainees overwhelmingly come from the poorest strata of society.

In England and Wales, about a third of men and half of women remanded to pretrial detention are poor enough to receive council housing benefits. About one in ten persons entering pretrial detention have no fixed abode and are in effect homeless at the time of their arrest. The vast majority (80 percent) of pretrial detainees expect to claim state benefits of some kind upon release.[2] Also in England and Wales, a 2009 report by the Prison Reform Trust found that 40 percent of children in custody have previously been homeless, and more than two in three adult pretrial detainees were unemployed at the time of their arrest.[3]

In the Australian state of Victoria, a quarter of the state's pretrial detainees come from 16 postcode (Zip code) areas—just over two percent of the state's total. Fifteen percent of all remand cases derive from only one percent of postcode areas. These postcodes include some of the most disadvantaged areas in Victoria.[4] In Scotland, half the prison population comes from home addresses in 155 (or 13 percent) of the 1,222 local government wards. In 2003, the overall imprisonment rate for men in Scotland was 237 per 100,000, but for men from the 27 most impoverished wards the rate was four times that (953 per 100,000).[5]

Some studies, while not focusing on the socioeconomic background of incarcerated persons directly, seek to measure detainees' and prisoners' levels of education and literacy. To the extent that formal education and literacy is related to employment prospects and income, it is possible to draw some cogent conclusions about relative poverty levels among incarcerated populations.[6]

A six-country study on prison conditions in Africa, found that "the majority of those in prison come from very poor backgrounds, often having received little education," with only a small proportion of prisoners having formal paid employment at the time of their arrest.[7] An audit of the prison population undertaken by Nigeria's Justice Ministry in 2005 concluded that about 85 percent of pretrial detainees were too poor to pay for a lawyer.[8] In India, one study estimated that 80 percent of the prison population has only a primary school education or is illiterate, while 50 percent are either unemployed or employed in low-paying agricultural activity.[9]

In the United States in the late 1990s (the latest period for which national data are available), 47 percent of inmates in local jails, of which the majority are pretrial detainees, had not completed high school or its equivalent. This was higher than the equivalent proportion for sentenced prisoners (27 percent of federal prison inmates, and 40 percent of state prison inmates), and significantly higher than the rate for the general population (about 18 percent).[10]

As the above example from the U.S. reveals, where socioeconomic data are available for both pretrial detainees and sentenced prisoners within the same penal system, pretrial detainees appear, on average, to be poorer and less educated compared to their sentenced counterparts.[11] This may be because people arrested for minor crimes, such as trespassing, loitering, and urinating in public, are often very poor or even homeless. In many countries, people with a verifiable address often receive a summons (citation) to appear in court or a ticket to pay a fine. But those without an address and those too poor to pay a fine end up in pretrial detention.

Why are poor and marginalized people more likely to be arrested and detained awaiting trial? While some of the reasons are self-evident—poor people lack the money for bail, to hire a lawyer, or pay a bribe—others are more subtle. Poor and marginalized people generally do not enjoy the social and political connections and influence (i.e. knowing someone viewed by the court as a person of substance who can vouch for their character and commitment to return for trial) which facilitates the release of pretrial detainees in many places. In Malawi, for example, the indigent regularly remain in pretrial detention because they cannot obtain two "sureties" or respectable members of the community to appear in court and guarantee their appearance at trial.[12] Poor people are also more likely to spend time in the open—on the streets and market places—where they become easy targets for arrest by overzealous and corrupt police officers.

## Cannot Afford Money Bail

In many jurisdictions, money bail (also known simply as "bail" or "bond") is used as a condition for the release of defendants awaiting trial. Typically this entails the deposit of a sum of money with the court or the police by the defendant or someone on his behalf, as a guarantee that the defendant will not abscond and will adhere to any other conditions of his release. In principle, such money is returned to the defendant (or whoever deposited the money on the defendant's behalf) upon finalization of the trial, provided the defendant did not contravene any of the conditions of his bail.

Money bail is discriminatory in its effect. Poor people often do not have the money needed to secure their release, or have to resort to multiple transactions to cobble together the funds, during which time they will remain in custody. In middle- and low-income countries, detainees also generally do not have bank accounts and access to formal loan facilities to borrow the needed money within a short period of time. Sometimes relatives can procure the money, but this often entails overcoming a number of logistical and financial hurdles. In developing countries, arrestees may not be able to make contact with their relatives to inform the latter of their arrest, because either party may lack access to a telephone. Moreover, in both developing and developed countries, relatives and friends of poor defendants typically have no savings and have to sell their few assets to procure the money necessary for bail. This can be a time consuming process that, even if successful, lengthens defendants' stay in pretrial detention.

Around the world, a significant number of people languish in pretrial detention simply because they are poor and do not have access to the necessary resources to post bail. In Sri Lanka, for example, defendants have the right to bail if their trial has not commenced within two years of their detention. Not only is this legal requirement routinely ignored by the courts, with many accused persons being held without bail or trial for three years and more, but, when money bail is granted, it is often set at a level beyond the financial means of detainees.[13] In one documented case, a woman accused of drug possession was held in prison with her baby, who was 8 months old at the time of her imprisonment, for a year, because she was unable to pay the 15,000 rupee (US$134) bail set for her.[14]

In some jurisdictions, such as in Bolivia, Brazil, Ecuador, and parts of Mexico, money bail may also include—in addition to a deposit serving as a guarantee of the defendant's compliance with his conditions of release—the fine that might be imposed should the defendant be convicted, plus the compensation or restitution he will likely be ordered to pay to the victims of his alleged crime. These two additional sums of money are not returned to a defendant if he is convicted. In such jurisdictions, the sums of money a defendant (or someone on his behalf) has to procure to secure his release awaiting trial can be considerable.

A study undertaken in the Mexican state of Nuevo León in 2006 found that these additional bail obligations can significantly increase the amount of money a defendant has to deposit with the court. The study randomly selected a representative sample of cases in which defendants were granted bail. The average amount of bail set to guarantee a defendant's compliance with his conditions of release was about 4,700 pesos (US$450 at the time). In just over a quarter of the cases, defendants were also obliged to deposit an amount to cover the potential damages accruing to the victims should the defendant be convicted. The average amount for damages was 40,709 pesos—almost ten times the traditional bail amount, and prohibitively high for the average Mexican.[15]

In Malawi, a key reason for overcrowding of the prison system is that prisoners cannot pay bail or provide any surety.[16] A 2011 survey of pretrial detainees in Sierra Leone found that the average bail amount set was 25 times the average weekly earnings of detainees. In other words, the average bail amount was equivalent to just more than six months' of the average earning of detainees.[17] In South Africa, about a third of all pretrial detainees granted bail are routinely unable to afford the amount set.[18]

As long ago as 1978, the Indian Supreme Court authorized the pretrial release of indigent defendants on personal bond (i.e. a promise to stand trial, also known as "release on own recognizance"). Noting that "the poor are being priced out of their liberty in the justice market," the Supreme Court observed that bail provisions in the Criminal Procedure Code "must be liberally interpreted in the interest of social justice."[19] Yet, over three decades later, money bail remains a prominent feature of India's pretrial justice regime, condemning impoverished defendants to await trial in detention.

Many of India's pretrial detainees are trapped in a quagmire of poverty and a slow moving justice system. As one commentator notes: "In a system where bail is available to those who can show proof of property and furnish financial surety, they [indigent defendants] have committed the crime of being poor... Being an undertrial [pretrial detainee] in India is an endless tale of oppression, of being forever stuck in brutish, overcrowded jails as a laidback judiciary languorously delivers its judgments."[20] In the Indian state of Maharashtra, for example, hundreds of pretrial detainees are eligible for bail but cannot come up with the surety required by the law to set them free. The state's judiciary's attitude towards the poor has been described as one "of mistrust and non-reliance."[21]

The inability of the poor to raise money for bail is not limited to the developing world. In the United States, of the defendants with a public attorney who are granted financial bail, about two-thirds are not released before adjudication, presumably because they cannot afford the amount of bail set by the court.[22]

A review of all defendants arrested in New York City in 2008 for minor (non-felony) charges found that a large number were unable to afford the financial bail set by the court. In almost three-quarters of the cases where bail was set, the bail amount was $1,000 or less. Yet, 87 percent of defendants required to post a bail amount of $1,000 or less were detained awaiting trial because they could not do so. Of these defendants, almost three out of four (71 percent) were accused of non-violent, non-weapons related offenses.[23] An investigation of criminal justice practices in the U.S. state of Mississippi came across numerous indigent defendants who could not afford to deposit bail as low as $100 and consequently remained in pretrial detention for months.[24]

According to the Bronx Freedom Fund, a New York City based NGO which provides loans to family and community members to post bail for indigent pretrial detainees, people's inability to afford bail has far-reaching consequences. "The unfortunate reality is that many clients [of the Bronx Freedom Fund] in poor communities of color like the Bronx are too poor to post even modest bail of $500, $1,000 or $1,500. Forced to remain behind bars, their lives destabilize: They lose their jobs; their physical and mental health deteriorates; and their families' social and economic network falls apart. In the face of these consequences and under the threat of continued incarceration, many defendants, whether guilty or innocent, plead guilty simply to get out of jail."[25]

Conditions of release other than money bail can also pose particular challenges for the indigent. For example, defendants are often released awaiting trial on the condition that they report to a police station on a regular basis. Individuals without access to private transport, too poor to afford the regular use of public transport, or who live in a rural area far from the nearest police station, find it difficult to meet such a condition. In a survey of rural inhabitants in South Africa, half the respondents indicated that they lived between 11 and 30 kilometers from the nearest police station, with 12 percent being more than 30 kilometers away. Just six percent of the respondents indicated they were able to drive themselves in private transport to the nearest police station, and 10 percent said they could use a commuter bus because of the limited availability of public transport in rural areas.[26] In northern Kenya, for example, people reportedly need to travel several hundred kilometers to reach a court, a journey that many cannot afford.[27]

### Criminalization of Poverty

The Special Rapporteur on Extreme Poverty and Human Rights' report to the sixty-sixth session of the UN General Assembly in 2011 discusses the difficulties the poor face in meeting the conditions of their pretrial release:[28]

Across developing and developed countries, release on bail pending trial is subject to increasingly stringent and onerous conditions which require individuals to, for example, demonstrate their connections with the community, have a fixed address or permanent employment, report regularly to police or make a cash deposit or post a bond as guarantee. These requirements are impossible for the poorest and most marginalized to meet in the vast majority of cases and, as a result, they are more likely to remain in detention pending a trial. This dramatically increases the likelihood that they will ultimately be convicted: not only does it put them in a vulnerable position whereby they will be more inclined to accept unfair "plea deals" or to make admissions of guilt in order to secure a swifter release, it contributes to the deterioration of the detainees' appearance and demeanour, impedes their ability to liaise with lawyers or obtain character witnesses and causes them to lose their employment or social housing, thereby creating a disincentive for the court to give a suspended or community service sentence.

## Cannot Afford Counsel

Poor people do not have access to private counsel, and most countries lack a comprehensive legal aid system for defendants too poor to afford their own lawyers. In countries where a rudimentary legal aid system operates, legal counsel is often provided only at the trial stage of legal proceedings, long after a decision has been made to detain a defendant awaiting trial. Yet, as discussed in Chapter Four, access to a lawyer at the early stages of the criminal justice process can be crucial in limiting abuse and torture at the hands of the authorities and in significantly enhancing defendants' chances of being released awaiting trial.

A 2011 UN Office on Drugs and Crime (UNODC) report on legal aid in Africa documented the dismally low availability of state-funded lawyers for indigent criminal defendants.[29] In numerous African countries, the scarcity of public defenders means that legal aid at public expense is restricted to capital cases:

- Liberia, with a population of some 3.8 million inhabitants spread over a country half the size of the United Kingdom, has 21 public defenders, of which all but two are recent law graduates with limited practical experience.
- Malawi, a country of 15.5 million people, has 18 legal aid lawyers, of whom 16 are junior or have fewer than five years' experience.
- Mozambique's legal aid system is comprised of 16 paralegals and 17 legal assistants, who service a population of 23 million people spread across a territory the size of France and the United Kingdom combined.
- Sierra Leone has three legal aid lawyers, for a population of 6.4 million people; the three provide services only in the capital city, Freetown.
- In Zambia, the Legal Aid Board has 21 lawyers on its staff to provide services

to a population of 13 million people in a country larger than Ukraine, Europe's second largest country.[30]

In many countries, especially in the developing world where state-financed legal aid is virtually nonexistent, there exists a general dearth of professional legal personnel. Lawyers are in such short supply that they can charge a premium for their services, putting them out of the reach by all but the wealthy. Moreover, in such places the vast majority of lawyers are based in their countries' largest urban centers, so that rural defendants have virtually no access to a lawyer. In Malawi, for example, a mere 220 registered lawyers were servicing a population of some 15.5 million people in 2011. With an average of one lawyer per every 70,000 inhabitants, only Malawians with considerable means can hope to obtain the services of counsel.[31] Sierra Leone and Rwanda have about 300 lawyers each for, respectively, six and ten million inhabitants. Angola, with a population of 18 million, has around 600 lawyers.[32]

Some developing countries have an abundance of lawyers, but their fees remain too high for the average defendant. Thus, Nigeria has more than 50,000 lawyers, the highest number of any country in Africa.[33] Yet, it is estimated that some three-quarters of pretrial detainees in Nigeria are too poor to afford a private lawyer.[34] Bangladesh has some 60,000 lawyers. In 2010, its prisons had a capacity for 29,000 inmates but contained 74,000, of which 72 percent were pretrial detainees. A review identified two blockages affecting the Bangladeshi prison system, of which one is the "lack of legal advice and legal assistance to prisoners."[35]

Even in middle-income countries, the dearth of state financed lawyers can be dire. In Sao Paulo, Brazil's most populous city, there are three public defenders providing legal assistance during the pretrial stage of the criminal justice process to more than 2,000 people arrested every month.[36] Research in the criminal courts of Istanbul, Turkey's economic and financial center, found that less than three percent of all criminal defendants have access to a government paid lawyer.[37]

The situation is better in developed countries, but only up to a point. In the United States, for example, an indigent defendant may not be imprisoned, even for a minor offense, unless afforded the right to counsel.[38] In the late 1990s (the latest period for which national data are available), at the end of their case some 66 percent of felony defendants in federal courts and 82 percent of felony defendants in large state courts were represented by publicly financed counsel.[39] (In the U.S., approximately 95 percent of criminal defendants are charged in state court.) These figures are indicative of both the extent of the U.S. legal aid infrastructure and the disproportionate manner in which the indigent are ensnared by the country's criminal justice system. Indeed, according to a U.S. government report, some 87 percent of defendants charged with felonies in the U.S. are indigent.[40]

However, while state funded legal aid is widely available in the U.S., the average quality of such services appears to be inferior to those provided by privately funded lawyers. A report by the Justice Policy Institute, an NGO, concludes that, "lack of quality defense may lead to pretrial detention. In places where [public]

> Even in middle-income countries, the dearth of state financed lawyers can be dire. In Sao Paulo, Brazil's most populous city, there are three public defenders providing legal assistance during the pretrial stage of the criminal justice process to more than 2,000 people arrested every month.

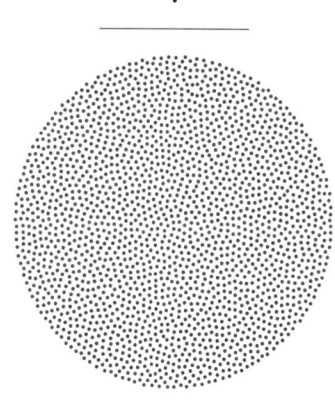

defender caseloads are very high or the court fails to appoint counsel in a timely manner, poor people accused of criminal offenses may spend a lot of time in jail before ever speaking to a lawyer or appearing in court."[41]

According to a U.S. government report, some **87 percent** of defendants charged with felonies in the U.S. are indigent.[35]

Only about half (52 percent) of defendants using a public defender or assigned counsel in the United States are released from jail prior to trial; by comparison, over three-quarters (79 percent) of defendants employing a private attorney were released before trial.[42] Moreover, of inmates who are granted financial bail, only a quarter are released prior to their trial if they have a court-appointed lawyer, compared to almost two-thirds (66 percent) if they use a private lawyer.[43] That is, defendants with court-appointed lawyers are significantly more likely to have financial bail set at amounts which they cannot afford.

Interestingly, conviction rates in both U.S. federal and large state courts are the same for defendants irrespective of whether they were represented by state financed or private counsel. Of those found guilty, higher percentages of defendants with state financed counsel were sentenced to incarceration.[44] This may be because pretrial detention is in itself a predictor of the risk a defendant faces of receiving a custodial sentence. These data imply that the quality of legal counsel and / or the time and resources at a lawyer's disposal are particularly significant during the pretrial stage of the criminal justice process.

A 2011 report, *System Overload: The Costs of Under-Resourcing Public Defense*, sums up the state of the U.S. public defender system as follows:

> There is a chasm between a "right to counsel" and a right to quality representation in judicial proceedings. Public defense systems serve millions of people in the United States every year. Yet many systems across the country have been in a state of "chronic crisis" for decades. The defender systems that people must rely on are too often completely overwhelmed; many defenders simply have too many cases, too little time and too few resources to provide quality or even adequate legal representation.[45]

According to a U.S. Department of Justice review, almost three-quarters (73 percent) of county-based public defender offices lack enough attorneys to meet national caseload standards,[46] while 23 percent of offices had less than half of the necessary attorneys to meet caseload standards. Only 12 percent of county public defender offices with more than 5,000 cases per year have enough lawyers to meet caseload standards.[47]

### USA: 30 Needless Days in Pretrial Detention[48]

Jonathon spent 30 days in the Baltimore city jail without once speaking to a public defender. He met his attorney in the courtroom on the day of his appearance. While Jonathon's defender "did a good job" in the courtroom, Jonathon knows that defenders "are overworked" and in his case did not conduct any investigation until the day of his court appearance. Having a defender involved earlier in the process could have saved Jonathon the 30 days in jail, which "shut [his] entire life down," and could have avoided the collateral consequences of being locked up that Jonathon continues to suffer, including being unable to get a full-time job—or even a job interview.

The U.S. is one of only a handful of countries that provides state funded lawyers to a large swath of defendants. In Italy, for example, deficiencies in the country's legal aid system result in a high proportion of poor defendants being denied competent legal services. While all defendants in Italy must be represented by counsel, the threshold for legal aid eligibility requires many poor defendants to go into debt to pay for their lawyer. Many of those who do qualify for legal aid miss out on the service because they are unaware that they can apply. In 2006, just over six percent of adult defendants received legal aid. The lack of adequate funding for legal aid services results in remuneration that is so low that many lawyers refuse appointment. Often, those who do accept appointment provide the accused with inadequate representation because they lack the funds to conduct even the most basic investigation of the case.[49]

In Germany, legal aid is available in limited circumstances, based on the seriousness of the offense and the vulnerability of the accused, including financial need. The process by which indigence is determined is complicated and places undue burdens on the accused. Moreover, funding for legal aid is inadequate, especially during the pretrial phase. Many services, such as the costs of investigation by the defense, are not borne by the state, discouraging lawyers from engaging in these activities.[50]

## Cannot Afford Bribes

Of course, the ability to afford bail or legal representation only really matters after arrest. Around the world, poor people are arrested because they cannot pay a bribe to a corrupt police officer. They are then denied access to counsel because they cannot bribe a corrupt guard or prosecutor, and often held for long periods of time in pretrial detention—at times indefinitely—because they cannot bribe a corrupt judge. In criminal justice systems where corruption is pervasive, defendants are likely to be released awaiting trial only if they have politically powerful allies or the means to bribe the arresting officer, prosecutor, or judicial officer overseeing their application for pretrial release.

Corruption flourishes in the pretrial phase because it receives less scrutiny and is subject to more discretion than subsequent stages of the justice process, and often involves lower paid and junior actors in the system. Unhindered by scrutiny or accountability, police, prosecutors, and judges are able to arrest, detain, and release individuals based on their ability to pay bribes. In many countries the financial and political incentives to corrupt the pretrial detention process are relatively numerous, rewarding, and risk free. That toxic combination—low levels of accountability combined with poor transparency around the processing of the case—is why so many pretrial detention systems are corrupt from start to finish.

There are many places where corruption is rife among police. Corrupt behavior may be especially prevalent among junior personnel who work under difficult and hazardous conditions for very little pay. These are typically uniformed officers who patrol the streets on a daily basis on the lookout for offenders. Ironically, such officers go about their daily routines with little supervision and imbued with considerable discretion about whom to arrest for which transgressions of the law. The combination of limited supervision, significant discretion, unpleasant working conditions, and poor remuneration serves as an incentive to engage in rent-seeking behavior. Corruption takes on a more systemic form when senior officers expect their subordinates to generate certain amounts of money every month by fleecing arrestees. In such a scenario, junior officers will seek to generate sufficient money though corrupt practices to both meet the demands of their superiors and to fill their own pockets.

In Bangladesh, for example, junior police officers earn very little. This is likely to have contributed to the arrest of Nur-A-Alam Nobi in Bogra, Bangladesh in 2010.[51] Nobi, a 23-year old barber, was arrested by police on the allegation that he was suspected of having stolen something as he was walking alone late at night. The arresting officers demanded a bribe of 200 taka (about US$3) for Nobi to be released. Nobi, who earned an average of 70 taka a day, and supported a wife and three-year old child, was unable to pay the amount demanded by the police. Consequently, Nobi was confined in a cramped cell with 80 other detainees for three weeks, until finally his case was dismissed when it became clear that there was no incriminating evidence against him and that he was unable to pay a bribe.

Nobi's case is a good example of how poor people become victims of police corruption. Nobi was walking alone late at night because he could not afford to travel by public transport and because his home was a long distance from his place of work. Nobi was thus accessible to police who were looking to make an arrest to extract a bribe. Someone with slightly more means—even within the impoverished context of Bangladesh—would have used a cheap cycle or motorcycle-rickshaw as transport home. Moreover, arresting, say, a middle class person entails risks arresting officers are unlikely to face when arresting poor persons. Wealthier people are more likely to have access to a lawyer, a local politician, or even a journalist friend who could expose the corrupt behavior of the police. While it is true that arresting poor people provides only modest returns, it is a low-risk activity for corrupt police, and they can simply arrest of a large volume of people.

### Bangladesh: 34 Corrupt Transactions over Four Months[52]

After a member of the Rezzak family was arrested, family members recorded the number of occasions on which they were forced to pay bribes and the amount they paid. The bribes were paid to secure basic provisions and safeguards during police custody and in hope of securing release on bail. Over the course of four months in 2008-09, the Rezzak family paid a total of 159,660 Taka (US$2,262) through a total of 34 corrupt transactions. The most significant proportion of this amount (a total of 75,000 Taka) was to detaining officers, to prevent torture and the fabrication of more charges against their relative. Other significant bribes were to lawyers and legal clerks. The remainder was for items that should have been provided by the state, including access to legal documents and food for the detained family member.

A 2002 UNODC study found that, on average, more than 70 percent of lawyers surveyed in three Nigerian states had paid bribes in order to expedite court proceedings, including the implementation of bail orders, the commencement of trial, and the expediting of trial proceedings. While most of these bribes were paid to court staff and police, a fifth of respondents stated they also had to make such payments to judges. In systems where judges do not have to provide transparent and defensible reasons why a defendant is being detained pending trial, chances are higher that some judges will accept bribes to release someone from pretrial custody. Moreover, more than 40 percent of Nigerian court users (i.e. members of the public who are not lawyers) experienced corruption when seeking access to the justice system, with a large proportion specifically stating that they paid a bribe to obtain bail.[53] According to the UNODC, "in particular the poor and uneducated, as well as ethnic minorities are more likely to be confronted with corruption... and to experience delays."[54]

Research on the Nigeria Police Force (NPF) revealed an organized scheme under which senior NPF officers expressly approve and profit from extortion committed by NPF personnel. There appears to be a standard practice whereby police personnel on some patrols are required to "deliver" certain amounts daily to their superiors. Failure to "deliver" can result in severe penalties, ranging from transfer to non-lucrative patrols to being dismissed from the force.[55]

Certain locations, such as Abuja, Nigeria's capital city, and some particular assignments such as the Ports Authority Police, are regarded as especially lucrative posts. Police officers routinely pay bribes of between ₦40,000 to ₦200,000 (approximately US$250 – US$1,250) in order to secure postings to these places—and then often must pay again to avoid being transferred out of these locations. The amount that must be paid depends on the rank and availability of positions in the desired location. Once they are in a position, those posted expect to reap rich returns on their investment.[56] Clearly, endemic corruption in Nigeria's police force will result in the arrest of those too poor to bribe their way out of unwarranted NPF attention. And corruption within the judiciary will result in excessive pretrial detention for those too poor to bribe their way out of jail. The net result is that Nigeria's pretrial detention population is overwhelmingly made up of those who are too poor to pay their way out.

Country reports from the office of the Special Rapporteur on Prisons and Conditions of Detention in Africa are full of examples of corrupt practices in respect of bail. In a visit to remand cells in Bangui in the Central African Republic, the Special Rapporteur found that "police demanded money [from the detainees] before release."[57] In a report on prisons in Malawi, the Special Rapporteur concluded that corruption was widespread.[58] In Benin, a prisoner told the Special Rapporteur: "The main problem is the judiciary. [The act of] prosecution in Abomey [a city in Benin] has become an avenue for getting money. If you do not have money, your case is never examined."[59]

A 2011 survey in Ghana found that almost a quarter of pretrial detainees (24 percent) were asked for a bribe by a state official to secure release. Of those who said a bribe was suggested, 27 percent said it was asked by police, nine percent by a magistrate, and nine percent by a clerk. Generally the bribe amount increased with the income of the detainee.[60]

In 2008, Chief Justice of the Indonesian Constitutional Court Jimly Asshiddiqie condemned the corruption endemic to the criminal justice system of Indonesia. "First the police 'squeeze' [bribe] those they arrest, demanding bribes," Justice Asshiddiqie said. "Then prosecutors squeeze the criminal. When he [the defendant] gets to court, the first man to squeeze is the registrar. And when he comes to the judges, they again squeeze the criminal, but they only get the bones."[61]

### Indonesia: The Cost of Corruption[62]

In 2008, Ary, a 22 year-old Indonesian man, was arrested and detained for purchasing a small packet of marijuana (cannabis). Ary was told by the police that for the equivalent of US$10,000 he would be free to go. Because his family did not have that amount of money, the police delayed filing charges against Ary for 50 days, holding him in pretrial detention while they negotiated with his family. Eventually the police agreed to accept US$500 and "reduce" the amount of marijuana seized so that Ary was charged as a user instead of a dealer. Ary's family then began negotiating with the next officials in the justice chain, the prosecutors. The prosecution stated that Ary's sentence would be five years. After selling belongings and borrowing from friends, Ary's family paid the prosecution US$2,000 to reduce the sentence request to nine months. After bribing the judge US$1,000, Ary was given a nine-month sentence.

An investigation of criminal justice practices in the U.S. state of Mississippi unearthed numerous complaints from indigent defendants that court-appointed lawyers pressure poor clients and their families to give them money on the side, promising that they can get a better class of service if they pay for it. In one representative case, a court-appointed lawyer told his client's family that he would deliver a good service for their son if they paid him $10,000. After accepting payment, the lawyer did little work on the case, leaving his client to languish in pretrial detention for a year. On the day of trial, the lawyer, who was ill-prepared, encouraged his client to plead guilty.[63]

> **USA: Lawyer Demands Bribe from 14-Year Old**[64]
>
> In 1998, 14-year old Carlos Ivy was arrested in Mississippi for the alleged robbery of $100 from an elderly woman. Ivy spent eight months in adult jail before he had his first conversation with a lawyer about the facts of his case. After one brief meeting with the lawyer, Ivy did not hear from him again for six months. The lawyer did not answer letters or return Ivy's grandmother's telephone calls.
>
> Ivy was desperate to get out of the county jail, where he was the only juvenile. During his stay there, he claimed to have suffered serious mistreatment, including having his head rammed into a wall, being choked, being deprived of food, being held in a cell for intoxicated inmates, and being stripped naked for a period of days. When the lawyer finally met with Ivy again, he stated that he was doing Ivy's case for free, and that it would help if Ivy's family could pay him some money. Ivy's grandmother was too poor to pay. As a result, the lawyer never investigated the case, spoke to any witnesses, or filed any motions on Ivy's behalf.

In Mexico, an important reason for corruption in pretrial detention is that the public prosecutor's power is largely unsupervised by the courts. With complete freedom to produce an accusation or release a suspect due to lack of evidence, public prosecutors and their police officers (investigating police) can set guilty people free if offered money.[65] According to one report:

> The most critical moment [in Mexico] for a citizen is when the preliminary investigation is being compiled. At this stage, the public prosecutor acts as the sole authority and knows that the evidence included in the case file will carry definitive weight in the proceedings. After the preliminary investigation, very little is contributed. As a result, there is a real threat of corruption. The evidence presented by the public prosecutor can favor the victim by exacerbating the crime committed against him or can benefit the accused by distorting events to lower the possibility of his being found guilty or, if the case, to reduce his sentence.[66]

## Lacking Influence

In places where corruption and patronage are pervasive, pretrial detainees are more likely to be released awaiting trial if they have politically influential allies or connections. In such settings politicians can, and do, exert pressure on criminal justice officials to ensure that their friends and associates who have been arrested are quickly released. Often a bribe has to be paid as well to a local official, but this only serves to underscore the challenge the poor face in such situations. Defendants do not need to have direct access to, for example, the national police minister to benefit from such an arrangement. Oftentimes, a phone call to a minor local politician or a friend who has access to, and some influence over, such a politician—a businessperson, a journalist or a land owner, for example—suffices.[67] Poor and marginalized people, who lack such connections, cannot avail themselves of this type of corruption.

As an International Crisis Group report on Pakistan observed: "Defendants with financial and political capital often evade punishment, while those without remain in jail, most often without being convicted or convicted on half-baked and concocted evidence. Few, even within the law-enforcement agencies, trust the trial process as a credible mechanism to combat serious crime."[68]

In settings where rights are subservient to patronage and influence, the rights of the poor become increasingly marginalized by a system which informally accommodates the needs of its elites. Unsurprisingly, in places where political patronage is pervasive, the country's elites care very little about promoting and maintaining efficient and fair criminal justice processes. Should they, their children, or their friends be arrested and detained, help is usually only a phone call away. The resultant neglect of the criminal justice system, through underfunding, and lack of proper oversight and management, reduces the system to one of dysfunction—or one that functions only *because of* corruption. Average periods of pretrial detention invariably begin to stretch into months and years, and the central purpose of the justice system ceases to be the provision of justice.

In Bangladesh, three-quarters of the annual budget for legal aid goes unspent year after year.[69] This is largely because those with money or connections do not need legal aid, and those who are poor or powerless are not given access to the funds. If the well-connected could not free themselves with a phone call, the legal aid funds would be more likely to be used. Similarly, in South Africa, where a group of four co-defendants have appeared in court 100 times without completing their trial, such inefficiency would be unthinkable if the defendants (or the victims in the case) enjoyed some social, economic and/or political influence.[70]

Corruption-related delays in holding trials also affect defendants' right to a fair trial. Delays, especially multiple postponements of trial dates, discourage witnesses from attending court hearings to provide testimony. In developing countries, where individuals disproportionately rely on their labor to earn a living, public transport is erratic and expensive, and many people live far from the nearest court, individuals suffer both direct and indirect economic losses by spending a day at court. This is especially so in respect of witnesses for the defense who cannot rely on the police to provide them with transport, for example. While the following account is from Nigeria, it applies equally to many developing countries: "On the part of witnesses, who might have been to court on some occasions probably three, four or five times without being attended to, they lose interest in the case especially where they had to come to court from a distant place at their own expenses."[71]

## Easy and Vulnerable Targets

In many countries, the formal criminal justice system often fails to provide justice and security to the indigent or protect their rights. According to the International Centre for Prison Studies, justice systems in poor countries exacerbate the poverty of the destitute "by bearing down most heavily on them and subjecting them to gross injustices, whilst not providing them with the protection they need."[72]

Poor people make easy targets for corrupt police officers or police who are under pressure to meet arrest quotas. Poor people are more likely to live on the streets or spend a lot of time on the streets. In developing countries, the indigent generally do not spend their days working in offices or factories and are unable to afford private or public transport. They are consequently more exposed to police surveillance as they walk long distances between their homes (typically outlying slums or informal settlements) and their places of work such as city-center markets and busy street corners to peddle home grown fruit or cheap goods.

ABand The poor are also at greater risk of committing certain petty offenses or transgressing municipal ordinances by virtue of their indigence, such as trespassing in an effort to find a place to rest or sleep, selling goods without a permit, urinating in public, and begging.

Children, especially poor children, are particularly vulnerable to arrest—and in the case of street children, readily available for arrest. The former UN Special Rapporteur on Torture, Manfred Novak, has estimated that one million children are behind bars, "many of them in prolonged pretrial detention" and the vast majority of them accused of "petty crimes or uncontrollable behavior."[73]

### Criminalization of Poverty, Part Two

The UN Special Rapporteur on Extreme Poverty and Human Rights laments the increasing criminalization of behavior which brings the poor into conflict with the law:

> With increasing frequency, States are also penalizing the performance of certain behaviours and actions which are associated with living on the street such as sleeping, sitting, lying, littering, lodging, camping or storing belongings in public spaces; public drunkenness; public urination; or jaywalking. Often these regulations are vaguely worded, allowing law enforcement agencies extensive discretion and enforcement authority, which threatens to violate legal and constitutional safeguards. By making these activities or behaviours illegal, States increase the exposure of persons living in poverty to abuse, harassment, violence, corruption and extortion by both private individuals and law enforcement officials.

> While these regulations are not explicitly addressed towards persons living in poverty, they affect them disproportionately. Owing to their lack of or limited access to housing, persons living in poverty rely more heavily on public spaces for their daily activities. Thus, individuals who have no choice but to live on the street find that daily life-sustaining activities can put them in danger of criminal sanctions. Although these types of measures are ostensibly neutral, studies show that authorities target those living in poverty, particularly homeless persons."[74]

In numerous jurisdictions, police performance is measured by, among other factors, the number of arrests undertaken within a set time period. This can apply to the total number of arrests undertaken by a police precinct, so that precinct commanders place pressure on their subordinates to institute a certain number of arrests on a recurring basis. It also applies to individual police officers whose performance is evaluated, and promotional prospects are influenced by, the number of arrests they undertake. In some jurisdictions police precincts and/or individual officers are given monthly arrest quotas they are expected to meet or surpass to avoid a negative evaluation of their performance. In such situations, the number of arrests tends to surge towards the end of every month as police officers scramble to meet their quota of arrests.

### Kyrgyzstan: Homeless and Available for Arrest[75]

Valera and Anwar were homeless teenagers, living on the streets of Bishkek, the capital of Kyrgyzstan. They were charged with stealing a computer from the orphanage where they used to live. The two boys spent ten months in pretrial detention, including four months in temporary detention isolation facilities and six months in pretrial isolation facilities. Kyrgyzstan law states that time in temporary isolation facilities should not exceed three days. Conditions were abominable—Valera and Anwar lived with eight other juveniles in a room built for four, and they were fed scraps of food, leftovers from a local bar. Throughout their detention the police tried to pressure the boys to confess to additional crimes, which they refused to do. They served a year before gaining their freedom.

A 2003 Human Rights Watch report on Kazakhstan found strong evidence that, "police as a rule do not arrest drug dealers, even when they know where the dealers are located, but prefer the more marginalized and impoverished users. Police must also reportedly fill arrest quotas, a holdover practice from the Soviet era, and they naturally seek easy targets for arrest."[76] Police in South Africa,[77] Russia,[78] and New York City[79] have also reported the use of arrest quotas, especially in respect of persons suspected of less serious crimes, and individual officers have claimed that they suffered negative consequences for not meeting their assigned quotas.

In some places there is intense pressure on the police to solve all serious crimes committed in their jurisdiction. The inability to solve such crimes is treated as a blemish on an investigator's record and often that of his superiors too. For individual officers this can lead to delays in promotion and increases in salary and related perks and, in high-profile cases, even to demotions or reassignment to less appealing positions or locations within the police organization. Under such pressures, officers will seek to arrest someone who is available (e.g. living on the street), too poor to post bail or retain defense counsel, and too marginalized to raise public concern about his plight.

### Ukraine: Arrest and Beatings to "Solve" a Crime[80]

In 2007, Vartan S., a Ukrainian who earns his living selling stationery at a marketplace, saw from some distance a corpse lying on the bank of the river on the outskirts of Kharkov where he often goes fishing. After consulting with his wife, they decided to inform the police. "I called from our home phone and I gave my name—this was my biggest mistake." When the patrol came, he was taken to the police station to provide a signed statement. And then, two days later he was detained in the street and taken to the police station where he was badly beaten. The police stripped the 41-year old Vartan naked and for 40 minutes they hit him on his head, neck, ears, and groin. Technically, Vartan was detained on the basis of having "behaved rudely towards the police agents on duty," But in truth the officers were trying to force him to confess falsely to killing the man whose body he found.

Vartan should never have been detained absent some credible basis for linking him to the crime. In fact, he has a solid alibi. The day the man was killed, Vartan was on his plot of land in Danilovka, 10 kilometers from Kharkov, and was seen there by several neighbors.

The ill effects of the torture on Vartan must have given pause to the police, because unexpectedly they arranged for him to be taken to a medical center. But the police warned him to insist that he was fine. Consequently, after two days of beatings, Vartan told the doctor that he had no complaints.

Fortunately, a lawyer from the Public Defenders' Office intervened and then, in front of the prosecutor, Vartan was able to explain that his confession was extracted under duress. He was released and the "rude behavior" charge was dropped and the prosecutor did not charge Vartan with manslaughter.

Vartan's lawyer explains that the police are evaluated on the basis of performance indicators, such as the proportion of murders that are solved or the total number of drug possession cases cleared. Thus, the police's desperate efforts to get someone—anyone—to confess to a murder.

## MARGINALIZED MINORITIES AND NON-CITIZENS

Discriminated-against minorities and foreigners are significantly overrepresented in many pretrial detention systems. This is so for a number of reasons, ranging from blatant discrimination and xenophobia to the more subtle consequences of minority or non-citizen status. For example, marginalized minorities and foreigners are often relatively impoverished and work on the margins of the formal economy (with foreigners prohibited from working legally in many places)—both factors which place members of such groups at disproportionate risk of being arrested.

In 2009, Advocacy Forum-Nepal, an NGO, interviewed almost 4,000 pretrial detainees in police detention centers as part of its regular efforts to identify persons in need of legal aid and / or who may have been tortured. Advocacy Forum found that some 65 percent of the detainees they came across were ethnic minorities or Dalits.[81] Dalits are considered "untouchable" and suffer widespread discrimination. Comprising the poorest of the poor, Dalits constitute some 13 to 15 percent of the Nepalese population. Advocacy Forum also found that female[82] and juvenile[83] Dalit detainees were disproportionately likely to be tortured while in pretrial detention—in the case of female Dalits, often at rates three times higher than non-Dalit detainees.

The situation of Dalits in India is equally dire:

> Dalits are disproportionately targeted by the police for a number of reasons. According to the NHRC [National Human Rights Commission], under a

> theory of collective punishment, the police will often subject entire Dalit communities to violent search and seizure operations in search of one individual. Dalit communities may also be perceived by the police as inherently criminal. Dalits and other poor minorities are disproportionately represented among those detained and tortured in police custody because most cannot afford to pay police bribes. Dalits are also likely victims of police misconduct because they are rarely informed of their rights, rarely have access to an attorney, and are not able to afford bail. Police officers' deeply embedded caste bias (most officers belong to the dominant castes) and a general lack of familiarity with legislative protections for Dalits, further compound the problem.[84]

High incarceration rates for indigenous people—both for pretrial detainees and sentenced prisoners—appear to be a global phenomenon.[85] In Canada, persons who self-identified as Aboriginal accounted for 21 percent of the total number of adults remanded into pretrial detention in 2008-09, even though Aboriginal adults comprise about three percent of the Canadian adult population.[86]

In Australia, over half (57 percent) of juvenile pretrial detainees in 2007-08 were indigenous defendants (Aboriginals and Torres Strait Islanders), despite indigenous people representing only 2.5 percent of the Australian population.[87] In effect, the pretrial detention rate for indigenous juveniles is over twenty times higher than the rate for non-indigenous juveniles.

Indigenous adult defendants in Australia are more likely to be refused pretrial release than non-indigenous defendants, even after controlling for other factors.[88] According to Western Australia's Law Reform Commission, indigenous people are more likely to be refused bail and "more likely to be unable to meet the requirements or conditions that have been imposed," such as having a stable place to live.[89] A 2005 survey of male indigenous pretrial detainees in South Australia found that over a third (36 percent) were homeless at the time of their arrest. And almost three-quarters anticipated no secure accommodation on release.[90]

In the U.S. between 1985 and 2007 (the last years for which data are available), black youth were disproportionately detained. Black youth were twice as likely as white and Native American youth to be detained for drug offenses.[91] In 2009, blacks accounted for 39 percent of all jail inmates (in the U.S. pretrial detainees charged with non-federal offenses are held in local jails) but only about 13 percent of the general U.S. population.[92]

A review of all defendants arrested in New York City in 2008 for minor (non-felony) charges found that a large number were unable to afford the financial bail set by the court. Blacks and Hispanics constituted 89 percent of all pretrial detainees held on bail of $1,000 or less, even though these two groups comprise only 51 percent of the city's population.[93]

In Texas, a review of 15,000 cases of people arrested for minor (misdemeanor) offenses in late 2010 found that over two-thirds (70 percent) of white defendants were released on bail compared to 45 percent of black defendants and 52 percent of Hispanic defendants.[94] These are cases where bail was granted by the courts but the defendants were unable to come up with the money needed to facilitate their release. The racial and ethnic disparity in the data is ascribed to the relative inability of many minority defendants "to raise the money necessary to post bond on even relatively minor cases."[95]

Social status is another factor which leads to discrimination by criminal justice agencies.[96] Examples of such discrimination can be found in the treatment of drug users and sexual minorities. Drug use is often harshly criminalized; in some countries more than a third of pretrial detainees are charged with drug related crimes.[97] Similarly, sexual minorities are criminalized in many countries for expressing their sexual preferences. In pretrial detention they often face a particular risk of torture and are held under considerably worse conditions than others.[98]

Limited information is available on the proportion of foreigners among national pretrial detention populations. The countries with the most comprehensive information are the member states of the European Union. A report on pretrial detention in the EU found that the proportion of foreigners in the pretrial population is "relatively high compared to the number of foreigners in the national population."[99] This is a diplomatic understatement. In EU member states for which data are available, 30 percent of all pretrial detainees are foreigners.[100] In at least seven EU member states—including larger states such as Germany, Italy, and Portugal – between one-third and two-thirds of all pretrial detainees are foreigners (Table 1).

Within the EU, foreigners are more overrepresented among pretrial detainees than among sentenced prisoners. In 2007, foreigners comprised 19 percent of sentenced prisoners among EU countries for which data are available, but 30 percent of all pretrial detainees among comparable EU countries. If this pattern holds for criminal justice systems generally, then foreigners are significantly overrepresented among pretrial detention populations around the world. The International Centre for Prison Studies (ICPS) provides information from almost 200 countries on the proportion of prisoners (both sentenced and pretrial detainees) who are foreigners. The ICPS lists 22 countries in which the proportion of foreigners exceeds one-third of the overall prison population, and 56 countries where foreigners comprise more than 10 percent of the national prison population.[101]

TABLE 1:

**Foreigners in pretrial detention as a proportion of all pretrial detainees, selected EU countries, 2007**

| Country | % |
| --- | --- |
| Austria | 64.5% |
| Belgium | 55.4% |
| Spain | 52.2% |
| Italy | 45.2% |
| Germany | 42.3% |
| Portugal | 37.7% |
| Ireland | 34.7% |
| Netherlands | 22.9% |

Source: A.M. van Kalmthout et al., Pretrial Detention in the European Union.

## THE MENTALLY ILL AND INTELLECTUALLY DISABLED

People remanded into pretrial detention often have higher rates of mental health problems than sentenced prisoners or the general population.[102] An international trend toward deinstitutionalization has led to significant reductions of the number of patients in psychiatric hospitals and an often concomitant increase in the number of pretrial detainees with mental health problems.

In Victoria, Australia, for example, there has been a decline in the seriousness of the criminal history of pretrial detainees, but an increasing rate of severe mental health and drug and alcohol abuse problems among detainees.[103] A legal aid worker in Victoria commented that the pretrial detention system "seems to have become the dumping ground for people with mental health problems and with intellectual disabilities ... There has been a massive increase of people with mental health issues who are in the remand system and who've got nowhere to go."[104]

An investigation at a large remand center for men in England found that about one-third of pretrial detainees could be classified as having a psychological disorder, and around five percent of detainees were acutely psychotic.[105] A report on all prisons in England and Wales by the Office for National Statistics discovered even higher levels of mental disorder among the prison population in general, and pretrial detainees in particular: a personality disorder was found in 78 percent of male pretrial detainees (compared to 64 percent of male sentenced prisoners), and psychosis was identified in 10 percent of male pretrial detainees (and seven percent of male sentenced prisoners).[106]

In the U.S., persons with a serious mental illness are also overrepresented among pretrial detainee populations. While approximately five percent of the U.S. population has a serious mental illness, in pretrial detention the proportion is around three times this figure. Persons with a mental illness on average spend longer periods in pretrial detention than do healthy defendants.[107]

People with an intellectual disability also tend to be over-represented in pretrial detention.[108] In Australia, for example, people with an intellectual disability are more likely to be detained awaiting trial than non-intellectually impaired.[109] Moreover, first time pretrial detainees in the Australian state of Victoria with intellectual disabilities are detained for twice the period of time compared to non-intellectually impaired detainees.[110]

In the UK, 20 to 30 percent of offenders and suspected offenders have learning disabilities or difficulties that interfere with their ability to cope within the criminal justice system.[111] A study by the Prison Reform Trust in the UK found that over three-quarters of prisoners with possible learning disabilities had difficulties filling in prison forms, and that "similar difficulties were likely to have occurred at the police station and in court" in respect of pretrial detainees with learning disabilities.[112] The study concludes that "people with learning disabilities or difficulties are discriminated against personally, systematically and routinely as they enter and travel through the criminal justice system."[113]

People with learning disabilities or difficulties who are in pretrial detention are sometimes denied medication and treatment—either willfully as a punishment, or to entice them to confess to the charges against them, or due to neglect and official indifference. This may further undermine a person's ability to understand legal proceedings, communicate with his lawyer, and resist official efforts to elicit a confession.

Finally, it is often assumed by the courts that defendants with mental disabilities do not have close community ties. This, and the fact that persons with mental disabilities are released awaiting trial on unrealistic conditions (e.g. to comply with a curfew order or to report regularly to a probation officer), results in defendants with mental disabilities being at greater risk of spending some time awaiting trial in pretrial detention compared to other defendants with similar backgrounds charged with similar crimes.

# LOW-RISK DEFENDANTS, PERSONS ACCUSED OF MINOR OFFENSES, AND THE INNOCENT

In theory, judicial officers' pretrial release and detention decisions are rational because they are based upon an acquired expertise about the risk factors presented by individual defendants. The theory has, however, not been substantiated by studies of bail decisions. In fact, in risk-of-flight studies, similarly situated defendants have received significantly different bail decisions. In some risk of re-offending studies, judicial officers accurately identified potential re-offending defendants in as few as five to 30 percent of the cases.[114] Judicial officers' decisions about who should be released pending trial are highly discretionary and often highly inconsistent. Most people in pretrial detention should not be there.

In a survey of detention decisions between 2004 and 2007 in the Mexican city of Monterrey, it was found that virtually all pretrial detainees resided in metropolitan Monterrey, and many of them were employed. It was also found that half of the detainees were over 30 years of age (past the age when persons are disproportionately likely to commit violent crimes), and two-thirds of the detainees were first time offenders.[115] On the face of it, these defendants posed a low risk of flight, offending while awaiting trial, or interfering with the administration of justice. In other words, they should generally not have been in pretrial detention.

A 2009 UNODC survey of 30 African countries sought to identify the characteristics of those in prison, in an effort to gauge the threat they might pose to society. Prison administrations were asked to estimate the proportion of prisoners in pretrial detention charged with "minor offenses" or convicted of such offenses (the survey conflated pretrial detainees and sentenced prisoners). According to the survey results, the proportion of prisoners who have been detained or sentenced for "minor" crimes is strikingly high in many countries. In Ghana it is 90 percent, followed by Malawi and Swaziland (85 percent), Zambia (79 percent), Djibouti (75 percent), and Burkina Faso, Burundi, Cameroon, and Mali (all 60 percent or higher).[116] Simply, put, these people were behind bars despite not having committed a serious crime, and despite posing no real threat to society.

An analysis of pretrial detention in five Brazilian cities found that between 2000 and 2004, judges routinely imprisoned large numbers of people accused of petty theft, even though this is a minor offense. In some places, over a third of those detained on this charge had spent more than 100 days in pretrial detention, and many spent longer on remand than the custodial sentences they eventually received.[117]

In Texas, the excessive use of financial bail results in the detention of a large number of defendants who are charged with minor crimes and who pose a low risk of absconding or committing a crime if released awaiting trial.[118] In New Orleans, almost 3,000 persons incarcerated in the local jail are pretrial detainees, the majority being held for drug possession, traffic violations, public drunkenness, or other nonviolent offenses.[119] This seemingly unnecessary use of pretrial detention is one reason why Louisiana (in which the city of New Orleans is situated) has the highest state-level incarceration rate in the U.S., at 850 prisoners per 100,000 of the general population.

**Romania: Four Years, instead of a Fine**[120]

In hindsight, Andrei should have just admitted to procuring a prostitute and paid the fine. But embarrassed at what his wife and two daughters would think, he decided to contest the charge and was placed in pretrial detention—where he spent four years. He turned 60 while languishing in Romania's pretrial detention system, and developed thrombophlebitis and thrombosis in his right leg. The rudimentary health care available to pretrial detainees could not address his condition, and eventually he pleaded guilty because sentenced prisoners can receive specialized medical attention. Being convicted will allow him to go to a proper hospital. Although Andrei is eligible for conditional release based on his good behavior, he's afraid his health will deteriorate further before it comes through.

In England and Wales, four out of ten pretrial detainees received a non-custodial sentence in 2009—that is, even after being found guilty, they were not held in prison because their offense was so minor.[121] Among juveniles, three-quarters of all pretrial detainees are either acquitted or given a non-custodial sentence.[122] Among adult pretrial detainees, around half of males and two-thirds of females are either acquitted or given a non-custodial sentence upon conviction. A senior probation officer in England commented that these statistics appear "even starker if one considers that amongst those ultimately sentenced to custody are the ones who receive a prison sentence virtually commensurate with the time already served on custodial remand. It would appear reasonable therefore to make the assertion that there are many people who are remanded into custody unnecessarily, or at least spend longer in prison than would otherwise be the case."[123] In Scotland, between a fifth and half of all pretrial detainees receive a non-custodial sentence.[124]

In New Zealand, about half of all persons who spend some time in pretrial detention receive a non-custodial sentence.[125] Studies of pretrial detainees in New South Wales, Australia, found that 56 percent of adult,[126] and 84 percent of juvenile,[127] pretrial detainees are released without a custodial sentence. In South Australia only about 30 percent of those remanded in custody serve additional time in prison following sentencing, whereas in Victoria, with its lower remand rate, about 60 percent of pretrial detainees spend additional time in custody after sentence.[128] In Chile, between 2005 and 2010, less than a quarter of pretrial detainees ended up being convicted and receiving a custodial sentence.[129] In Germany, generally only a bit over half of all convicted pretrial detainees (56 percent in 2006) receive an unconditional custodial sentence, with some 40 percent receiving a suspended custodial sentence and five to 10 percent receiving a fine.[130]

Where custodial sentences are imposed, there is some evidence to suggest that "imprisonment appears at least in some times and places to be used in order to 'cover' pretrial detention: that is, pretrial detention is retrospectively justified by imposing a prison sentence."[131]

According to the Criminal Justice Agency of New York, in 2003-04, in "22 percent of non-felony cases with a detained defendant, the defendant was ultimately acquitted or the case was dismissed."[132] Among New York City defendants arrested in 2008 on non-felony charges and given bail under $1,000, 24 percent were acquitted.[133]

In England and Wales, around one in five pretrial detainees are acquitted.[134] In New Zealand, too, about a fifth of all persons who spend some time in pretrial detention end up being acquitted of the charges against them.[135] A review of cases coming before three large criminal courts in South Africa found that around half of arrestees end up being released because the charges against them are withdrawn.[136]

## CONCLUSION

As this chapter has sought to demonstrate, pretrial detainees around the world are disproportionately poor.

The widespread use of money bail is discriminatory in its effect, and is one prominent reason why the poor are held in pretrial detention and why those with means are released. The indigent simply do not have the resources needed to secure their release. Even in rich countries, where endemic corruption in the justice sector is typically rarer and state-financed legal aid schemes provide some access to justice for the poor, albeit of often low quality, money bail results in persons being detained awaiting trial simply because they lack the means to deposit the requisite bail with the courts.

The fact that the poor cannot afford private counsel in most places, and that state-financed legal aid systems are underfunded and understaffed virtually everywhere, implies that the indigent are at the mercy of their interrogators. This is aggravated by the fact that legal aid schemes rarely provide legal services to defendants prior to their first court appearance. As a result, poor defendants typically have no recourse to a lawyer within the first few hours or days of their arrest. Yet, it is within this timeframe that police often exert pressure on arrestees to confess to real or imagined crimes, often sealing the latter's fate. Indeed, the UN Working Group on Arbitrary Detention has noted that empirical research shows those in pretrial detention have a lower likelihood of obtaining an acquittal than those who remain at liberty before their trial. This "deepens further the disadvantages that the poor and marginalized face in the enjoyment of the right to a fair trial on an equal footing."[137]

Corruption flourishes in the pretrial phase of the criminal justice process. All over the world, poor people are arrested because they cannot pay a bribe to the corrupt police officer, then denied access to counsel or family because they cannot bribe the corrupt guard or prosecutor, then held indefinitely—or found guilty—because they cannot bribe the corrupt judge. The ability to put cash in the right hands often makes the difference between freedom and detention. Once in custody, pretrial detainees are wholly at the mercy of the detaining authorities. They or their families are often forced to pay for access to services and treatment to which they are entitled under national and international law, including food, drinking water, medication, or contact with family members. Additionally, they are forced to pay to "prevent" torture or other mistreatment, and demands for bribes are often combined with the threat or actual use of torture.

The disproportionate use of pretrial detention against the poor and otherwise marginalized is, on its face, unjust and unfair. Yet, such practices may be defended by some if they result in the detention of individuals who pose a serious threat to public safety and the sound administration of justice. The available evidence tends to suggest otherwise, however: many pretrial detainees do not pose a flight risk; are suspected of only relatively minor, non-violent offenses; and often do not receive a custodial sentence upon conviction. Moreover, a significant number of pretrial detainees are never convicted of the charges which led to their detention in the first place. Their only crime is being poor.

# Circumstances of Detention and Impact on Detainees and their Communities

## INTRODUCTION

Places of imprisonment are tense and overcrowded facilities in which all prisoners struggle to maintain their self-respect and emotional equilibrium despite violence, exploitation, extortion, and lack of privacy. Prisoners face stark limitations on family and community contacts, and typically have few opportunities for meaningful education, work, or other productive activities. Such hardships are particularly deplorable in the context of pretrial detention, where detainees should be considered innocent but where, paradoxically, conditions are often worse than they are for those who have already been found guilty.

Persons in pretrial detention have not been convicted of a crime.[2] They should be considered innocent and as far as practicable be treated as such. Pretrial detainees become convicts only once their guilt has been proven in front of an impartial tribunal. Many pretrial detainees around the world are arrested and detained on flimsy evidence, with a significant number eventually having the charges against them withdrawn or being acquitted of their charges. A large number of detainees receive a noncustodial sentence upon their conviction because of the relatively trifling nature of their crimes, or receive a sentence that is actually less than the amount of time they have been in pretrial detention.

This chapter first examines how and why conditions are worse for pretrial detainees than for sentenced prisoners, then looks closely at those conditions, including the types of facilities used and the frequency of violence and abuse. The chapter also examines the impact of pretrial detention on the health of detainees and their communities, as well as the economic impact. It concludes by considering the idea that excessive pretrial detention actually increases crime.

## WORSE OFF THAN CONVICTED PRISONERS

It is a cruel irony of pretrial detention that pretrial detainees are typically treated worse than convicted inmates. In comparison to sentenced prisoners, pretrial detainees are more likely to go hungry, be victims of violence (at the hands of guards or fellow detainees), suffer overcrowding, and be denied access to health care. Unlike convicts, pretrial detainees suffer from instrumental abuse and violence at the hands of the police to entice them to confess or reveal the whereabouts of a suspected accomplice.

The physical, mental, and economic consequences of pretrial detention not only detrimentally affect detainees but also their families and wider communities. Incomes and employment lost as a result of lengthy periods of pretrial detention often hurt detainees' families more than detainees themselves. Pretrial detainees are often at considerable risk of being subsumed into criminal gangs common to many prison settings or falling ill from a communicable disease—infections (one social, the other medical) which released detainees introduce into their communities when they are eventually released.

Many prisons are not equipped, and prison officials do not see it as their function, to provide more than the bare minimum of services to pretrial detainees. Even the bare-bones accommodations that are available to sentenced prisoners in some places, such as medical care or exercise facilities, are often denied to pretrial detainees. A UNICEF report describes this phenomenon for juvenile detainees, but the words could be applied equally to adult pretrial detainees:

> It is, somewhat paradoxically, during the pre-trial period that a child or young person is likely to face the worst conditions of detention and when relevant standards are likely to be most abused. In comparison with sentenced juveniles, he or she is at much greater risk of, for example, being in contact with adults (e.g. in police cells), being held in unhealthy accommodation, lacking supervision by specially trained staff, being without an activity programme, and having to remain in closed quarters up to 23 or even 24 hours a day.[3]

In Nigeria, pretrial detainees "live in the most terrible conditions, occupying the most crowded cells… In addition, there is a lot of hostility meted out to them by warders. They are treated most roughly and when food is not enough, they are the unlucky ones who have to go hungry. They are seen as 'parasites' who come to 'eat up' the food meant for convicts. The awaiting trial inmates, though not yet found guilty, are treated as if they had been and even worse."[4]

As the situation in Nigeria described above exemplifies, in poorer countries pretrial detainees often receive less food than the already meager rations given to convicted prisoners. In Kenya, pretrial detainees are given half the food ration of convicted persons, ostensibly because they do not work.[5] In Zambia, human rights monitors found that pretrial detainees are allowed to eat only after convicted prisoners are fed, which often leaves them with virtually nothing to eat.[6]

The deplorable conditions and treatment imposed on pretrial detainees often reflect the problems of an underfunded criminal justice system. But it is an established principle of international law that prison conditions that infringe prisoners' human rights are not justified by a lack of resources. When a state deprives a person of liberty, it assumes a duty of care for that person. The human rights of all prisoners are established in international law by a number of conventions and covenants which have treaty status. States signing and ratifying them bind themselves to observe their provisions.[7]

The tendency for pretrial detainees to be incarcerated under worse conditions than convicted prisoners is, moreover, not confined to low-income countries. In South Africa, a middle income country, the UN Working Group on Arbitrary Detention found conditions of overcrowding and the incidence of disease to be much worse for pretrial detainees than convicted prisoners.[8]

In England and Wales it is widely acknowledged that pretrial detainees "occupy some of the worst accommodation in the entire prison estate."[9] Among other abuses, pretrial detainees in England and Wales are more likely to be included in an "overcrowding draft," a sudden and usually unexpected shipment to another prison. This makes it difficult for detainees to become familiar with the routine of any one institution and for their families, friends, and lawyers to plan visits.[10] In Scotland, too, conditions in custody for pretrial detainees are "at best equivalent, but most commonly worse, than those of convicted prisoners," according to an official Scottish Prison Service report.[11]

International norms and standards prohibit compulsory physical labor for pretrial detainees because they have not been convicted of any crime, and enforced work is seen as a punishment. Yet, in Zambia, for example, pretrial detainees are compelled to engage in hard physical labor. According to a Zambian pretrial detainee, "Everyone must work, even those that are sick. The labor may consist of breaking stones for three to four hours a day. There is no payment. Both remandees and convicts must work."[12] In Pakistan, remand prisoners are also routinely forced to perform labor.[13] This is in contravention of Pakistani law and in breach of the International Covenant on Civil and Political Rights which Pakistan ratified in 2010.[14]

Several factors make the conditions under which pretrial detainees are held worse than those for convicted prisoners. These include the types of institutions in which pretrial detainees are held, the transitory nature of the pretrial detention population, the lack of clarity in some places about who is responsible for pretrial detainees, and the deliberate abuse of pretrial detainees to induce confessions and guilty pleas.

As discussed in the next section on the circumstances of pretrial detention, pretrial detainees are often held in police lockups for extended periods of time. Such lockups are designed to accommodate persons for short periods of time only. Space for exercise and recreational opportunities is limited and frequently nonexistent. Moreover, the location of lockups within police premises exposes detainees to abuse and torture by police.

The uncertain status of pretrial detainees—not convicted, but not at liberty—can lead to neglect and official indifference. Prison administrators regard their main mandate as the custody and rehabilitation of convicted prisoners and see pretrial detainees as a group whose imprisonment is temporary and somewhat incidental to their work. A UN Special Rapporteur on Torture found that "discriminatory treatment suffered by pretrial detainees, who may be held longer than some convicts, has been justified by the heads of some facilities on the grounds that their guilt being not yet proven, there is less responsibility and obligation, and consequently less resources, allocated to care for them."[15]

The transitory nature of the pretrial detention population can make it difficult for prison authorities to anticipate how many pretrial detainees they will be responsible for at any given time, which can lead to overcrowding and shortages of beds, food, and medicine. The lack of resources in the pretrial situation is often

> In some countries, especially in places where the police and prosecutors lack the human and technical resources to undertake proper investigations, confessions are crucial to the state's ability to convict serious criminals.
>
> In Nigeria, for example, **over 90%** of criminal prosecutions are based exclusively on confessions.[18]

justified by the impossibility of planning for inmates whose length of stay in the facility cannot be determined in advance. In countries where educational opportunities for pretrial detainees exist in theory, these are often wanting in practice. In England and Wales, for example, pretrial detainees are typically last when benefiting from such services because education staff consider their time is better spent concentrating on the convicted population.[16] In police lock-ups, the physical constraints usually render any educational or vocational activity impossible.[17]

Many facilities for convicted prisoners, especially in developed countries, separate prisoners according to a variety of criteria, including the danger they pose to fellow inmates and their level of psychological wellbeing. Many prison systems have low-, medium- and high-security facilities, for example. But in general, no such separation takes place for pretrial detainee populations. In most countries, an 18-year old accused of minor theft, for example, may be confined with persons ten years his senior accused of serious violent crimes. Moreover, pretrial detainees do not benefit from the progressive reduction of security that occurs for many convicted prisoners, which moves the latter to incrementally more "open" regimes based on good behavior and time served.

Given the relatively high turnover rate of pretrial detainees, plus the limited space and chaotic conditions in many police lockups and remand centers, being detained can be particularly difficult for persons with special needs and vulnerabilities. Compared to places of confinement for convicted prisoners, pretrial detainees are at greater risk of not being segregated according to age and gender. The pretrial confinement of juveniles with adults is a common occurrence in many jurisdictions, especially within police lockups. While rarer, the risk of women being detained with men is greater for those awaiting trial compared to convicted prisoners. Under these circumstances the risk of exploitation and victimization is high.

There is also an instrumental reason for the particularly bad treatment and poor conditions afforded pretrial detainees. In numerous jurisdictions, police and prosecutors seek to use the period of pretrial detention as an opportunity to obtain confessions that will lead to convictions. In some countries, especially in places where the police and prosecutors lack the human and technical resources to undertake proper investigations, confessions are crucial to the state's ability to convict serious criminals. In Nigeria, for example, over 90 percent of criminal prosecutions are based exclusively on confessions.[18]

A multi-country study found that "most prison systems in practice frequently deny to the remand population access to many of the facilities, rights and privileges granted to convicted inmates… in some cases, such deprivations amount to an inducement to plead guilty in order to obtain better conditions of confinement."[19] A Canadian study found that the detention of accused persons is an "important resource that the prosecution uses to encourage (or coerce) guilty pleas from accused persons."[20] Similar findings have been made regarding the French and Hungarian justice systems.[21]

Human rights monitors visiting several former Soviet states, including Belarus and Moldova, have suggested that pretrial detention conditions are maintained at deplorable levels expressly to force people to incriminate themselves and be sent to prison colonies where conditions are better.[22] Indeed, detainees in Russian SIZOs (*sledstvenny isolator* or investigative isolator units for pretrial detainees) have been known to beg for the authorities to convict them.[23] In addition to the difference in physical conditions, people in prison colonies may be eligible to benefit from amnesties, conditional release, and a number of rehabilitation programs to which pretrial detainees have no access.[24]

# CIRCUMSTANCES OF DETENTION

## General Conditions

Official neglect, insufficient funding, and acts of omission lie behind the predominantly dismal conditions faced by pretrial detainees around the world. This is manifest in overcrowded and inadequate places of detention that offer little food and poor or non-existent health care, and with few or no opportunities for exercise, study, or recreation.

Corrupt officials who siphon away the limited public funds assigned to pretrial detention systems aggravate these problems. In addition, the abuse and torture of pretrial detainees by criminal justice officials, especially police officers and prison guards, and, at times, other inmates, is typically intentional, aimed at securing confessions or maintaining control. Before discussing these more deliberate abuses, it is important to understand the general conditions of detention, focusing first on police lockups and then remand centers.

### Police Lockups

Defendants are held in police lockups, often for extended periods of time, for a variety of reasons. In some places, prisons or remand centers are already overcrowded and lockups are used as an overflow mechanism to lessen the pressure on the prison system. Police stations are frequently located in close proximity to the local court in which arrestees have to make an appearance for their bail hearing and eventually to stand trial. In resource-poor settings, police vehicles and fuel are in short supply. It is consequently more practical for the police to keep detainees at police stations from where they can more easily be transported to the local courthouse for remand hearings and trial proceedings.

It is also convenient for police investigators to have detainees close by and accessible, especially in places where the police rely disproportionately on admissions and confessions to solve crimes, and where detainees do not have the benefit of a lawyer shielding them from protracted periods of questioning and interrogation. More ominously, in numerous jurisdictions police officers seek to exploit the poor conditions of detention common to lockups as an inducement for defendants to plead guilty. A guilty plea and conviction gets detainees transferred to a prison with generally better conditions.

Police lockups are typically designed to hold people for short periods of time only: for a few hours as arrestees' paperwork is processed before they are taken to court, or overnight or possibly over a weekend, to await the next court sitting. Conditions in lockups become progressively more oppressive the longer detainees are confined in them. The lack of natural light, fresh air, and even a proper chair or bed to rest on, are tolerable only if the confinement is brief. Yet, in many places people are confined to lockups for days, weeks, and even months.

Conditions at police lockups—especially those which accommodate detainees for longer periods of time—have been variously described by human rights reporters as "filthy,"[25] "terrible,"[26] "substandard,"[27] and lacking opportunities for exercise or recreation.[28] Police lockups are notorious for "overcrowding and long stays for persons in police cells, substandard physical conditions and design faults, lack of access to health and mental health care, vulnerable persons being inappropriately held in police cells, abuse of detainees, poor sanitary conditions, lack of adequate accommodation, juveniles being held with adults, and absence of consistent training in duty of care and custodial role of police lockup staff."[29]

Poor conditions and treatment in police lockups are aggravated—and the worst cases invariably concealed—by the fact that lockups are often under less external scrutiny than prisons or remand centers.[30] Occasionally, abusive conditions in police lockups come to light as a result of supranational inspection mechanisms. In most countries visited by the UN Special Rapporteur on Torture, people in police custody slept on the floor without anything but the clothes they were wearing when they were arrested. Arrestees did not have beds, mattresses, or blankets, had no toilets apart from a hole or a bucket in the corner, had no toilet paper, and often had no food or water. The cells were generally dirty, overcrowded, and lacked sufficient light and fresh air. In many countries, suspects are confined in such conditions for weeks or even months, according to the Special Rapporteur.[31] In the Central African Republic, for example, pretrial detainees are kept in police lockups for up to 18 months.[32]

The lack of space and resultant overcrowding in police lockups can have fatal consequences. Overcrowding was one of the main causes of the deaths, by suffocation, of about 100 detainees in a police cell in Malawi. The detainees had been forced into a small cell (7 meters by 3 meters) even though ten prisoners had suffocated to death in that same cell the previous night.[33]

Police stations rarely have the facilities to separate different categories of detainees to protect the vulnerable. In one police lockup in Equatorial Guinea, monitors found 40 people, including pregnant women, children, and men together, stuffed into a dark and filthy room with no beds and not enough room to lie down.[34] Even in a developed country like Australia, police lockups can produce a problematic mix of detainees:

> Persons detained in police cells can be an explosive mix of drunks, remand prisoners who should be kept separate from sentenced prisoners, persons needing to be kept separate because of their offences, first timers, those at risk of self-harm, young people, women and the physically and mentally ill.[35]

In some places, such as Sierra Leone, for example, police are not legally obligated to provide food for detainees in lockups.[36] Even where police are required, in theory, to provide food, police stations are often not equipped with a kitchen, or the kitchen and food allotment are only intended to feed the officers themselves. Consequently, a common complaint from detainees confined to police lockups for longer periods is about the lack of food. In the Central African Republic, pretrial detainees in police holding cells receive food "once a day in small quantities and of poor quality."[37]

In poorer countries the police often claim it is not their responsibility, but rather the task of families, to provide suspects in police cells with basic necessities to ensure survival. In Equatorial Guinea, for example, families have to bring bottles with water and plastic bags with food. Since most police lockups have no toilets, detainees use the same bottles to urinate and the plastic bags to defecate. Detainees in Togo's lockups are not provided with food or drinking water, and must rely on their families for these necessities.[38] If they have no family to call upon, detainees are dependent on their fellow detainees to ensure their survival.[39]

### South Sudan: Police Lockups[40]

In 2011, 95 percent of the South Sudan police budget was spent on salaries, leaving little funding for infrastructure and equipment. Police stations and holding cells are generally derelict structures, including thatched mud huts, metal containers, or trees to which detainees are chained. Police detainees are not provided with food. Many rely on relatives to bring them meals or on the generosity of other inmates, while others go days without eating.

### Remand Centers and Prisons

Although conditions in remand centers or sections of prisons allocated to pretrial detainees are usually better than police lockups, they are often marked by high levels of overcrowding. In addition, prison authorities often designate their oldest, most decrepit facilities for pretrial detainees, while using newer facilities to house sentenced prisoners. The former UN Special Rapporteur on Torture described "the combination of severe overcrowding and antiquated infrastructure" as in itself "degrading treatment," proscribed by international law.[41]

Expert testimony provided to a commission investigating abuse in U.S. prisons sums up a number of consequences of overcrowding for incarcerated populations.

> Prisoners in overcrowded correctional settings interact with more unfamiliar people, under extremely close quarters that afford little or no privacy or respite, where their basic needs are less likely to be addressed or met. Indeed, overcrowding operates at an individual level to worsen the experience of imprisonment by literally changing the social context or situation to which prisoners must adapt on a day-to-day basis. In addition to these direct, individual level effects, however, overcrowding changes the way the prison itself functions. For one, prison systems responding to the press of numbers often forego the careful screening, monitoring, and managing of vulnerable or problematic prisoners – in part because there are too many of them to assess in a conscientious way and in part because the system lacks the capacity to address their special needs anyway.[42]

Overcrowded detention centers and their staff are less able to provide detainees with adequate supervision, food, clothing, bedding, clean water, and adequate health care. Good hygiene, opportunity for exercise, and a healthy diet—essential to prevent the spread of communicable disease—are more difficult to maintain if detainees have to share beds, crowd ablution facilities, and are restricted to their cells for most of the time because guards are unable to cope with the number of detainees under their supervision.

Prison Occupancy Rates in 2010 – 2011

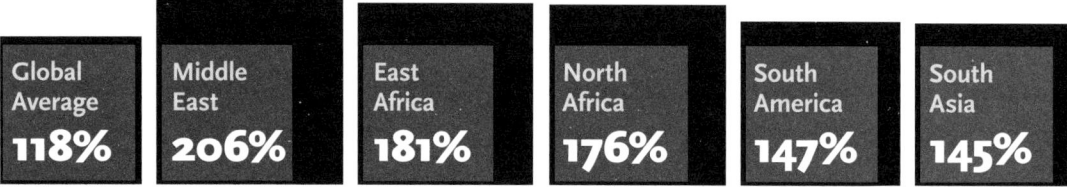

Globally, prison occupancy rates hovered around 118 percent in 2010-11, according to data collected by the International Centre for Prison Studies.⁴³ The global figure masks significant regional variations. Regions with particularly high occupancy rates are the Middle East (206 percent), East Africa (181 percent), North Africa (176 percent), South America (147 percent), and South Asia (145 percent). These data do not distinguish between prisons for convicted prisoners and pretrial detention centers—partly because pretrial detainees and convicts are not confined separately in many countries—and do not include police lockups where overcrowding levels are typically highest.

In many Latin American countries, prisons are old—sometimes dating from colonial times—and consist of structures which were not specifically designed to serve as detention centers. In Argentina, 10 of the 54 prisons in the province of Buenos Aires were not constructed for the purpose of incarcerating people. Moreover, three of the prisons were constructed before 1883, and four between 1913 and 1951. In Bolivia, of the country's 18 prisons, three were constructed before 1901, and another three between 1935 and 1957. In Guyana, of the five prisons in the country, three were built before 1860. Of Nicaragua's eight prisons, three were not originally built to be prisons.⁴⁴

Many African countries accommodate most of their prisoners in facilities dating back to colonial times, when both the overall population and prisoner numbers were much lower. Zambia's prison system, for example, consists of infrastructure built before independence in 1964 to accommodate 5,500 prisoners. In late 2010, the country's aging prisons housed 15,300. Mukobeko Maximum Security Prison, a facility built in 1950 for a capacity of 400, housed almost 1,800 inmates (433 percent of its capacity).⁴⁵ Lusaka Central Prison, a facility built in 1923 with a capacity of 200, housed 1,145 (573 percent of capacity). At many Zambian prisons, overcrowding is often so severe that inmates cannot lie down at night. Prisoners at Lusaka Central Prison, for example, sleep in shifts. Elsewhere detainees reported sleeping on their sides, up to five on a mattress, unable to turn over.⁴⁶

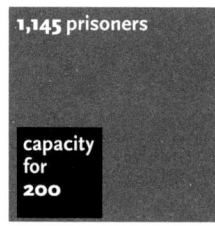

In Nigeria, all detention facilities visited by the Special Rapporteur on Torture in 2007 were severely overcrowded, with some facilities operating at double or triple the actual capacity, resulting in extremely poor physical and sanitary conditions. In Port Harcourt Prison, where 92 percent of all prisoners were awaiting trial,

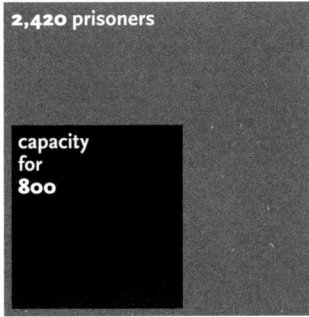

2,420 detainees were held in a prison with the capacity for 800.[47] In early 2012, Onitsha Prison held 898 inmates of which only 53 had been convicted. The prison is designed to accommodate 326 inmates.[48]

Bangladeshi prisons house three times the inmates they were built for. The situation in several individual prisons is far worse. Narayanganj Prison, for example, holds over 1,700 prisoners in facilities designed for 200.[49] The Bangladesh Prison Directorate points out that massive overcrowding makes it impossible for its prisons to deliver United Nations defined minimum standards of adequate light and air.[50]

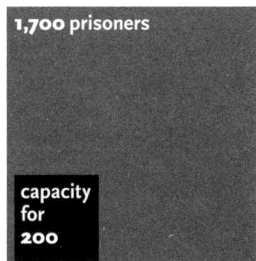

Particularly bad conditions have been documented in the pretrial institutions of the former Soviet bloc. These conditions are routinely judged by human rights monitors to be vastly worse than conditions faced by convicted prisoners in the same countries. Nigel Rodley, then the UN Special Rapporteur on Torture, described pretrial facilities in the Russian Federation as places where there was insufficient room for everyone to lie down, sit down, or ever stand at the same time, and where detainees all bore festering sores and boils:

> When the door to... a general cell is opened, one is hit by a blast of hot, dark, stinking (sweat, urine, faeces) gas that passes for air. These cells may have one filthy sink and a tap, from which water does not always emerge, near a ground-level toilet around which the inmates may drape some cloth for a minimum of privacy and to conceal the squalor of the installation. There is virtually no daylight from covered or barred windows, through which only a small amount of fresh air can penetrate.[51]

More recent accounts suggest that while conditions in some Russian facilities may have improved somewhat, extreme overcrowding, poor sanitation and lighting, and inadequate food remain common.[52]

Overcrowded prisons can literally become death traps. Honduras, whose prisons are overcrowded by some 50 percent, has suffered repeated prison fires which have killed pretrial detainees and convicted prisoners alike, as there is no effective separation between the two groups. In 2012, a fire at Comayagua prison killed more than 350 people, most of whom were pretrial detainees.[53] The Comayagua blaze was the third fatal Honduran prison fire within a decade: in 2003, 61 prisoners were killed in a fire at a prison in La Ceiba,[54] and in 2004 the death toll was 170 from a fire in a San Pedro Sula prison. In all cases, pretrial detainees were among those killed.[55]

The International Committee of the Red Cross (ICRC) annually visits more than 2,500 places of detention, which together hold about half a million people, in around 70 countries worldwide. An ICRC expert summarized detention conditions globally: "Existing infrastructures can't deal with rising prison populations, and the problem is getting worse across the board... not just in developing countries."[56]

## Violence and Abuse

Pretrial detention centers, like the prisons that house convicted offenders, are often violent institutions. Violence in prisons is a well-documented, nearly-universal phenomenon, driven by forced confinement, lack of resources, an entrenched culture of violence, and the presence of gangs and individuals prone to violence. Many of the factors that make prisons such violent places can also be found in the pretrial detention context, including overcrowding, a lack of guards, and official indifference. Such factors arguably have an even more detrimental effect on pretrial detainees, who are often unfamiliar with detention and the culture of violence. In addition, there are some characteristics specific to pretrial detention that makes it particularly prone to violence and abuse. These include the failure to segregate pretrial detainees according to their proclivity for violence, and failure to separate pretrial detainees from sentenced prisoners.

The violent and abusive conditions under which pretrial detainees are incarcerated is, in part, a product of the overcrowding and underfunding of prison systems detailed in the previous section. Overcrowding and concomitant lack of resources lead to violence in virtually all detention settings, whether pretrial or for convicted prisoners. However, it is worth noting that overcrowding and lack of resources are often worse for pretrial detainees than for sentenced prisoners, and hence the violence arising from it may be expected to be worse, too.

Overcrowding makes it hard for prison staff to protect pretrial detainees from violence at the hands of other prisoners. A related problem is the lack of guards in pretrial detention centers. This may stem from an overall lack of resources throughout the criminal justice system, or from the belief that pretrial detainees do not require the same level of oversight as sentenced prisoners. In Benin, a prison visited by the Special Rapporteur on Prisons and Conditions of Detention in Africa had 397 prisoners being guarded by six wardens, a guard-to-prisoner ration of 1:66.[57] In the Central African Republic and Burkina Faso the nationwide ratios are, respectively, 1:72 and 1:38, while Malawi's ratio is 1:10.[58] These may be extreme cases, although a dearth of data on staffing levels in developing countries—where the ratio is likely to be the most extreme—makes this difficult to verify. In the majority of European countries the ratio of guard to prisoner is between 1:1 and 1:3.[59]

The lack of prison wardens means that in some cases guards will allow prisoners to discipline themselves, tacitly approving inmate-on-inmate violence as a form of discipline and control. In Togo, prison staff delegate much of their authority to the *bureau interne*, a group of prisoners who effectively control all aspects of life within the prison and detention facilities. Providing one group of inmates with such sweeping authority contributes significantly to an environment characterized by abuse of power, corruption, and violence.[60] Pretrial detainees placed in such an environment are easily preyed upon.

In Benin, assault and battery of detainees by fellow prisoners, at the command of the guards, is common, occurring "on the least pretext, like an argument among inmates... with 45 lashes with a baton [being] not uncommon."[61] In Malawi it has been reported that cell leaders (known as *nyapalas*) are used in a supervisory capacity. Allegations abound of *nyapalas* being involved in assaults on other prisoners and also in sex trafficking.[62] Other allegations directly implicate *nyapalas* in the administration of discipline.[63]

In Mexico, *autogobierno*, or self-rule, has become more common as prison overcrowding has increased. In 2010, self-rule was practiced in 37 percent of Mexico's prisons, up from 30 percent in 2009, according to the country's National Human Rights Commission. The commission classifies self-rule as inmates being permitted to manage internal functions "such as controlling keys... and overseeing dormitories."[64]

The UN Subcommittee for the Prevention of Torture, in its 2010 report on Honduras—where pretrial detainees are commonly mixed with sentenced prisoners—described the existence of prisoner self-rule and lack of effective control by the authorities.[65]

> The Subcommittee noted that the shortage of staff assigned to the prisons had given rise to a regime of self-governance, under the control of "coordinators" and "subcoordinators" who are prisoners who act as spokespersons in dealings between the authorities and the rest of the prison population [...] From talking with inmates, the Subcommittee learned that the coordinators and subcoordinators are in charge of keeping order and assigning spaces in each wing. This was accepted by the prison staff with whom the Subcommittee spoke, who also revealed that they never enter some wings, such as those where the members of *maras* [a notorious criminal gang] are held...
>
> The system of corruption and privileges described above has spread to all aspects of daily prison life, and covers the obtaining of beds, mattresses, food, air conditioning units, televisions and radios. According to repeated and concurring statements by prisoners, weekly fees ranging from 15 to 20 lempiras are to be paid to the coordinators for cleaning and maintaining order in the wing.
>
> The self-governance regime also applies to food; the prison staff admitted that all food portions are handed over directly to the coordinators, who take responsibility for distributing them. According to certain accounts, some of the food is distributed and some is sold to the prisoners.
>
> A number of inmates stated that they had been beaten as punishment by other inmates or by prison staff, on orders from the coordinators, and that sometimes the coordinator himself administered the "punishment".

Lawlessness also plagues Venezuelan prisons. With a guard-to-prisoner ratio of 1 to 60, Venezuela's 34 prisons, originally designed to hold approximately 14,000 inmates, house over 50,000 people, of which two-thirds are awaiting trial. Every year several hundred inmates die in riots and gang fights. In the first 11 months of 2011, for example, 457 inmates were killed and over 1,000 seriously injured while in custody.[66] According to an Inter-American Commission on Human Rights report, 4,506 prisoners were killed and 12,518 injured as a result of prison violence in Venezuela over a twelve-year period, 1999-2010.[67]

### Venezuela: Armed Prisoners and No Guards[68]

Through a stench of urine infused with marijuana, inmates of Venezuela's La Planta prison brandish machine guns, rifles and grenades while enjoying music blaring from a 6-foot high stack of speakers. Guards are nowhere to be seen as other inmates sharpen knives and carry pistols. One even keeps hold of his gun as he plays soccer on a five-a-side court within the prison walls. "If the guards mess with us, we shoot them," said one prisoner.

At La Planta, in the ill-named El Paraiso (Paradise) district of Caracas, prison guards patrol only the perimeter. Inmates say they even fail to enter when violence breaks out. "I've seen a man have his head cut off and people play football with it," Pedro [a prisoner] said. Walls display scorch marks from grenades and bullet holes from regular gunfights. Built in 1964 for 350 inmates, La Planta now houses 2,436, according to a whiteboard near the entrance. Many sleep on the floor in communal areas as rats scurry around them.

Human rights monitors have documented many instances of sexual violence tolerated or even abetted by detention authorities. In both Moldova and Russia, independent monitors concluded that prison officials placed sexual predators strategically within pretrial detention centers to help "keep order" in the facilities.[69]

In New York City's main jail (in the United States, "jails" house primarily pretrial detainees) a guard was convicted in 2010 for orchestrating the beatings of teenage inmates as part of a rogue disciplinary system. As a result of this incident the City of New York Corrections Department interviewed hundreds of teen inmates and concluded that under a practice known as "the Program," guards were deputizing inmates, often in the teen jail, and pitting them against one another in fights as a way to keep order and extort them for phone, food, and television privileges.

In addition to overcrowding, lack of guards, and official indifference, there are three structural factors specific to pretrial detention that increase the likelihood of violence and abuse: the failure to segregate violent pretrial detainees from the nonviolent; the failure to segregate male, female, and minor pretrial detainees; and the failure to segregate pretrial detainees from sentenced prisoners.[70]

Such separation is the norm among sentenced prisoners, but often absent in the pretrial setting. For example, sentenced prisoners are often classified according to their proclivity for violence, with more violent offenders placed in more secure facilities. But this type of segregation is not done for pretrial detainees, exacerbating the risk of violence and abuse. Similarly, pretrial detention centers lack the inducements to shape detainee behavior. Prison officials often use disciplinary sanctions on violent prisoners, while offering modest rewards (for example, television privileges) for detainees who avoid violence. Some prison systems even employ cognitive therapies, such as conflict resolution and stress management techniques, to combat violent behaviors. But such violence-prevention measures are not available in pretrial detention. Pretrial detainees cannot be given time off for good behavior, as their release schedule is contingent on the speed of the state's investigation and subsequent trial, and therapeutic interventions are not provided to populations which are—at least in theory if not in practice—considered short-term and transient.

The failure to segregate pretrial detainees presents particular risks to vulnerable populations, such as juveniles and children. Violence against children perpetuated by adult detainees with whom they are housed has been reported in many countries, "putting them at risk of threatening behaviour, blackmail, or even rape by older prisoners."[71]

According to the Special Rapporteur on Torture:

> The lack of separation was particularly disturbing with regard to police custody and pretrial detention, stages in which children found themselves in an environment characterized by tension, fear, abuse and violence. Once in prison, the separation was in some cases enforced only during the night, leaving children exposed to adults throughout the day. In some cases, children were not separated from adults outside of the cell during recreation time, e.g., in Paraguay and the Republic of Moldova. In a few instances, children were left to be guarded by older detainees, who not only lacked the specific training but might abuse their position.[72]

Many of the most shocking accounts of physical and sexual abuse of children in pretrial detention derive from the failure of governments to house children separately from adults. Lack of segregation of children has been reported in places where monitors say there is officially no juvenile justice system separate from the adult system, including Belarus, Burundi, Equatorial Guinea, Nepal, Nigeria, Pakistan, and Ukraine.[73] In some places separate juvenile systems exist in theory, but in practice children are often housed with adults in police lockups and pretrial facilities.[74] In Angola, the Working Group on Arbitrary Detention reported that children whose birth certificates were lost or never issued because of the country's civil war were housed in detention with adults as a result and faced sexual abuse in custody.[75]

In developed countries, too, there exist numerous documented cases of awaiting trial juveniles being confined with adults. In respect of Slovakia, the UN Committee Against Torture has expressed concern about the placement of juvenile pretrial detainees together with adults.[76] Although rarer, a number of countries also do not consistently separate male and female detainees, leaving women vulnerable to sexual assault.[77]

U.S. law requires the separation of juvenile and adult pretrial detainees. However, this protection does not apply to defendants 17 years and younger sent to adult court to be tried for serious offenses. Such defendants—some 5,600 at any given time in 2010, according to federal Bureau of Justice Statistics—lack protection from adult detainees.[78] In jails intended for adults, juveniles face an elevated risk of physical attacks, including sexual assault. Juvenile inmates are 36 times more likely to commit suicide in adult jails than in youth detention centers, according to data included in a 2007 Centers for Disease Control and Prevention task force report.[79]

In the U.S., budget pressures are pushing some juveniles accused of lesser crimes into adult jails even while their cases remain in the juvenile justice system. Their numbers have nearly doubled in recent years, from 1,009 in 2005 to almost 2,000 in 2010. The state of Florida passed a law in 2011 enabling counties to send teenagers accused of less serious crimes in juvenile court to adult jails instead of youth detention facilities. Costs drove the change: detaining an inmate in one of the state's juvenile facilities costs counties roughly $280 per day, while jail accommodation costs $80.[80]

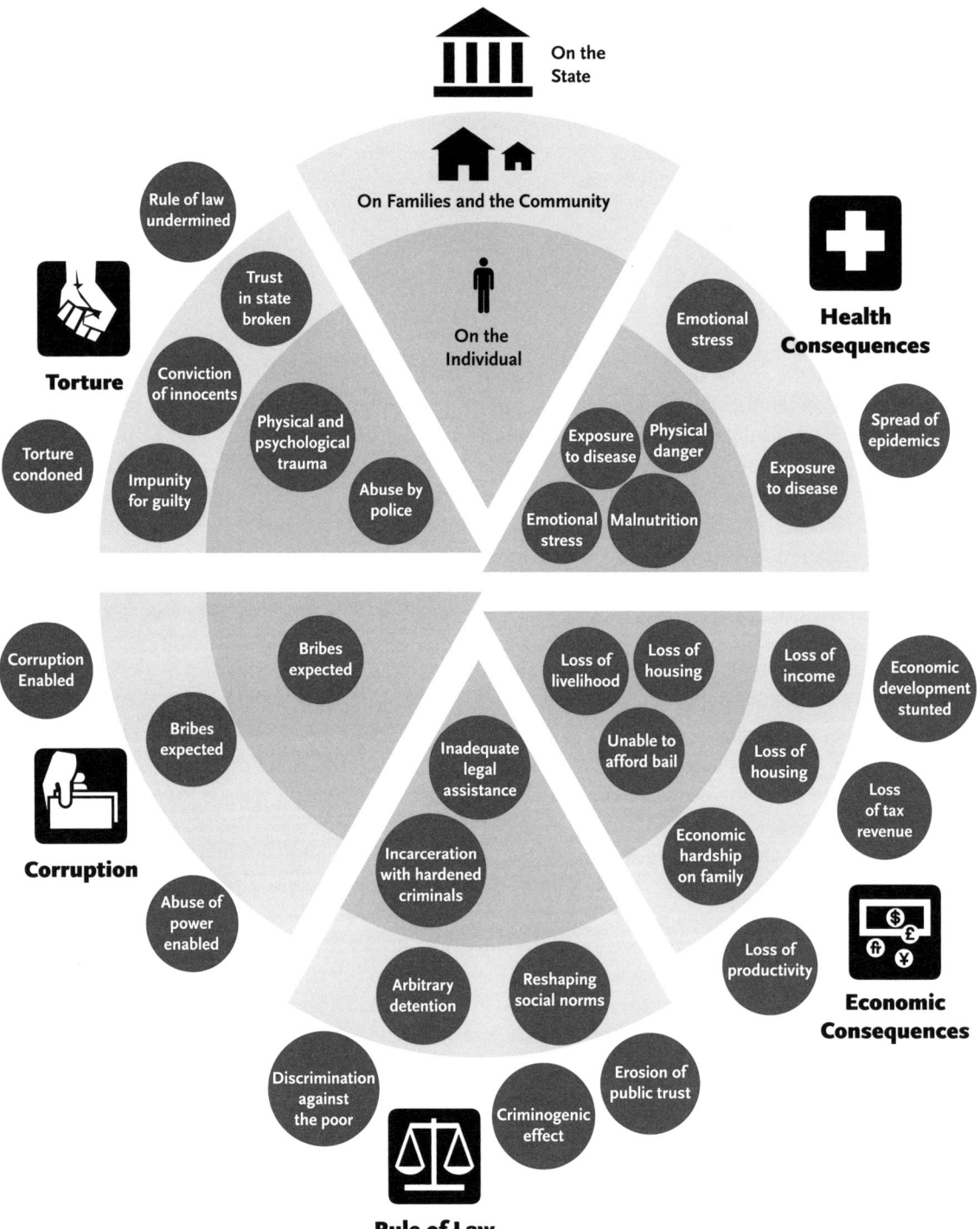

Another second structural factor heightening pretrial detainees' vulnerability to violence is that in a number of places, especially in resource-poor countries, pretrial detainees are not consistently separated from convicted prisoners. In Cameroon[81] and Zambia,[82] for example, pretrial detainees are housed together with convicts, leading to frequent harassment of the detainees. In India, a study of 24 sub-jails (local prisons) in the Indian state of Maharashtra found that in all of them pretrial detainees and convicted prisoners were mixed.[83] In Uruguay, "as a general practice, there is no separation whatsoever between pretrial detainees and convicted prisoners."[84] In El Salvador, the UN Committee Against Torture expressed concern about the authorities' "failure to separate accused persons from convicted prisoners, women from men and children from adults."[85]

The failure to separate pretrial detainees from convicted prisoners augments the risk of violence. When mixed with convicted, long-term prisoners, pretrial detainees are exposed to a violent offender subculture. In some prisons, daily life is dominated by violence, abuse, drug addiction, and internal gang structures. A 2010 investigation at the Parappana Agrahara Central Prison in Bangalore, India, found that more than a quarter of inmates in the 18-21 years age group had rectal damage due to sexual abuse. The youngsters, most of whom were pretrial detainees, were reportedly sodomized by hardened criminals, with whom they were forced to share space in the overcrowded prison.[86] Pretrial detainees, who are newcomers and who sometimes have little experience with gangs and violence, run a particularly high risk of victimization.

## Torture and Ill-Treatment

Torture is common in pretrial detention. In fact, around the world, pretrial detainees are more likely to be tortured than sentenced prisoners are. Three primary factors put pretrial detainees at particular risk of torture: in the initial days and hours after arrest, torture is often used to extract a confession; there is less scrutiny of pretrial detention by oversight bodies; and the extremely poor detention conditions and serious overcrowding of pretrial detention facilities often in themselves amount to cruel, inhuman, or degrading treatment or punishment.

Reports from various Special Rapporteurs on Torture, the European Committee for the Prevention of Torture, UN treaty bodies, and non-governmental organizations show that criminal suspects are at risk of torture and other ill-treatment at all stages of their detention, from the moment of their apprehension until their release.[87] Pretrial detainees' exposure to torture is examined below, through the three distinct stages within the pretrial phase of the criminal justice process: during apprehension, in police custody, and in remand detention.

### Inter-American Commission: Torture Prevalent at the Pretrial Stage

According to a report by the Inter-American Commission on Human Rights, most cases of torture and cruel, inhuman and degrading treatment in Mexico take place during the preliminary investigation of crimes as a method to obtain confessions. "This general pattern in Mexico has also been observed in a significant number of hearings, petitions and cases examined by the Inter-American human rights system and has been the subject of consistent pronouncements of UN human rights protection mechanisms."[88]

### Upon Apprehension

The torture of pretrial detainees often begins at the first contact with police and security officers—well before detainees are taken to police premises or other detention facilities. Some police and security forces employ "capture shock," the deliberate use of violence during apprehension to disorient the arrestee and break down his resistance.[89] In Nigeria, for example, it is common practice to shoot suspects in the legs and feet after they have been apprehended, to prevent them from fleeing or as a means to make them confess.[90] The treatment of the prisoner's wounds—or lack of treatment—then depends on the detainee's willingness to confess.[91]

Once apprehended, suspects risk being tortured before being brought to police premises. Suspects are sometimes tortured in police vehicles in order to extract confessions, or they are taken to a separate location where they are tortured before being taken to a police station for interrogation. In Kenya, some police are known to place suspects in the back of a car and then drive them around for hours or even days while beating them.[92] In Indonesia, detainees are reportedly taken to private houses upon arrest, where they are tortured, sometimes for several days.[93] The police often benefit from broad discretion in their treatment of suspects during arrest. Effective methods of recording arrests and monitoring treatment during transfers are often absent, allowing officers to avoid being held accountable.

### In Police Custody

In countries as diverse as Azerbaijan, Ecuador, Equatorial Guinea, Georgia, Mauritania, South Africa, and Uzbekistan, torture, beating, burning with cigarettes, electric shock, and other physical abuse are reportedly most likely to occur during the first hours of detention, especially in police custody.[94] In police custody, investigating authorities have direct control over suspects and an immediate interest in securing a confession. Suspects are often interrogated without the presence of a lawyer or any independent monitors, allowing officials ample opportunity to exert pressure through ill-treatment.

The majority of cases of torture encountered during the fact-finding missions of a UN Special Rapporteur on Torture, Manfred Nowak, took place during the initial period of police detention. In 11 of the 15 countries visited by Nowak during his term of office, torture in police custody was found to be pervasive. Novak repeatedly expressed concern that excessive reliance on pretrial detention, combined with pressure on police to obtain confessions, leads directly to police torture of criminal suspects.[95] "In many countries, torture of criminal suspects who are in police custody (before transfer to pre-trial detention facilities) is practiced in such a widespread or systematic manner that every other 'new arrival' at pretrial detention centres shows clear marks of beatings and other forms of torture."[96] Torture and ill-treatment occurs primarily as a means of forcing suspects to confess, or otherwise testify against themselves.[97] In Kenya, a defense attorney noted that the torture of suspects is most severe at the point of arrest, and then improves as the process moves toward the courtroom: "From the time of arrest the [officers] were very brutal, including being brutal in front of the suspect's family, and they continue their abuse at a police station. Their treatment gets better only once [the suspects] are brought to court."[98]

In Kyrgyzstan, the worst human rights abuses from law-enforcement officials take place not in prisons or pretrial detention centers (SIZOs) but in temporary detention facilities (IVS)[99] administered by the police.[100] Conditions in IVS facilities, which tend to be in the basement of police stations and not intended for prolonged detentions, are often extremely poor. Food is usually only bread and tea, and sanitation facilities are usually unavailable.

Allegations of police beatings and unlawful and prolonged detention in IVS facilities are common. "People are sometimes held there for three weeks and then are told what they 'did,'" a human rights activist reported. Police investigators, themselves under pressure to increase the proportion of "solved" cases, sometimes charge pretrial detainees with a host of unsolved crimes and reportedly use beatings—or the threat of beatings—to extract confessions. "Somebody who is there for stealing a chicken, for example, suddenly finds out that he's become a major criminal overnight, with a long list of crimes," another human rights activist said. A former detainee confirmed this, saying:

> The police take advantage of the fact that all the power is in their hands. They drag you out of the cell, supposedly for interrogation, and then begin blackmailing you, saying that you should "admit" to five or six other crimes you didn't commit. If you refuse, then they start to beat you and threaten you: "If you don't agree, we'll put you in a maximum-security cell."[101]

In many countries the police are not always adequately resourced or trained to use modern techniques of crime investigation. Often under intense pressure to solve cases, coercing a confession sometimes appears to be the easiest and perhaps the only way of securing a conviction at trial. In Brazil, evidence obtained by police during interrogation is often the primary or only basis of conviction.[102] This both provides an incentive for the police to abuse detainees, and makes the consequences of torture particularly harsh.[103] In Moldova, "torture and other cruel inhuman or degrading treatment in police custody remains widespread and systematic."[104] According to a coalition of Moldovan NGOs, the desire to collect evidence through torture is a primary reason that the Moldovan justice system practices pretrial detention.[105]

### Togo: Torture to Extract a Confession[106]

Kadissoli Abalbedue, aged 27, accused of stealing food from a shop, was arrested by the gendarmerie in 2007. He was beaten during the arrest, then taken to the gendarmerie post. The police chief cuffed Abalbedue's hands and his legs together behind his back, so that his spine was painfully bent. He lay face down on the floor of the main office, with a chair placed over his upper back and neck. He was left like this for 30 minutes.

Later, the chief returned and again forced Abalbedue to lie down with his hands cuffed behind his back. While in this position, several officers beat his back and the soles of his feet with wooden clubs for more than 30 minutes, until he confessed to stealing the food.

Abalbedue spent three days in the gendarmerie post. During that time he was always handcuffed. Every day he was tortured in a similar manner. On the second day, he was beaten with a rope belt usually worn by the gendarmes. The gendarmes continued to beat him, even after he confessed, because they thought he was lying and wanted to know where the stolen goods were hidden.

---

In Brazil, Human Rights Watch interviewed scores of pretrial detainees who described being tortured while in police custody.

> Inmates were typically stripped naked, hung from a "parrot's perch" and subjected to beatings, electrical shocks, and near-drownings. Many detainees remained for long periods in the precincts where they suffered the abuse, enduring continuing contact with their torturers... Although Brazil's national prison law mandates that prisoners have access to various types of assistance, including medical care, legal aid and social services, none of these benefits are provided to the extent contemplated under the terms of the law... The situation is particularly bad in police lock-ups, where severely ill and even dying prisoners may remain crowded together with other inmates.[107]

Even when police coercion falls short of torture, it can still be startlingly abusive. In Japan police often use prolonged interrogation sessions to coerce suspects into confessing to crimes, whether or not the suspects are guilty.[108] Magistrates in Japan routinely grant prosecutors' requests to detain individuals for 23 days before indictment. During this period, suspects are required to submit to interrogation for up to 8 hours a day. Suspects' counsel may not be present during the interrogations.[109]

### In Remand Detention

After judicial review, detainees are frequently placed in pretrial detention facilities, also known as "remand detention," to await trial. But as noted above, the nature of these facilities can vary greatly, and pretrial detainees can be housed with violent sentenced prisoners. While in pretrial detention facilities, they are no longer under the control of authorities interested in a confession, but remand detainees are still subject to being tortured by or with the knowledge of prison officials. Pretrial detainees are abused by guards and fellow detainees as a means of punishment, intimidation, or to extort money.

Upon arrival at remand prisons, detainees risk being exposed to abusive "welcome treatments" which can be practiced by prison guards as a means of intimidation and subordination, or by other detainees to introduce newcomers to the established inter-detainee power structures. Reports of abusive initiation ceremonies such as beatings by prison guards or painful and degrading physical exercises in front of other detainees emanate from many countries. In Jordan, detainees reported that a "welcoming committee" of up to 20 officers forced them to strip to their underwear in the courtyard and subjected them to heavy beatings. When they lost consciousness, the detainees were revived with cold water and beaten again. The beatings lasted for days and no medical treatment was provided for their injuries.[110] In Togo, detainees were subjected to beatings by fellow detainees if they did not pay an "arrival fee,"[111] while in some Chinese detention centers staff instruct veteran detainees to torture new arrivals.[112]

Another form of initiation is detention in "welcome cells," allegedly for quarantine purposes or to classify detainees before placement in normal cells. Conditions in such cells are typically worse than elsewhere in the facility and detainees are often shackled or handcuffed for the entire period.[113] These "welcome cells" are usually used as punishment cells for normal detainees, suggesting that new arrivals are placed in them as a means of intimidation and punishment rather than for administrative reasons. The two extremes of complete isolation or serious overcrowding[114] are common, and cause a higher risk of torture and other ill-treatment for new arrivals.

In countries where corruption is widespread, pretrial detainees are easy victims of authorities who may torture them in order to extort money. In Indonesia, corruption is a "quasi-institutionalized practice" and detainees are "spared" from ill-treatment in return for the payment of money.[115] Sometimes the most basic amenities, such as food and water, are withheld unless a bribe is received.[116] Corruption in detention facilities can have deadly consequences for detainees who are entirely dependent on authorities

> Magistrates in Japan routinely grant prosecutors' requests to detain individuals for 23 days before indictment. During this period, suspects are required to submit to interrogation for up to 8 hours a day. Suspects' counsel may not be present during the interrogations.[109]

**Indonesia: Torture to Extract Money**[117]

Eko, aged 28, a student from Central Java, was arrested by six police officers at his home, based on an order from the head of the police drug unit. Eko was kicked and punched by the officers and then taken to the local police station where he was interrogated. During interrogation he was electrocuted, had his fingers smashed with a hammer, and was beaten by four police officers for one hour. Following this treatment, Eko confessed, and the police offered to drop some charges in exchange for money. Eko did not receive any medical treatment for his injuries.

Eko was kept in police custody for two months and then transferred to a local prison where he spent six months. At the police station visitors had to pay a bribe to see him. The prosecutor at the district court offered to reduce the charges in exchange for money. The prosecutor was informed about the ill-treatment and the confession under torture, but this did not affect the outcome of the trial.

Detainees are often denied access to complaint mechanisms, a competent lawyer, or independent judge. As a consequence, they may feel forgotten by the outside world, and the severe conditions and excessive length of detention can motivate them to confess to a crime just so they can be transferred to a regular prison facility and escape the state of limbo in which they have no idea when, or if, they will be released or tried.[118]

Children in pretrial detention facilities are particularly at risk of torture and abuse, according to human rights monitors. In at least 78 countries, it is legal to beat children in criminal detention, and beatings are inevitably not limited to places where they are legal.[119] In Moldova, corporal punishment and forced labor in juvenile facilities is applied liberally "to prepare minors for life in adult prisons."[120] In places ranging from Yemen to Brazil to Laos as well as the U.S. and the UK, children reported to researchers numerous incidents of sexual abuse by guards, beatings, having meals withheld, administration of electric shocks, use of painful restraints, and being forced to stay in uncomfortable positions for hours.[121]

For children and adults alike, the conditions of pretrial detention are often miserable, marked by overcrowding, lack of resources, violence, and abuse. Appalling conditions can be found in developed and developing countries, and at each stage of the criminal justice process. These conditions frequently have a disastrous effect on detainees' mental and physical health, as examined in the next section.

# HEALTH CONSEQUENCES OF DETENTION FOR DETAINEES AND THEIR COMMUNITIES[122]

Pretrial detention has a detrimental effect on the mental and physical health of detainees, and also poses a public health problem for the communities that detainees come from and eventually return to. Pretrial detainees are often sick or malnourished before their detention, making them more likely to spread and contract disease. The high turn-over and poor conditions of most pretrial detention centers make them a vector for the spread of disease, and few such facilities have appropriate health services. Pretrial detention is notoriously hard on the mental health of detainees because of the poor overall conditions and long periods of waiting and uncertainty. And when pretrial detainees are finally released and return to their families and communities, they bring with them the health problems—often communicable—that they picked up in detention.

The vast majority of the world's pretrial detainees are people from poor and marginalized communities with little access to health services. Many pretrial detainees have a history of disease exposure, drug use, and alcohol consumption; are likely to have lived in overcrowded premises often lacking proper sanitation; and may suffer from malnutrition and water-borne diseases. These health problems do not improve in pretrial detention.

## Detention Conditions and Disease

Prisons in general—and pretrial detention centers in particular—aggravate existing health problems and serve as vectors in the spread of communicable diseases. Neglected chronic diseases, infectious and noninfectious diseases, inconsistent antibiotic use, prolonged exposure to the elements, and poor nutritional status all influence the frequency and severity of disease in places of confinement. Further, the prevalence of assault, ill-treatment, and torture adds to the risk pretrial detainees face of contracting infectious diseases through open wounds or weakened immune systems.

A survey of pretrial detainees in Ghana in 2011 found that a fifth of the respondents had been ill at the time of their arrest, but that 80 percent of all respondents said they fell ill after their arrest. That is, all of the detainees ill on arrest remained ill, and 75 percent of those not ill on arrest subsequently fell ill to malaria, diarrhea, and tuberculosis, among other diseases. Pretrial detention effectively quadrupled the rate of ill-health among detainees in Ghana. In nearby Sierra Leone, a similar survey found that pretrial detention doubled the rate of ill-health among those arrested and detained.[123]

The poor physical condition of many police lockups, remand centers, and prisons promotes the spread of disease.[124] Overcrowding, poor nutrition, lack of exercise, limited access to health care, violence, risky sexual practices, high rates of injecting drug use, sharing razor blades, and tattooing make places of detention a perfect habitat for the spread of infectious diseases.[125] Both convicted prisoners and pretrial detainees face extreme health challenges in most parts of the world.

Prison populations exhibit much higher rates of communicable diseases, including HIV,[126] tuberculosis (TB), hepatitis C, and other sexually transmitted infections, than does the population at large.[127] HIV prevalence in sub-Saharan African prisons has been estimated at two to 50 times that of non-prison populations, while average TB incidence in prisons worldwide has been estimated at more than 20 times higher than in the general population.[128] The alarming spread of HIV/AIDS in prisons and the high turnover of prisoners and pretrial detainees across the continent have led epidemiologists to identify prisons as an important and often overlooked engine of the African AIDS epidemic.[129] Incarceration has also been established as a risk factor for HIV infection in Asia,[130] and Latin America.[131] While undoubtedly an extreme case, an account of the spread of HIV/AIDS in Lithuania is indicative of how prisons are extremely effective vectors for the spread of infectious diseases. In 2002, 263 inmates at a prison in Lithuania tested positive for HIV. Yet before these tests, Lithuanian officials had counted just 300 cases of HIV in the whole country.[132]

Similarly, TB infections spread quickly among detainees, and are particularly likely to be diagnosed late and inadequately treated, increasing the risk of transmission and the risk of drug-resistant strains of the disease developing.[133] TB rates in prison are up to 100 times higher than in the outside population. In some countries, a quarter of all TB cases are among prisoners.[134] In 2005, prisoners accounted for 27 percent of Russia's TB cases, even though prisoners comprised less than one percent of the population.[135] In Georgia, 1,300 cases of TB were reported among the prison population in 2010. This infection rate of 5,417 cases of TB per 100,000 of the prison population compared to 98 cases of TB per 100,000 of the general population.[136] In other words, the rate of TB was over 55 times higher among prisoners than among the general population.

In Eastern Europe, overcrowding has been a principal driver of the extensive tuberculosis epidemic in pretrial detention centers and prisons.[137] In Estonia, "closely connected to the overcrowding of prisons is high prevalence of tuberculosis and sexually transmitted diseases among prisoners," according to a 2009 UN report.[138] In Azerbaijan, authorities reported that overcrowding was both a cause of tuberculosis and also the main obstacle to segregating active TB cases from the rest of the population.[139]

## Mental Health of Pretrial Detainees

Just as overcrowding and poor conditions drive the spread of disease in pretrial detention centers, they also increase the incidence of mental illness. Imprisonment is known to negatively affect prisoners' mental well-being.[140] Factors which contribute to this include overcrowding, violence and intimidation, enforced solitude, lack of privacy, a dearth of meaningful activities, and inadequate mental health services. In many countries, people with mental disorders are disproportionately likely to be incarcerated, whereupon their mental disorders are usually further exacerbated by the stress of imprisonment.[141]

It is possible that people who are found to suffer from a mental illness while in pretrial detention were suffering from it before their detention. However, it is documented that only a small proportion of pretrial detainees receive psychiatric help in the year before entering detention. This raises the possibility that many of those suffering mental health problems in custody developed those problems as a result of pretrial detention.[142]

Suicide—one of the most extreme manifestations of mental illness—is the single most common cause of death in many correctional settings. A survey of 36 member states of the Council of Europe revealed that almost 3,000 prisoners died in penal institutions in 2003, of which a bit over half were suicides.[143]

According to the World Health Organization, prisoners not only have higher suicide rates compared to their counterparts in the community, but suicide rates among pretrial detainees are considerably higher than among convicted prisoners. Among pretrial detainees the suicide rate is ten times that of the outside community, while convicted prisoners have a suicide rate three times higher than in the outside community.[144] In 2002, more than a third (38 percent) of prison suicides in England and Wales were committed by pretrial detainees, even though they constituted only 19 percent of the total detainee population.[145]

Pretrial detainees are at heightened risk of committing suicide during the initial period of their confinement.[146] This is not surprising, given the often particularly unpleasant, abusive, and oppressive conditions pretrial detainees face within the first days of their arrest. These initial stressors, collectively termed "confinement shock," include, for example, the experience of being torn out of their familiar social environments, of being isolated, and of losing control over their lives. Bullying, which has been shown to be more common among pretrial detainees, is a further contributor to suicides and self-injury among detainees.[147]

Suicide is particularly high among youths in detention. In the United States, jail inmates under 18 years have the highest suicide rate of all inmates.[148] Moreover, youths held in jails for short periods of time—which would be disproportionally pretrial detainees—are at particularly high risk of suicide. Juvenile suicides are especially concentrated in the first week of custody (48 percent), with almost a quarter of suicides taking place on the day of admission to jail (14 percent) or on the following day (nine percent).[149] For juvenile pretrial detainees, who may be experiencing their first separation from parents or caregivers, feelings of depression, anxiety and hopelessness are exacerbated.

In many penal systems, pretrial detainees are considered ineligible for work, educational or vocational programs.[150] Such enforced idleness "fosters a lowering of self-esteem, loss of skills, and inevitable institutionalization."[151] Not knowing the outcome of their impending trial can also place a detainee under considerable strain and has been identified as a significant contributing factor in incidents of self-harm.[152]

## Access to Health Services

Physical and mental health services are inadequate, oftentimes nonexistent, in many prison systems around the world. Only 15 of Zambia's 86 prisons have health clinics or sick bays, and many of the clinics have little capacity beyond distributing paracetemol, a pain reliever. In 2010, the Zambia Prisons Service employed 14 trained health staff—one physician (who worked as an administrator, not a clinician), one health environmental technician, nine nurses, and three clinical officers—serving a prison population of 15,300 prisoners.[153] In Peru, 63 physicians are in charge of caring for almost 50,000 prisoners, and 28 out of 66 prisons do not have medical staff at all.[154]

As inadequate as health services may be for convicted prisoners, health services are frequently even more lacking in remand facilities. The right of persons newly detained to be seen by a health professional upon admission to state custody is widely disrespected. Many low-income countries do not seem to involve their ministries of health in prison health service delivery, and even where they are involved, pretrial detention is unlikely to be a priority for improving care.[155] The absence of qualified medical personnel to conduct intake screenings may contribute to the difficulties of detection and management of tuberculosis and sexually transmitted diseases, among other conditions.[156] Moreover, peer education, which may be among the most effective health programs in prisons,[157] is unlikely to be developed or sustained in the high-turnover environment of pretrial detention.

Even where health services are present in remand facilities, there is often a reluctance to start treatment for infectious diseases that require a sustained period of therapy, such as for tuberculosis,[158] HIV, or hepatitis C. Authorities may also be less likely to be concerned about ensuring continuity of care and support for people in temporary custody (even if "temporary" custody turns out to be of long duration), including continuing treatment initiated before arrest and detention.

Access to health care is also manipulated by authorities as a form of punishment or to force a confession. Human rights organizations have documented instances of interrogation in police custody of people who were badly injured during their arrest,[159] and of people in withdrawal or otherwise suffering from drug dependency.[160] These cases exemplify the practice of using the pain of withdrawal symptoms to coerce confessions. This cruel treatment of people living with drug dependency has been recognized as a form of torture by the UN Special Rapporteur on Torture.[161]

In Zambia, pretrial detainees, in particular, suffer from restricted access to medical care. According to a 2010 Human Rights Watch report there is a contentious relationship between the Prisons Service and police on the subject of pretrial detainee security and responsibility for escorting and transporting detainees. As a result, pretrial detainees have less access to medical care than their convict counterparts.[162] One senior prison officer justified his colleagues' behavior as follows: "With remandees, we fear to take them [to the hospital] because we are afraid they will run away – the police will say we let them go deliberately. The police are supposed to take them to the clinic, but it's rare, so normally they don't go."[163] Such uncertainty and fears over responsibility for escapes lead to denial of treatment.

If access to health care is worse for pretrial detainees than it is for sentenced prisoners, access to mental health care for pretrial detainees is worse, still. Although global data is woefully lacking, it is estimated that mental health care for pretrial detainees in developed countries is wholly inadequate, and in developing countries is virtually nonexistent.[164]

## Health Consequences for Families and Communities

Pretrial detainees infected with HIV/AIDS, tuberculosis, or other infectious diseases are likely to pass these on to their families and communities after their release. The high incidence of disease, lack of health care, and transitory populations that mark pretrial detention contribute to broader public health consequences as released prisoners spread disease to the rest of the population.[165] The effect of this on poor households and communities can be devastating and may impoverish households reliant on the good health and labor of each of its members.

Given that most persons incarcerated—especially those that have not been convicted—have a high likelihood of eventually being released, the health of detainees is a fundamental public health concern. Prisons have been documented as structural factors fuelling outbreaks of HIV and TB in Africa, Eastern Europe, Russia, and elsewhere.[166] In South Africa, where an estimated 40 percent of prison inmates are reported to be HIV positive, some 25,000 prisoners are released every month. Many of these are former pretrial detainees who have been granted bail, are acquitted, or have had their charges withdrawn.[167]

In Latin America, diseases in prisons are so abundant that they threaten the health of the general population, according to health experts who spoke at a 2006 seminar sponsored by the International Committee of the Red Cross (ICRC) and the Peruvian National Prison Institute. According to the ICRC, tuberculosis is up to 100 times more common in Peruvian prisons than among the general population, while AIDS is about six times easier to contract in Peru's largest prison, San Juan de Lurigancho, than in the streets of Lima, according to Doctors Without Borders.[168] Diseases are spilling from detention centers into the public at large due to the vast amount of traffic in and out of prisons—and pretrial detention centers in particular.[169]

A U.S. study found that high rates of incarceration, including, to a somewhat lesser extent, pretrial detention, can have the "unintended consequence of destabilizing communities and contributing to adverse health outcomes."[170] According to the study, rates of sexually transmitted infections and teenage pregnancies consistently increased with increasing imprisonment rates. Moreover, the population released from incarceration presents an above average risk of infecting community members with sexually transmitted infections.[171]

In Russia, where the emergence of multidrug resistant strains of TB present a public health crisis, pretrial detention centers and prisons "became an 'epidemiological pump' for spreading the disease throughout the general population."[172] Ex-prisoners and detainees, often with improperly treated TB that had mutated into the multidrug resistant form of the disease, returned to cramped housing complexes where, during wintertime, unventilated apartments provided ideal conditions for transmission to relatives, friends, and neighbors. The annual rate of new TB cases among the general population in Russia more than doubled in the 1990s to 88 cases per 100,000 inhabitants.[173] By the late 1990s, hundreds of TB cases were also being recorded among Russian prison staff.[174] It was only the spread of TB to the general population—through the vector of prison guards in particular—that impelled the government to act. Recently, new medical treatment regimens have helped slow the spread of TB in Russian custodial settings, according to the WHO.[175]

It is important to recall that not only are pretrial detainees presumed innocent in the eyes of the law, but most of them are in fact innocent. Yet their innocence does not protect them from contracting life threatening diseases in pretrial detention. Nor does it prevent them from passing those diseases on to their spouses, children, and neighbors, ultimately sickening and destabilizing whole communities. In these instances, pretrial detention is truly, in the words of penal reform expert Vivien Stern, "a death sentence."[176]

## ECONOMIC IMPACT ON DETAINEES AND THEIR FAMILIES

It stands to reason that individuals held in pretrial detention experience financial losses as a result of the detention, as do their families. An individual who is detained cannot work and is likely to lose his job. Nor, in most cases, can he engage in education or job training. And his detention doesn't just take away income—it also adds an array of expenses, from lawyers to bribes to having to pay for food or a bed in detention. These financial impacts are not felt by the detainee alone, but extend to his family as well.

Pretrial detention disproportionately affects individuals and families living in poverty. When an income-producing member of a family is detained, the rest of the family must adjust to the loss of that income. In the developed world, these losses may be ameliorated by the state's safety net, which may provide supplemental income, food assistance, and even housing assistance to the poor. But the economic impact of pretrial detention can be especially severe in poor, developing countries where the state does not provide reliable financial assistance to the indigent and where the families of detainees are expected to provide food, bedding and clothing for the detainee because the state does not. This situation is exacerbated in parts of the developing world where it is not unusual for one breadwinner to financially support an extended family network.

### Manifold Impacts of Detention on the Poor: from the Special Rapporteur on Extreme Poverty

The 2011 report of the Special Rapporteur on Extreme Poverty and Human Rights to the UN General Assembly sums up the many consequences of pretrial detention for the poor:[177]

> - The economic and social costs of detention and incarceration can be devastating for persons living in poverty. Detention not only means a temporary loss of income, but also often leads to the loss of employment, particularly where individuals are employed in the informal sector.
>
> - Families are forced to use their limited income or sell assets to pay for bail, legal assistance, access to goods and services within penal facilities (e.g. food or telephone usage), or travel to visit the detainee. Children's education is also often disrupted when their parents are detained. In this context, detention represents a serious threat to the financial stability of the detainee's whole family and serves to perpetuate the cycle of poverty.
>
> - Detention and incarceration can also have serious health implications for the poorest and most vulnerable, who are likely to be subject to the worst treatment and conditions, including overcrowded cells, inadequate hygiene facilities, rampant disease transmission, and inadequate health care. In some cases, overcrowding in prisons can have such a severe effect on detainees that the conditions may even amount to a form of cruel and inhuman treatment.
>
> - Those who are poor and vulnerable are therefore likely to leave detention disproportionately disadvantaged financially, physically, and personally. After their release they will have depleted assets, reduced employment opportunities, limited access to social benefits, and severed community ties and family relationships, and will be subject to added social stigmatization and exclusion, diminishing even further their prospects of escaping poverty.

Below is a more detailed examination of the financial consequences of pretrial detention for detainees and their families, as measured by income and employment, education, and a variety of detention-related expenses.

## Income and Employment

Persons detained awaiting trial cannot work or earn income while detained, and frequently lose their jobs, even when their time in pretrial detention is relatively brief. In England and Wales, for example, half of men and two-thirds of women who were employed at the time of arrest lost their jobs as a result of their pretrial detention.[178] If the period of detention is lengthy, detainees' future earning potential is also undermined. Those who are self-employed—common to people working in much of the developing world—are at risk of bankruptcy, losing their goods through theft, missing sowing or harvesting season, or foregoing their trading space at the local market.

> In England and Wales, half of men and two-thirds of women who were employed at the time of arrest lost their jobs as a result of their pretrial detention.[178]

In Mexico, a study estimated the amount of income lost, as a result of their detention, by the country's pretrial detainees who were employed at the time of arrest, as 1.3 billion pesos (or about US$100 million) in 2006.[179] In Argentina, the collective amount of income lost per year by pretrial detainees was calculated at nearly 40 million pesos (or over US$10 million) in 2006.[180]

A U.S. study of young men awaiting trial found that arrests, more than convictions, lead to lower earnings. This seems surprising, given that an arrestee is at least legally considered innocent.[181] But many prospective employers do not consider this legal nicety, seeing an arrest as an indicator of guilt and refusing to hire those with an arrest record.

Pretrial detainees are not only at risk of losing their employment at the time of detention, but also risk long-term unemployment or underemployment after release. The stigma of detention, combined with lost education or training opportunities, severely limits detainees' lifetime earnings. This is exacerbated by the fact that most pretrial detainees are between ages 20 and 40, which should be their wage earning peak. Income lost at this point in their lives almost certainly cannot be regained.

In countries that have Social Security or some other form of retirement program, the income lost today by a pretrial detainee will also hurt him later in life due to reduced contributions to the retirement plan. In Mexico, lost Social Security contributions caused by pretrial detention have been estimated at 17.6 million pesos (US$1.4 million) annually.[182]

For every pretrial detainee who loses his job as a result of detention, there is a family paying the price. In some cases, his spouse—and even his children—must find work to make up for the lost income. But in other cases, his spouse must quit work because of the demands imposed by incarceration, including court appearances, prison visits, and taking food and other necessities to the incarcerated spouse. For the already-poor, the loss of income can be crippling. If, for example, the detainee and his spouse are subsistence farmers, it is likely impossible for the spouse to take on any additional work. In such a scenario, the spouse may be forced to sell the family's belongings, hastening the descent into abject poverty.

### Benin: Lost Income, Thwarted Ambitions[183]

A prisoner in Benin, who had been in pretrial detention for 30 months, reported that his family was trying to raise money to find a lawyer. As a result of his detention, his wife's plans to start a business—a hairdressing salon—had to be abandoned and she was forced to work instead in the far less lucrative trade of street hairdressing. Not only had her small enterprise been scuttled, but her working hours were reduced by fruitless visits to the prosecutor and her daily visits to take food to the prison. In addition, her expenses increased because of travel demands. Her husband's arrest pushed her from the brink of middle class stability to the edge of poverty.

In Sierra Leone, a survey of pretrial detainees found that virtually all detainees (94 percent) were economically active in some way at the time of their arrest. Moreover, 80 percent of the detainees had children (an average of 2.7 children per detainee with children), of whom almost three-quarters (74 percent) were dependents younger than 16. Some 42 percent of detainees had one or more dependent spouses reliant on them, and almost a quarter (23 percent) of the detainees had one or more dependent parents reliant on them. The average total number of dependents of a detainee was 4.2.[184] A similar survey in Ghana found that the average total number of dependents per pretrial detainee was 7.9.[185]

Particularly in socially conservative societies, it can be difficult for families

## Consequences of Pretrial Detention

- X is detained
- Held in detention
- Assaulted as part of the interrogation
- X can no longer harvest and sell vegetables at the market
- X's wife has to borrow money from neighbors to buy medicine and food for X and to pay bribes to visit the prison where he is held

to support themselves without a male income provider, as women have limited opportunities for employment. In these cases, the pretrial detention of a male wage earner is practically a guarantee of dire poverty. In Afghanistan, for example, the families of detained men are commonly reduced to begging because no other options for earning income are available.[186]

### Poland: Three Months in Pretrial Detention, 30 Jobs Lost[187]

After three years of renovations and construction, Krzysztof P. was about to open a new boutique hotel and restaurant in the Polish city of Krakow. Before he could do so, Krzysztof and a dozen members of the construction crew were arrested by the police. The police sealed the hotel and froze its bank accounts. Krzysztof was charged with transgressing the building code and the law for the protection of historical monuments. The prosecutor alleged that the construction of the hotel was done without a permit, which Krzysztof disputed, and that the hotel's new roof obstructed the chimneys of neighboring building thus "endangering the life and health of its inhabitants."

The arrested members of the construction crew were released within 48 hours, but Krzysztof spent three-and-a-half months in pretrial detention. Although Krzysztof was eventually released, 30 hotel employees lost their jobs due to his pretrial detention and resulting delays in the hotel's opening.

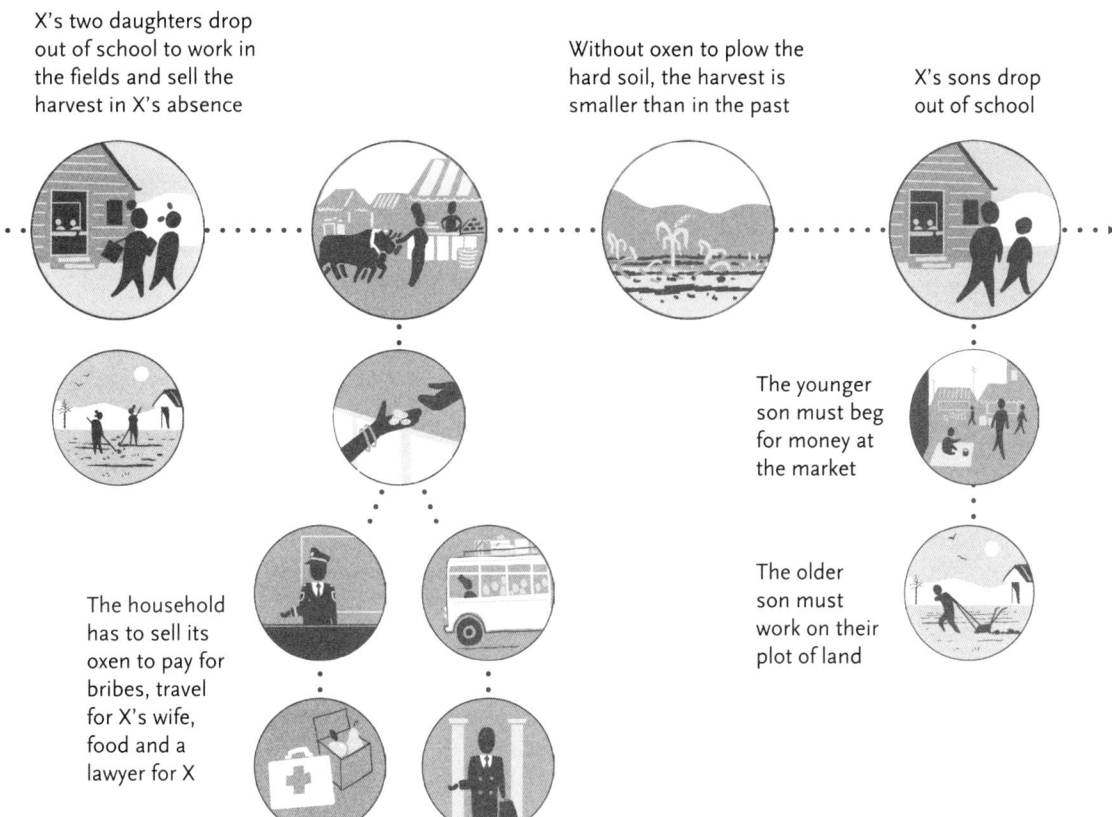

## Education

Many pretrial detainees are young adults, some of whom will have their education interrupted as a result of their detention. Other detainees may have their job training interrupted, making it harder to find a job upon release and limiting their lifetime earning potential. Education and training opportunities are virtually nonexistent in pretrial detention, even if they are available to convicted prisoners.

In addition, the education of children is often disrupted when a parent is detained. These children have to take on new roles, including providing domestic, emotional, or financial support for other family members. According to an NGO report, such children "may have to move to a new area, a new home or a new school because of imprisonment."[188] A review of the literature on children whose mothers are detained found that those "children's lives are greatly disrupted... resulting in heightened rates of school failure and eventual criminal activity."[189] Particularly in developing countries, children are commonly forced out of school and into work, to replace the lost income of detained adults.

There is a body of research—focused primarily on sentenced prisoners—linking the imprisonment of parents to negative outcomes for their children, including increased propensity for violence and other antisocial behaviors, increased likelihood of suffering anxiety and depression, and decreased school attendance.[190] Although it is not clear that a parent's incarceration is by itself responsible for increased likelihood of criminality in the child, it is clear that children of detained parents are more likely to one day be imprisoned themselves.[191]

For juveniles, pretrial detention interrupts their education, making it more difficult for some to return to school and find employment. Indeed, "economists have shown that the process of incarcerating youth will reduce their future earnings and their ability to remain in the workforce, and could change formerly detained youth into less stable employees."[192] The failure of detained juveniles to return to school affects public safety: according to the U.S. Department of Education, school dropouts are three-and-a-half times more likely than high school graduates to be arrested.[193]

Some argue that prison can be used by prisoners to improve their skills and human capital by, for example, completing their high school education, earning university credits or degrees, and developing occupational skills through formal training programs or work assignments. However, such opportunities are typically denied to pretrial detainees, even where they are available to sentenced prisoners. Prison administrators do not see it as their responsibility to provide educational or occupational opportunities to pretrial detainees, focusing rather on convicted prisoners in need of rehabilitation.

## Detention-Related Expenses

Entering pretrial detention not only limits one's income and earning potential—it actually costs money. In developing countries, authorities often fail to provide basic necessities, so detainees must pay for food, water, clothing, and bedding. Commonly, they must also pay bribes for "privileges" such as making a phone call, securing a place to sleep, and avoiding or lessening beatings. The annual cost to detainees of these extra-legal payments has been estimated at 539 million pesos (US$42.3 million) in Mexico,[194] and 9 million pesos (US$2.3 million) in Argentina.[195] It is important to bear in mind that Mexico and Argentina are not considered developing countries and that the impact of bribes paid by pretrial detainees in poorer countries may be more severe when considered as a proportion of detainees' income or net worth.

In Equatorial Guinea, for example, a male detainee kept in police custody for several months was forced to pay for food and drinking water. Kept in a cell that was partially open to the sky, he had no protection against malaria-carrying mosquitoes. He was repeatedly denied a hearing before a judge, access to a lawyer, or contact with his family.[196] To calculate the costs to the man and his family, it would be necessary to add up—at a minimum—the man's lost income (both immediate and lifetime), the burden on his spouse, the lost educational opportunities for his children, the direct costs of his food and water, and the costs of his contracting malaria.

### Indonesia: Hidden Costs of Detention[197]

Ms. Rina, aged 24, from West Sumatra, was arrested by police officers after allegedly stealing a mobile phone and money two weeks earlier in order to buy drugs. The officers took Ms. Rina directly to the theft victim's house to broker a "peace deal," meaning that she could avoid further judicial proceedings by paying the amount of 7,700,000 IDR (about US$820) directly to the victim. Ms. Rina rejected this settlement because she could not afford the amount. She was transferred to South Jakarta Polres (or district command), where she was interrogated. Ms. Rina was then temporarily detained in a cell she had to share with one other woman and seven men, before being interrogated for a second time on the same day.

Subsequently, Ms. Rina was transferred to another cell with seven to ten women. Every cell had to pay 250,000 IDR (about US$27) in rent and so-called "peace settlements," a fee for not being harassed. In addition, each prisoner had to pay 30,000 IDR (about US$3) per month for electricity and laundry. The payment was made either to the head of the cell, who would forward the money to the guards, or directly to the guards. Detainees who refused to pay were beaten by the guards or had to work for other inmates in return for them settling their "debts."

In addition to lost income, the families of pretrial detainees must wrestle with legal fees, the cost of bribes to corrupt criminal justice officials, and other expenses. When an income-earner is detained, family members must adjust not only to the loss of that income but also to costs of supporting that family member in detention, including travel to visit the detainee, food and personal items for the detainee, and, often, bribes to guards. In Nigeria, "pretrial detainees reported that they are forced to pay for food, bathing, contacting family members, receiving visitors, and medication."[198] Wealthier detainees may have to absorb the cost of private defense counsel (although, as noted earlier, wealthier people are unlikely to find themselves in pretrial detention).

### Brazil: Impact of Detention on a Poor Household[199]

The following is an abridged account of the socioeconomic impact of pretrial detention on the detainee's wife and children. The account is contained in a report produced by a group of Brazilian NGOs:

Sonia, who lives in the neighborhood of Benfica in Rio de Janeiro, explained that her husband was arrested in October 2008 on suspicion of receiving stolen goods. She is now left to look after four children by herself. In addition, she has to provide such items as soap, toilet paper, shaving cream, and razors for her husband. Her only regular income is the R$90 (US$40) per month she receives from the *Bolsa Família* program for her children attending school. She tries to find work where she can, but this is normally nothing more than a day's cleaning for which she receives some R$60. In addition to her family's basic needs, Sonia has to meet the cost of a lawyer, of buying food for her husband at the market, and of travelling to see him four times a month (at R$10 per round trip). Crucially, Sonia must also find R$150 per month to pay her rent. Sonia knows that if this situation continues, she and her children will eventually lose their home. Sonia's story is not exceptional, and it is therefore no surprise that women with a partner in prison risk becoming involved in drug dealing or other illegal activities in order to support their families.

In Malawi, neither the police nor any other government agency provides food to detainees at police stations. The detainees are entirely reliant on friends and relatives for their meals. This places a terrible burden on the families concerned, especially when a breadwinner is detained. For detainees without families, the situation is even more dire as they are dependent on fellow detainees for food.[200] Detainees are not supplied with a uniform and are permitted to wear their own clothing, as is the practice internationally. However, if a detainee's clothing is no longer suitable, the police service does not supply alternative clothing and detainees are dependent on their relatives to supply them with clothing.[201] Moreover, detainees are not provided with the means to wash their clothes, but are reliant on their relatives to provide them with soap, or must send their clothes home with relatives to be washed.[202] The police service also does not provide sanitary napkins to female detainees.[203]

Below are case studies about two pretrial detainees in Malawi, including an analysis of the financial costs the defendants and their families suffered as a result of detention.[204]

*"Mr. L." (detained for nine months)*

In December 2009, Mr. L., a 46-year-old farmer who lives outside Lilongwe, was arrested for theft. His income at the time of arrest was average for Malawi: about MK80,000 ($530) per year. Once in pretrial detention, Mr. L. did not have any means of contacting family members and no knowledge of bail or court procedures. Fortunately for Mr. L., a group of paralegals conducted a clinic about detainees' rights at the prison where he was kept. These paralegals discovered that Mr. L. had been in detention for nine months even though the state's case against him was weak (e.g. no one witnessed him commit the alleged theft). The paralegals alerted the prosecutor's office, which withdrew the charges against Mr. L. for lack of evidence.

*Costs incurred by Mr. L. and his family ($1,975)*: Mr. L.'s nine months in pretrial detention was financial devastating for him and his family. Mr. L. suffered losses of nearly $2,000—a real fortune in Malawi. Moreover, Mr. L. lost his farm and had to work as a tenant farmer, dropping his income from MK80,000 to only MK10,000 ($66) (Table 1).

TABLE 1:

**Expenses and losses incurred by Mr. L. and his family as a result of his pretrial detention**

MEASUREABLE ECONOMIC COSTS

| Description | Losses in MK |
| --- | --- |
| Wife hospitalized upon his imprisonment due to stress. | 10,000 |
| Skin disease contracted while in pretrial detention required treatment. | 3,500 |
| Wife's visits Mr. L. at police cells, prison, and at court (food: MK30,000; transport: MK9,000; medicines and sundries: MK20,000). | 59,000 |
| Property stolen from Mr. L.'s home while he was in detention (batteries, battery charger, bicycle, seeds, tobacco, maize, chairs, radio, and farm equipment). | 80,000 |
| Mr. L.'s wife requires medicines and treatment after contracting skin disease from Mr. L. | 5,600 |
| Nine months of lost income (MK6,670 x 9). | 60,000 |
| Diseases contracted in detention make it impossible for Mr. L. to resume work productively for some months after his release. | 80,000 |
| TOTAL COSTS | MK298,100 ($1,975) |

### "Mr. B." (detained for five months)

In April 2009, Mr. B., age 41, from the Lilongwe area, was arrested on a charge of "theft by servant" when his employer accused him of stealing a radio. Mr. B. was not bailed and spent five months in pretrial detention until he was tried, acquitted, and released.

*Costs incurred by Mr. B. and his family ($1,606)*: Mr. B. and his wife suffered expenses and losses of a bit over $1,600. The eventual figure is likely to be higher as Mr. B. lost a well-paying job upon his arrest. Upon his release he obtained a much lower paying job in the informal economy (Table 2).

TABLE 2:

**Expenses and losses incurred by Mr. B. and his family as a result of his pretrial detention**

MEASUREABLE ECONOMIC COSTS

| Description | Losses in MK |
|---|---|
| With the arrest, Mr. B. lost his job with annual salary of MK144,000. He now works in the informal economy but receives no more than MK36,000 annually. | 108,000 |
| My B.'s wife had a small business selling clothes that contributed about MK75,000 a year. The business went bankrupt because of the time she spent providing support to Mr. B. in pretrial detention. | 75,000 |
| Mr. B.'s wife incurred expenses to visit Mr. B. at the police station (MK1,400), at court (MK7,200), and at the prison (MK42,000) over a five-month period. | 50,600 |
| Cost of clothes, soap, and sundries supplied to Mr. B. by his wife. | 1,000 |
| Mr. B. was assaulted by other prisoners: cost of treatment at clinic. | 1,000 |
| Mr. B. contracted skin disease in prison: cost of (unsuccessful) treatment. | 880 |
| Mr. B.'s wife began to suffer from high blood pressure problems upon Mr. B.'s arrest: treatment and medication. | 8,000 |
| TOTAL COSTS | MK 242,480 ($1,606) |

# CRIMINOGENIC IMPACT OF DETENTION

It is likely that the overuse of pretrial detention does not reduce crime, but in fact actually increases it. Excessive pretrial detention, as discussed above, impoverishes individuals and their families, leading some into the underground economy or even outright crime. Where pretrial detainees are mixed with experienced criminals, the detainees can actually learn to become criminals in pretrial detention. The overuse of pretrial detention can also destabilize communities, breaking down social norms against committing crime, while at the family level this destabilizing effect can lead the children of pretrial detainees to eventually commit crimes themselves.

The excessive and arbitrary use of pretrial detention may bring about conditions which often quite directly increase the number of potential offenders in a society. To the extent that pretrial detention leaves the detainee without a job and reduces his prospects of finding one, it may lead him to making a living by whatever means necessary. This is especially true if being in pretrial detention exposed him to criminal gangs and culture, and taught him about crime.

There is significant evidence to show that prisons serve as "schools" or "breeding grounds" for crime.[205] Prisons psychologically harm their inmates, making their adjustment to society upon release more difficult, with one consequence being that at least some of them will turn to crime. Much of the literature on the effects of incarceration argues that the confined spaces of prisons reinforce certain forms of negative behavior. For example, by examining the social learning contingencies that exist in prisons, it was found that prisoners face "overwhelming positive reinforcement" by the peer group for a variety of antisocial behaviors, so much so that even staff interacted with the inmates in a way that promoted a pro-criminal environment.[206]

A U.S. study has shown that once juveniles are detained awaiting trial, even when controlling for prior offenses, they are more likely than non-detained juveniles charged with a crime to engage in future delinquent behavior, with the "detention experience increasing the odds that the youth will recidivate."[207] The failure of previously detained juveniles to return to school affects public safety as, according to the U.S. Department of Education, school dropouts are three-and-a-half-times more likely than high school graduates to be arrested.[208]

In a 2008 report on Brazil, the then UN Special Rapporteur on Extrajudicial, Summary or Arbitrary Executions, Philip Alston, noted that:

> In most prisons, the state fails to exert sufficient control over inmates, and lets gangs (or other prisoners in "neutral prisons") sort out amongst themselves matters of internal prison security. Selected inmates are often given more power over other prisoners' daily lives than guards. They assume control of (sometimes brutal) internal discipline and the distribution of food, medicine, and hygiene kits. This practice often results in allowing gang-leaders to run prisons.[209]

Even when a new inmate has no gang affiliation whatsoever, Alston noted that the inmate may be required by prison administrators to pick a gang with which to be affiliated. Prisoners who refuse are often assigned to a gang by the prison administration. "The state practice of requiring gang identification essentially amounts to the state recruiting prisoners into gangs. Ultimately, this contributes to the growth of gangs outside prison and elevates crime rates more generally."[210]

As is the case with convicted prisoners, pretrial detainees invariably face similar criminogenic influences, especially if detained for extended periods under crowded and poor conditions. The risk is greater in places where convicted prisoners and pretrial detainees are not separated, or where pretrial detainees charged with minor offenses are incarcerated together with detainees suspected of having committed serious crimes—both common scenarios in many overcrowded prison systems around the world.

A review of 20 EU countries found that nearly all the countries surveyed mix pretrial detainees and convicted prisoners for activities, primarily due to the lack of resources to do otherwise.[211] An official survey conducted in England and Wales found that in 88 percent of prison establishments, pretrial detainees and convicted prisoners were mixed for activities and in 67 percent they shared residential accommodation. In male prisons, 38 percent of pretrial detainees shared cells with convicted prisoners.[212] As discussed earlier in this chapter, in the developing world it is common for pretrial detainees to be mixed with sentenced prisoners throughout their detention.

Little research has been undertaken on the broader social impact of excessive pretrial detention, specifically on communities and society as a whole. However, there is research on the impact of mass incarceration as seen in countries such as the U.S., Russia, Belarus, Ukraine, and South Africa (all countries with incarceration rates in excess of 330 per 100,000 of the general population). It is likely that the effects of mass pretrial detention are similar to those of mass incarceration:

> When most families in a neighborhood lose fathers to prison, the distortion of family structure affects relationship norms between men and women as well as between parents and children, reshaping family and community across generations. And, while families in poor neighborhoods have traditionally been able to employ extended networks of kin and friends to weather hard times, incarceration strains these sustaining relationships, diminishing people's ability to survive material and emotional difficulties. As a result, incarceration is producing a deep social transformation in the families and communities of prisoners – families and communities, it should be noted, that are disproportionately poor.[213]

High rates of incarceration, including pretrial detention, can have the "unintended consequence of destabilizing communities."[214] Removals from, and releases to, communities disrupt relationships and weaken social norms, in that maintenance of these norms is based on long-term relationships. Existing social norms that once militated against committing crime are undone by the pressures of mass pretrial detention and the concomitant economic losses; increased crime follows.

If, at the macro level, excessive pretrial detention is likely to have a destabilizing and criminogenic effect on communities, at the micro level, it is likely to have that same effect on families—especially the children of pretrial detainees. The imprisonment of parents has been linked to negative outcomes for their children, including increased propensity for violence and other antisocial behaviors, increased likelihood of suffering anxiety and depression, and decreased school attendance.[215] Children of incarcerated parents are also more at risk of sexually transmitted infection and/or teen pregnancy.[216] Although it is not clear that a parent's incarceration is by itself responsible for increased likelihood of criminality in the child, it is clear that children of imprisoned parents are more likely to one day be imprisoned themselves.[217]

# CONCLUSION

Although an individual's pretrial detention may last only a few weeks, the impact can be felt over the rest of his life—and indeed, into the next generation. A book on the English bail system, *Bail or Custody*, provides an example of the impact pretrial detention has on a detainee and his family, showing the far-reaching impact pretrial detention can have.[218] The example is about a 29-year-old truck driver who lived with his wife, his retired-father-in-law, and his eight-year-old son in a council house in England. He was arrested in connection with a robbery and held in pretrial detention after police successfully opposed bail. When the case was scheduled for trial, the police withdrew their objection and bail was granted. After almost four weeks in pretrial detention, the defendant found he had lost his job and the rent on the house where he had lived for seven years was in arrears. He and his family were evicted. The mental strain of the situation caused the defendant's wife to suffer a nervous breakdown and so disturbed his son that he had to be given psychiatric treatment. The defendant's time in detention made it difficult to get work, yet he could not obtain unemployment benefits because he was awaiting trial and was not, according to the local labor bureau, available for work. Four months after his arrest, the defendant was tried and acquitted. But the damage was done.

In most countries, pretrial detainees suffer real privations as a result of generally deplorable conditions of detention. In many places, the conditions of detention—including the availability of food, proper bedding, health care, sanitary ablution facilities, and the level of crowding—are considerably worse than the conditions under which convicted prisoners are incarcerated. This is an outrageous state of affairs given that pretrial detainees have not been convicted of a crime and, indeed, a substantial proportion of detainees are not convicted of the crimes of which they have been charged.

In a large number of jurisdictions, the poor conditions of detention serve an instrumental purpose. The more depraved the conditions under which defendants are detained awaiting trial, the greater the incentive to admit guilt and thereby be transferred to a prison for convicted prisoners. In many places, the abuse and torture of pretrial detainees is rife as police investigators seek to extract confessions. This leads to the innocent being convicted and the real culprits going unpunished, thereby undermining public trust in the justice system.

In virtually all cases, it is poorer detainees—the poorest of the poor—who languish under the worst conditions of confinement. Without money to bribe a guard or cell leader, such detainees are most likely to be allocated the worst spaces in overcrowded cells and the last to receive the meager rations authorities provide for pretrial detainees. Unable to afford a lawyer, indigent detainees are also at greatest risk of being abused and tortured by police wishing to extract a confession or bribe, or both.

For pretrial detainees who contract disease or who are damaged physically or psychologically by torture during their detention, the long-term effects are so great as to be nearly incalculable. A man who emerges from pretrial detention having contracted HIV risks passing it to his wife or partner(s). He will have a shorter lifespan and reduced earning potential, which can affect the educational attainment and hence income potential of his children. And the disease will cost his family in the form of medical bills and the wages they forfeit while caring for him. For even a wealthy family, this scenario is disastrous. For an already poor family, it is a nightmare.

An obvious solution to the many problems enumerated in this chapter would be to improve the conditions of pretrial detention. A better solution would be to sharply curtail its overuse.

# The Causes of Arbitrary and Excessive Use of Pretrial Detention

## INTRODUCTION

International human rights treaties emphasize the essential distinction between people who have been found guilty, convicted by a court of law, and sentenced to prison, and those who have not. Because of the presumption of innocence, the law views prisoners awaiting trial (or awaiting the outcome of a trial) differently from those found guilty. The presumption of innocence is universal, and to treat a detainee as anything other than presumed-innocent is to violate international human rights norms.

International standards require that states only use pretrial detention when reasonable grounds exist to believe that the arrestee has been involved in the commission of the alleged offense, and there is a demonstrable risk that the person concerned will abscond, interfere with the course of justice, or commit a serious offense.[1] These standards also mandate the widest possible use of alternatives to pretrial detention.[2]

Further, the decision to detain a person cannot be arbitrary. As the UN Human Rights Commission has ruled, "The notion of 'arbitrariness' is not to be equated with 'against the law,' but must be interpreted more broadly to include elements of inappropriateness, injustice, lack of predictability and due process of law."[3] As a result, pretrial detention "must not only be lawful but reasonable and necessary in all the circumstances."[4]

Using pretrial detention excessively and / or arbitrarily is not only a violation of international norms, but often unnecessary. Most pretrial detainees pose no threat to society and should not be in detention. Many of those held in pretrial detention will have their charges withdrawn due to a lack of incriminating evidence, while others will be acquitted at trial. Still others will be found guilty of minor, non-violent offenses for which imprisonment is inappropriate or for which the maximum custodial sentence is less than the time spent awaiting trial.[5] Yet, globally one out of three prisoners is in pretrial detention and in many places the majority of prisoners are pretrial detainees. Too many states use pretrial detention excessively, rather than as the last resort it is intended to be.

The overuse of pretrial detention reflects a fundamental lack of coherence over how the presumption of innocence should be balanced against the need to protect the public. Even in states with well-functioning, well-funded criminal justice systems, the presumption of innocence is more of a theory than a reality. Often, the criminal justice professionals—from police to prosecutors to judges—entrusted to apply the principle of innocent-until-proven-guilty have little clarity as to what the concept means, or how it should function in practice.

Myriad factors drive the global overuse of pretrial detention. Many of those factors stem from various violations of the right to be presumed innocent. For example, numerous jurisdictions allow courts to engage in "preventive justice"—to detain individuals for fear that they will commit a crime if released, based on the fact that they have been charged with a crime. Some jurisdictions have restrictive laws that openly flout the presumption of innocence, while others may have appropriate laws on the books, but ignore limits on pretrial detention in practice. And still other jurisdictions may have imprecise laws that lead to the arbitrary application of pretrial detention.

Politics and public pressure also play a role in the excessive use of pretrial detention. As this chapter explores, public fears about crime and populist "tough on crime" policy responses result in many people being locked up who should be released pending trial. Relatedly, there is often a dearth of political will to challenge the tough-on-crime approach. The powerful influence of police and prosecutors, as well as official corruption, are also factors.

There are other, more mundane, reasons for the excessive or arbitrary use of pretrial detention. Procedural factors, such as the lack of time allocated to bail hearings, can increase pretrial detention. A lack of coordination between the state's criminal justice agencies, or inadequate resourcing for criminal justice systems, may result in police agencies lacking the human and technological resources to forensically investigate crimes. An almost universal dearth of quality legal assistance for arrestees during the pretrial stage of the criminal justice process often aggravates such systemic weaknesses.

Many—probably most—countries in the world use pretrial detention excessively and arbitrarily because of the factors listed above. Indeed, a number of the causes are linked and reinforce one another. Imprecise laws, for example, both impede effective collaboration between criminal justice agencies and foster corruption. Corruption, in turn, frequently leads to arbitrary detention practices and siphons away scarce resources available for providing state-funded legal assistance to the indigent. To understand why pretrial detention is so grossly overused, it is necessary to explore in greater detail its many causes.

## THE PRESUMPTION OF INNOCENCE: AN ELUSIVE ASPIRATION

The presumption of innocence is a fundamental right accorded in international law to anyone who has been charged with an offense. Under this right, accused persons should not be declared guilty until a court has established their guilt, and pretrial detention should be the exception rather than the rule. However, while international standards protect the individual right to liberty, pretrial detention is—within limitation—acknowledged as a legitimate exception to this right.

The presumption of innocence is based on widely held ideas about the limits to state power in a free society. While even democratic states have extensive powers to investigate, prosecute, and punish, they cannot do so in violation of individuals' autonomy and dignity. The presumption of innocence seeks to protect individuals against arbitrary and excessive state action. However, even in places like Europe where there are strong legislative and jurisprudential checks on state power, the presumption of innocence is "not a factual but a normative assumption."[6]

A review of the literature and European standards on the presumption of innocence provides little legal guidance on what the concept means in practice:

> [The] literature seems to be utterly divided on the standards that can be deduced from the presumption of innocence curtailing pre-trial detention. Moreover, the European institutions fail to give any standards. The literature shows that existing rules can be either confirmed or rejected by the presumption.... This indicates that the presumption of innocence can be seen as an important but abstract principle operating in the background.... The presumption of innocence is thus a principle that has little *operational* value with regard to pre-trial detention when trying to improve or criticize it.[7]

Given this lack of clarity, states use pretrial detention in ways that override the presumption of innocence. Pretrial detention has become "a popular preventive instrument serving the purpose of security, and hence an intensively used one." As Western countries in particular have become increasingly obsessed with reducing the risk of crime, they have turned to pretrial detention as a strategy.[8] Countries such as Chile, Colombia, Costa Rica, El Salvador, Nicaragua, and Panama explicitly permit judicial officers to detain defendants as a preventive strategy.[9]

Preventive justice is the polar opposite of the presumption of innocence. Yet preventive justice easily validates itself in the eyes of policymakers, even in the absence of empirical data. As Laurence H. Tribe has noted:

> Once the government has instituted a system of imprisonment openly calculated to prevent crimes committed by persons awaiting trial, the system will appear to be malfunctioning only when it releases persons who prove to be worse risks than anticipated. The pretrial misconduct of these persons will seem to validate, and will indeed augment, the fear and insecurity that the system is calculated to appease. But when the system detains persons who could safely have been released, its errors will be invisible. Since no detained defendant will commit a public offense, each decision to detain fulfills the prophecy that is thought to warrant it, while any decision to release may be refuted by its results.
>
> The inevitable consequence is a continuing pressure to broaden the system in order to reach ever more potential detainees. Indeed, this pressure will be generated by the same fears which made preventive detention seem attractive in the first place.[10]

The pressure on judges to use preventive justice compounds the already difficult task of translating the theory of the presumption of innocence into the reality of detention/release decisions. That complex process of making rights real often results in vague laws and the arbitrary application of pretrial detention.

# IMPRECISE LAWS LEAD TO ARBITRARY APPLICATION

International law calls for the following practices to protect people accused of a crime from the arbitrary and excessive application of pretrial detention:

> - Following arrest, people accused of criminal misconduct are entitled to a prompt, often automatic, appearance before a judicial officer, who reviews the propriety of the arrest and decides whether pretrial detention or imposition of some form of bail is appropriate.
>
> - All such hearings should carry a presumption in favor of pretrial release and a sense that pretrial restrictions should be proportional to the particular case and the charges brought.
>
> - Pretrial detention must be warranted by specific conditions, such as: the arrestee poses a risk of flight, a risk to the conduct of the investigation or judicial proceeding, or a risk of further criminal activity.
>
> - Courts must have a range of alternatives to pretrial detention available to them, which affords them flexibility in determining what sort of bail or other pretrial restriction, short of detention, is appropriate to the circumstances.

However, in practice many states disregard these international standards, even where national legislation closely mirrors these principles.[11] The problem is that international standards are vague: a state may comply with them on paper, yet violate them in practice.[12] As some legal scholars have noted, "there is scope for legitimate disagreement as to precisely what is meant by expressions such as 'promptly', [and] 'without undue delay' vis-à-vis the need that an accused be expeditiously brought before a court for a bail hearing and subsequently stand trial."[13]

The task of translating theory into practice usually falls to judges, who are asked to rule on pretrial detention versus pretrial release. Most bail regimes ask the courts to consider several criteria in bail decision-making, and to take numerous factors into account in making a determination.[14] This is inherently difficult, and judges often do not have enough information to make such an important decision.

In addition, the judicial officers who make these complex decisions tend to be junior magistrates or judges with little courtroom experience. In England and Wales, for example, the lay magistrates who make many of the bail decisions are non-professionals who receive only limited training. Faced with uncertainty, complex criteria, and lack of information, many judges err on the side of detaining arrestees, despite laws and norms favoring pretrial release, and even though most arrestees pose no risk to the community.[15]

Studies have documented the arbitrary work of judicial decision makers, as identical cases produce a wide variety of rulings by judicial officers. As one such study noted, even well intentioned decision makers are subject to "random fluctuations in attention, perception, mood, and so on."[16] Given that pretrial detention can influence an arrestee's likelihood of entering a guilty plea, receiving a conviction, and receiving a custodial sentence, these "random fluctuations" can change an arrestee's life.[17]

According to many scholars, even professional assessors have difficulty making detention/release judgments accurately enough to justify the detention of people against whom no criminal charge has been proven.[18] Jack F. Williams of Georgia State University's College of Law concluded that "studies on predicting dangerousness have shown that experts are accurate at predictions of dangerousness about one-third of the time and that experts overpredict dangerousness, yielding a false positive rate of sixty percent."[19] While systematic risk assessment tools offer an intriguing new avenue, most jurisdictions leave arrestees prey to the impressions of an official who understands that detention produces 100 percent compliance, regardless of its injustice.

As Williams notes, an assessment of dangerousness is prone to faulty prediction, leading to the arbitrary application of pretrial detention, or even outright abuse. The discretion granted to judges in making detention/release decisions can result in arbitrary fluctuations based on the rate of crime or the public's fear of crime. And the potential for abuse makes groups such as ethnic minorities and migrants particularly vulnerable to excessive pretrial detention.[20]

The wide discretion granted to judges is compounded by the vagueness of legislation governing the maximum length of pretrial detention. For example, the European Convention on Human Rights stipulates that accused persons must have a fair and public hearing within a "reasonable time," without specifying the meaning of "reasonable."[21] While some E.U. member states have set maximum time limits for pretrial detention, these often come with legislative provisions enabling extension of pretrial detention after expiration of the statutory time limit.[22] An assessment of 15 E.U. member states in 2011 found that France, Ireland, Lithuania, Romania, and Spain have no maximum period of pretrial detention. Germany and Poland allow extensions with no upper limit, while the Czech Republic and Slovakia have maximum periods of up to four years.[23]

### Bolivia: Misfiled Paperwork Leads to Pretrial Detention[24]

Luis didn't realize that the house was still registered to his parents' name. They were deceased, and ownership had passed to him and his brother, but no papers had been filed to document the change. When Luis sought to borrow money against the value of the house, he was charged with fraud and became ensnared in Bolivia's legal system. Although Luis posed no threat to society and should have been released on bail, vague laws governing pretrial detention resulted in his being detained for two months without trial in a San Pedro jail because of the error, only achieving release through bribes paid by Luis's wife, Mariela. She paid approximately $8,000 USD, some in Bolivianos and some in U.S. dollars, to achieve his release.

Equally vague laws govern the use of alternatives to pretrial detention. Typically, judicial discretion alone determines whether an arrestee is offered an alternative to pretrial detention. A review of pretrial detention laws and practices in the 27 E.U. member states found that the introduction of alternatives to pretrial detention resulted in virtually no reduction in the number of detainees incarcerated as a proportion of all prisoners. The authors of the review concluded, "even in countries where alternative measures are explicitly mentioned in law, in some cases, the law itself does not give an explicit objective of these alternatives...even the conditions under which they might be applied are lacking."[25]

The reluctance to use alternatives to pretrial detention can be seen in data from two countries. In 2006 and 2007, Latvian courts imposed house arrest in 15 cases, money bail in 32 cases, and pretrial detention without bail in 27,000 cases.[26] Similarly, between 2005 and 2007, Hungary made 381 orders of "geographic ban" (barring arrestees from leaving a specified geographic area without prior authorization), 153 orders of house arrest, and almost 15,000 orders of pretrial detention.[27]

And while some countries have (admittedly vague) laws that allow alternatives to pretrial detention, others refuse to even consider such options. Fewer than one-third of E.U. member states have provisions allowing courts to require accused persons, in lieu of detention, to not engage in particular conduct, to adhere to supervision, to submit to electronic monitoring, or to live under house arrest, and scarcely more than half have provisions for the release of individuals who report to the police on an imposed schedule. In many cases, the refusal to consider alternatives to pretrial detention comes in response to public pressure.

## RESTRICTIVE LAWS PROMOTE PRETRIAL DETENTION

While some laws and practices governing pretrial detention are vague and arbitrary, others are overly narrow and needlessly restrictive. So while even persons charged with serious offenses are presumed innocent until convicted by a court, some jurisdictions *require* pretrial detention for persons charged with certain crimes.[28] Austria, for example, requires pretrial detention for anyone charged with a crime that carries a minimum penalty of 10 years or more (although there are some exceptions), and Belgium requires it for crimes carrying a penalty of more than 15 years.[29] A number of Latin American countries have a list of offenses—typically consisting of relatively serious crimes such as robbery—for which pretrial detention is mandatory. These laws clearly violate the international norm that pretrial detention should be an exceptional measure.

Some jurisdictions, while not prohibiting pretrial release outright, restrict courts' ability to release certain categories of accused persons before trial. In South Africa, for example, a person charged with a serious violent crime must be detained awaiting trial, unless he produces evidence which satisfies the court that exceptional circumstances exist which should permit his release.[30] In the United States, a 1984 law creates a rebuttable presumption as to both dangerousness and flight risk in respect of persons charged with, inter alia, serious drug offenses (those carrying penalties of ten years or more) and offenses involving the use of a firearm in crimes of violence or in drug trafficking crimes.[31] The law's restrictive provisions have been upheld by the U.S. Supreme Court.[32]

Another international norm routinely violated in statute is the limitation on arrestees' time in facilities under the control of their interrogators or investigators. This time should not exceed the time required by law to obtain a judicial warrant of pretrial detention, which, in any case, should not exceed a period of 48 hours.[33] In a number of jurisdictions, however, the domestic legal framework provides for lengthy and even indefinite periods of detention in police custody. Regulations which provide for extended police custody only in "exceptional circumstances" often become standard practice. Some countries provide for maximum periods of police custody of up to 12 days (instead of the international norm of 48 hours), including some that have provision for repeated and indefinite extensions.[34] Others provide vague allocations of "reasonable time."[35]

## FLOUTING LIMITS ON DETENTION

Many jurisdictions have legislation stipulating, appropriately, that police custody may last for only 24 or 48 hours (or in rarer instances, 72 hours). However, in practice such laws are routinely ignored.[36] For example, in Mauritania, the U.N. Working Group on Arbitrary Detention found that police custody is not extended in writing as required by law; in most of the police stations visited by the Working Group, authorities were not able to produce extension authorizations despite a number of detainees claiming to have been in detention considerably beyond the permitted 48 hours. The Working Group also found that prosecutors often obscure such violations through authorizations written after the fact.[37] Prosecutors and judicial officers rubberstamp applications for extended custody without looking into the merits of individual requests. Some prosecutors, the Human Rights Council reported, lack "professional distance" from police authorities and instead collude in ways that violate arrestees' rights.[38]

In Kenya, police flout the statutory requirement that persons be brought before a judicial authority within 24 hours of arrest by transferring arrestees between police lockups, which allows them to describe the transfer as a release and fresh detention, thus starting a new 24-hour cycle.[39] The U.N. Human Rights Council has reported flagrant non-compliance, in several countries, with the rule that all detainees must be brought before a judicial authority within 72 hours.[40]

The Malawi Constitution requires that arrested persons be brought before a court within 48 hours of arrest for charging and a bail hearing.[41] However, an audit of five police stations in 2010 found that police custody regularly exceeded 48 hours. In Lilongwe, Malawi's capital, 13 percent of arrestees had been in police custody for more than five days at the time of the audit.[42] In Nepal, time limits are also frequently flouted, with one report indicating that persons detained by the police were taken before a court within the time limit in only about half of all cases.[43]

## PUBLIC PRESSURE AND POPULIST POLICY RESPONSES

Public policy is not developed in a vacuum. Examples abound of policymakers exploiting public fear of crime—or, conversely, being driven by it—to restrict the pretrial release of defendants awaiting trial.

In 1989 the Irish Supreme Court took the position that preventive detention—denying pretrial release because the accused may commit an offense while out on bail—amounts to a denial of the presumption of innocence.[44] The court held that, "The accepted method of preventing the commission of future offences is the threat of conviction and punishment…. [A]ny imprisonment before conviction has a substantial punitive content and it would be improper for any court to refuse bail as a mark of disapproval of former conduct."[45]

However, a plebiscite overturned the 1989 Irish Supreme Court decision. Pressure from the Irish police, who argued that "bail banditry" had become a problem, resulted in a 1996 referendum that amended the Irish Constitution to allow for the refusal of bail to a person charged with a serious offense. Despite opposition to this constitutional change by, among others, the Law Reform Commission of Ireland, the popular vote carried the proposal.[46]

A 1997 South African law requiring arrestees accused of serious violent crimes to present evidence in order to obtain pretrial release followed a period of rising crime and fear of crime in the country in the mid-1990s. In a 1999 ruling, the South African Constitutional Court upheld the restrictive law.

In Latin America, the number of pretrial detainees vastly exceeded the number of sentenced prisoners, until a wave of reforms in the 1990s—including reforms specifically aimed at decreasing pretrial detention—largely succeeded in addressing the problem. However, as increasing violent crime and increasing fear of crime—both fed by the drug war—became prevalent in the region, a counter-reform backlash took hold.[47] Between 1999 and 2007, ten Latin American countries adopted counter-reforms which restrict the right to pretrial release, either through legislation or executive decree.[48]

Public concerns about crime—or, at least, the translation of such concerns into official policy—are often based on perception, rather than facts. In a number of developed countries, the use of pretrial detention has increased, even as violent crime has declined. In Australia, the total number of convicted prisoners increased by around 20 percent between 1995 and 2004; over the same period, the number of pretrial detainees jumped almost 150 percent. An underlying reason for this trend has been a hardening of public and official attitudes towards people abusing alcohol and drugs and, relatedly, toward people with mental health problems. An analysis of trends among pretrial detainees in the Australian state of Victoria, for example, showed declines in seriousness of criminal history at the same time as there were indications of increasingly severe drug and alcohol abuse and mental health problems. These changes in detainee characteristics are one of the significant reasons for Victoria's increase in pretrial detention numbers in recent years.[49]

In many jurisdictions, alarmist media reporting on judges deemed "soft" on crime for releasing someone awaiting trial who is charged with a serious offense, or who subsequently commits an offense, places pressure on judges to err on the side of detention rather than release. In other places, such as Ukraine, judges are reluctant to use alternatives to pretrial detention because professional success depends on being perceived as tough on crime.[50] As one Dutch judge commented, "If you are skilful, you can detain virtually anyone."[51]

A similar fear of being perceived as soft on crime dogs many politicians. In some countries, interference by politicians in the operational functions of the police and even prosecution is rife. Police may carry out arrests on the orders of a political or an administrative authority (such as a governor, government representative, or the military) rather than on the basis of an independent investigation into an alleged criminal offense.[52] Where politicians and prosecutors campaign for election based on their crime-fighting bona fides, it is not surprising to find high rates of pretrial detention, even if the overuse of pretrial detention has not been shown to reduce crime.

## DEARTH OF POLITICAL WILL

For politicians and government officials, seeking to reduce pretrial detention is a risky business. In the United States, for example, controversy over the furlough of a convicted murderer and accusations of being soft on crime in the 1988 presidential campaign "changed the course of that race."[53] Thus, pressure for reform often comes not from politicians or officials, but from international bodies or as the result of intolerable prison conditions abruptly exposed due to a disaster such as a prison fire or riot. However, even in such cases, official enthusiasm for reform is often short-lived because of political risk and the popular backlash governments may face when they seek to reduce pretrial detention numbers.

In India, for example, various state governments and the federal government have set up several committees to suggest ways to reform the country's prison system, including the overuse of pretrial detention. One of the most well-known and comprehensive of these was the All India Committee on Jail Reforms, 1980-1983, which submitted 639 recommendations to the central government on all areas of prison administration and prisoner rights.[54] Yet, "almost all of the recommendations of this and other committees lie gathering dust without the political will to implement them."[55] This remains so, even though the Supreme Court and the High Courts in India have commented at length upon the deplorable conditions inside prisons and the resulting violation of prisoners' rights. The National and State Human Rights Commissions in India have also, in their annual reports, drawn attention to the appalling conditions and urged governments to introduce reforms—all to little avail.[56]

In neighboring Bangladesh, government commissions were set up in 1957 and in 1978 to recommend prison reforms. In both cases, the process of implementing these has been extremely slow. The recommendations contained in the Bangladesh Jail Reform Commission Report of 1980 remain largely unimplemented. In 2002, the government set up a Ministerial Committee for Jail Reforms, headed by the state minister for home affairs.[57] Almost a decade later, the recommendations remain unimplemented.

In Nigeria, the federal government has frequently expressed an ostensible interest in improving prison conditions and access to justice for pretrial detainees.[58] The establishment of a Presidential Taskforce on Prison Reforms and Decongestion led to the release of some 8,000 prisoners in 1999. However, no long-term policy was adopted to address the problems of pretrial detention and within a few years the country's prisons were as congested as they were before the release. In 2001, then Minister of Interior Chief Sunday Afolabi said that the government would review prison laws and initiate prison reforms. In 2002, then President Olusegun Obasanjo described the situation of inmates awaiting trial as "inhuman."[59] Over the next five years, the number of committees and reports built up:

› A 2005 report by the National Working Group on Prison Reform and Decongestion (which reviewed 144 Nigerian prisons) lamented the high proportion of prison inmates who were pretrial detainees.

› An Inter-Ministerial Summit on the State of Remand Inmates in Nigeria's Prisons was established in 2005 to review the report of the previous Working Group on Prison Reform. It recommended the federal government address prison crowding and the problem of pretrial detainees, with special attention to a shortage of defense counsel.

> The Presidential Committee on Prison Reform and Rehabilitation was established in 2006. President Obasanjo said that the federal government would implement the committee's recommendations.[60]

> Another committee, the Presidential Commission on the Reform of the Administration of Justice, followed. The president asked the commission to undertake a case-by-case audit of various categories of inmates, such as pretrial detainees.

> In 2007, the Committee on the Harmonization of Reports of Presidential Committees Working on Justice Sector Reform reiterated the commission's recommendations.

At the time of writing, none of the aforementioned working groups, summits, committees, and commissions had changed Nigeria's pretrial justice system or reduced the number of prisoners awaiting trial. Over the last 20 years, the proportion of pretrial detainees has consistently hovered between two-thirds and three-quarters of all prisoners confined in Nigeria's overcrowded prison infrastructure.[61]

Nigeria represents, perhaps, a particularly egregious case in which promises have been broken and the federal government's own appointees' findings ignored, but it is fair to say that political considerations block penal reform in general—and the reduction of pretrial detention in particular—throughout the world.

## POLICE AND PROSECUTORIAL INFLUENCE

Police and prosecutors nearly always favor pretrial detention over pretrial release. The police are typically convinced that a defendant is guilty, and the prosecution service, working closely with the police, adopts this position.[62] For police and prosecutors, the excessive use of pretrial detention offers two important benefits. First, pretrial detainees are guaranteed to stand trial, cannot interfere with witnesses and the criminal investigation, and do not pose a risk to public security. Second, pretrial detainees—especially those without legal representation—are at the largely unfettered beck and call of detectives and prosecutors for repeated questioning, and are more likely to cooperate with their interrogators by making admissions or confessions.

In the United States, prosecutors have the authority to pursue a plea agreement and bargain with an arrestee. Federal prosecutors, who prosecute the most serious violent crimes and drug-related offenses, have discretion over pretrial detention, which allows them to use it as a bargaining chip during plea negotiations. This system "converts pretrial detention from a method of protecting society from crimes committed by criminals out on bail into a tool which helps prosecutors obtain information or convictions."[63] Threatening someone with pretrial detention can be persuasive: pretrial detainees are more likely to be convicted and, if convicted, given a custodial sentence compared to similar arrestees who await their trials at liberty.[64] Even for detainees unaware of this dynamic, it may be tempting to accept the plea bargain, rather than endure indefinite pretrial detention.

Studies undertaken in Canada and the United States provide empirical support for the contention that pretrial detention may pressure arrestees to plead guilty, even if they are innocent.[65] The literature suggests that there are numerous reasons that a detainee may opt to plead guilty. For example, he may not want to be in the legal limbo pretrial detention implies, and a conviction may prompt a move to a less crowded custodial facility. Moreover, if a guilty plea will not involve additional prison time, detainees have an obvious motivation to plead guilty.[66] A Canadian study found pretrial detainees made 2.5 times as many guilty pleas as those released on bail, and that the prosecution is much more likely to coerce a guilty plea if an arrestee is in pretrial detention.[67] Another study found that juveniles are more likely to plead guilty if they are in pretrial detention.[68]

In contrast, if arrestees are released pretrial, they are more likely to resist pleading guilty and have their charges withdrawn. A U.S. study found that arrestees released pending trial are more likely to work with a lawyer and try to mount a vigorous defense in order to avoid a prison term.[69] A Canadian study found that arrestees at liberty awaiting trial were 2.3 times more likely to have their charges withdrawn than those who had been detained.[70]

> **Kyrgyzstan: Arrested for One Crime, Charged with 24 More**[71]
>
> Six months into his stay at a pretrial isolation facility in Kyrgyzstan, 30-year-old Anatoli suffered a heart attack. He was taken to the hospital but returned to detention after a week and handcuffed to a bed. An orphan from a young age, Anatoli supported himself from the sale of scrap metal and was accused of stealing some from a geological expedition. While he admitted to this crime, he was innocent of the 24 additional unresolved cases the police attributed to him in an effort to meet a quota of "solved" cases. Some of these crimes—such as supposedly stealing a mobile phone from a theatergoer at a performance on a day when the theater was actually closed—never even occurred. His legal aid attorneys obtained an acquittal for all but three of the cases and Anatoli was released through an amnesty after serving nine months in pretrial detention.

The judiciary's role in upholding the law, including the principle of presumed innocence, might moderate prosecutorial zeal for pretrial detention. However, in many jurisdictions the judiciary slavishly follows the direction of the prosecution in respect of bail decisions.

In Poland, official data for the years 2001–2007 reveal that the courts comply with prosecutors' requests for pretrial detention in approximately 90 percent of cases. Appeals to a higher court against the initial detention decision only very rarely alter the outcome.[72] According to a study published in 2004, Belgian prosecutors request pretrial detention in virtually all cases (92 percent), with the prosecution's request being granted in 63 percent of cases.[73] In France, pretrial detention hearings have been described as "little more than a procedural formality, with ... inappropriate weight being placed on the perceived guilt of the accused."[74]

Judicial deference to the prosecution is especially prevalent in the countries of the former Soviet Union. Russia transferred the right to make pretrial detention decisions from the prosecution to the judiciary in 2002, only to see judges approve at least 90 percent of all prosecutorial applications for pretrial detention.[75] In

Armenia, Georgia, and Ukraine, courts grant over 90 percent of requests for pretrial detention.[76]

Even in jurisdictions with a long tradition of judicial independence in other areas of criminal justice, courts usually adhere to prosecutors' detention requests. Research suggests the Crown Prosecution Service (C.P.S.) in England and Wales usually follows police recommendations in respect of bail, and that judicial officers follow suit.[77] One study in England and Wales found that in 86 percent of cases, judicial officers followed the prosecution's request to detain a defendant awaiting trial.[78] The study concluded that "the C.P.S. recommendation was very influential on the magistrates' remand decision," noting that "magistrates simply 'rubber stamp' the [prosecution's] decision."[79] One analyst observed that "the 'presumption' in favour of bail is, in practice, illusory and that, in contrast, there is a strong working presumption in favour of remanding the accused in custody if that is what is requested by the CPS."[80]

## CORRUPTION

Official corruption is a major factor in the global overuse of pretrial detention. Police officers, prosecutors, and judges in many countries are underpaid; consequently, these actors may make decisions about arrest, investigation, charge, and pretrial detention to generate income, rather than to uphold the law or protect public safety.[81]

Corruption among police officers may include arrests to exact a bribe, to meet arrest targets, or to harass sections of the community.[82] Corruption among prosecutors may include charging an arrestee with an offense that is more serious than the evidence warrants. This is done for a variety of purposes, including inducing a person to confess and/or plead guilty to a lesser charge, or to extract a bribe.[83] And corruption among judges may result in pretrial release for those who can pay bribes and pretrial detention for those who cannot.

In many developing countries, the police and the judiciary are seen as the two most corrupt institutions, according to Transparency International.[84] The organization's 2013 Global Corruption Barometer identifies the police as the institution most often reported as the recipient of bribes; almost three in 10 of those who had contact with the police worldwide report paying a bribe. The judiciary follows in second place, with almost a quarter of those who had contact with judges reporting paying a bribe.[85]

Corruption and excessive pretrial detention are mutually reinforcing. A criminal justice system that overuses pretrial detention is susceptible to corruption, and an environment marked by corruption will likely lead to over-reliance on pretrial detention. The two form a vicious cycle: a dysfunctional justice system leads to corruption, and corruption undermines rational and rights-based pretrial justice practices.[86]

### Ghana: Torture Motivated by Profit

In a 2011 survey of male pretrial detainees in Ghana, almost half (49 percent) said they had been tortured by a state official after their arrest, with a third suffering permanent physical injury as a result. Being tortured was significantly associated with being bribed. Among those detainees from whom a bribe was solicited (about a quarter of surveyed detainees), 70 percent were tortured. The majority (74 percent) of detainees tortured said this was done to extract a confession, while 11 percent said it was done for "punishment." [87]

Corruption is so prevalent in the pretrial phase because it is the part of the criminal justice process that receives less scrutiny and is subject to more discretion than subsequent stages, and often involves lower paid and junior actors in the system. Relatively unhindered by scrutiny or accountability, police, prosecutors, and judges arrest, detain, and release individuals based on the ability to pay bribes. In many countries, the financial and political incentives to corrupt the pretrial detention process are numerous, rewarding, and risk free. That toxic combination—low levels of accountability combined with poor transparency around the processing of cases—causes systematic corruption in many pretrial detention systems.[88]

In criminal justice systems with pervasive corruption, only arrestees with political connections or the means to bribe officials achieve pretrial release. A review of arrest and detention practices in 21 African countries found that in many places, the release of persons wrongfully arrested and the prompt handling of investigations depend on bribes rather than observance of legal procedure.[89] In addition, pretrial detention has been used to interfere in commercial disputes; for example, in Senegal, the police arbitrarily arrest and detain taxi drivers for days at a time, without charge, during disputes between taxi drivers' associations.[90]

The African Policing and Civilian Oversight Forum reports that in some countries police routinely round up the poor, women, homeless children, migrants, and refugees in mass arrests, then subject them to beatings, sexual abuse, and extortion.[91] In Kenya, for example, police have executed nightly raids in shantytowns without search or arrest warrants, beating residents and demanding money under threat of arrest.[92] In Nigeria, police are known to detain sex workers as a way to extort sexual favors; the practice is known as "fringe benefits."[93]

Ironically, widespread corruption may lead to the overuse of pretrial detention by judges seeking to demonstrate that they are *not* corrupt. That is, corrupt judges make a show of placing almost all arrestees in pretrial detention, as a way to distract attention from their releasing those arrestees who pay bribes. According to the International Bar Association, judges in Brazil have increased their use of pretrial detention partly in response to accusations of corruption.[94]

### Pakistan: Multiple Bribe Points [95]

Pakistan's *The International News* reported on bribery in 2011. The article described the experience of a man named Umair, who had been in pretrial detention for six years and described paying a multitude of bribes. His relatives paid bribes to get access to him; he had to bribe an officer to be produced in court for his own trial. Another official sought a bribe for an expedited appearance before a judge and the opportunity to share a meal with his family within the court's corridors.

## PROCEDURAL FACTORS

In many criminal justice systems, the very process of deciding between pretrial detention and release is warped in favor of detention. For example, the bail hearing may be too brief to consider all the facts or make an accurate determination of the likelihood that the arrestee will abscond if granted pretrial release. In many jurisdictions, it is impossible to challenge a pretrial detention decision once it is made, or the structure of the system may make it impossible for the detainee to get in front of a judge.

In general, courts devote minimal time to considering the question of bail. Although determining whether to deprive a presumed-innocent person of his liberty pending trial is one of the most serious decisions a state can make, it is often made in an instant. In England and Wales, one study found that courts processed 62 percent of remand cases in less than two minutes each.[96] A study of London magistrates' courts found the remand decision was made in five minutes or less in almost 90 percent of cases.[97] In South Australia, the median time taken for contested bail hearings is about five minutes.[98] A study in Cook County in the United States found a judge processing 101 cases in 75 minutes. As one observer reflected, "The Cook County Bond Court is not a legal system. It is a machine. Its mantra is efficiency over justice. Mechanized administration over individual rights."[99] These processing periods prevent judicial officers from adequately considering available alternatives to pretrial detention or a defendant's personal circumstances, such as his character, health, mental state, and financial situation. Such quick decisions increase the risk of arbitrary imposition of detention without bail.[100] They also lead to the assignment of bail without regard for finances, effectively denying pretrial release to poor people.

Once people are in pretrial detention, it is very hard to get out. The European Convention on Human Rights confers the "right to periodic review of loss of liberty on the basis that the initial grounds for detention may no longer exist."[101] A 1989 ruling by the European Court of Human Rights held that an opportunity to review the lawfulness of pretrial detention must be provided at "reasonable intervals."[102] Yet an assessment of 15 E.U. member states in 2011 found that eight had restrictions on the right to a regular and reasoned review of the decision to remand in custody.[103] In some E.U. member states, no legislative provisions for periodic review of pretrial detention decisions exist. In these countries, the defendant and/or his legal representative has to proactively seek such a review or appeal against the initial pretrial detention decision.[104] Outside the European Union, many jurisdictions have no provision for review of the decision to keep a person in pretrial detention.[105] India and Bangladesh, for example, routinely extend pretrial detention without the detainee appearing in person before a judge.[106]

In Nigeria, a practice called a "holding charge" increases the frequency and duration of pretrial detention. This practice empowers any magistrate—a low-level judicial officer—to order pretrial detention for any arrestee charged with a capital offense, such as armed robbery or murder. The arrestee is to be held in pretrial detention pending the conclusion of the police investigation. As the Nigerian Bar Association notes, a magistrate does not need to review evidence before ordering a holding charge: "the only trigger for this remand order is a police charge sheet accusing the person in question of committing a capital crime."[107]

Most importantly for the police, the magistrate has the power to order pretrial detention using the holding charge, but he does not have the power to grant bail or conduct a trial—only a more senior judicial officer can do that. But, in practice, more senior judges are often not informed that a holding charge has been issued. Thus, once they have obtained a remand order under the holding charge, the police enjoy almost unfettered power to keep an arrestee in pretrial detention as long as they deem necessary.[108] Individuals have been kept in jail for years under the holding charge for crimes they did not commit. Nigeria's Presidential Commission on the Reform of the Administration of Justice found 110 individuals who had been in pretrial detention for more than 10 years.[109] While the states of Lagos and Ondo have abandoned the practice, other jurisdictions maintain it.[110]

Another procedural contributor to excessive pretrial detention is the suspension or violation of habeas corpus (in those jurisdictions that provide for it). Detainees' lack of awareness of their rights, lack of access to courts and lawyers, and ineffective or corrupt judicial authorities all contribute to such violations.[111] Some jurisdictions require a prosecutor's approval to bring a detainee before a judge, which allows prosecutors and police to prevent judicial review.[112] In other places, the costs involved make filing a writ of habeas corpus effectively impossible.[113]

## LACK OF COORDINATION BETWEEN CRIMINAL JUSTICE AGENCIES

A fair and effective pretrial justice system, especially one that minimizes the use of pretrial detention, requires the coordination—and, at times, active collaboration—of a range of criminal justice agencies, including police investigators, prosecutors, defense lawyers, judicial officers and, ideally, agencies tasked with supervising defendants released awaiting trial. Given the multiplicity of agencies and professions involved in the pretrial justice process, effective coordination is a perennial challenge in most jurisdictions.

The lack of coordination between, and even within, criminal justice agencies typically lengthens the duration of police investigations. Prosecutors need to communicate and consult with one another to avoid case files collecting dust on a detective's or prosecutor's desk. Arrestees need to be brought before court in a timely manner for their initial remand hearing or, once in pretrial detention, to be returned to court for reviews of their pretrial detention at regular intervals. Court-based hearings can typically proceed only with the presence of the arrestee, a police investigator, witnesses, a judicial officer and, in many cases, defense counsel. A lack of coordination bars the progress of such hearings.

In less developed countries, coordination can be a particular challenge. Rural courts often do not have full-time sitting judicial officers, and a lack of transport or guards can result in detained defendants not being brought to court in a timely manner. The following account from Sierra Leone provides a glimpse of the coordination required to get a detainee to court for trial.

> For a detainee's case to be heard at the given date requires six things to perfectly coincide. First, the Magistrate must arrive to town on the pre-determined date. Second, the complainant/plaintiff must be present. Third, relevant witnesses must be [present]. Fourth, the prosecuting police officer must be present. Fifth, the detainee must be present. And sixth, the preceding court cases must not take longer than anticipated. However, the requirements needed for a case to proceed are infrequently met. Often, a lack of fuel, backed up court cases at another site, and unforeseen logistical problems arise and cause an absence. Witnesses rarely come to court as the costs associated with going to court are high and in many cases insurmountable (basic travel costs, etc.). Prosecuting officers often do not show up. Interviews with officials at [X] Prison suggest that prisoners are not always transferred to court on the day of their hearing. Moreover, court cases often take longer than expected and the queue of cases is never quite finished.[114]

Similar problems have been reported in India and Nigeria, and evidence suggests they exist in many other jurisdictions.[115] Once a person has been remanded to pretrial detention, a lack of communication and coordination among different criminal justice agencies may mean that he is literally lost in the system.

In Nigeria, there is a "near total failure of coordination and information management between the various agencies at the state and federal levels involved in the criminal process."[116] The police, a federal agency, have primary responsibility for investigating crimes. Most crimes, however, are state crimes, prosecuted by state-level prosecutors, and overseen by the state directors of public prosecutions (DPPs). Trial courts are mostly state courts. Cases may stall because the police transfer an investigator from one state to another, without notification to the relevant state prosecutors who will require the officer as a witness.[117] DPPs have no control over the police, and case files often go missing between the agencies. If their records get lost, detainees can be condemned to remain in pretrial detention almost indefinitely.

A presidential committee's audit of Nigeria's prison system in 2005 found that almost 30 percent of pretrial detainees had been affected by poor coordination between agencies. Four percent of pretrial detainees were in custody because their case files were missing, eight percent because the police investigator had been transferred, and another 17 percent because of delays in the investigation.[118]

Malawi has similar problems. The DPP has nominal authority over the police prosecutors who handle the vast majority of all criminal prosecutions, but in practice a separate ministry and hierarchy of command actually supervises.[119] Moreover, the referral of cases by local prosecutors to regional and national headquarters strictly follows the police bureaucracy. For example, a homicide docket cannot be sent directly to the DPP's office without first being channeled through the police's regional prosecutions office, which invariably results in delays.

Agencies in the United States also exhibit poor coordination. In his analysis of the pretrial detention crisis[120] in the late 1980s, the chief of the Program Services Branch Probation and Pretrial Services Division of the United States Courts concluded that "notably absent while the crisis was continuing was any type of systematic analysis of the situation. The various agencies charged with detention have issued reports and hold regular meetings about the problem among themselves… [but] these scattered efforts do not add up to a coherent plan based upon the input of all relevant parties."[121] In both developed and developing countries, presumed-innocent people are behind bars because of bureaucratic ineptitude.

It is essential that criminal justice practitioners coordinate their efforts more carefully and thoroughly. They should also regularly review their efforts and performance, and jointly identify and address shortcomings.

## THE ROLE OF LIMITED RESOURCES

Although the overuse of pretrial detention is costly to states, a criminal justice system's lack of resources actually increases pretrial detention and the costs associated with it. The lack of material and personnel resources results in more people being kept in pretrial detention for longer periods.

Where the police and prosecution have limited investigative abilities due to a lack of forensic equipment or qualified investigators, or both, they must solve crimes by catching people in the act or through the use of confessions.

One consequence of limited investigative abilities is that police focus on minor offenses, because it's typically easier to catch people in the act of, for example, theft or urinating in public, while investigating a serial killer or a white collar criminal requires greater resources. A 2009 study by the United Nations Office on Drugs and Crime found that in most of the 30 African countries surveyed, less than half of pretrial detainees and convicted prisoners had been charged with serious offenses. In Ghana, Malawi, Swaziland, and Zambia, over three-quarters of all prisoners were incarcerated for minor crimes.[122] While the presumption of innocence makes all pretrial detention inherently suspect, the pretrial detention of individuals not even accused of major crimes has a particularly low likelihood of protecting public safety.

Another consequence of the lack of resources is an overreliance on confessions, in lieu of proper police investigations that can be resource-intensive. This leads to the use of pretrial detention to coerce confessions. In Nigeria, a 2008 report by the Presidential Committee on Police Reform acknowledges that "the standard of Police investigation is very low and hardly goes beyond taking statements and coercing suspects to confess."[123] The Nigerian police often lack the capacity to prosecute serious crimes. For instance, out of 5,883 robbery suspects held in four of Nigeria's most populated prisons between 2000 and 2005, only 48 robbery convictions were secured and 4,014 were acquitted.[124] In countries where conviction rates are low because of a lack of criminal justice capacity, there is a temptation to use pretrial detention not to "attain its primary goal of upholding order and security and facilitating investigations, but rather, as…a form of sanction."[125]

In addition, the lack of criminal justice resources can cause delays that lengthen pretrial detention. For example, many resource-poor jurisdictions do not have the technical systems to track arrestees as they move through the system, or to track persons released awaiting trial.[126] So people are kept in pretrial detention simply because the system lacks capacity to monitor them if they are released pending trial. In jurisdictions that lack the photocopiers to produce duplicate case files, the original case file containing all pertinent materials must be shared among police, prosecutors and judges. At best, this causes delays—and at worst the files or parts of them get lost, resulting in indefinite pretrial detention.[127]

A scarcity of police vehicles or fuel to run them can slow down the pretrial process and thereby increase both the average duration of detention and the average number of detainees. In Nigeria, despite a policy recommendation that the Nigeria Police Force should have at least 30,000 vehicles, the force was reported in 2008 to have only 5,900 serviceable vehicles—less than a fifth of the recommended minimum.[128] More recently, a shortage of fuel for police vehicles in Malawi in 2011-12 significantly restricted the police's ability to transport pretrial detainees to court for bail hearings or trial proceedings.[129] In Harare, the capital of Zimbabwe, pretrial detainees could only be transported to court two days a week in 2011, which created a huge case backlog.[130]

### Kyrgyzstan: Extended Pretrial Detention Due to Fuel Costs[131]

A former inmate from the southern town of Kyzylkyya in Batken province described his experiences in a local IVS (*Izoliatory vremennogo soderzhaniia*), where suspects are confined until a prosecutor determines whether to pursue the case. Officially, the maximum time a suspect can spend in an IVS is ten days after being formally charged:

> In the old days, maybe you'd sit in the IVS for a month [while under investigation] before they took you to the Jalalabat prison. But now they only have one jeep to transport the prisoners in, and they only want to make one trip. So they wait until they have eight or ten prisoners, and then they take them all together. It usually takes six months to a year. If you want to go to the prison earlier, the police go to your parents and ask them for ten litres of petrol. Then they order an ordinary taxi to take you to Jalalabat. I sat in the IVS in Kyzylkyya for over a year. We got a bit of bread and hot tea in the morning and evening. Our relatives could bring us some more stuff, but if you don't have police connections, nothing gets through; my mother couldn't get me anything for eight months.

Even the shortage of something as simple as a typewriter or courtroom can substantially increase pretrial detention. For example, in Zambia prosecutors generally draft police dockets by hand because they lack a computer or typewriter. When dockets are illegible the court sends them back, delaying trials.[132] Similarly, many jurisdictions in poor countries lack an adequate court infrastructure. Judges may share courtrooms and therefore curtail their hours, or may not be able to find an available courtroom and thus postpone hearings.

The lack of resources is not limited to criminal justice systems in developing countries. An Australian study found that many defendants were detained awaiting trial because judges felt there was insufficient personnel to manage their release and ensure their return for trial.[133]

Lack of resources also undermines alternatives to pretrial detention, increasing the likelihood that courts will remand awaiting trial prisoners into pretrial detention. In many countries legislation provides for a wide range of alternatives, but lack of funds foreclose many of them. The U.S. federal system, for example, provides for home electronic monitoring and the placement of detainees in halfway houses as alternatives to pretrial detention, but some federal districts have no resources to provide them.[134]

Even where resources are in short supply, it is essential that criminal justice systems invest in data collection. Increasing data collection capacity can enhance the performance of the criminal justice system throughout the pretrial detention phase, and improve both day-to-day operations and more long-term planning and evaluation.

Many jurisdictions, in the developed and developing world alike, are marked by a shortage of personnel. A lack of judges is the most obvious shortage, resulting in adjournments and incomplete trials.[135] But pretrial detention can also be exacerbated by the lack of police, guards, prosecutors, court officers, and administrative staff. Perhaps most damaging to the presumption of innocence is the lack of legal representation for defendants, which is explored in the next section.

# INADEQUATE LEGAL REPRESENTATION AND ASSISTANCE

The vast majority of arrestees lack the education, knowledge, or skills necessary to protect their right to be presumed innocent. They cannot adequately mount an application for pretrial release as they are ignorant of the (often vague) legal and factual criteria courts use in their pretrial decision making process. Unrepresented arrestees have great difficulty preparing their criminal case because, even if they do know the basis of the accusation or charge, they do not necessarily understand what a proper defense requires. Those detained awaiting trial do not have the liberty that would enable them to trace and interview witnesses, scrutinize the evidence against them, study the relevant law, and prepare their defense.[136]

The availability of legal representation and assistance—especially at the very early stages of the criminal justice process—can make a significant difference to arrestees' likelihood of being remanded into pretrial detention and, in cases where they are detained, how long they are held. An initiative in four Nigerian states, under which lawyers known as duty solicitors were stationed at police stations around the clock, reduced the number of pretrial detainees by almost 20 percent and the duration of pretrial detention by 72 percent over a one year period.[137] In Malawi, the introduction of paralegals who provide legal advice and assistance to arrestees and defendants at police stations, remand centers, and courts, almost certainly played a significant role in reducing both the number and proportion of pretrial detainees in that country.[138]

A study involving nearly 4,000 lower-income arrestees in the United States found that legal representation made arrestees more than twice as likely to be released on their own recognizance from pretrial custody and more than twice as likely to have bail reduced to an amount they could afford. The study found that delaying representation until after the pretrial release determination was the "single most important reason for lengthy pretrial incarceration of people charged with nonviolent crimes. Without counsel present, judicial officers made less informed decisions and were more likely to set or maintain a pretrial release financial condition that was beyond the individual's ability to pay."[139] Other U.S. studies link the provision of counsel at the bail process to early release, enhanced satisfaction with the criminal justice process, and financial savings to courts and prisons.[140]

### USA: Pretrial Detention without a Lawyer

According to an American Bar Association report, in some places throughout the United States, poor persons accused of crime are placed in pretrial detention "for months or even years before they have a chance to speak with a lawyer."[141] In the state of Georgia, for example, an individual was arrested for loitering and spent 13 months in pretrial detention without seeing a lawyer or judge, or even being formally charged. In Mississippi, a woman arrested for stealing $200 from a casino slot machine spent eight months in pretrial detention because she was unable to afford bail. Eventually, without receiving any effective legal representation, the woman pled guilty. She was sentenced to time served.

Few countries provide arrestees with free legal assistance, especially at the pretrial stage of the criminal process. Many less developed countries have few, if any, lawyers available outside of major towns and cities, so that even arrestees with some means are unable to procure private counsel.

Europe has more developed legal aid provisions than any other region. Yet, a three-year study deemed legal aid in many E.U. member states "inadequate," noting that "a variety of factors prevent access to competent legal assistance at all stages of the criminal process."[142] In many E.U. member states, the law does not provide for a right to legal assistance immediately following arrest and in some states, such as the Netherlands, a lawyer is not allowed to be present during police interrogations.[143] Even where the law provides for a right to legal assistance at the early stages of the criminal process, various practices and procedures often limit access to legal assistance in practice, especially for those who cannot afford to pay for it.

In the United States, fewer than a dozen states out of 50 ensure legal representation within the initial 48 hours after arrest,[144] and a number of states do not provide lawyers at any part of the bail stage of the criminal justice process.[145] Even arrestees who do have access to a state-funded lawyer can find it challenging to meet with counsel because overcrowding in pretrial detention centers leads to frequent movement of detainees. The chief of operations of the Federal Defender Service Unit of the Legal Aid Society in the United States commented on the problem:

> Many of our clients are bounced around like ping pong balls between institutions. They are awakened in the middle of the night in preparation for

> a trip to court and when they arrive they are exhausted and have difficulty concentrating.... Defense counsel are unable to operate under the present system and still provide constitutional representation for their clients.[146]

In Brazil, the vast majority of persons charged with a serious offense do not have access to proper legal assistance during the pretrial phase of criminal proceedings. An investigation of 6,500 cases of robbery in the state of São Paulo in 1999-2000 showed defense lawyers made requests for provisional liberty before trial in only a quarter of robbery cases. Moreover, defense lawyers were not even present during 22 percent of cases in which their clients made their first appearance before a judge, despite the fact that this should render all subsequent proceedings null and void.[147]

In Africa, state budget allocations for legal aid are typically minimal. A survey on legal aid in Africa found that while national laws—often entrenched as constitutional provisions—establish a right to legal aid, access to legal aid is not available at all stages of the criminal justice process, and is particularly rare at police stations and only sometimes available in prisons and the lower courts, all of which disproportionately affect pretrial detainees.[148]

It is in the interest of criminal justice systems everywhere to collaborate with civil society organizations to improve the delivery of pretrial services. Such collaboration can improve the efficiency of the pretrial detention phase, which is especially important where the state is unable or unwilling to provide legal aid itself.

## CONCLUSION

The causes of the arbitrary and excessive use of pretrial detention are many and often interrelated. Jurisdictions burdened by high levels of pretrial detention also frequently use detention in an arbitrary manner, detaining persons accused of minor offenses for which custodial sentences are inappropriate. As this chapter has sought to demonstrate, numerous jurisdictions are plagued by challenges and weaknesses which coalesce to produce sustained pretrial detention crises.

Problems around the arbitrary and excessive use of pretrial detention begin with definitional and normative challenges around the practical meaning of the presumption of innocence. While many policy makers and senior criminal justice officials pay lip service to the importance of upholding the presumption of innocence, political and societal forces intent on minimizing the risk of crime undermine its operational use. The factual and legal distinction between a person suspected of having committed a crime and a convicted offender has been blurred. Laws justifying the detention of defendants on the basis of their potential future actions—a preventive approach—undermine the presumption of innocence around the world.

The presumption of innocence's limited operational value is further eroded by imprecise and restrictive laws dealing with pretrial detention. Many jurisdictions lack clear laws limiting the length of pretrial detention or the right to a regular review of continued confinement prior to trial. In developed and developing countries alike, laws abound which restrict the judiciary's ability to release defendants awaiting trial. Such laws are not produced in a vacuum; public pressure and populist policy initiatives often produce them. Moreover, a lack of political will in many countries serves to undermine coherent policy initiatives which have the potential to address the excessive and arbitrary use of detention.

Mundane reasons for the excessive and arbitrary use of pretrial detention, such as inadequate criminal justice agency coordination or resources, are almost ubiquitous worldwide. As with the other causes of the excessive and arbitrary use of pretrial detention, these two factors complement one another. A lack of resources makes coordination—through such tools as electronic file transfers—more difficult. Insufficient police vehicles or fuel may delay an investigation or prosecution while pretrial detention continues.

Inadequate legal representation or assistance plays an important role in aggravating the excessive and arbitrary use of pretrial detention, as well. The availability of legal support, especially during the early stages of the criminal justice process shortly after arrest, can make a significant difference to arrestees' likelihood of being remanded into pretrial detention and, in cases where they are detained, the duration thereof. Yet, even in regions with relatively developed legal aid mechanisms, such as Western Europe and parts of the United States, the law does not always provide for a right to legal assistance immediately following arrest or during the bail stage of the criminal justice process.

The problems inherent in the arbitrary use of pretrial detention run deep, as described in the next chapter, which looks at the negative impact of excessive pretrial detention on the rule of law.

# The Implications for the Rule of Law

## INTRODUCTION

The overuse of pretrial detention harms people, communities, and states in direct, measurable ways. Excessive pretrial detention, as documented throughout this report, contributes to torture, corruption, the spread of disease, and a host of other ills. But it also has the less visible, arguably more insidious, effect of undermining the rule of law. Often, one of the victims of excessive pretrial detention is the criminal justice system itself.

This report has thus far focused on the people who are hurt by the overuse of pretrial detention, and the many ways in which they are harmed. But there is important and potentially long-lasting collateral damage: the harm done to the ideas and practices of basic fairness, due process, and equality before the law.

This chapter explores the association between pretrial detention and violations of the procedural norms that most societies claim to live by, as well as some of the potentially far reaching consequences for the rule of law in those societies. A fair, functioning criminal justice system honors the rights to liberty and the presumption of innocence, and observes the attendant limits on arrest and detention, as well as guarantees of ready access to counsel designed to protect each of us. When these are missing, the result is not solely too many people locked up awaiting trial—it also bends the arc of criminal law towards injustice and so corrodes the rule of law.

At its extremes, excessive pretrial detention begs the question of whether states acknowledge the relevant norms as binding sources of law. On paper, international law—reflected in numerous treaty provisions, and authoritative interpretations applicable around the world and in particular regions—holds that pretrial detention should be the exception, rather than the rule, used for the narrow and specific purposes of ensuring that a defendant is brought to trial and does not interfere with the legal process. It is clear that the patterns of excessive pretrial detention documented in this book are violations of fundamental norms. The ability to detain a person who is presumed innocent is one of the most profound and draconian powers the state has. And yet it is hard to find another legal concept that is not only so readily ignored in practice, but treated as if it does not mean what it plainly says.

In every region of the world, legislators foreclose any chance of pretrial release for broad and /or vague categories of crimes, heedlessly following the blithe pronouncements of tough-on-crime politicians. Prosecutors openly adopt lockstep policies in opposition to release, and judges seem to forget that each case is to be decided on its own merits before routinely dispatching defendants into remand custody. The evidence compiled in this report suggests strongly that pretrial detention is overused: it is employed far more than necessary to cover those relatively exceptional cases where society, and the legal process, cannot be safeguarded by any means other than locking the accused behind bars. Such overuse degrades the rule of law and damages the relationship between the public and the criminal justice system.

The potential for such damage is intertwined with the ease with which pretrial detention lends itself to direct abuse of those in custody. Physical and psychological violence (and neglect), extortion, and other forms of corruption are more common during pretrial detention than in other stages of the criminal process. In holding cells or police lockups, custodians are free to act without significant procedural constraints or outside observers of their conduct. Even the most formal elements of the pretrial phase—relating to the judicial processes by which liberty or detention are determined—typically present the judicial officer with wide latitude to detain and little oversight in the form of defense counsel or reviewing courts. Because this "front end" of the criminal process is less formally regulated and generally far more neglected (in oversight terms) than later stages, the dangers are not merely those collateral to detention such as physical abuse or corruption. The conduct of the process itself can become distorted and devalued.

This chapter looks at several forms of procedural abuse relating to pretrial detention: arbitrary arrest, lack of access to counsel, prolonged or indefinite detention, lack of redress, and lack of accountability. It also looks at the results of these abuses, including the mass release of prisoners due to overcrowding, and the damage to public confidence in the criminal justice system. Taken together, these abuses and their consequences present a potent threat to the integrity of law enforcement. This section also explores the possibility that the loss of credibility is reflected in public opinion, representing an erosion of confidence in the relevant institutions and even in the rule of law as a credible governing principle.

## ARBITRARY ARREST AND DETENTION

Overuse of pretrial detention is often associated with two other violations of fundamental freedoms: arbitrary arrest and detention, which are themselves notorious gateways to other grave abuses. Where police officers have the motive and the means to arrest illegally, they will often have subsequent reason and ability to detain someone, frequently acting outside of legal norms. When researchers examined files for the 179 juvenile detainees at Malawi's Zomba Central Prison in 1999, they discovered not one had been lawfully detained.[1] Sri Lanka's police roundups are often so random that officers frequently do not bother to file formal arrest reports. Although three-quarters of Sri Lankan detainees ultimately have their cases dismissed or are acquitted, they spend months, even years, in illegal detention.[2] According to Zambian pretrial detainees, police arrest and detain family members when their primary targets cannot be found.[3] One female detainee told Human Rights Watch investigators that Zambia's prisons are congested because "they arrest entire families when they just are looking for one person. They will arrest six at a time, even old ladies who can't walk."[4]

In Mexico, the government's highly publicized arrests and detention of those it claims are linked to organized crime have been derisively described as "a catch and release" program due to the authorities' frequent failure to formulate formal charges against people who have been publicly rounded up on questionable grounds:[5]

> It's practically a daily ritual: Accused drug traffickers and assassins, shackled and bruised from beatings, are paraded before the news media to show that Mexico is winning its drug war. Once the television lights dim, however, about three-quarters of them are let go. ... Records obtained by The Associated Press showed that the government arrested 226,667 drug suspects between December 2006 and September 2009, the most recent numbers available. Less than a quarter of that number were charged.[6]

Where arbitrary arrests have led to conviction, the excesses of pretrial detention may be to blame. In its review of cases in five Mexican states, Human Rights Watch linked a high percentage of those crimes that are "solved" to incriminating statements made under duress:

> [I]n nearly all cases, the only evidence offered by authorities of suspects' guilt was incriminating statements given following torture or other abuse. There appeared to be no independent evidence to corroborate these coerced statements and *it is not clear what evidence established reasonable suspicion about the individuals prior to their detention.* To the contrary, the evidence in several of the cases we researched strongly suggests that authorities erred in targeting these particular individuals. For example, court records establish that a victim of torture who was accused of kidnapping a civilian was not even in Mexico when the alleged kidnapping took place.[7]

In recent years, Mexico has expanded the use of a form of pre-charge detention, known as *arraigo*, which allows officials to detain someone without charges for up to 40 days in order to facilitate a criminal investigation—and can be renewed for up to an additional 40 days. *Arraigo* detainees are held, it seems, everywhere—in prisons, converted apartment buildings, and, as is now officially acknowledged, on military bases.[8] The legal threshold standard for an *arraigo* order is loosely defined.[9] In theory, *arraigo* requires a suspected link to organized crime, but in practice that requirement is of little significance. Although government statistics are murky,[10] data from the federal prosecutor's office (PGR) acknowledged 8,595 people held under *arraigo* between January 2008 and October 2012 with perhaps half again as many held by state authorities.[11] *Arraigo's* ostensible "detain to investigate" purpose is itself a troubling inversion of accepted law and practice, but the greater problem is that it undermines the role of judges in safeguarding the presumption of innocence and is an invitation to the abuse of detainees. Echoing concerns from numerous national and international sources, the nongovernmental Mexican Commission for the Defense and Promotion of Human Rights has stated that "*arraigo* violates among others, the rights of personal liberty, legality, presumption of innocence, due process and the right to an effective recourse."[12]

Special courts (created by a much questioned agreement between the government and the Federal Judicial Council and designed to issue orders for *arraigo*, home searches, and wiretaps) routinely (95 percent of the time) grant prosecutors' requests for this pre-charge detention—which typically lasts the full 40 days.[13] The PGR asserts that its prosecutors are able to formulate charges against those detainees in 90 to 95 percent of the cases. However, even government officials now acknowledge that once they bring those charges before ordinary criminal courts, prosecutors overwhelmingly fail to demonstrate sufficient evidence to initiate a proceeding.[14] According to available figures, only slightly more than three percent of those detained under *arraigo* have ultimately been convicted of a crime, which suggests that the *arraigo* net is cast far too broadly and that *arraigo's* benefits to investigation are negligible.[15]

The lengthy detentions made possible by *arraigo* increase the possibility that *arraigados* will be subjected to torture or other cruel, inhuman or degrading treatment.[16] A 2008 United Nations field mission examined medical records for about 70 of the 130 detainees held at the National *Arraigo* Center, a large holding facility in Mexico City. According to the records, nearly half of the *arraigados* showed signs of recent violence.[17] The *arraigos* ordered between mid-2008 and mid-2010 generated 120 formal complaints to the National Human Rights Commission; of these, 77 alleged torture, the most of any category of complaint. Aside from the extended length of detention, *arraigo* raises the risk of abuse because it formally leaves the prosecution and its agents, rather than the judge, as the responsible legal authority, thus reducing oversight and detainee protection.[18] Little judicial supervision is available, and some authorities have even made the cynical argument that *amparo* (a fundamental writ that can be used like *habeas corpus*) does not apply since an *arraigo* detention does not qualify as a deprivation of liberty—its "purpose" being to aid investigation, not detain.[19]

Perhaps not surprisingly, *arraigo* has encountered some hostility from judges, including those on Mexico's Supreme Court, which in 2005 declared *arraigo* unconstitutional.[20] That decision likely prompted the government of President Felipe Calderon to insulate *arraigo* from legal attack by successfully insisting, during negotiations for the 2008 constitutional reform, that *arraigo* be expressly included in the constitution.[21] Having made *arraigo* a central weapon in a disastrous "war on drugs" that has left 70,000 dead and countless disappeared, tortured, or traumatized, the Calderon government and its successor have failed to act on calls from numerous rights groups, jurists, and on at least nine separate occasions, an organ of the United Nations, to eliminate the practice.[22]

*Arraigo* brings into relief the vices of Mexico's pretrial justice regime: detention before investigation or charge, lax judicial oversight (some of which is dictated by statute), prolonged detention, detainee abuse, and ultimately, ineffectiveness in building criminal prosecutions. Like other abuses linked to excessive pretrial detention, *arraigo* further fuels suspicion and cynicism regarding criminal justice processes and institutions.[23]

In Nigeria, a scheme somewhat similar to *arraigo* allows police officers to detain an individual over long periods before he is charged, often with the intent to extort bribes. In this arrangement, an arrestee is brought before a magistrate who has limited jurisdiction, and a "holding" charge is assigned, although the police have not conducted an investigation and are not yet in a position to proffer formal charges. Such holding charges are frequently used for serious crimes (armed robbery, for example) over which magistrates lack jurisdiction. Nigerian law permits the magistrate to remand the individual to pretrial detention while the police investigate and obtain legal advice from the prosecution service, but does not grant the magistrate the power to otherwise move the case forward. If the police or prosecutors simply fail to move on the case, the detainee is effectively in limbo, at the mercy of authorities who can often keep him there indefinitely until he pays a bribe or is able to find a lawyer to intervene. While Nigerian detainees under the holding charge are ostensibly under a lawful remand order, their custody is essentially indefinite, since no court is truly seized of their case. Relief is available if the detainee can find counsel willing to challenge his detention before a court of general jurisdiction, but for many, that may be next to impossible.

A 2007 Nigerian Supreme Court judgment effectively validated this practice on the grounds that police need to ensure that suspects remain in custody while the alleged crime is investigated and proper charges are formulated.[24] This practice, and the court's defense of it, prompted profound cynicism from observers. The Nigerian Bar Association characterized the holding charge as a grant of "unfettered powers to keep the accused person as long as they [i.e. the state authorities] want, even when the delay in arraignment is entirely their fault," and noted the "many recorded cases of detention where the threat of a holding charge has been employed by the police to extort money from individuals."[25]

Arbitrary detention is of course corrosive to the rule of law—and even more so when it is unacknowledged or takes place before charges are even filed. Practices such as *arraigo* and the holding charge breed cynicism about the criminal justice system, and that cynicism is furthered when a country's highest court steps in to defend the practice.

## RESTRICTED ACCESS TO LEGAL COUNSEL

Restricting detainees' access to counsel—especially during the earliest period of detention when the risk of mistreatment is greatest—is often used to ensure that the police are able to hold defendants pretrial. Police often view their job as gathering enough incriminating information to warrant a judicial remand order at the initial court appearance, which typically occurs within 24 to 72 hours of arrest. Not surprisingly, police see defense lawyers as a hindrance, and seek to prevent arrestees from having legal representation.

Police can exploit pretrial detention to keep a suspect from a lawyer even where the law provides for counsel. In Zambia, for example, the law provides for free legal assistance for those facing felony trials who cannot afford a lawyer, and for lesser offenses, defendants may request legal aid. Yet 60 percent of adult male prisoners and some three-quarters of adult female and juvenile prisoners in six Zambian prisons reported having no legal representation whatsoever.[26]

Even children appearing before the Zambian High Court are rarely represented by counsel. As one teenager reported: "I had no representation, I stood on my own behalf. It was my first time in a police station or in court. I was just speaking, and I was scared. So I didn't know what I was saying.... As young people, it is very threatening to see the inside of the court. Even if you are not guilty, you end up pleading guilty."[27] Without advocates at their side, defendants can get pushed around, haphazardly funnelled through a process which they recognize is unfair but are powerless to navigate effectively. One inmate at Zambia's Choma Prison reported that he did not intend to plead guilty, but the magistrate decided he should plead guilty and "checked it on the form."[28]

Although the criminal procedure code of Azerbaijan guarantees criminal defendants access to legal counsel immediately after arrest, police are typically allowed to detain individuals during a period of "operational search activities" that can last several days. During this time, detainees are generally not granted access to a lawyer.[29] It is unsurprising, in this permissive context, that "[p]re-trial detention has become the rule in Azerbaijan. Most suspects are given pre-trial detention, especially if they are accused of serious crimes. The refusal by the prosecutors to choose pre-trial detention is extremely rare."[30]

The practice of forcing arrestees into pretrial detention by denying them access to counsel is not limited to developing countries. Monitoring of more than 1,000 European trials by the Organization for Security and Co-operation in Europe revealed that judges regularly failed to inform defendants of their right to counsel; as a result, only defendants knowledgeable and intrepid enough to demand a lawyer obtained representation.[31] Other recent studies of several longstanding EU member states and Turkey demonstrated that the right to counsel is severely undermined in both law and practice, resulting in far less protection against the potential for arbitrary pretrial detention.[32]

Even when access to counsel is permitted, police or prosecutors frequently delay it until *after* the police have interrogated a suspect—regardless of the dictates of international or domestic law. In other instances, police and prosecutors may seek to undermine the effectiveness of defense counsel. In Brazil, it is common for the authorities to wait until just before the suspect is brought before the judge to assign defense counsel, and the absence of an opportunity to learn about the case negates much of the benefit of representation.[33] Amnesty International found that police in the Philippines, regarded to be systematically involved in torture of detainees, have solved the problem of interfering defense counsel (a right of each detainee under Philippine law): they torture suspects until they waive their right to an attorney.[34]

Until recent reforms, Mexico's judiciary routinely rationalized the denial of counsel during the initial interrogation by elevating the evidentiary value of pretrial confessions extracted by the police (without defense counsel present) over that of a statement made in open court in the presence of defense counsel and the judge. The perverseness of this logic, particularly in the context of police notoriously prone to extortion and abuse of detainees, signaled the extent of the system's dependence on the authorities' unfettered ability to detain.[35] The conventional wisdom is that in Mexico the police "detain in order to investigate" rather than vice versa.[36]

When authorities refuse a detainee contact with counsel, they transform the legal process into a much more one-sided affair. Without representation, the defendant's chances of gaining release before trial diminish considerably. Once deprived of liberty, and stripped of much of his capacity to assist in his own defense, a defendant—even if represented—faces a much greater chance of conviction simply as a result of the earlier decision to hold him in pretrial detention. In a rigorous analysis of the link between pretrial detention and case outcomes, the New York City Criminal Justice Agency (CJA) found that cases with a non-felony defendant who was released until the case ended had a 50 percent conviction rate, while non-felony defendants detained throughout had a conviction rate nearly double that (92 percent). The CJA found that "pretrial detention had an effect on conviction after controlling statistically for the number and severity of arrest charges, the offense charged, the defendant's criminal history, demographic characteristics, borough, and length of case processing, among other factors."[37]

The CJA concluded that, "pretrial detention has an adverse effect on case outcomes, especially the likelihood of conviction."[38] A 2009 study of criminal cases in the Mexican state of Nuevo Leon conducted by the Justice Initiative and the Monterrey-based NGO Renace found that those detained at different stages of the process consistently experienced a slightly (ranging from approximately 4.5 percent to 10.5 percent) higher rate of conviction than their counterparts who were at liberty during the process, although the researchers cautioned that this difference might also reflect other related disadvantages accruing to detention, including less access to adequate counsel and the fact that judges' views of the likelihood of convicting defendants may be reflected in their decisions regarding bail and pretrial release.[39]

Clearly, defendants who are in pretrial custody are at a distinct disadvantage in terms of preparing their defense. Their options are much more limited in meeting with counsel, who will have to travel to a detention center. Meetings in custody may well be constrained by the circumstances of space and privacy that the facility provides. Moreover, a detained defendant may simply not be able to provide exculpatory documentation to his counsel. One recent project in Rio de Janeiro used a social worker to help document that defendants have a stable domicile. The study found that this simple ability to demonstrate an address made a significant difference in the defense's ability to convince the judge to grant pretrial release.[40] Denial of access to counsel sets off a chain reaction that increases the defendant's likelihood of being held in pretrial detention, which in turn increases his likelihood of being convicted.

## DURATION OF DETENTION

Disregard for the critically important time limits on different phases of pretrial detention is also common. International law and most domestic legal frameworks call for individuals to be brought before a judge within a few days of arrest, in large part to guard against abuse. In many jurisdictions, legislation provides that police custody may last for only up to 24 or 48 (sometimes 72) hours, often renewable for a limited number of times by a judicial officer. However, in practice such laws are routinely ignored in a number of places.[41] For example, in Mauritania, the UN Working Group on Arbitrary Detention found that police custody is not extended in writing as required by law and in most of the police stations visited by the Working Group authorities were not able to produce extension authorizations despite a number of detainees claiming to have been in detention considerably beyond the permitted 48 hours. The Working Group also established that prosecutors often cover up the fact that people are held beyond the legal time limit for custody.[42] Prosecutors and judicial officers rubberstamp applications for extended custody without looking into the merits of individual requests. Some prosecutors seem to lack the "professional distance" from the police authorities and instead collude to violate defendants' rights in the name of fighting crime.[43]

In a pattern frequently recounted in Kazakhstan and other parts of Central Asia, detainees, defense lawyers, and human rights investigators report that police falsify the starting point of detention, registering individuals into custody only after hours in the back of a police car, or even days of illegal detention in a clandestine "safe" house where they are illegally interrogated and often abused.[44] Similarly, Kenyan police have been accused of holding suspects in police cars for hours, often while torturing them, in order to extract a confession or "soften up" the suspects before they are brought to a police station and their detention "officially" begins.[45]

Mexico City authorities failed to bring detainees before a judge within the constitutionally mandated time frame in half of all cases, according to one 2003 study.[46] Human Rights Watch's Zambian prison study found that 97 percent of the prisoners interviewed had not seen a magistrate or judge within 24 hours of arrest, as Zambian law requires. In fact, many had been held for months—and some more than two years—without ever having seen a judicial officer to review their detention. Overall, the surveyed male inmates were held in pretrial detention for an average of four months, and female inmates for an average of one month, prior to seeing a judge or magistrate for the first time. One bitter pretrial detainee at the Lusaka Central Prison told investigators, "It is better even to be found guilty.... I have [been detained] four years now, but my case is not disposed of."[47]

Despite legal limits intended to ensure a reasonably prompt trial and restrict the overall length of pretrial detention, it can reach alarming lengths, far beyond permissible bounds, with no visible repercussions for those responsible. Official Nigerian figures suggest that the average duration of pretrial detention is nearly four years, and trending higher. While the methods by which these data are collected is unclear,[48] it almost certainly means that shockingly long detention is at least not infrequent and—as evidenced by the abuse of holding charges, described above—that the system is either unwilling or unable to effectively monitor and prevent unlawfully prolonged detention.[49]

In India, a combination of corruption, court delays, and a striking propensity for lost case files has given rise to epic miscarriages of justice, with detainees spending 20, 30, even 50 years awaiting trial.[50] Sri Lankan law, which sets a flat maximum of 12 months detention prior to trial regardless of the nature of the offense, has proven of little assistance to the 23 percent of pretrial detainees who had been incarcerated for more than a year as of 2009.[51]

Malawi's constitution requires that arrested persons be brought before a court within 48 hours of arrest to be charged and for a bail hearing.[52] However, an audit of five police stations in 2010 found that arrestees were regularly kept in police custody for more than 48 hours. For example, in the capital city of Lilongwe, 13 percent of arrestees had been in police custody for more than five days at the time of the audit.[53] In Nepal, time limits are also frequently ignored, with one report indicating that persons detained by the police were taken before a court within the time limit in only just over half of all cases.[54]

Homicide defendants in Malawi's four central prisons can wait ten years for trial because of a combination of prosecuting authorities' failure to acknowledge that they are unable to put together an effective case and defendants' lack of access to legal advice.[55] In many cases, defendants could have left jail sooner by actually pleading guilty to manslaughter and simply serving the sentence for that crime.

Most of the situations cited above involve detention periods that simply flout local law: defendants are forgotten or trapped, or both, by detaining authorities who manage to avoid judicial oversight. However, countries have also ratified extremely long detentions in national law. Spain, for example, permits up to four years of pretrial detention for persons accused of any crime that carries a prison sentence of more than three years.[56] Slovakia also has a four year limit. Portugal's is two-and-a-half years, while in Luxembourg defendants can be jailed for a period equal to their expected sentence before protections are triggered that would typically lead to their release. Prosecutors in Azerbaijan routinely extend the three months statutory period for pretrial detention up to five times, according to the U.S. State Department's country report.[57] Such deliberate flouting of international and domestic law—or manipulation of laws to contravene international norms—weakens the rule of law and people's sense that the system is fair.

## LACK OF REDRESS AND ACCOUNTABILITY

The damage done by violations of the rules is often compounded by failures of accountability. In many cases, people who suffer abuse through the pretrial detention process actually have fewer avenues for recourse than convicted prisoners. Unfortunately, the relevant institutions provide precious little relief for abuse, even when a detainee is able to lodge a complaint before a judge. Judges everywhere are particularly loathe to remedy arbitrary arrest or prolonged detention because it would typically mean releasing before trial someone who may be guilty of the crime alleged; across different countries and legal systems, courts look for ways to consider the initial taint "cured" so as to avoid release. Not only do a significant number of states, such as Belgium, set no limit on the duration of pretrial detention, but some have no mechanism for penalizing the failure to bring the case to conclusion and hence end pretrial detention within a reasonable time.[58]

Despite the universal prohibition on torture and the use of coerced confessions, only a relative handful of countries take seriously the obligation to inquire further into defense allegations that incriminating statements were extracted under unlawful pressure. In Spain, for instance, Amnesty International documented a pattern of physical abuse of criminal suspects by police for the purposes of obtaining confessions, which is facilitated by collusion between the police and the judiciary to ensure that investigations of torture do not prosper. Police officers support one another by refusing to report or testify about abuse of detainees, and police insist on being present when abused detainees are examined by physicians, dissuading detainees for reiterating the allegations. Police often file retaliatory charges against detainees who have alleged abuse, claiming that the detainees resisted arrest or were abusive toward the police.[59]

A UN mission to Honduras on the prevention of torture found that while police stations typically feature a register of detainees, the register is often incomplete, or has been altered by the police with impunity.[60] Meanwhile, police stations typically do not record complaints of ill-treatment by detainees.[61] Detainees are not routinely examined by medical personnel upon arrival, an important safeguard against abuse.[62] Even when detainees arrive injured at detention, police have discretion over whether the accused can see a doctor, which often precludes the documentation of abuse detainees have suffered during arrest.[63] Of some 50 cases in Central Asia where detainees made official complaints about torture, virtually all also alleged that judicial and/or prosecutorial officials failed to investigate the allegations.[64] Too often, judges systematically credit the denials of the police over the allegations of detainees.

Internal accountability mechanisms offer the promise of review and possible accountability for official malfeasance. But such internal accountability mechanisms frequently lack independence, and instead serve as window dressing. Investigators who will have to work with, or even answer to, the subject of the investigation, have a palpable incentive to find in favor of the accused abuser. Where accountability mechanisms lack the bureaucratic muscle to make an independent stand, they become complicit. A junior employee assigned to investigate his boss or other officers with greater seniority faces a dilemma, and the greater the pattern of institutional malfeasance the greater the likelihood that the office as a whole will conform to the prevailing norm. Reports from the Philippines, for example, indicate that members of the bodies charged with investigating claims of police abuse are "often either subordinate" to or otherwise know the persons accused of the violation, "and often do not act in the interest of those making complaints."[65]

External oversight bodies which lack the political will or legal authority to compel cooperation, obtain evidence, and impose meaningful sanctions clearly engender in the eyes of frustrated observers a sense of police impunity and the belief that predatory officials will be able to continue with business as usual. When it was founded in 2001, Nigeria's Police Service Commission appeared to be a potent oversight body with far ranging powers to investigate police misdeeds. And such power seemed necessary: the Nigeria Police Force killed between 2,500 and 7,200 "armed robbers" between 2000-2004,[66] and killed 785 "armed robbers" during a particularly busy 100-day period in 2007.[67] But the Nigeria Police Service Commission did not investigate any of these killings—because it had delegated investigative authority back to the police force itself.[68] The commission's existence, then, arguably does little to stem the tide of extrajudicial killings by police—but does much to sow cynicism among Nigerians.

The weakness of some accountability mechanisms can be seen in low reporting rates. A lack of complaints can indicate lack of faith in the mechanism's effectiveness, or even fear that lodging a complaint will trigger reprisals. For example, police in Honduras are known to engage in torture, which is likely abetted by the total absence of institutional safeguards against torture in police custody. Yet the number of detainee complaints of abuse was described as "extremely low" in a United Nations field report. The UN investigative mission emphasized that:

> ... staff assigned to police stations should systematically provide information to all persons deprived of their liberty about the right to make a request or complaint regarding their treatment in custody. Every request or complaint must be promptly dealt with and replied to without undue delay, and steps must be taken to ensure that the detained person does not suffer prejudice as a consequence of making the complaint.... Police personnel should not interfere in the complaints procedure or screen complaints addressed to the competent authorities, and should not have access to the content of the complaints.[69]

The absence of oversight mechanisms and the corresponding lack of accountability can indicate that the police and prosecuting authorities are stronger than the rule of law. Where such mechanisms exist but are ignored or deliberately weakened, they promote cynicism.

## MASS RELEASES DUE TO OVERCROWDING

The overcrowding that sometimes results from excessive use of detention can undermine confidence in the system in unexpected ways. Responding either to budgetary concerns, court orders, or the threat of enforcement actions against overcrowded conditions, authorities sometimes engage in "outlet valve" releases of "excess" prisoners who would otherwise fit the legal criteria for continued custody. These releases do not represent an improvement in detention practice (e.g., better decision-making about who should be detained, or a move toward greater respect for international norms). As somewhat arbitrary acts designed to meet other exigencies, mass releases may simply reinforce the view among those affected that the rules of the game can always be trumped by external considerations. In addition, such agency may be perceived as a threat to public security that would undermine confidence in the responsible institutions.

Some U.S. municipalities have been forced by overcrowding litigation to release detainees rapidly, without the time or resources to determine which pretrial detainees should remain in detention because, for example, they are likely to abscond. In Philadelphia, the jail system operated under a series of court orders and consent decrees for two decades (from the mid-1970s to the mid-1990s) obligating the authorities to engage in mass releases which had the effect of superseding and rendering nearly meaningless pretrial release decisions made in municipal court at the first appearance stage. Because those most likely to abscond were no longer those most likely to be detained, rates of failure to appear during the period of the consent decree rose to three-to-four times the normal level:[70] the detention-heavy practices had boomeranged, ultimately weakening the criminal justice system's control over those pretrial detainees who posed the highest risk.[71]

In mid-2010, almost 1,000 convicted criminals were released from Irish prisons before serving their full custodial sentence. In effect, almost a fifth of Ireland's prison population was released prematurely. The figures highlight the pressure on cell space within the prison system, which forced officials to push temporary release numbers to their highest levels in more than 15 years. The revelation came just days after it emerged that a man jailed for the fatal assault of a teacher had 64 previous convictions and was on temporary release at the time of the attack.

The irony here is twofold—and not lost on the public. The overcrowding occurs because so many people are being held in pretrial detention, even though they have not been convicted. But the official response to this overcrowding (which, again, is caused by holding too many presumed-innocent people) is to release a large number of those prisoners who have been found guilty.

## IMPACT ON PUBLIC CONFIDENCE

Perhaps most troubling about the distortions of law and process described above is that if such patterns of official misbehavior permeate public consciousness, they may undermine confidence in those particular actors, institutions, and processes. The abuses relating to pretrial detention stretch across the police, courts, and corrections systems. Prolonged conduct of this sort (and the impunity that accompanies it) almost certainly breeds profound cynicism among the agents in these institutions. It clearly appears to corrode trust among the detainees on the receiving end.[72] It is unclear how much the broader public becomes aware of what happens to those jailed awaiting trial. Existing research across the relevant institutions suggests that to the extent the public is aware of the systemic abuses attendant to excessive pretrial detention, it results in deep mistrust, apathy, and perhaps even a lack of confidence in the broader legal system.

Public attitudes towards law enforcement are influenced by the concept of procedural legitimacy: that individuals recognize the criminal justice system as legitimate—and therefore more or less voluntarily submit to it—as long as the system operates in a manner that is fair. Research findings strongly suggest that for the public, the fairness of the *outcome* is less important than the *way* in which authorities act.[73]

More recent conceptual writing has suggested that legitimacy is constructed as much by the governed as by their public officials. Drawing from political science, Anthony Bottoms and Justice Tankebe argue convincingly that across cultures and geographical boundaries, the mechanisms of legitimation are essentially the same.[74] They argue that even clever use of "presentational rules" to cloak self-serving or abusive behavior will do little to fool people who have experienced or witnessed corrupt officials in action.[75] Whatever legitimacy people may attach to the formal norms, they will view the law in practice as legitimate only to the extent they perceive it as serving the public interest, and not corrupt or abusive.

Much of the research in this area concerns police, for whom such findings have especially profound implications. Police operate in public, and cumulatively they come into contact with enormous numbers of people. People tend to share widely their encounters with the police, and as they spread, these accounts shape the perceptions of the police among third parties who may never have experienced any, or similar encounters. Among particular groups, individual encounters may be used to exemplify what criminologist David Smith calls a community's "grand narrative" about their treatment by the police: in interactions among group members, individual anecdotes reinforce other anecdotes, news accounts, and opinions, multiplying and generalizing a perception of the police.[76]

Prisons are less of a daily fixation for the public and the media than the police are,[77] and detainees are simply less visible to, and less able to communicate with, the general population.[78] Their mistreatment is less likely to have the viral impact on public perceptions of the relevant officials than encounters with police that may be recorded and can readily by recounted by people still at liberty. Nonetheless, powerful accounts of prison abuse or scandal, when publicized, can go a long way to shaping public perceptions. In the case of the 2010 overcrowding and release scandal in Ireland, opposition politicians were quick to highlight the impact on public confidence in government institutions:

> The only response of the Government to overcrowding is the flawed operation of the temporary release system. Yesterday's newspapers highlighted that over 200 people sent to jail for non-payment of fines were released at the gates of prisons. What message does this send about the administration of justice and respect for our laws?[79]

Two years later, the former head of Ireland's largest prison publicly complained that although the overcrowding was a scandal that also led to physical abuse and sexual assault, the "biggest scandal of all is that the public has become conditioned that it's normal."[80]

Although pretrial detention shares some characteristics with prison, including its relative isolation and ominous lack of transparency, pretrial detainees remain more palpably under the jurisdiction of a court and subject to its processes, compared to convicted prisoners for whom the courtroom is a memory. It therefore seems more likely to be experienced by detainees as part of the criminal justice process, rather than as a discrete ecosystem, or as an entirely separate episode from the legal process itself in the way that a lengthy prison term might be viewed. The malfeasance of one's custodians may simply reinforce the negative impressions left by corrupt or negligent court clerks or judges—and vice versa, particularly since it may be judicial officers as much as jailers who are responsible for unwarranted detention or who offer to sell release for a price.[81]

## CONCLUSION

The overuse of pretrial detention has many different causes, and many different and negative outcomes. Most of those outcomes can be quantified, both individually and collectively, such as the number of people detained and the human hours of productivity lost. But the excessive use of pretrial detention also has outcomes that are harder to measure, if no less pernicious. It damages the rule of law and undermines the criminal justice system. When people are arbitrarily arrested or denied access to counsel, it hurts the entire system. When pretrial detention stretches for weeks or even months, legitimacy is lost.

If national governments wish to maintain the legitimacy of their criminal justice systems, they must enact and enforce pretrial detention laws that reflect the contents and values of international standards and norms, and ensure that these laws are understood and consistently applied by judges, prosecutors, and other criminal justice actors. To avoid undermining the rule of law, the use of pretrial detention must be both made more rational and reduced, as discussed in the next chapter.

# Reducing the Arbitrary and Excessive Use of Pretrial Detention

## INTRODUCTION

It is important to acknowledge that there are valid reasons for states to use pretrial detention. Crime and insecurity are major concerns in some places, and some states simply lack the resources to operate an efficient criminal justice system that moves people through pretrial detention quickly. In addition, pretrial detention can be a tool of justice, to prevent a suspect from absconding, intimidating witnesses, or interfering with the investigation. However, governments around the world grossly overuse pretrial detention. This chapter will look at how excessive incarceration in general, and pretrial detention in particular, can be sharply curtailed—including in places marked by crime, insecurity, lack of state resources, and inefficient criminal justice systems—without compromising public safety.

There are many paths to successful reform. This chapter looks first at the political conditions that can create fertile ground for reforming the overuse of pretrial detention, even in environments where excessive pretrial detention is common. The next section describes changes in law and policy that have reduced the arbitrary and excessive application of pretrial detention, followed by sections on the use of data to assess the use of pretrial detention and on coordination among criminal justice agencies. Subsequent sections of this chapter examine reducing over-incarceration, the roles of lawyers and paralegals, and government programs that have succeeded in reducing pretrial detention.

Reforming the use of pretrial detention is both urgent and possible. By focusing on the conditions and actions that have made reducing pretrial detention possible in various places around the world, it is possible to identify strategies that can decrease the excessive use of pretrial detention in every jurisdiction.

## POLITICAL CONDITIONS THAT SUPPORT PRETRIAL DETENTION REFORM

As noted earlier, in the chapter examining causes of the overuse of pretrial detention, politicians and voters often support a tough-on-crime approach that favors excessive pretrial detention. However, this is not universally true, and some political circumstances can actually work in favor of reform. Few countries have the resources and conditions that made the reform and reduction of pretrial detention possible in Finland and Singapore, which are described below. However, many states possess one or two similarities to these countries, and reformers should look to exploit these to their advantage when seeking to implement rational and rights-based pretrial justice policies.

## The Finnish Case

Finland has one of the lowest rates of pretrial detention worldwide: less than one-fifth of its prison population is comprised of pretrial detainees, at 10-15 detainees per 100,000 inhabitants.[1] Its overall incarceration rate is lower than the Scandinavian average. Yet during the 1950s the country's incarceration rate exceeded most of Europe's, with a rate four times as high as the Scandinavian average. Between 1966 and 2004, the Finnish parliament undertook 25 legislative reforms, all seeking to reduce the use of incarceration.[2] This revolutionary and sustained decline in the use of imprisonment and pretrial detention over the last 50 years provides a number of instructive points for reformers, starting with the political conditions that made Finland's transformation possible.[3]

To begin with, Finnish authorities have demonstrated a widespread political will and consensus to reduce prisoner numbers. Civil servants, the judiciary, prison authorities, and, crucially, elected officials, all shared a commitment to reducing incarceration. Finland is a unitary state with a single written criminal code. Nationally organized institutions administer justice, making policy implementation relatively straightforward.

An unusual media market also made reform possible in Finland. Some 90 percent of Finns read a newspaper daily, one of the highest rates in the world, and almost 90 percent of newspapers are sold by subscription. This means that newspapers do not have to be alarmist: they do not rely on startling headlines to sell newspapers at a newsstand. During Finland's period of reform, crime control never became a central issue in Finnish elections.

With the political will for change and a non-sensationalist media in place, a relatively small group of experts was able to drive the reform process. These professionals had close personal and professional contacts with senior politicians, but they themselves were civil servants in the justice ministry. An intensifying era of Nordic cooperation that emerged in the 1960s also prompted change, including the promotion of liberal ideas about crime and criminal justice policy. The exchange of ideas among Nordic countries, including legislative models developed by Finland's neighbors, especially Sweden, strongly influenced the Finnish penal reforms of the 1960s and 1970s. In making the case for liberal penal policy, reformers referenced positive experiences gleaned from other Nordic countries and the need for inter-Nordic harmonization.

These conditions led to the creation of improved laws and policies, but, as this chapter will discuss in more detail later, good laws will not create change without good practice. Finland's judiciary and prosecution service had the freedom and the will to implement good practices because they enjoy constitutionally guaranteed independence, because they (as well as the police) are permanently appointed non-partisan career officials, and because Finnish judges and prosecutors have training in criminology and criminal policy. In cooperation with universities, Finland provides regular courses and seminars for judges and prosecutors to improve their knowledge of pretrial detention and sentencing practices.

This political atmosphere made it possible for Finland to develop social and situational crime prevention strategies, decriminalize certain conduct, introduce alternatives to imprisonment and pretrial detention, expand diversionary mechanisms and mediation, and introduce juvenile justice mechanisms that allowed social welfare and child protection measures to address misconduct by all children under 15 and many of those aged 15-17.

## Singapore's Education

Far from Scandinavia, Singapore has also benefited from a concerted and sustained policy initiative that substantially reduced its number of prisoners. After peaking in 2002 with 18,000 prisoners, Singapore's prison population declined to just under 13,000 in 2010 (the latest year for which data are available), with the imprisonment rate declining from almost 400 per 100,000 of the general population to around 250. Although this is still a high rate of imprisonment, the sustained reduction in prisoner numbers over an eight-year period is remarkable. The use of pretrial detention in Singapore has also declined, and in 2010 less than eight percent of the prison population was comprised of pretrial detainees, an exceptionally low proportion by global standards.

A reduction in recidivism from 44 percent for the 1998 release cohort to 27 percent for the 2008 release cohort significantly contributed to the declining prison population. The Rehabilitation Framework, developed in 2000, and the Yellow Ribbon Project, launched in 2004, transformed Singapore's recidivism rate. The project engages the community in accepting ex-offenders and their families, including signing up thousands of employers willing to hire ex-offenders and organizing numerous community activities to raise awareness.[4] Under its auspices, some 1,700 volunteers, almost as many as regular prison staff, provided training and counseling for prisoners in Singapore in 2008.

Annual public opinion surveys undertaken by the Singapore Prison Service find that more than 80 percent of the Singaporean public is aware of the Yellow Ribbon objectives and 70 percent are willing to accept ex-offenders either as friends or colleagues.

Like Finland, Singapore has a number of advantages in promoting and implementing penal reforms. Singapore is a democracy, but the same ruling party has been in power since Britain granted the nation self-government in 1959, making for policy continuity. Moreover, the government benefits from a strong state apparatus and an experienced and qualified civil service. Singapore is a relatively small country—both in terms of population (about five million) and physical size—which, no doubt, facilitates the deployment of publicity campaigns such as the Yellow Ribbon Project.

Some of the commonalities of the Finish and Singaporean experiences are useful in highlighting those factors which facilitate penal reform. These include a political system which can sustain a policy position without being driven off course by the day-to-day vagaries of public, media, or party political opinion; a system of government which has the capacity to implement policy; and a broad social consensus about the utility of the reform.

### Costa Rica and the Dominican Republic

Costa Rica and the Dominican Republic represent the only two successful examples of sustained penal reform efforts in Latin America, but their examples suggest what's possible in countries quite different from Finland and Singapore. In both countries reformers introduced change at the highest level of government—the presidency and the respective ministry—with continuity a key to the reforms' success. As one study summarized, "Continuity has been uninterrupted in the reform programme [of both countries]. It is indispensable for the penitentiary reform to outlast the different administrations and for it to last from eight to ten years in order to become consolidated. In Costa Rica the process started in 1975 and it has been able to survive for eight administrations. In the Dominican Republic it started in July 2003 and it is into the third administration."[5] As seen in the following section, even modest reforms to those particular practices which tend to increase pretrial detention and other misuses of incarceration are possible and often produce significant and positive change.

## LAWS AND POLICIES TO REDUCE PRETRIAL DETENTION

Without good laws, consistently good practice is impossible. Moreover, explicitly bad laws abet and encourage practices which undermine the presumption of innocence. While some of the proposals below represent compromises with the principle of presumed innocence inasmuch as they make a distinction between minor and major offenses, history suggests that political forces make it palatable to treat as innocent people accused of minor offenses. Such laws form a foundation to scale back pretrial detention, and may lead to greater changes and further reduction in the use of pretrial detention. This section examines specific laws and policies that have been shown to reduce pretrial detention.

*Laws should provide judicial officers with wide discretion to release defendants awaiting trial.* Some countries classify numerous offenses as "non bailable"—that is, persons charged with such offenses cannot be released awaiting trial.[6] In many Mexican states, for example, courts cannot grant pretrial release to any person charged with robbery, serious assault, stock theft, or assisted suicide.[7] Ecuador's non bailable offenses include all crimes punishable with prison terms of five years or more, as well as all hate, sexual, or domestic-violence crimes.[8] Austria bars pretrial release for most persons charged with a crime that carries a minimum penalty of 10 years or more.[9] In Zambia, a person charged with theft of a motor vehicle and who has previously been charged with the same offense cannot be released on bail.[10] South Africa requires any person charged with a serious violent crime to adduce evidence satisfying the court that exceptional circumstances exist which in the interest of justice permit the defendant's pretrial release—essentially placing the onus on the defendant to show why he should be released awaiting trial.[11] Changing these policies to allow judicial discretion will decrease the arbitrary imposition of pretrial detention.

*Laws should ban pretrial detention where logical.* Mexico's federal constitution prohibits pretrial detention for persons charged with offenses for which the potential sentence upon conviction excludes imprisonment.[12] Chile also addresses pretrial detention in cases where the potential sentence excludes imprisonment, but requires such suspects to show they have local family ties to avoid detention.[13] A number of Mexican states prohibit pretrial detention for juveniles charged with "non-grave" or minor offenses, and prohibits it altogether for children under the age of 14 years.[14] Brazil prohibits pretrial detention for persons charged with an offense for which the potential maximum sentence is four years of imprisonment or less, provided such a person is not charged with a crime involving domestic or family violence committed against a vulnerable person (i.e. a child, woman, elderly person, or physically disabled person) and has not previously been convicted of a serious crime.[15] Ecuador's laws stipulate that pregnant women cannot be held in pretrial detention.[16]

Unfortunately, these laws have limited effects, and tend to exist in places where other conditions support excessive use of pretrial detention. Their language may cover a very limited number of people—for example, Mexico imposes imprisonment for most offenses. In addition, some of these laws only require that individuals be released if they make bail, which may be set too high to help many suspects. However, they represent foundations on which to build and models that other jurisdictions could follow; correctly applied, they would decrease pretrial detention.

India has a stronger bar on mandatory pretrial detention. The law requires that a person charged with a bailable offense be granted bail by the police or the courts. If the defendant is unable to furnish any surety within a week of arrest, the person is deemed "indigent" and released on a personal bond without sureties for his appearance.

*Laws should set an upper time limit on the legally permitted duration of pretrial detention.* France, for example, requires the length of pretrial detention be "reasonable," given the seriousness of the alleged offense and the complexity of the investigations, and stipulates the maximum length of pretrial detention—ranging from four months to four years—based on the maximum penalty the defendant would face if convicted.[17] Denmark uses a "proportionality principle," generally disallowing pretrial detention in excess of two-thirds of the expected custodial sentence.[18] Under Greek law, lengths of pretrial detention vary according to the nature of the alleged offense, ranging from six months to one year, and only permitting pretrial detention longer than 18 months in exceptional circumstances.[19] In the Netherlands, once a defendant has been remanded in custody the trial must commence within 104 days.[20] Moreover, pretrial detention in the Netherlands must terminate as soon as the pretrial detention period together with the period of police custody equals the anticipated custodial sentence upon conviction.[21] Poland stipulates that pretrial detention should not exceed three months, but permits extension by nine months. Thereafter, only the appellate court can extend the duration of pretrial detention.[22] In England and Wales, legislation governs the maximum period of pretrial detention, and if a trial has not commenced within the statutory time limit the defendant must be released on bail. Only a few enumerated exceptions allow for an extension of the maximum period of pretrial detention.[23]

*The law should provide for a variety of alternatives to pretrial detention.* It is important that judges have a wide range of flexible bail conditions available to them. Such alternatives to pretrial detention can include precluding defendants from engaging in particular conduct, leaving or entering specified places or districts, or meeting specified persons. They may also include ordering defendants to remain at a specific address; report on a periodic basis to a court, the police, or other authority;

surrender passports or other travel documents; or provide financial or other forms of security so as to guarantee attendance at trial.[24]

> ### Alternatives to Pretrial Detention: The Danger of "Net Widening"
>
> England and Wales introduced conditional bail in the late 1960s in an attempt to reduce the number of pretrial detainees. Since then, the use of conditional bail has steadily increased. Today a majority of defendants released on bail by the courts have conditions attached to their bail. The police were empowered to impose conditions on police bail in 1995, and police conditional bail has also risen.
>
> These increases raise the specter that conditional bail, rather than narrowing the net of detention, increases the net of conditions. Suspects who might have been released on their own recognizance now must satisfy conditions. Empirical evidence relating to the effectiveness of the increased use of conditional bail is sparse. Anthea Hucklesby's 2001 study suggests that police conditional bail has been subject to net widening.[25] George Mair's 2002 study also found that only half of cases of conditional bail displace the use of custodial sentences.[26]
>
> The Law Society of England and Wales finds that the defense are increasingly offering a package of conditions as part of a bail application, which may preempt a remand in custody, but raises the concern that this implies "an acceptance that the defendants would be refused unconditional bail," and that as a result, bail conditions are "frequently imposed unnecessarily."[27]

Unfortunately, a review of pretrial detention laws and practice in the 27 E.U. member states found little evidence that the introduction of alternatives to pretrial detention resulted in a reduction in the number of detainees incarcerated as a proportion of all prisoners. But, as noted above, these kinds of options give judicial actors something on which to build.[28] Other modifications prescribed in this chapter, especially the education of judicial system actors and the public, may make such programs more effective in decreasing pretrial detention.

*Laws and guidelines should regulate the use of conditional bail.* While in most cases preferable to pretrial detention, conditional bail does restrict the liberty of defendants, especially when courts impose multiple conditions simultaneously. Judicial officers must carefully weigh the advantages and disadvantages of each condition in order to find appropriate forms of intervention that can serve as an effective alternative to detention. Judicial officers should verify that defendants are able to meet the requirements they set. Without this verification, conditions act as de facto pretrial detention. The U.N. Office on Drugs and Crime has developed the following considerations for judicial officers evaluating conditional bail:[29]

> Requirements to appear in court should not be excessive in number. Scheduled hearings should be meaningful in that they move a case toward completion.

> Where bail is considered necessary to ensure the appearance of the accused for trial, courts should set bail amounts that are proportionate to the defendant's

means. Otherwise, high bail amounts discriminate against the poor.

> Judicial officers should tailor restrictions of movement as narrowly as possible and take the defendant's circumstances into account. Legitimate activities such as going to a job should remain possible.

> Before requiring a defendant to surrender certain documents, judicial officers should consider whether the defendant needs the documents to work, withdraw money, or interact with the state bureaucracy. In some countries, courts may order that the counsel for the defendant take possession of such documents, with leave to allow their appropriate use.

> Judicial officers should limit direct supervision in the community, an intrusive alternative that greatly limits freedom and privacy.

*States should take prison overcrowding into account.* A 2001 law requires South African courts to consider release of those detained on unaffordable bail if overcrowding poses a material and imminent threat to the human dignity, physical health, or safety of pretrial detainees who are unable to pay their bail amounts, and who have been charged with less serious offenses.[30] Over an 18-month period in 2009–2010, prison authorities made applications with respect to some 34,700 pretrial detainees, and the courts released 23,200.[31]

*States should make provisions to address the fact that even low bail amounts may be unaffordable.* South Africa also took action to address unaffordable bail amounts for poor detainees. In 2007–2008, some 8,300 persons who were granted bail were held in pretrial detention in South Africa because they could not afford the bail amounts set at R1,000 (U.S.$ 125) or less. Half of those pretrial detainees had bail set at under R500 and many under R100.[32] South Africa took action, releasing those who could not afford small bail fees, and developed a protocol to address the problem of unaffordable bail fees. All those with bail set at less than R1,000 have the right to reappear before the court if within 14 days of the court having granted bail they have not managed to raise the monies. By 2010, the number of pretrial detainees with bail amounts less than R1,000 had decreased by 47 percent, to 4,458.[33] These measures not only reduced the number of persons in pretrial detention, but also improved the functioning of the courts at several of the pilot sites where the reform was tested.[34]

*Laws should dictate a system of mandatory review* as a check on unnecessary delays and to reduce the burden on the defendant of finding "new facts" with which to present a fresh bail application. Defendants cannot be expected to understand the reasons for delays in the prosecution of cases and the onus should be on the prosecution to show to a court at regular intervals why the continued detention of a defendant is necessary and reasonable. Evidence suggests that effective regular review can be at least as effective as statutory time limits in controlling the length of pretrial detention. Neither Finland nor Sweden limits the duration of pretrial detention, but an effective review process ensures short average periods of pretrial detention.[35]

*Laws should require the review of bail decisions.* A number of Latin American jurisdictions have incorporated the automatic review of bail decisions into their respective criminal codes. Costa Rica, El Salvador, Paraguay, the Dominican Republic, and Venezuela all require that bail applications be reviewed every three months.[36]

Unfortunately, legal changes do not always prevent the excessive use of pretrial detention. For example, both Bolivia's and Malawi's new codes of criminal procedure contain fixed limits on the amount of time defendants can be held in pretrial detention. Yet prolonged detention remains a problem in both countries due to factors such as judicial corruption, lack of public defenders, poor case-tracking mechanisms, and judicial officers who claim to be ignorant of the new law.[37] In Russia, the country's judiciary routinely ignores laws promoting the release on bail or personal recognizance of defendants charged with economic crimes and stipulating that seriously ill detainees need not await trial in jail.[38] In the early 1970s, the U.S. Congress and state legislatures enacted "speedy trial" acts to ensure that criminal cases were decided quickly. These laws set specific deadlines which, if not met, could lead to dismissal of cases. The mere adoption of these laws, however, has generally failed to shorten disposition times.[39]

In a similar vein, the Italian criminal procedure code contains abundant language aimed at curbing excessive use of pretrial detention. It requires "serious circumstantial evidence of guilt," specific facts to support allegations that the accused might tamper with evidence, and requires authorities to name "specific conduct" or previous convictions to support an allegation of likely repeat offense. Yet representatives of the Italian criminal bar association allege that Italian courts systematically violate the principle that pretrial detention remand must be a last resort. They added that the police use pretrial detention as an "investigative tool" to compel defendants to incriminate themselves and others in exchange for release or for the substitution of home arrest.

In spite of these challenges, it's clear that states can implement a number of laws to decrease pretrial detention. Where practice falls short, some of the measures described below, such as the use of data and the intervention of legal practitioners to invoke the law, can build on the foundation that the right laws supply.

# THE ROLE OF DATA IN ASSESSING THE PROBLEM

Obtaining and understanding data on a criminal justice system's performance is no easy task. This is especially the case with respect to pretrial justice, the efficient delivery of which requires the coordinated actions of a range of criminal justice agencies and the people who work within them. As one expert has said of the dearth of reliable criminal justice data and research worldwide, "most of the penitentiary systems do not provide meaningful data."[40]

It is important for justice systems to have effective information management systems that provide current, accessible information on the status of cases and defendants. The UNODC *Handbook on Prisoner File Management* highlights the importance of maintaining accurate files:

> Creating and maintaining prisoner and detainee files is an essential tool for protecting and upholding [human rights] standards...an essential component of effective prison management and plays an important part in improving the transparency and accountability of prison administrations....[41]

When it comes to preventing or decreasing the abuse of pretrial detention, data about judges' decisions to release defendants pending trial can aid reform. This data includes the charges against individuals released, the conditions imposed on them, and characteristics such as employment status. It also includes the results of release decisions, such as the number of released defendants who abscond, (re) offend while awaiting trial, or interfere with the administration of justice. Showing that most released defendants comply with the conditions of their release should help the argument for reducing the use of pretrial detention. By correlating information about defendants with the results of release decisions, data can point the way to releasing additional defendants pretrial, if the data show that indicators such as being charged with a nonviolent crime or having a job make defendants more likely to comply.

Judicial officers could also improve their bail decisions if states collected statistical evidence. This evidence could facilitate the authorization of catch-all categories establishing the risk that a defendant would abscond, offend, interfere with witnesses, or otherwise obstruct justice. Statistical analysis could unlock component parts of a release-on-bail decision and develop a weighting scheme informed by objective measures. It could measure which conditions effectively prevent negative outcomes without unduly disadvantaging the poor or imposing lengthy pretrial detention.[42]

However, even basic data on the number of pretrial detainees and the length of their detention can prompt targeted and effective interventions. In Brazil, for example, the National Council of Justice (*Conselho Nacional de Justiça*, or CNJ), a statutory body, created an ad hoc initiative called the *mutirão* (literally, "the help that members of a family give to one another"), in an effort to deal with the backlog of cases underlying the country's high pretrial detention numbers. The number of pretrial detainees more than quadrupled between 1995 and 2009 in Brazil.[43] A small team based in Brasília coordinated the assembly of groups of judges, drawn from different areas to examine a single state's caseload.

Between 2009 and 2011, after examining 383,893 cases, the *mutiroes* freed almost 10 percent of the defendants: 36,893 people who had been detained irregularly. Hundreds of these people had spent far longer in pretrial detention than the sentences for the charges they faced could have brought. In one state, Bahia, the *mutirão* discovered that while the prison authorities had recorded a prison population of between 10,000 and 11,000 in January 2009, there were actually around 15,000 people in detention facilities, approximately a third of whom were awaiting trial.[44]

In Ecuador, the law limits the period that pretrial detainees may be held after indictments have been issued but before conviction or sentencing, to six months in the case of less serious crimes and one year in the case of serious crimes. A review of pretrial detainees identified almost 12,000 being held in violation of these principles in August 2007. Lawyers employed by a reformed and better-resourced criminal defense system identified these cases and ensured that the detainees were released or brought to an expedited trial. By September 2009, all of them had been released.[45]

In 2003, a census of three Kenyan prisons, including the main Nairobi remand center, found that 86 percent of pretrial detainees accused of bailable offenses had been granted bail but could not meet the conditions set by the court.[46] A number of defendants were released pending trial, following a reduction in money bail amounts or other changes in condition of release.

In 1999, a number of Malawian NGOs conducted a study of the conditions of juveniles in three of Malawi's largest prisons. The study found that of the 179 young people in the juvenile section in Zomba Central Prison, not one had been lawfully detained. None of the juveniles had legal representation or had been charged with offenses that would justify remand to prison.[47]

These ad hoc undertakings suggest what can be achieved by data collection mechanisms that gather relevant pretrial justice indicators on a sustained and real-time basis. At its most basic, every criminal justice system should know who is in pretrial detention. That is, states should have information on every pretrial detainee's demographic background (e.g. age, gender), the charge(s) he faces, the date the detention began, and the date of the next court appearance. The dearth of data hamstrings judicial officers who seek to make decisions that will support the integrity and credibility of the justice system, protect the community, and assist in the protection of the defendant's rights. Data could give judges information about the extent to which bail and pretrial detention practices achieve their lawful aims. The availability of data on issues such as failure to appear, the reasons for failing to appear, offending on bail, and interference with witnesses and victims is generally so poor that the effectiveness of pretrial detention cannot be analyzed with any degree of accuracy.[48] As Australian scholars Sarre, King, and Bamford note, "To facilitate quality assurance, reliable data must be collected and made publicly available. To understand the contribution of each set of decision-makers to remand rates requires systematic, comparable and accessible data on remand hearings and remand outcomes."[49]

A more sophisticated data collection mechanism will seek to identify bottlenecks within the criminal justice system as a prelude to developing interventions which can address these most effectively. For example, in the early 2000s, the Nizhny Novgorod Project on Justice Assistance developed a "jail monitor" to measure the duration of pretrial detention for different stages of the criminal justice process (Table 1).[50]

TABLE 1:

**Average number of days between various pretrial stages, Nizhny Novgorod**[51]

| Stage of proceeding | 2001 | 2002 | Jan. 2003 |
| --- | --- | --- | --- |
| From arrest to arrival at SIZO* | 6.8 | 2.9 | 3.0 |
| From arrival to indictment | 51.5 | 48.6 | 44.0 |
| From indictment to verdict | 36.8 | 36.7 | 36.0 |
| From verdict to end of appeals | 36.0 | 36.6 | 29.0 |
| From adjudication to exit from SIZO | 30.3 | 24.0 | 18.0 |
| Total time in detention (days) | 161.3 | 148.9 | 130.0 |

* SIZO is the Russian acronym for a pretrial detention center.

This approach pinpoints where delays are occurring within the broader pretrial justice system. In Table 1 we can see, for example, that detainees covered by the Nizhny Novgorod project spent roughly a third of their total time in pretrial detention from arrival at a pretrial detention center (SIZO) up to the point of being indicted or charged. That is, the police took 6-7 weeks to finalize their investigation for the prosecution to then proceed to trial. As a result of this analysis, the Nizhny Novgorod project persuaded the police to employ assistant investigators to expedite the police's investigative work.

Data collected at the Ikoyi Prison in Lagos, Nigeria, on the duration of each detention for all persons exiting pretrial detention (which includes those being sentenced to detention following trial) revealed, contrary to the expectation of most Nigerian criminal justice officials, the average stay was 73 days and one-third of detainees exited within a week, most having been released on bail.[52]

However, four percent of pretrial detainees at Ikoyi Prison remained in pretrial detention for more than a year, and researchers from the Lagos State Attorney General's office, the Lagos-based CLEEN Foundation, and Harvard University determined that these individuals accounted for almost half the prison space occupied at the prison over time. An additional four percent of pretrial detainees were held between six and 12 months. In general, the prosecution of defendants who stayed in pretrial detention for above average lengths of time was discontinued or withdrawn (after an average of 121 days in pretrial detention) or dismissed by the courts (after an average of 111 days). Completing within six months all of the cases where a defendant was in pretrial detention for at least a year would reduce the remand population by 17 percent.[53]

A comprehensive approach to data gathering and analysis provides a foundation for substantial change, not just in the overuse of pretrial detention but in penal reform in general. As the Twelfth United Nations Congress on Crime Prevention and Criminal Justice observed in 2010, "Successful initiatives tend to be those founded on empirical understanding validated by key stakeholders."[54]

## COORDINATION BETWEEN CRIMINAL JUSTICE AGENCIES

In many jurisdictions, a lack of coordination and cooperation between the various criminal justice agencies responsible for pretrial justice contributes to the duration of pretrial detention. Even with limited resources, addressing this disconnect can achieve substantial change. As the cases below illustrate, regular meetings at the local level to address bottlenecks in the criminal justice system can have a significant effect.

In 1998, the government of Uganda appointed a Case Management Committee comprising senior local representatives of the various criminal justice agencies—including police, probation, prosecution, prisons, magistracy, and judiciary—to address an extreme backlog of criminal cases. Monthly committee meetings tracked the progress of cases through the system from the very beginning of the criminal justice process, identifying the major bottlenecks and seeking solutions. For example, cases could be transferred from police to court more quickly and an available magistrate could begin taking evidence from available witnesses to ensure faster disposal of simple cases. The committee also developed a joint simplified procedure to discontinue the prosecution of certain cases in which the defendant had not been formally arrested. This procedure disposed of some 600 cases clogging up the system in a single district.[55] Other actions to cut delays include better control of case files, statistical reports to identify bottlenecks, trials held on consecutive days to reduce adjournments, and steps to encourage better witness attendance at court.[56]

Uganda has established similar case management committees nationally under the auspices of the Chain Link Initiative. In addition to improving coordination among criminal justice agencies, the initiative has improved case management through coordination with citizens. For example, in one district a chief magistrate assigned a clerk to monitor the grounds around the court premises to ensure that persons waiting there knew what to do and where to go. The court's entrance now has posters and guides for court users in multiple languages.[57]

Malawi established Court Users' Committees meeting regularly at the local, regional, and national levels to identify problems and develop local solutions. The committees enable justice system actors to address temporary crises and reduce the caseload by referring appropriate cases for diversion or to traditional authorities for local settlement. They also encourage the police to speed up investigations and gather evidence before defendants are remanded in custody, rather than afterwards.[58] In an example of the committees' success, a team of paralegals, supported by prison officers, raised the matter of overcrowding of a particular prison at the local Court Users' Committee meeting. In response, the chief magistrate of the area visited and inspected the prison in question. The following day he returned with three magistrates, police prosecutors, and court clerks and released a number of pretrial detainees to ease the congestion.

Malawi's National Taskforce of Court Users' Committees has developed guidelines to encourage members to speed up case processing times and reduce the use of pretrial detention.[59] These include:

> Police applications for warrants of arrest shall be made after investigations have been finalized unless good reasons can be advanced for doing otherwise.

> Trials involving minor offenses should be finalized within three months of the defendant's arrest.

> Objections to bail should cite good reasons.

> Trials of minor offenses should be conducted on the day of pleas, with police summoning witnesses in advance.

> Frequency of trial adjournments should not exceed three in total.

> Witnesses present at court should be heard whenever and wherever practicable.

**More than 90 percent** of Liberia's prisoners are pretrial detainees.

In Liberia, the Ministry of Justice established a Case Flow Management Committee in 2004 to address prison overcrowding. More than 90 percent of Liberia's prisoners are pretrial detainees and defendants charged with minor offenses often spend long periods in detention awaiting trial. The committee reviews the individual files and status of pretrial detainees and makes a monthly recommendation to the solicitor-general to drop charges in appropriate cases.[60]

In Bangladesh, the Madaripur Legal Aid Association (MLAA) participates monthly in a Case Coordination Committee meeting designed to manage cases efficiently, thus reducing backlogs and prison overcrowding. At the meeting, the MLAA's paralegals present the committee with cases that need immediate attention. These typically have to do with pretrial detainees not having trial dates set, persons who have been in pretrial detention for long periods of time, and pretrial detainees not knowing how to deposit bail money to facilitate their pretrial release. The committee members, who represent various criminal justice agencies, work together to provide quick and practical solutions to urgent problems. Each meeting begins with an update on the status of previous cases and ends with a plan for resolving pending problems.[61]

The South African government developed an Integrated Justice System initiative following the end of apartheid to transform the criminal justice system "into a modern, efficient, effective and integrated system."[62] As part of the initiative, the Court Centre Project (CCP) brings together representatives from the safety and security, justice, correctional services, and welfare departments at the local level to create an integrated team to expedite the court process. Team members ensure that case files are ready for trial two days in advance, and ensure the timely delivery of files as well as detained arrestees at trial. CCP also provides improved information management. A user-friendly and simple computer-based data-capture and -management program stores information contained in each case file and charge sheet. The system manages the court rolls, and tracks and controls the pretrial detention period of detainees. The system also allows for the identification of trends, such as the number of juveniles standing trial, the length of cases, and the number of dockets that are missing. In response to this data, the CCP established reception courts, where all first appearances, remands, bail applications, and guilty pleas are heard. This ensures that courts can prioritize trial-ready cases.

Most of the initiatives described above require a relatively modest application of effort on the part of criminal justice officials. The impact of monthly meetings between members of agencies working together to expedite cases has been impressive and should be replicated elsewhere.

## REDUCING THE NUMBER OF PEOPLE WHO COME INTO CONFLICT WITH THE LAW

The criminal justice system is akin to a funnel. The large end represents encounters with the law when the police stop and question people. The funnel narrows as the police arrest some people they stopped, and summon others to court. It narrows again as some of those arrested will be charged, and again to prosecutions, to convictions, and to the imposition of a custodial sentence.[63]

The narrowing of the funnel at each stage varies by jurisdiction. In countries where police are numerous and efficient, arrest numbers may be high. In places where prosecutors have a duty to prosecute all cases in which sufficient evidence exists of the probable guilt of the suspect (the so-called "legality principle"), prosecution rates tend to be high. Countries with corrupt police but under-resourced criminal justice systems may have many arrests but few prosecutions and convictions.

In the United States, which has tough penal laws and imposes custodial sentences relatively frequently, most arrests do not result in conviction and imprisonment. U.S. law enforcement makes some 13-14 million arrests annually, or about 4,500 arrests per 100,000 of the general population. Relatively few of these are for violent crimes. In 2009, for example, U.S. police made 13.7 million arrests, of which 582,000 were for serious violent crimes, 1.3 million for minor assaults, and 1.7 million for property crimes. Other arrests were for vandalism, transgressing liquor laws, drunkenness, disorderly conduct, and curfew and loitering law violations (2.2 million), drug abuse violations (1.7 million), and driving under the influence (1.4 million).[64]

Over a typical year, the United States gives a custodial sentence to 700,000 to 750,000 people, or about 250 persons per 100,000 of the population. Of these, 200,000 to 250,000 go to prison for violating a condition of their parole. In short, of the 13–14 million annual arrests, only about five percent culminate in a custodial sentence.[65] However, most arrestees spend some time in pretrial detention—some just a few hours at the police station, but most at least overnight pending a bail hearing. Many, however, will spend weeks in detention before making bail, being acquitted at the end of their trial, or receiving a non-custodial sentence upon conviction. The U.S. criminal justice system moves quickly compared to others, so that the average period of pretrial detention tends to be low. In other countries, however, where defendants can wait months and years for trial, an arrest can lead to long periods of detention.

Countries with long pretrial detention durations will naturally see the strongest results from lowering arrest rates. The major ways to decrease arrest rates are crime prevention, decriminalization, and alternatives to incarceration such as restorative justice.

## Crime Prevention

The following four principal approaches all contribute to a reduction in offending and crime and, thereby, arrest and pretrial detention:

> Crime prevention through social development (or social crime prevention). This includes social, educational, health, cultural, and environmental measures that help reduce the risks of offending and victimization. Social approaches offer support to the most vulnerable populations or geographic areas.

> Situational crime prevention approaches. Such approaches seek to reduce the opportunities for and benefits of offending, as well as increasing the risks of being caught, primarily through the design of the built environment.

> Community or locally-based crime prevention. Such measures help to change the conditions in neighborhoods that influence crime, victimization, and the resulting insecurity.

> Prevention of recidivism. Such programs focus on the social reintegration of offenders.

A growing number of countries are adopting broad public safety policies that include a component devoted to prevention. The International Centre for the Prevention of Crime (ICPC) identified 37 countries in this category in 2008, and 57 in 2010.[66]

After a global review of crime prevention policies, the ICPC concluded that key elements of successful policies include a sense of trust between the population and public institutions, particularly the police, justice, and the educational sector; the active participation of the population involved in prevention strategies; and prevention strategies which constitute public policies in and of themselves, which are not annexed to other policies. They also specify that prevention strategies must benefit from adequate and specific resources in terms of funding and governance.[67]

Modest crime prevention interventions can have a significant impact on reducing offending behavior. For example, a review of 13 studies in the United States and United Kingdom found that improved street lighting—an example of situational crime prevention—resulted in a decline in reported crime in public spaces by about a fifth.[68]

### Colombia: Crime Prevention Initiative Reduces Homicide Rate in Medellín[69]

Medellín, Colombia's second largest city, achieved a remarkable plunge in crime between 2002 and 2007. The city had the highest rate of homicide in the world in 1991 at 381 murders per 100,000, and while it halved over the next 10 years, in 2001 it was still one of the highest rates of homicide globally. The control exerted by armed groups of drug traffickers, paramilitaries, and guerrilla groups in many parts of the city maintained a high rate.

The Medellín mayor's office played a key role in implementing local regulation to control the consumption of alcohol and the carrying of guns in public spaces, focusing attention on areas with the highest rates of violence. Through a peace and reconciliation program, *Projectos Urbanos Integrales* (Integrated Urban Projects), the city undertook large-scale investment to provide public services to informal settlements on the mountainsides surrounding the city, particularly transport, education, housing, and the creation of green spaces. Selling these as an investment in the city as a whole, stressing solidarity and the need to reduce inequality, the city worked with civil society organizations, whose presence in, and knowledge of, their neighborhoods, as well as their legitimacy within them, had sustained independence from armed groups in preceding years. Between 2002 and 2007 homicide rates in the city fell from 174 to 29 per 100,000, a startling achievement.[70]

## Decriminalization

Decriminalization is the abolition of criminal penalties in relation to certain acts, sometimes replaced by regulatory permitting or fines. A number of countries have decriminalized acts over the last few decades such as loitering, being a "rogue and vagabond," hawking, being an "idle or disorderly person," the possession or recreational use of certain drugs, consuming alcohol in public, breastfeeding in public, homosexuality, prostitution, and public nudity.

According to the U.N. Office on Drugs and Crime, jurisdictions that have decriminalized vagrancy have thereby significantly reduced rates of both pretrial detention and overall imprisonment.[71] In Uganda in the 1990s, 50 percent of the young persons in pretrial detention centers had been charged with "being idle and disorderly"; the removal of this offense from the statute book in 1999 reduced the number of young persons in pretrial detention dramatically.[72]

The United States would see a significant plunge in pretrial detention and in incarceration rates if it were to decriminalize the possession of marijuana. In 2010, arrests in the United States for possession of marijuana exceeded 750,000 people, including more than 50,000 in New York alone, some whom possessed less than 25 grams of the drug.[73]

## Restorative Justice, Alternative Dispute Resolution, and Diversion

Restorative justice focuses on the needs of victims, offenders, and the involved community, instead of satisfying abstract legal principles or punishing the offender. Victims typically take an active role in the process, while offenders are encouraged to take responsibility for their actions.[74]

Restorative justice understands crime as an offense against an individual or community, rather than the state.[75] It involves both victim and offender and focuses on their personal needs. In addition, it supports the offender in avoiding future offenses. Restorative approaches to crime date back thousands of years and many traditional societies still use them. Restorative justice typically does not include arrest, or, therefore, pretrial detention. It may proceed in a courtroom or within a nonprofit or community organization. It typically proceeds with much more speed than formal courtroom processes, as well.

### Sierra Leone: The Customary Justice System[76]

With only 250 lawyers in Sierra Leone (90 percent of whom work in the capital), most people in Sierra Leone trust and rely on customary law for justice problems such as domestic violence, child abandonment, forced marriage, corruption, police abuse, economic exploitation, abuse of traditional authority, and denial of the right to education and health care. Almost 60 paralegals trained by Timap for Justice help address individual justice-related problems, as well as community-level problems, by drawing on both customary and formal institutions. In general these approaches do not involve pretrial detention, because most proceedings do not involve jail time and happen swiftly.

In numerous developing countries throughout most parts of Africa, and large parts of Asia and Latin America, customary justice systems dominate dispute settlement.[77] The United Kingdom's Department for International Development estimates that in many countries on these three continents people address 80 percent of their disputes to traditional or customary legal systems.[78]

A survey of some 2,500 Liberian households in 2008–2009 found that more respondents favored taking disputes of a criminal nature to a customary forum rather than a formal forum or court, even with respect to serious offenses such as murder and rape. Of all the cases the households had taken to a forum—for disputes of both a criminal and civil nature—over a 12-month period (some 2,000 cases in total), they consistently preferred the outcome and "service" they received from the informal over the formal forum (Table 2).[79]

TABLE 2:

Liberia: Respondent satisfaction by forum, % of all cases taken to either a "customary" or "formal" forum

|  | Customary | Formal |
|---|---|---|
| Outcome was fair | 92.3 | 85.0 |
| Somewhat or very satisfied with the outcome | 89.3 | 78.2 |
| Somewhat or very satisfied with respect shown | 89.2 | 75.7 |
| Would return to this forum | 90.5 | 76.4 |

Afghans, to take another example, widely use community-based dispute resolution mechanisms—the workings of which most citizens, especially outside urban areas, understand better than formal courts—to resolve criminal (and civil) matters. These mechanisms handle over 80 percent of disputes in Afghanistan.[80]

Diversion programs using a restorative approach to justice vary from country to country. They may include formal police caution, conciliation, community service, or individual, family, or group therapy. In principle, diversion refers to the channeling of certain criminal cases away from the criminal justice system, usually on certain conditions. It may require offenders to acknowledge responsibility for the offense and agree to make amends for the crime, often by performing community service or compensating the victim. Sometimes the offender is sent to a course or program to deal with a specific problem.

In practice, diversion programs represent an expansion of default practice. If countries investigated, prosecuted, and imprisoned all suspected offenders, the system would be unable to cope with the numbers. Consequently, police and prosecutors exercise a degree of discretion in deciding whom to take action against and whom to ignore. Jurisdictions that incorporate diversion into a legislative framework provide structures and guidelines to criminal justice officials who might otherwise exercise their discretion in an arbitrary or discriminatory manner, and generally exercise greater diversion than they would without an official policy and clear guidelines.[81]

A review of legislation relating to diversion worldwide indicates that many countries provide diversion to drug- and alcohol-dependence treatment programs, some of them in ways that decrease pretrial detention.[82]

Jurisdictions seeking to decrease pretrial detention specifically and over incarceration generally need to develop specific criteria to assess a case's suitability for diversion, such as the nature of the offense, admission of guilt, the age of the accused, and the victim's preferences. Specific criteria will make decisions regarding diversion efficient, and thereby decrease pretrial detention—not just for the defendant in a diverted case, but also for defendants in cases that benefit from a more efficient system. Thailand successfully reduced its 250,000 inmates in 2002 to 185,000 by 2008, 28 percent of whom were pretrial detainees, through a diversion program. It included the development of community mediation centers to settle minor disputes within communities, the encouragement of the use of prosecutorial discretion not to prosecute under certain circumstances, the initiation of drug diversion programs, and the inclusion of pretrial diversion among the mandates of a new probation department.[83]

Papua New Guinea cut the number of juveniles in pretrial detention by 62 percent between 2001 and 2007 through a diversionary protocol.[84] A Juvenile Justice Working Group consisting of 21 government and community agencies collaborated to establish a comprehensive juvenile justice system, based on restorative justice, Melanesian traditions, and contemporary juvenile justice practices.[85] Activities included the implementation of a Police Juvenile Policy and Diversionary Protocol encouraging police to use pretrial detention as a last resort for juveniles. The protocol encouraged police to issue cautions or refer children to community mediation rather than formally arresting them, particularly for minor and non-violent crimes. A specialized Police Juvenile Policy Monitoring Unit monitors police compliance with the protocol, and a network of NGOs has been trained to document abuse and provide care, support, and advocacy where required.

The program also provides diversion at the court level through a Juvenile Court Diversion Programme. When children come before the court charged with minor crimes, the court has the discretion to refer them to community mediation rather than proceeding with the formal trial. Local mediators have been accredited to facilitate resolutions between the child, his parents, the victim, and community members. In addition, Juvenile Court Magistrates throughout the country have received training on juvenile justice principles to ensure child-sensitive handling of children by the formal court system and the imprisonment of children only as a last resort.

In a program targeted to accused adults and children, South Africa reduced the average period in which it addresses disputes through the Community Peace Programme which it established in the mid-1990s. The program seeks to mobilize local knowledge and capacity around issues of dispute-resolution and community-building. Groups of residents in poor communities facilitate the resolution of local disputes and support local entrepreneurs who are engaged in projects and enterprises that address the root causes of local conflicts. Centered on activities in 180 sites across the country, the program has achieved an average dispute resolution time of three days and a 99 percent success rate in finding solutions to disputes, 91 percent of which are of a nature that might carry jail time and pretrial detention under other models of resolution.[86]

South Africa's Child Justice Act, implemented in 2010, provides for the possibility of diversion in all matters involving juveniles in conflict with the law. Within the first six months of its operation (the latest period for which data are available), almost 8,000 juveniles were diverted from the formal criminal justice process. Over the same period the number of juveniles in pretrial detention in South Africa declined from 425 to 290.[87] By late 2011, the number of detained juveniles had declined to a record low of 196.[88]

Places where customary legal proceedings continue to have the trust of the people can typically avoid the excessive use of pretrial detention; many may be able to avoid almost all of its use. The Lilongwe Declaration on Accessing Legal Aid in the Criminal Justice System in Africa has this to say about the role of non-formal means of conflict resolution:[89]

Traditional and community-based alternatives to formal criminal processes have the potential to resolve disputes without acrimony and to restore social cohesion within the community. These mechanisms also have the potential to reduce reliance upon the police to enforce the law, to reduce congestion in the courts, and to reduce the reliance upon incarceration as a means of resolving conflict based upon alleged criminal activity. All stakeholders should recognise the significance of such diversionary measures to the administration of a community-based, victim-oriented criminal justice system and should provide support for such mechanisms provided that they conform to human rights norms.

## THE ROLE OF LAWYERS AND PARALEGALS[90]

Particularly in countries where legal processes do not work efficiently and effectively, lawyers and paralegals have the potential to make a positive contribution to decreasing a country's reliance on pretrial detention in a variety of ways and at various stages of the criminal justice process. For example, in countries where the proportion of prisoners who are in pretrial detention is high, legal advisors can identify those people in pretrial detention who are eligible and suitable for release and help them seek their release and push for their rights. Interventions between the different stages of the criminal process—for example, during the period between charge and trial—can help to ensure that relevant procedural steps (such as the transfer of case materials from police to prosecutor) occur in a timely fashion.

Ensuring accused persons' access to effective legal assistance at all stages of the pretrial justice process involves particular demands, and requires:

> - an effective mechanism for ensuring that suspects and defendants know of their right to legal assistance, and can make an informed choice in legal representation free from undue influence;

> - an effective mechanism to allow arrestees to contact a suitably qualified lawyer or paralegal without delay;

> - legal services structured and managed to allow the provision of prompt and qualified legal assistance;

> - ready access by lawyers and paralegals to arrestees in police detention, remand centers, and prisons, and facilities for lawyers and paralegals to consult with arrestees in private; and

> - appropriate training and accreditation, and systems of monitoring, to ensure that lawyers and paralegals have the necessary knowledge and skills.

### Nigeria: University Law Clinics

The Network of University Legal Aid Institutions (NULAI) Nigeria was established in 2003 as a non-governmental, non-profit organization to promote clinical legal education, legal education reform, legal aid, access to justice, and the development of future public interest lawyers. NULAI promotes pretrial detention work among law clinics in Nigeria and throughout Africa. Beginning in 2008, six legal clinics in Nigeria, catalyzed by NULAI, started to specialize in pretrial detention, providing litigation support, dispute resolution mechanisms, legal aid, and paralegal services. In 2009, NULAI signed a Memorandum of Understanding with the Legal Aid Council of the Nigerian Ministry of Justice to collaborate on building a network of legal and paralegal personnel for prison visits, data collection, and the provision of legal aid to those in pretrial detention in Nigeria. NULAI is also working to build a network of university-based law clinics around Africa that provide pro-bono legal services to the indigent while training a new generation of skilled law students committed to public service.

## The Importance of Paralegals in Many Jurisdictions

Paralegals can perform many of the functions listed above, and in many cases represent the best hope that significant numbers of defendants can receive legal assistance. As a World Bank report concludes, paralegals provide "first aid" in access to justice in many African countries:

> ...properly construed, paralegal services should be viewed as especially necessary in sub-Saharan Africa because of the poor extent of access to justice available to most Africans. In systems suffering from high prisoner remand populations and extensive court delays, there can be little or no case for bolstering the private legal profession or even the government public defender offices while the more urgent need for paralegal services is neglected. Paralegals should be viewed as a priority in building credible systems of justice in Africa.[91]

This section will discuss the role of paralegals in decreasing the abuse of pretrial detention, and the mechanisms that allow them to expand their role to serve the needs of many populations. Paralegals can and do provide primary legal aid services in numerous developing countries, decreasing the remand population, unnecessary detention, and case backlogs, and supporting the speedy processing of cases, diversion of young offenders, and the "equality of arms" between the defendant and the prosecution during the bail process in court. Given the relatively simple nature of the legal processes that lessen pretrial detention—prosecuting cases requires more expertise—it's an issue particularly ripe for address by paralegals.

In many countries, a lack of legal recognition inhibits the effective use of paralegals, as does the resistance of professional bar associations. Jurisdictions that allow paralegals access to people in police or prison custody can expect to decrease the overuse of pretrial detention. England and Wales require that police treat accredited paralegals who work under the supervision of a fully qualified lawyer as lawyers in most respects, and research on the system has shown that accredited paralegals provide competent advice and assistance.[92]

### Evolving Recognition for Paralegals

Since 2004, international legal and regulatory frameworks have supported the existence of paralegals as service providers in the criminal justice process. The *Lilongwe Declaration on Accessing Legal Aid in the Criminal Justice System in Africa* specifies that the delivery of effective legal aid to the maximum number of persons requires reliance on non-lawyers, including paralegals.[93] The African Commission on Human and Peoples' Rights adopted the *Lilongwe Declaration* and its associated *Plan of Action* in 2006, and the U.N. Economic and Social Council followed suit in 2007. In 2010, a conference of South Asian states on prison overcrowding issued the *Dhaka Declaration on Reducing Overcrowding in Prisons in South Asia* and called on governments in South Asia to make paralegals available in all prisons and at all stages of the criminal justice process.[94]

The U.N. *Principles and Guidelines on Access to Legal Aid in Criminal Justice Systems* urges states to recognize the role paralegals or similar service providers play in providing legal aid services.[95] Moreover, states should, in consultation with civil society and justice agencies and professional associations, introduce measures to:

> develop, where appropriate, a nationwide scheme of paralegal services with standardized training curricula and accreditation schemes;

> ensure quality standards and adequate training for paralegal services, including operation under the supervision of qualified lawyers;

> ensure paralegals' access to police stations, facilities of detention, pretrial detention centers, and prisons; and

> allow court-accredited and duly trained paralegals to participate in court proceedings and advise defendants when there are no lawyers available to do so.

At the national level, some countries have started adopting policies and passing legislation to promote paralegals within their criminal justice systems. For example, legislation in Malawi and South Africa recognizes paralegals as legal service providers. In Sierra Leone, a new legal aid law (passed by the legislature in 2012 but not promulgated by the executive at the time of writing) provides for a legal framework for institutionalizing and scaling-up community based paralegal programs throughout the country.[96]

Paralegal schemes—whether enjoying official recognition or not—have had a significant, measurable impact on pretrial detention populations in a range of countries. In Bangladesh, a paralegal program operating in three prisons resulted in the release of almost 2,000 pretrial detainees over four years.[97] In Malawi, over a seven-year period the Paralegal Advisory Service contributed to a fall in the proportion of prisoners held pretrial from 35 percent to 17 percent.[98] In Sierra Leone, paralegals operating in one prison reduced the pretrial population by 50 percent in one four-month period in 2009.[99]

Working in five prisons in Rwanda, ten paralegals conducted awareness raising sessions for 3,000 pretrial detainees over a one year period, preparing detainees for their next court appearance by role playing bail applications, applications for release, pleas in mitigation (for defendants who wished to plead guilty), and cross-examination. Between October 2009 and October 2010, the paralegals assisted with the pretrial release of almost 200 detainees, and the permanent release (through a dismissal of charges) of 625 pretrial detainees.[100]

According to an International Development Law Organization (IDLO) report, paralegals are especially effective during the early stages of the criminal justice process, and consequently have a particular role to play in decreasing pretrial detention.[101] They can screen cases in prisons, police stations, and courts; filter the caseload; and advise and assist those in conflict with the law at police stations, courts, and in prisons. Paralegals can, moreover, advise defendants on the law and procedure so that they understand the status of their case and how to navigate the criminal justice system in their own case. They can also link all the actors involved in the criminal justice process and facilitate communication and coordination to speed the application of justice. In advising pretrial detainees, they can make it possible for people to invoke legal limitations on pretrial detention and improve the success of bail applications.

Uganda's Paralegal Advisory Services (PAS) has been giving legal advice and assistance to pretrial detainees held in police stations, remand centers, and prisons since 2005. In 2007, PAS expanded its operations with 38 paralegals and 39 social workers, working in 38 prisons covering 57 percent of Uganda's prison population. An evaluation of PAS's work over an 11-month period between August 2009 and June 2010 revealed that its paralegals and social workers contributed to the release of almost 24,000 pretrial detainees (Table 3).[102]

TABLE 3:
**Pretrial detainees released following PAS intervention, August 2009 – June 2010**

| Nature of release | PAS intervention | No. released |
|---|---|---|
| Mediation and diversion | Arrestees / detainees diverted from the criminal justice system | 1,245 |
| Police bail | Detainees helped to obtain police bail through negotiations with police and tracing of sureties | 8,527 |
| Release after maximum bail period expired | Detainees educated and successfully requesting release after completing maximum pretrial detention period of 60 days for minor offenses | 3,351 |
| Bail in court | Detainees obtaining bail using the advice offered by paralegals in trainings on self-representation during bail proceedings | 2,652 |
| Other releases | Cases dismissed, discharged or acquitted after follow-up by paralegals through the criminal justice institutions | 8,182 |
| Total | | 23,957 |

Between 2005 and 2010, the number of pretrial detainees as a proportion of all prisoners in Uganda declined from 63 percent to 55 percent. At prisons where PAS operated, the proportion of pretrial detainees declined to 25 percent compared to 75 percent for prisons where PAS was not active.[103]

## Paralegals in Malawi Provide Pretrial Counsel: A Case Study

In October 2009, the Paralegal Advisory Service Institute (PASI) in Malawi deployed four full-time paralegals to two new project sites. One is a rural site in the village of Mangochi, and one is an urban site in Kanengo in the main industrial zone of Lilongwe, the capital city. At both project sites PASI began to provide paralegals at police stations for adult arrestees and detainees, augmenting PASI interventions focused on prisons and courts.

An evaluation of the new service revealed that PASI's paralegals assist pretrial detainees in a variety of ways. They provide support to arrestees making bail applications at the police station and court, trace relatives and sureties for bail, and screen and refer delayed cases for expeditious processing. Paralegals not only provided key information to improve the success of bail applications but made it possible for detainees to make bail. PASI also made a fairly big impact on dropped charges. Helping the detainee to understand the charges, the laws, and police procedures empowered defendants to argue their cases by, for example, providing a better explanation or alibi, all of which contributed to dropped charges.

The evaluation also revealed that PASI's paralegals sped up the time elapsing between arrests, charges, and the final disposal of minor cases by employing a number of activities originating at the police stations, such as tracing family members, witnesses, and sureties; awareness raising and information dissemination among arrestees (e.g., explaining the right to bail, discussing pleas to a lesser charge); and preparing detainees for their court hearings. Such efficiency gains bring about both individual and institutional benefits.

TABLE 4:
Average case processing times for persons suspected/charged with minor crimes, Mangochi and Kanengo

|  | Mangochi | | Kanengo | |
| --- | --- | --- | --- | --- |
| Time periods | 2009 | 2010 | 2009 | 2010 |
| From arrest to laying of charges | 1-4 days | 1-2 days | 3-4 days | 2-3 days |
| From laying of charge to disposal of case (without trial) | 2-3 days | 1 day | 2-3 days | < 2 days |
| From arrest to conclusion of case (with trial) | 2-3 months | 1 month | 1-2 months | 1 month |

Table 4 demonstrates that speed of case handling increased at both project sites such that at the 30-day point from arrest most cases were completed. Prior to the initiative, case handling took two or three months.

The same investigation found that PASI's public outreach and education programs had impact in ways relevant to pretrial detention, as the following table shows.

TABLE 5:
**Indicators of public trust in the police and PASI's role in furthering these, according to Mangochi and Kanengo police officers**

| Impacts indicating increased trust | PASI's role |
|---|---|
| More witnesses attending court, leading to a more efficient criminal justice process. | • PASI traced and contacted defense witnesses to ensure their attendance at court and provided them with guidance on what to expect and do in a courtroom setting.<br>• PASI helps to convene Court User Committee meetings where coordination issues are discussed and solutions thereto developed. |
| Improved public understanding of bail issues and increased number of defendants on police and court bail. | • PASI helped to improve community understanding of the law and the pretrial process, conducting 4-5 awareness sessions per site affecting about 4,000 people, and putting out posters in the communities explaining bail and related laws. |
| Improved community-police relations and better communication between police and community members. | • Addressing problems between the community and the police over bail issues at both project sites, bail became a key PASI subject at community outreach events. |
| Better understanding of how the justice system works by defendants and their families. | • PASI educated suspects and defendants about their rights and the operations of the pretrial justice process, including the average likely length of detention and possible reasons for delays. |
| Vigilantism has dropped and the public is more willing to cooperate in investigations and take suspects to the police. (Misunderstandings about bail contributed to acts of vigilantism against defendants released awaiting trial.) | • The incidence of vigilantism against awaiting trial defendants declined over the evaluation period.[104]<br>• Knowledge of the law surrounding pretrial release improved (see Table 6). |

The same study also looked at pretrial detainees' knowledge before and after PASI's intervention. The table below shows that PASI increased detainees' knowledge of the law by some 40 to 50 percent.

TABLE 6:
**Knowledge of the law: Pretrial detainees not exposed to PASI paralegal clinics (2009) versus those exposed (2010)**

| Multiple choice questions (correct response) | Kanengo % correct | | Mangochi % correct | |
| --- | --- | --- | --- | --- |
| | 2009 | 2010 | 2009 | 2010 |
| For how many days can a suspect be kept in police station cells? *(2 days)* | 56% | 98% | 45% | 100% |
| Which bail is free? *(police bail)* | 87% | 100% | 48% | 98% |
| When can a suspect apply for bail? *(first appearance)* | 36% | 99% | 26% | 96% |
| Who cannot be admitted as a surety? *(your spouse)* | 62% | 89% | 26% | 96% |
| What is the maximum number of days a case can be adjourned before it is dismissed? *(15 days)* | 32% | 80% | 23% | 98% |
| At which time must the detainee be informed of the reason for his or her arrest? *(as soon as possible upon arrest)* | 59% | 95% | 64% | 100% |
| Which is a legitimate objection to bail that can be raised by a prosecutor? *(defendant is a flight risk)* | 61% | 100% | 61% | 98% |
| Which of the following cannot help the detainee to communicate with lawyers and members of his/her family upon arrest and detention? *(the court)* | 28% | 99% | 18% | 94% |
| What does the law say a convicted prisoner can do if he or she is not happy with the conviction or sentence? *(appeal)* | 87% | 100% | 57% | 100% |
| Reasonable force may be used by the police to...? *(effect arrest)* | 49% | 97% | 24% | 96% |
| **AVERAGE OF ALL SCORES** | 56% | 96% | 39% | 98% |

These improvements in knowledge tend to decrease the use of pretrial detention because defendants are empowered to assert their rights. The same study found improvements in police understanding of the same issues, which decreases violations of suspects' rights.

PASI's program, in which almost 2,000 of the 2,800 pretrial detainees counseled by the added paralegals went home more quickly, alleviated poverty for affected families. Ninety percent of families in Malawi live at a subsistence level, which means that the cost of visiting a detained relative and providing supplies, as well as lost income from the between 80 and 90 percent of pretrial detainees who were family breadwinners, could be extremely disruptive. PASI's work also saves the state money in three ways: (i) providing a needed service to pretrial detainees which the state should be providing in many cases; (ii) reducing police caseloads and the number of people in pretrial detention at any one time, thus saving money for police, courts, and prisons; and (iii) reducing pretrial detention and thereby returning workers to farms and businesses—a benefit to the broader economy.

## Legal Practitioners' Role at the Police Station

Lawyers and paralegals can have a significant impact by identifying, advising, and representing those who may be eligible for pretrial release at the point of decision-making about pretrial detention, at the investigative stage, or following the commencement of formal criminal proceedings. One role of legal practitioners is to speed the process; another is to provide legal assistance to defendants. Using their knowledge of the law and their client's circumstances, lawyers and paralegals can identify individuals who are eligible for release from the police station, and can assist them in proving their suitability for release. They can identify juvenile offenders and block their classification as adults. Legal practitioners can also inhibit police abuse of detainees and locate relatives and others who can assist detainees.[105]

Availability at short notice is a key requirement for those legal advisors working at the investigative stage of the criminal process. The demand for legal assistance in these circumstances is difficult to predict, and requires a speedy response. Ad hoc arrangements rarely answer this need. Effective legal assistance at the investigative stage of the criminal process requires:

> - an effective and accountable mechanism for ensuring that suspects are informed of their right to legal assistance, and allowed to contact a lawyer or paralegal, without delay;
> - a method of funding legal assistance that ensures access to assistance during a review of eligibility;
> - legal services structured and managed to allow a suitably qualified adviser to provide assistance without delay, and by a method (for example, by telephone or in person) appropriate to the seriousness and complexity of the alleged offense and the suspect's circumstances.

To meet these demands, a range of police station advice and assistance schemes —using a mixture of private lawyers, public defenders, and paralegals—has been established in several countries.

England and Wales provide suspects who have been arrested and detained by the police with state-funded legal advice and assistance irrespective of their financial circumstances. Law firms under contract with the Legal Services Commission provide advice at the police station. The contract requires them to have the staff available and procedures in place to ensure that a lawyer or paralegal is always available at short notice. Paralegals working under the supervision of a lawyer often provide advice.[106]

Ukraine has three Public Defender Offices established by the International Renaissance Foundation, an NGO, to pilot new models of legal aid in criminal cases. Together, they employ 26 defense lawyers, providing legal advice and assistance to people detained by the police. Each office ensures that a lawyer is always on duty and available to provide assistance to a detainee at short notice.[107]

In Nigeria, since 2005 the Rights Enforcement and Public Law Centre has operated a police-duty solicitor scheme under an agreement between the National Police Force, the Legal Aid Council, and the Open Society Justice Initiative. With the consent and support of the police, the Federal Ministry of Justice, and the Legal Aid Council, this non-governmental partner serves the major police precincts of four states: Imo, Kaduna, Ondo, and Sokoto. Duty solicitors attend designated police stations on a 24-hour schedule, and the police must permit access. The duty solicitors advise suspects and detainees and advocate on their behalf, applying for bail or discharge from detention. Twenty duty-solicitors comprising four Legal Aid Council lawyers and sixteen Youth Service lawyers work as duty-solicitors in the project states. Over an 18-month period between January 2008 and June 2009, the duty solicitors had contact with over 3,500 pretrial detainees, of which 2,600 were released from detention. Detainees assisted by the duty solicitors spent an average of eight days in pretrial detention, compared to a period of many months typical for Nigeria.[108]

The table below lists the achievements of the Rights Enforcement and Public Law Centre in reducing pretrial detention.

TABLE 7:

**Number of persons released through intervention of police-duty solicitor schemes in four Nigerian states, 2005-2010**

| Year | No. of releases |
| --- | --- |
| 2005 | 432 |
| 2006 | 2,548 |
| 2007 | 2,332 |
| 2008 | 2,601 |
| 2009 | 3,394 |
| 2010 | 2,579 |
| **Total** | **13,886** |

Source: Rights Enforcement and Public Law Centre

In Sierra Leone, the NGO Timap for Justice employed ten paralegals in mid-2009 to work at police stations in three districts of Sierra Leone; today it employs 58.[109] Timap reaches and assists over half of all arrestees who come through the police stations in its three target districts. Over a one year period in 2011-2012, the paralegals provided assistance to 5,781 people in police stations. They succeeded in securing police bail in half of the cases. In addition, they succeeded in getting the charges dropped entirely in 28 percent of the cases, usually due to mistakes of identity, misunderstandings of facts, or lack of evidence.[110] Timap is thus successful in securing release—either without charge or on bail—for approximately 80 percent of the people its paralegals assist in police stations.

**Legal Practitioners' Role at the**

## Remand Hearing and at Court

Legal advice and assistance at remand hearings can have a significant impact on the pretrial detention population, both in terms of the number of people in pretrial detention and the time spent in pretrial detention. For example, data from the United States show that defendants in Baltimore, Maryland, who were given legal representation were required to provide about a third less bail, were significantly more likely to be released on their own recognizance, and spent significantly less time in pretrial detention before final disposition of their cases than unrepresented defendants.[111]

An experiment in a German court district revealed that the early assignment of defense counsel—at the remand hearing before the beginning of trial—resulted in average pretrial detention periods two months shorter compared to those defendants who did not have access to a lawyer. The systematic assignment of lawyers during the remand hearing stage and beyond, it was concluded, reduced the average time spent in pretrial detention by 16 percent.[112]

A legal practitioner who has interviewed an unrepresented detainee before a court hearing can advise the detainee about the right to apply for bail (if applicable in the legal system) and how to present facts that are relevant to such an application, such as the names of relatives who may be able to raise bail deposits or act as sureties. Even in systems that do not generally permit non-lawyers to speak for litigants at a pretrial hearing, pragmatic judicial officers may often allow a paralegal to speak for an indigent defendant on matters of bail.[113]

Paralegals can improve the quality of self-representation among defendants, especially during the pretrial phase of the criminal justice process. Awareness-raising and education on self-representation, demystifying the court processes through role playing, and providing expertise about the bail process and the grounds on which judicial officers typically base their pretrial release decisions all perform this function. As a result, defendants become more active players and partners in the administration of justice, typically resulting in more successful bail applications at court. This, in turn, may help to check corruption in the criminal justice institutions. Knowledge of the processes and procedures of the criminal justice system by the public reduces vulnerability to manipulation and extortion of money by corrupt officials.[114]

## Legal Practitioners' Role at Prison

Lawyers and paralegals can assist detained defendants who never received bail in preparing and lodging bail applications. They can train prisoners individually to prepare bail applications or offer group workshops to inform remand prisoners about court procedures, court etiquette, and their options for gaining representation by a lawyer or acting for themselves. Just as contacting detainees' relatives at the police station has proven invaluable to people who might have no other means of contact, lawyers and paralegals offering assistance in prison can contact relatives and other sources of help with bail.

As part of their prison-based work, legal practitioners typically seek to identify pretrial detainees whose remand warrants have expired, who have been in pretrial detention longer than the statutory maximum allows, who wish to plead guilty, and who are terminally ill. These identifications can lead to release, changing the conditions of bail, granting bail where it was previously refused, setting a new trial date, accepting a guilty plea, or discharging a matter. Between 2007 and September 2011, PASI paralegals in Malawi facilitated 91 camp courts in which magistrates visited prisons and addressed cases, resulting in 1,490 successful bail applications, 603 cases where charges against the defendants were withdrawn, and 858 cases where either a new court date was set or the duration of the remand warrant extended.[115]

In a number of African countries, paralegals conduct regular prison-based clincs aimed primarily at guiding pretrial detainees to apply the law in their own case. The paralegals use a range of participatory learning and forum theatre techniques, including role plays, games, and songs, that enable detainees to, for instance, apply for bail, make a plea in mitigation (should they wish to plead guilty), cross-examine witnesses and police officers, and make an appeal.

In 2008, the Bangladesh Ministry of Home Affairs and the Prison Directorate initiated a project to reduce the country's pretrial detention population, including a scheme to bring a group of paralegals to three prisons. Paralegals in this project gather information on the legal status of pretrial detainees and then present this information to a judge or lawyer and request the appropriate action. The paralegals also hold clinics in prison to educate pretrial detainees on basic legal procedures, from arrest to appeal, so that detainees can apply criminal law and procedures in their own cases if they lack the means to engage legal assistance. Paralegals also provide assistance to locate pretrial detainees' family members.

Bangladesh's paralegals also work with prison officers to screen and filter pretrial detainees whose cases require attention, typically because legal time-limits have been exceeded or bail is appropriate. From time to time, paralegals target groups such as pretrial detainees charged with homicide whose cases seem to have stalled in the criminal justice process and assist the authorities to push these cases along quicker.

Between 2008, when the Bangladesh project launched, and early 2012, paralegals have succeeded in obtaining the release of almost 2,000 pretrial detainees. Moreover, in two of the project prisons, all pretrial detainees under the age of 18 years had been released by April 2012.[116]

In Kenya, Muslims for Human Rights (MUHURI), an NGO that provides paralegal services to defendants, has offices inside a number of prisons, which are open every weekday. Overcoming initial resistance by pretrial detainees and prison wardens, both of whom suspected paralegals of intending to report on them, MUHURI's paralegals provide basic legal advice and legal aid clinics, and contact relatives and counsel for detainees. They also monitor respect for human rights at the prisons they visit, making impromptu cell visits and reporting concerns to their own leadership for follow-up with senior prison administrators.

The role for legal practitioners in addressing the excessive use of pretrial detention is broad, especially in places where laws intended to limit detention might not be enforced without oversight, and where defendants might not be able to afford counsel. Paralegals clearly represent a powerful tool in many jurisdictions, and programs using them should be expanded.

# GOVERNMENT PROGRAMS THAT REDUCE PRETRIAL DETENTION

A number of programs implemented by criminal justice agencies in countries around the world have effectively reduced the use of pretrial detention. This section presents interventions that decrease pretrial detention at the point of arrest, interventions involving prosecutors, interventions involving courts and judicial officers, and interventions held at prisons and remand centers.

## Interventions at the Point of Arrest

Police summons and police bail both can have the effect of decreasing pretrial detention. The first alleviates the need to arrest a suspect, book him at the station, and then hold him just to appear in court and get a court date. The second requires arrest and booking, but eliminates detention afterward, releasing the arrestee on bail.

### Police Summons

In many cases where offenses are minor, empowering police to issue a summons rather than make an arrest is effective and appropriate. It saves police time and resources and, crucially, reduces the number of people detained in a police lockup before their first court appearance.[117]

> **A.B.A. Standards: Components of an Effective Citation Release Process**[118]
>
> The American Bar Association (A.B.A.) pretrial release standards encourage the use of summons in cases involving minor offenses. The standards state: "[A] police officer who has grounds to arrest a person for a minor offense should be required to issue a citation in lieu of taking the person to the police station or to court. In determining whether an offense is minor, the police officer should consider whether the alleged crime involved the use or threatened use of force or violence, possession of a weapon, or violation of a court order protecting the safety of persons or property."
>
> A.B.A. stipulates the need for:
>
> › Accurate and reliable information by the police about the identity, background, and living situation of the person being considered for a citation.
>
> › Workable criteria for determining eligibility for citation release.
>
> › Training of law enforcement to make informed decisions regarding citation release.
>
> › Minimizing the period of time between the issuance of the citation and the defendant's first scheduled court date.
>
> › The capacity for rapid response to track defendants who miss their first court date.

In 2011, the U.S. state of Kentucky required police to issue a summons for dozens of minor offenses, such as possession of marijuana or drug paraphernalia, as long as police believe the suspect is no danger to himself or others and will appear in court to answer the charge. Advocates argued for the change based on likely cost savings.

The U.S. city of New Orleans implemented a similar measure in mid-2008, making the use of a summons mandatory for most cases of nonviolent municipal offenses. The effect was dramatic: the portion of people suspected of committing offenses in this category given a summons, instead of being arrested and held, increased from less than 25 percent to 41 percent in 2009 and 68 percent by late 2010, as the graph below shows.

FIGURE 1:

Changes in the proportion of summons issued versus arrests for suspected infringements of the New Orleans Municipal Code, 2008-2010*

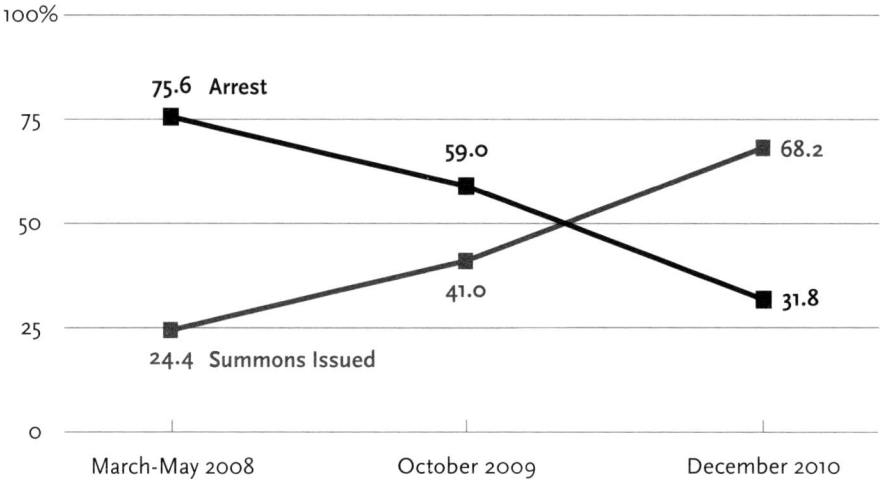

* Excluding public intoxication and domestic violence.

Requiring the police to issue a citation in lieu of an arrest for minor offenses saves police resources and lowers pretrial detention. These police-empowering programs should be expanded around the world.

**Police Bail**

Empowering police to release suspects on bail, either before or after charging them, rather than detaining them in custody until a judge can set bail also decreases pretrial detention.[119] These programs require defendants either to report back to the police station or appear at a magistrates' court on a particular date. In practice this means that defendants, once charged and bailed, must appear at the local magistrates' court for a first hearing.

England and Wales have police bail programs. "Custody officers," police officers of at least sergeant rank, decide whether defendants detained at a police station should be released, continue to be detained, charged, or bailed. The program seeks to make custody officers independent of the investigative process, and therefore less incentivized to make sure that a particular suspect will be present at trial at any cost to suspects and the taxpayer. Their role is to protect the rights and welfare of suspects and evaluate any evidence that releasing a defendant could result in damage to evidence or failure to appear at trial. They can make bail conditional or unconditional, and have relatively free rein in setting conditions, but must stipulate the reasons for conditions in the custody record. Arrestees can appeal to magistrates' courts to vary the conditions of their police bail.

This program effectively prevents unnecessary detention in England and Wales, as the release of 86 percent of arrestees on bail before their first court appearance in 2001 reflects.[120] A similar program in South Africa has had less success, according to research findings from a study conducted in three large South African courts during 2007, which found that only three percent of suspects and defendants were granted bail on or before their first court appearance. South Africa's program places more restrictions on release, and a 1996 decision in which the Constitutional Court declined to list the factors that should be present in the denial of bail appears to have set a tone.[121]

The success of police bail in England and Wales suggests that additional jurisdictions should establish such programs; South Africa's example suggests that the design of the program and the guidance given to police and prosecutors will determine the success of police bail in decreasing pretrial detention.

## Interventions Involving Prosecutors

Prosecutors' role in decreasing pretrial detention can occur through prosecutorial discretion, early engagement of prosecutorial offices, and changes in prosecutorial policy.

### Prosecutorial Discretion

Prosecutorial discretion can be a powerful mechanism to reduce the number of people entering the criminal justice system, and thereby the number of pretrial detainees and courts' caseloads. In some civil law jurisdictions, prosecutors have very little discretion; an investigating judge makes the decision to prosecute after a preliminary inquiry, or law requires that every case be prosecuted where sufficient evidence exists to do so. In other civil law systems the prosecutor has discretion to prosecute, to dispose of a case upon the fulfillment of conditions by the accused person, or not to proceed at all. Some civil law systems grant this discretion on a limited basis. In common law systems, exercising discretion whether to prosecute is generally a key function of the office of the public prosecutor. The exercise of discretion may depend on a range of factors over and above the adequacy of evidence.

Most jurisdictions involve some prosecutorial discretion in the decisions as to whether to recommend the release of a suspect on bail, whether to make a plea offer to a lesser charge, or whether to allow a person to be diverted from the formal justice process, though these latter two issues require judicial approval in some countries.[122]

The *U.N. Guidelines on the Role of Prosecutors* requires a legal or regulatory framework that guides the exercise of discretion to ensure fairness and consistency.[123] Moreover, reform strategies that aim to reduce the size of the pretrial detention population should consider:[124]

- increasing prosecutorial discretion to divert suitable cases away from the criminal justice system;
- introducing guidelines and enhancing the training of prosecutors to exercise their discretionary powers appropriately;
- developing tools for the prosecution services to assess suitability for diversion; and
- providing guidance and information to prosecutors on community programs to which offenders may be diverted.

### U.N. Guidelines on the Role of Prosecutors: Alternatives to Prosecution[125]

The Eighth United Nations Congress on the Prevention of Crime and the Treatment of Offenders issued the following guidelines on the role of prosecutors in finding alternatives to prosecution:

18. In accordance with national law, prosecutors shall give due consideration to waiving prosecution, discontinuing proceedings conditionally or unconditionally, or diverting criminal cases from the formal justice system, with full respect for the rights of suspect(s) and the victim(s). For this purpose, States should fully explore the possibility of adopting diversion schemes not only to alleviate excessive court loads, but also to avoid the stigmatization of pre-trial detention, indictment and conviction, as well as the possible adverse effects of imprisonment.

19. In countries where prosecutors are vested with discretionary functions as to the decision whether or not to prosecute a juvenile, special consideration shall be given to the nature and gravity of the offence, protection of society, and the personality and background of the juvenile. In making that decision, prosecutors shall particularly consider available alternatives to prosecution under the relevant juvenile justice laws and procedures. Prosecutors shall use their best efforts to take prosecutory action against juveniles only to the extent strictly necessary.

In Russia, the number of people in pretrial detention centers (SIZOs) declined consistently for the period 2005–2011. While a significant decrease in the number of defendants remanded into pretrial detention before trial and declining crime rates in general likely played the strongest role in the decrease, prosecutors may have also had a role.[126] Harvard researcher Todd Foglesong argues that prosecutors also became more discriminating in their assessment of the need for pretrial detention. Between 2005 and 2010, when the total number of suspects identified by the police fell 36 percent, the number of applications for detention fell 45 percent (Figure 2).

FIGURE 2:
Pretrial detention population and detention orders in Russia, 2003 – 2010

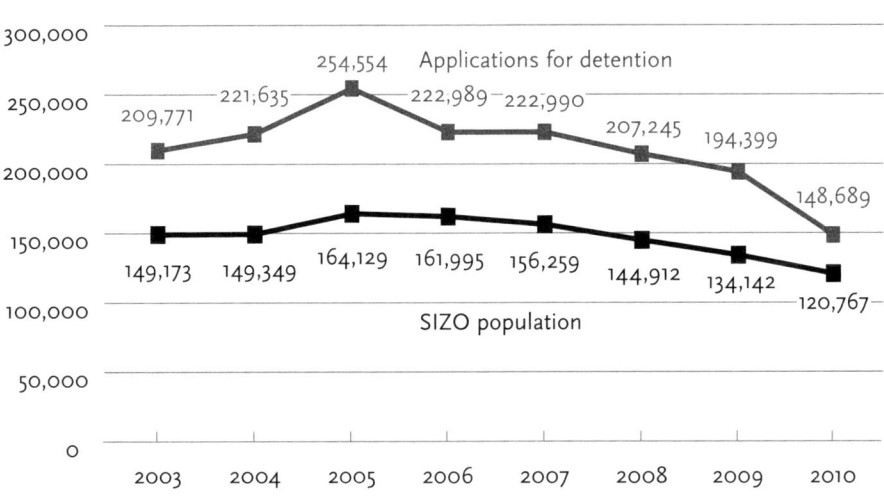

Sources: Russian Judicial Department and Federal Prison Service.

While prosecutorial discretion, when it competes with judicial discretion, doesn't always contribute to the liberalization of a system, it's clear that under the right circumstances giving prosecutors a role in reducing unnecessary detention can decrease its overuse. Experienced prosecutors, those with trial experience who know what a conviction will require, are well-equipped to screen cases and terminate the detention of anyone unlikely to be convicted of a charge.[127] A study of defendants charged with serious crimes in the 75 largest U.S. counties found that prosecutors drop 23 percent of all felony cases; clearly, the dropping of charges will decrease pretrial detention.[128]

### Early Engagement by the Prosecutor's Office

The sooner a prosecutor has the opportunity to review a case for its suitability to go to trial, the more this review will decrease pretrial detention. The national standards of the National District Attorneys Association in the United States provide that its members, prosecutors who work at the local and state level, have the responsibility to screen cases "at the earliest practical time."[129] Sensitive to the fact that inexperienced prosecutors may have difficulty assessing a case's merit, it further stipulates that prosecutor offices should provide training and guidance to the lawyer assigned this task.

The U.S. city of Philadelphia launched a number of interventions in 2008 to reduce its pretrial detention population, following an increase by 50 percent between 2000 and 2008. Prosecutors had a strong role in each measure, beginning with a change in the formulation of charges. Early in 2010, prosecution offices began to stipulate charges according to the available evidence—that is, what could be proven in court—replacing the practice of formulating the highest charge police allegations would support. The head of the prosecution offices' Pretrial Division described the new approach thus: "[In the past] if a fact pattern read that someone had smashed a store window, the lead charge likely would have been burglary, and the bail magistrate would have set bail consistent with that charge, when, without further proof of intent to commit a crime inside, that case probably would have ended in a verdict supporting vandalism. Now, without further proof of burglary, we would decline the burglary charge and charge vandalism only."[130] Because Philadelphia judges use the most serious charge facing a defendant to determine bail, this had a direct effect on rates of release.[131]

Prosecutors and defendants also began to participate in a discovery court dedicated to working out discovery issues prior to trial. The U.S. discovery procedure involves the exchange of information between the prosecutor and accused person (or her counsel) in a criminal matter prior to trial, and the process had become a major contributor to the length of the trial process in Philadelphia. Without key evidence, the prosecution could not assess a case and make a plea offer, and the defense was unable to respond. Within a year of opening the discovery court, the proportion of cases in trial court that had incomplete discovery dropped from 61 percent in 2009 to 21 percent in 2010.[132]

Philadelphia's pretrial detention population shrank by more than 10 percent, from 9,231 in 2009 to 8,273 in 2010. In October 2010, the city launched an initiative entitled Strategic Management Advance Review and Consolidation Readiness and Trial (S.M.A.R.T.). Under the program, prosecutors began providing defendants with a relatively early plea offer—the best he can expect to receive—in support of early finalization of the case. According to the supervising judge of the trial division of the Philadelphia criminal trial courts, "The [S.M.A.R.T.] offers are more reasonable and based on what actually can be proven. The assistant district attorneys are now giving the best offer sooner. As a result, pleas are up."[133] In November and December 2010, the trial courts accepted 2,026 guilty pleas, compared with 1,363 for the same two months in 2009. Moreover, 47 percent of cases were resolved within six months in 2010, up from 39 percent in 2009.[134]

Prosecutors' role in determining which cases should go to trial has the potential to reduce pretrial detention, and actions that speed prosecutors' involvement tend to speed the process of ending such detention.

**Prosecutorial Policy**

Given the significance of prosecutors in determining pretrial detention, prosecutorial policy should instruct prosecutors to request the detention of defendants awaiting trial in a sparing manner and to deal with cases involving pretrial detainees expeditiously. The ethics code for prosecutors in South Africa, for example, reminds prosecutors that they should not oppose the release of detained defendants if the interest of justice so permits, and that prosecutors have a constitutional obligation to ensure trials proceed without unreasonable delay. Moreover, cases where the defendant is in pretrial detention must receive preference, and bail applications and bail appeals should be "dealt with as a matter of urgency as the liberty of the accused is at stake."[135]

The South African prosecution service has also developed Awaiting Trial Detainee Guidelines, which contain detailed guidance on how prosecutors can reduce the use of pretrial detention and fast-track cases involving pretrial detainees. For example, guidelines encourage prosecutors to consider diversion and other restorative justice mechanisms as a means of avoiding prosecution and the unnecessary pretrial detention of defendants.[136]

In England and Wales, the Crown Prosecution Service has assumed significant responsibility around the management of maximum periods allowed for pretrial detention. Its National Standard for the Effective Management of Prosecution Cases Involving Custody Time Limits places responsibilities on prosecutors and their managers for managing the prosecution of pretrial detainees, for whose cases it designates Custody Time Limit (C.T.L.), including:[137]

> - Prosecutors must note the expiry date on the cover of documents filed in C.T.L. cases.
> - Duplicate monitoring systems, one electronic and one paper, must note the expiry date and where the responsibility for monitoring lies. In the event of a revision to the expiry date, it must appear in the systems within 24 hours.
> - Managers in prosecutorial offices must carry out a weekly check of the Case Management System diary to ensure adherence to the monitoring system and monitoring of all live C.T.L. cases.
> - Any C.T.L. file requiring action must be handed to a named prosecutor; it cannot be left on a desk.
> - In the event of the discontinuation of a C.T.L. case, the prosecutor's office must confirm the decision in writing immediately and send it to the court to speed release.

A number of policies contribute to a low rate of pretrial detention in England and Wales; these guidelines are certainly of value and countries around the world should adopt similar measures.

### Interventions Involving Courts and Judicial Officers

Entities such as the International Centre for Prison Studies have identified the allocation of political responsibility for prisons to the Ministry of Justice instead of the Ministry of the Interior (or Police/Public Security) as an important element in promoting reform of pretrial detention.[138] In a 2008 report they argue:

> Particular dangers can arise if there is not a clear distinction between the department responsible for the police and the administration of prisons. The police are responsible for investigating crime and arresting criminals. Once a person has been detained or arrested, he or she should as soon as possible appear before a judicial authority.
>
> If prisons are under the control of the police or within the same government department, there is a risk that investigating authorities may use pretrial detention as a tool of the investigative process or as a means to force prisoners to confess to the charges made against them.[139]

This potential for abuse points to the need to invest authority in judicial officers and the need to create strict guidelines for the police-led measures described above.

Judicial control over investigations and prosecutions has driven a decline in pretrial detention (and incarceration rates generally) in such places as Russia in the early twenty-first century. In this period Russia reformed the criminal procedure code to provide for judicial control over investigations and prosecutions. A significant decision shifted the power to place defendants in pretrial detention away from prosecutorial control and to the courts.[140]

Judicial officers also play a key role in the handling of individual decisions about pretrial detention. They typically make the final decision on release and conditions, including bail. It's important that judges assume the role of overseeing prosecution and police by reviewing—not rubber stamping—their recommendations. Pressure from the media and politicians to err on the side of detention makes this difficult, but training and support can counteract the problem. The right culture can prompt judicial officers to take a role in the founding of courts on prison grounds to handle simple matters, as described in the section on the role of prison personnel. India's more than a decade of alleviating pretrial detention in this manner was sparked by the actions of the country's chief justice in 1999. Judicial officers also have an important role to play in ensuring that such courts observe rules of evidence and due process.

A study of England and Wales' success in maintaining its low pretrial detention population credits a professional and experienced core of judicial officers that deal with pretrial decisions, noting the replacement of lay magistrates with district judges in many jurisdictions, and the resulting improvement in outcomes:

> District Judges are legally qualified, have greater presence and clout within courts and arguably have greater confidence in their decisions than the majority of magistrates. They also sit much more frequently than magistrates. Arguably, this means that they are more likely to take a chance and release defendants who pose bail risks. They are generally more knowledgeable about any initiatives in place in the courts which aim to divert defendants from custody. As a result they are more likely than magistrates to use such initiatives.[141]

States that support a knowledgeable base of judicial officers and provide options for conditional release will likely see improved management of their pretrial detention population.

**Pretrial Evaluation and Bail Support Services**
A number of countries have instituted pretrial evaluation and bail support services to rationalize the decision-making process regarding pretrial detention.[142] Pretrial evaluation and bail support services have two broad goals: First, to allow—to the maximum extent possible—pretrial release pending adjudication; and second, to assure that defendants appear in court to face their charges and ensure they do not pose a threat to the public.[143] While the scope and responsibilities of individual pretrial service programs vary, fully developed programs generally perform both evaluation and support services.[144]

Pretrial evaluation occurs in the period between the arrest and the hearing at which a judge makes the determination to either release or detain a defendant pretrial. The evaluation process identifies each arrestee's personal characteristics and any risk he may pose to the criminal process and society. Identifying the potential risks permits the criminal justice system's actors, including judges, prosecutors, and defenders, to make more rational pretrial decisions and recommendations and consider the most appropriate release conditions, reserving pretrial detention for exceptional cases where the risks cannot be managed by other means.

### England and Wales: Bail Information Schemes

England and Wales began using court-based bail information schemes in the early 1990s. They provided verified information to the prosecution service in cases where defendants were at risk of being remanded to pretrial detention, with the aim of persuading prosecutors that most defendants could be released to await trial. Evidence suggests that these schemes had some success in diverting defendants away from custodial remands.[145] Further, studies have documented that bail information makes prosecutors less likely to request a remand in custody, and the defense more likely to apply for bail.[146] However, these programs decreased significantly after the mid-1990s due to changes in funding.[147] As described below, the countries' schemes for juveniles have been quite successful.

Pretrial evaluation begins upon arrest and can be broken down into the following activities:

> *Collection of relevant information:* Information typically gathered on a defendant includes length of residence at past and present addresses, family ties and relationships in the community, employment status and history, financial conditions and means of support, and prior criminal record.[148] Interviews with defendants provide most of this information.

> *Verification of information:* Pretrial evaluation professionals verify information gathered in interviews, typically calibrating thoroughness to the seriousness of the charge and the nature of the information. Verifying defendants' identities, their addresses, and other locations where they can be reached after release is the top priority. Arresting officers, criminal record retrieval systems, family members, official documentation, and employers provide verification. The time and resources available to the person collecting information affects the nature of this process.

> *Risk assessment:* Analyzing the information assists the court in determining whether to release a defendant and whether to impose conditions. Risk assessments typically use instruments such as point scales or pretrial release guidelines that assign weights to variables such as the nature and seriousness of the crime charged, and a defendant's prior criminal record, employment status, housing situation, and family ties. Risk assessment scales should be evidence-based and regularly validated and refined.

> *Development of the opinion:* In addition to the information gathered and a score on a risk assessment scale, some pretrial evaluation services recommend a decision with respect to release and conditions. In many cases the person responsible for drafting the opinion attends hearings to answer queries that arise.

Evidence from a five year federal pilot study of pretrial evaluation schemes in the United States suggests that pretrial evaluation schemes not only reduce pretrial detention, but may also reduce the incidence of crime committed while on bail. In ten demonstration districts throughout the country, 90 percent of arrestees evaluated under the scheme were released awaiting trial but pretrial offending was cut in half.[149]

Most jurisdictions that offer pretrial information schemes also provide bail support (also called "bail supervision"). These services assist arrestees in completing their pretrial release period without re-offending or failing to appear in court.[150]

Released arrestees who miss a court appearance may do so because they do not know their date or forget it or willfully put it out of their minds. Bail support programs have developed innovative ways—such as posting or emailing reminder letters, telephoning arrestees on the morning of their court appearances, and providing a written note with the next court date to the arrestee at every court appearance—to get arrestees to appear in court on the due date.

Supervising arrestees in between court dates to curtail re-offending or witness tampering may involve linking participants with social services such as drug treatment, education and training, job development, housing services, and family counseling.[151] Providing a rigid structure to an arrestee's daily activities can redirect him. These services may involve weekly appointments with a pretrial services officer, which give the state a mechanism to identify absconded arrestees in advance of a court date. Many programs provide bail support to arrestees who would suffer particular hardship in pretrial detention, such as juveniles, single parents, and those with mental health problems.

General principles of best practice for bail support programs garnered from the international literature include:[152]

> arrestees must be able to choose between bail support and pretrial detention;
> programs should emphasize support and intervention over supervision and monitoring;
> a holistic approach, with a broad needs assessment and response, providing information, support, and intervention as required;
> coordination between criminal justice agencies and social support agencies, to provide access to pathways across different service systems; and
> programs must be adaptable and responsive to local conditions.

Programs such as the Pretrial Services Agency for the District of Columbia in Washington D.C. reflect at least some of these principles. It interviews about 20,000 defendants for risk assessment purposes per year and provides supervision services for some 12,000 defendants released awaiting trial annually. The agency calls for the use of the least restrictive conditions of pretrial release to reasonably assure public safety and appearance in court, the use of detention when those assurances cannot be met, and the sparing use of financial bail.

Since its beginning in 1963, the agency has succeeded in reducing the use of money bail. The agency and its staff have persuaded the courts to release defendants on their own recognizance or some other non-pecuniary condition or, where the courts are concerned about an arrestee's likelihood of failing to appear, by providing supervision as part of the condition of release. The proportion of arrestees released without money bail increased from zero in 1962 to 80 percent in 2008, as shown below (Figure 3). In 2008, 15 percent of defendants were held without bail and only 5 percent were granted money bail.[153]

FIGURE 3:

Proportion of defendants granted pretrial release on non-financial conditions, selected years 1962 – 2008, Washington D.C.

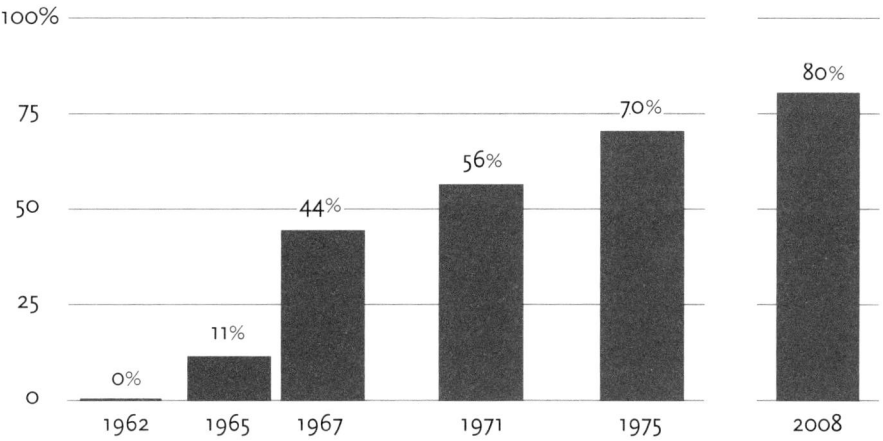

Mexico began making pretrial services available to juveniles in 2011. A Mexican NGO, the *Proyecto Presunción de Inocencia en México* (Presumption of Innocence Project) in close collaboration with the state government of Morelos, the Unidad de Medidas Cautelares para Adolescentes (Supervisory Measures Unit for Juveniles, UMECA) provides risk evaluation and bail support services for juvenile defendants in Morelos. UMECA's trained professionals provide risk assessment and supervision to defendants deemed safe to release but at relatively high risk. Based on the program's success, Morelos introduced similar services for adult offenders, and a number of additional Mexican states, including Baja California, have announced intentions to follow suit.[154]

The three key objectives of England and Wales' joint effort to provide bail supervision and support to juveniles are to reduce the use of pretrial detention, increase defendants' attendance at court, and reduce offending on bail. The program stipulates that defendants who would otherwise be granted bail without supervision or released on their own recognizance without any condition should not receive its services.[155]

A review of bail supervision and support schemes for juveniles across the United Kingdom, including those operating in Scotland and Ireland, concludes that only 20 percent of juveniles on bail supervision and support schemes fail to abide by the conditions of their release. Approximately 30 percent of defendants not given bail supervision had similar failures. These results suggest supervision is highly effective, because the unsupervised group had a lower risk assessment than the supervised group.[156] A separate review undertaken by the Youth Justice Board of the Ministry of Justice for England and Wales found that, over a two-year period, 94 percent of juveniles on bail supervision programs attended all the hearings relating to the matters for which they had been placed on a bail program. While baseline data for appearance rates prior to the introduction of the scheme are not available, the study notes that "where individual schemes have provided information the results are encouraging...the indications are that the level of offending on bail can be lower where young people are provided with adequate support and supervision, that keeps them active and focused, than without."[157]

A small Scottish study that evaluated an experimental bail supervision scheme for young people aged 16 to 25 in Edinburgh and Glasgow found that 18 percent of young people on the Edinburgh scheme committed offenses while on the program, compared to 27 percent of those not receiving supervision. Similarly, in Glasgow 33 percent of those on bail supervision programs offended, compared to 40 percent of those on bail who had not received services. As in England and Wales, the groups had not been assigned randomly and those on supervision had been deemed high risk; many of them had previously offended on bail.[158]

Preliminary research on bail supervision programs in the United States has also been positive.[159] One study found that in the Southern District of Iowa a concerted effort to increase pretrial service interviews and risk assessments led to a 16 percent increase in the identification of arrestees appropriate for release and a 15 percent increase in the pretrial release rate. The court appearance rate increased by 2.6 percent while pretrial criminal activity fell 1.7 percent and revocations of release pending trial due to technical violations fell 2.8 percent. An independent review of the effort concluded that "the project was successful in its goal of utilizing alternatives to detention when appropriate to increase pretrial release rates while assuring court appearance and community safety."[160]

Another study randomly assigned arrestees charged in three U.S. counties to be released under supervision. Ninety percent of these individuals were not rearrested and made all court appearances. In both measures the group outperformed arrestees who had been released without supervision, including the group deemed sufficiently low risk to be released on their own recognizance with no conditions.[161]

A study of bail supervision programs for adult arrestees in three counties in New York found that intensive supervision was very effective in preventing flight and re-arrest.[162] At one of the program sites, while eight percent of people on intensive supervision were rearrested whilst on pretrial release and three percent failed to appear or absconded, 51 percent of people released without supervisions failed to appear at trial or absconded, and 42 percent were re-arrested before trial.[163]

Given the positive findings about pretrial supervision programs, their expansion throughout the world has the potential to improve pretrial detention rates and improve public safety.

## Interventions Benefiting Detainees at Prisons and Remand Centers

Officials at prison and remand centers have a role to play in shortening the time between arrest and trial through camp courts, and in obtaining pretrial release after a remand to custody. Both will have an overall effect of decreasing pretrial detention.

### Camp Courts

Many factors cause delays in bringing prisoners to court. Fuel shortage can prevent transport from prison to court in Malawi[164] and vehicle and personnel shortages have prevented transport in India. One study found that only 62 percent of pretrial detainees from the Bangalore Central Prison were produced in court on their remand date during the course of 2007.[165] Camp courts, which bring the court to the prison to handle simple procedural matters such as bail applications, guilty pleas on minor charges, or for the dismissal of cases for multiple detainees at a time, can address these problems.

A program in Liberia has focused since 2009 on Monrovia Central Prison, which houses the vast majority of Liberia's pretrial detainees. Magistrates from six magisterial courts around Monrovia visit the prison to hold pretrial hearings six days a week, with one visiting each day. The courts release detainees who have been in detention for longer than their possible custodial sentence and withdraw charges where case files have gone missing or where the police's case has weakened (e.g. because a crucial witness has disappeared or changed his testimony). Liberia's total prison population at any one time is around 1,500 inmates, of which 85–95 percent are pretrial detainees. Over the course of about a year and a half, some 1,500 pretrial detainees gained release through the program.[166]

In early 2012 the state governor of the Nigerian state of Ondo commissioned Nigeria's first court to be built on prison premises. The court is to be built at Olokuta Prison in the state capital of Akure, which holds four times the detainees for which it was designed, the vast majority of them pretrial detainees.[167]

India has held *jail adalats* (literally "prison court") frequently since 1999. A review of 73 Indian prisons and sub-jails found that *jail adalats* disposed of over 5,000 cases over a one year period (Table 8).[168] A review of monthly camp courts in Bihar, India, shows that they have been highly effective at reducing the backlog of bailable cases and other simple criminal cases. On one occasion, camp courts held all over the state disposed of 5,383 petty criminal cases on a single Saturday.

TABLE 8:

**Frequency and disposal rate of *jail adalats*, April 2007 – March 2008, selected Indian prisons**[169]

| State / territory | No. jail adalats held | No. cases referred by prisons | No. cases disposed of | Disposal rate (%) |
|---|---|---|---|---|
| Delhi | 23 | 736 | 436 | 59.2% |
| Andhra Pradesh | 58 | 3,544 | 1,874 | 52.9% |
| Chhattisgarh | 68 | 580 | 208 | 35.9% |
| Jharkhand | 8 | 145 | 76 | 52.4% |
| Maharashtra | 33 | 638 | 405 | 63.5% |
| Karnataka | 8 | 136 | 136 | 100.0% |
| Tamil Nadu | 143 | 3,734 | 580 | 15.5% |
| Uttar Pradesh | 78 | 4,405 | 1,407 | 31.9% |
| Total | 419 | 13,918 | 5,122 | 36.8% |

It's important that camp courts not decrease pretrial detention at the expense of justice, however. Because *jail adalats* can convict defendants who plead guilty to minor offenses, human rights advocates have expressed concern about their procedural correctness.

> Those opposed to *jail adalats* argue that these courts are not just. They are short in procedure and exploit the vulnerability of the poor prisoners. Those who have the means are released on bail and the poor are given a dubious choice. They can stay in prison and await a trial for months or years, or they can opt to confess and be released after recording a conviction for the period (of imprisonment already) undergone.[170]

These concerns underscore the need to ensure that there are clear and enforceable procedures which dictate the process by which *jail adalats*—and camp courts more generally—are conducted. Moreover, judicial officers running such proceedings should be extra vigilant in ensuring that any confessions of guilt are made voluntarily and are supported by the evidence the state has garnered against individual arrestees.

**Second Appearance Schemes**

The prison service in England and Wales operates "second appearance schemes" to identify defendants who have been remanded in pretrial detention once they are received into prison. Second appearance schemes prepare reports containing verified information on defendants for their second appearance. The scheme aims to obtain pretrial release for eligible defendants and thereby prevent them from being remanded back into detention at their second court appearance. Prison-based schemes limit the potential for net-widening, but they also have a limited scope.[171] The program in England and Wales causes the release on bail of about six percent of people on the basis of bail information provided in prison.[172]

Prisons offer the last opportunity to shorten pretrial detention, but programs based in them can be quite powerful and should be adopted worldwide.

# CONCLUSION

Many countries use pretrial detention excessively due to a lack of recognition of the value of reform from the highest levels—including ministries, the parliament and executive bodies—on down to the electorate. Judges, prosecutors, and police may feel public pressure prevents them from using alternatives to detention.[173]

It is consequently important to engage with, and raise the awareness of, politicians and decision makers about the negative consequences of the excessive and arbitrary use of pretrial detention, and to address concerns, including public opinion and public safety, they may have about reducing the use of detention. Reform efforts must define the problems associated with the excessive use of pretrial detention as both solvable and politically palatable.

Criminal justice actors such as the police, prosecution, and judiciary should be involved in the development of strategies and programs such as those outlined above. They should receive practical trainings on diversion, alternatives to pretrial detention, criminal justice coordination and caseflow management, and on good practices worldwide and the potential benefits of improved practices. A consultative process will generate commitment and support by all key actors and, consequently, sustainability.[174] Representatives of civil society, including victims' support organizations, should be involved in the consultative process, to increase public acceptance, understanding, and involvement.

Public awareness activities to engender broader support for pretrial justice reform are an important component of generating societal consensus.[175] In many jurisdictions—arguably an increasing number as democratic regimes have grown in the post-Cold War era—the public has considerable influence on the determination of criminal justice policies by politicians, as well as on courts' determinations as to pretrial release. The public should consequently be informed about the harmful consequences of excessive and irrational pretrial detention and the purpose and justification of rights-based reforms. Much of the public's and politicians' support for draconian pretrial detention practices comes from the belief that detention is an effective way of dealing with crime. Providing basic facts about pretrial detention—for example, that the majority of pretrial detainees are typically suspected of committing minor offenses or that many pretrial detainees will end up being acquitted of the charges against them—can change the public's view of pretrial release. To this end, the public should have accurate data and reformers must nurture the cooperation of the media.

This chapter has offered a number of measures which have effectively reduced pretrial detention in jurisdictions around the world. As works both scholarly and policy-related have noted, criminal justice reform, such as reforming policies that lead to excessive pretrial detention, fail when local conditions and contexts are not taken into consideration. Interventions which show much promise in one or more places may not succeed at all in others.[176]

To succeed, reformers must adapt the programs described herein to the particular history and culture of the target community. For instance, in countries where tension with indigenous groups has led to political unrest, civil war, and widespread human rights abuses by the military, criminal procedure reforms must take account of how the system had previously acted as a tool for the oppression of ethnic minorities. Similarly, in societies historically plagued by injustice and inequality, inclusion of a broad sector of society and a more bottom-up approach will likely prove critical to meaningful reform.[177] It's clear, however, that reform can be achieved, and that the benefits will extend to every level of society.

# Conclusion

The global overuse of pretrial detention is a massive, if largely unnoticed, form of human rights abuse. It directly affects at least 15 million people each year, many of whom will wait months or even years—in conditions worse than those experienced by sentenced prisoners—for their day in court. Many more people are indirectly affected: they suffer from a spouse's lost income or a parent's absence; they spend money and time on jail visits or food and blankets for the detainee; they contract HIV or hepatitis C from the detainee upon his release. Broader society is also affected by the overuse of pretrial detention, in the form of wasted human potential, lost productivity, the spread of disease, and the misuse of state resources.

Excessive and arbitrary pretrial detention is not just a human rights violation, but also the nexus of other abuses and ill effects. The overuse of pretrial detention is linked to torture, corruption, and the spread of disease; it stunts economic development and undermines the rule of law.

These bad outcomes are entirely avoidable.

The international and regional standards and norms are clear: a person is to be presumed innocent until proven guilty and—except in rare instances—should be released pending trial. Simply put, many of those held in pretrial detention pose no threat to society and should not be there. Yet in the developed and developing world alike, pretrial detention remains the default setting of most criminal justice systems.

As this report has sought to document, reform is possible. Pretrial detention can be reduced, saving state resources—and upholding the law—without risking public safety.

Perhaps most shocking is not the extent or cost of this particular form of rights abuse, or the fact that it persists despite clear prohibition. What is most shocking is how little attention it receives and how little is known about it. The writing of this report required years of research by a large team of people, since no single source provides a thorough picture. Indeed, information about pretrial detention, its scope, causes, and effects, is scattered across hundreds of NGO papers, UN reports, government databases, and witness accounts. This report represents the first effort to paint a comprehensive portrait of the problem.

In fact this report is, if nothing else, a plea for further investigation of and attention to the global overuse of pretrial detention—an enormous, overlooked, and easily remedied human rights violation.

# Appendix: International and Regional Standards, Norms, and Jurisprudence

Following is an overview of key international and regional norms, standards, and jurisprudence addressing limitations on, and the grounds for, pretrial detention. That is, this appendix examines the limited circumstances under which pretrial detention can be justified, and the many circumstances under which it should not be used. This section does not address the norms, standards, and jurisprudence regarding conditions of pretrial detention.[1]

## INTERNATIONAL STANDARDS, NORMS, AND JURISPRUDENCE

The guarantee of personal liberty is a key element in the protection of human rights to which virtually all states have committed themselves, both legally and politically, at global and regional levels. It is a consistent feature of the numerous international and regional treaties, standards, and norms discussed below that any deprivation of liberty should always be objectively justified and should last only so long as this can be demonstrated as necessary under carefully circumscribed circumstances.[2]

International human rights treaties emphasize the important distinction between people who have been found guilty, convicted by a court of law and sentenced to prison, and those who have not. Prisoners awaiting trial or the outcome of their trial are regarded differently because the law sees them as innocent until found guilty. Underpinning the legal considerations of the applicability of pretrial detention are the right to liberty[3] and the presumption of innocence.[4]

Pretrial detention is covered by several international human rights treaties. Article 9(3) of the International Covenant on Civil and Political Rights states that:

> Anyone arrested or detained on a criminal charge shall be brought promptly before a judge or other officer authorized by law to exercise judicial power and shall be entitled to trial within a reasonable time or to release. It shall not be the general rule that persons awaiting trial shall be detained in custody, but release may be subject to guarantees to appear for trial.[5]

The UN Body of Principles for the Protection of all Persons under any form of Detention or Imprisonment elaborates this further:[6]

> Except in special cases provided for by law, a person detained on a criminal charge shall be entitled, unless a judicial or other authority decides otherwise in the interest of the administration of justice, to release pending trial subject to the conditions that may be imposed in accordance with the law. Such authority shall keep the necessity of detention under review.

Similarly, the UN Standard Minimum Rules for Non-custodial Measures (the "Tokyo Rules"), provide that:[7]

- pretrial detention shall be used as a means of last resort in criminal proceedings, with due regard for the investigation of the alleged offense and for the protection of society and the victim;
- alternatives to pretrial detention shall be employed at as early a stage as possible;
- pretrial detention shall last no longer than necessary and shall be administered humanely and with respect for the inherent dignity of human beings; and
- the offender shall have the right to appeal to a judicial or other competent independent authority in cases where pretrial detention is employed.

International standards permit detention before trial under certain, limited circumstances only.

In 1990, the Eighth UN Congress on the Prevention of Crime and the Treatment of Offenders established a two-part test for the application of pretrial detention.[8] First, to overcome the right to liberty there must be grounds to believe that the individual committed the offense(s) under investigation. That is, there must be a reasonable suspicion. Second, because this criterion alone is not enough to legitimize pretrial detention, one of the following grounds must also apply: risk of the suspect absconding, risk of the suspect committing further serious offenses, and risk of the suspect interfering with the administration of justice.[9]

Although international standards provide for the legitimate use of pretrial detention, there are circumstances in which its ostensible legitimate use becomes a violation of the right to liberty and the presumption of innocence. In its consideration of state reports, the UN Human Rights Committee[10] has noted that in certain circumstances pretrial detention may not be consistent with the presumption of innocence. For example, pretrial detention should not be permitted if the duration is excessive, or is set according to the length of sentence if guilt is established, or if it is applied automatically.[11]

According to the UN Human Rights Committee, pretrial detention should be used only where it is lawful, reasonable, and necessary. Detention may be necessary "to prevent flight, interference with evidence or the recurrence of crime," or "where the person concerned constitutes a clear and serious threat to society which cannot be contained in any other manner."[12]

The UN Human Rights Committee has also ruled that pretrial detention cannot be arbitrary: "The notion or 'arbitrariness' is not to be equated with 'against the law,' but must be interpreted more broadly to include elements of inappropriateness, injustice, lack of predictability and due process of law."[13] As a result, pretrial detention "must not only be lawful but reasonable and necessary in all the circumstances."[14]

The seriousness of the alleged offense with which the defendant is charged is often used by courts as a justification for pretrial detention. However, while it may be a factor to take into consideration, it cannot alone justify pretrial detention. The Eighth UN Crime Congress laid out a number of other factors that may be taken into consideration when deciding whether or not to detain an individual pending trial:

> In considering whether pre-trial detention should be ordered, account should be taken of the circumstances of the individual case, in particular the nature and seriousness of the alleged offence, the strength of the evidence, the penalty likely to be incurred, and the conduct and personal and social circumstances of the person concerned, including his or her community ties.[15]

In its jurisprudence, the UN Human Rights Committee has emphasized that domestic authorities must interrogate whether less restrictive measures than pretrial detention, such as bail and other conditions attached to pretrial release, can adequately secure the attendance of defendants at trial. Pretrial detention must be satisfactorily explained and supported by factual information. Vague and unsubstantiated assertions are insufficient. Moreover, a state cannot assume that a defendant will abscond, tamper with evidence, or obstruct the investigation of the case based on passive reasons, such as the foreign nationality of the defendant. Any risks associated with the pretrial release of a defendant must be investigated fully by the state.[16]

# REGIONAL STANDARDS, NORMS, AND JURISPRUDENCE

### Africa

The African Charter on Human and Peoples' Rights provides that "[e]very individual shall have the right to have his cause heard."[17] This includes the right to be presumed innocent until proven guilty by a competent court or tribunal; the right to defense, including the right to be defended by counsel of one's choice; and the "right to be tried within a reasonable time by an impartial court or tribunal."[18]

The African Charter, moreover, holds that "every individual shall have the right to liberty and to the security of his person. No one may be deprived of his freedom except for reasons and conditions previously laid down by law. In particular, no one may be arbitrarily arrested or detained."[19]

As support for these rights the African Commission on Human and Peoples' Rights[20] cites its "Resolution on the Right to Recourse and Fair Trial"[21] which states: "[p]ersons arrested or detained shall be brought promptly before a judge or other officer authorised by law to exercise judicial power and shall be entitled to trial within a reasonable time or to be released."[22]

The African Commission has stated that the requirements of a tribunal include "fairness, openness, and justice, independence, and due process."[23] A detainee must have "recourse to national courts" to challenge detention.[24]

The African Commission has held that "a military tribunal *per se* is not offensive," but warned of the lack of independence of the process when the military tribunal is under an "undemocratic military regime" in which the military has subsumed the authority of the executive and the legislature.[25] The tribunal must not only be impartial, but must also have the appearance of being impartial. In *Amnesty International and Others v. Sudan* in which national legislation permitted the president, his deputies and senior military officer to appoint individuals to special courts, the commission held that "[t]he composition alone creates the impression, if not the reality, of lack of impartiality."[26]

The African Commission has little jurisprudence determining what classifies as arbitrary detention. The commission held that t5he detention of individuals who protested the annulment of the presidential elections in Nigeria in 1993 and were held without charges for over three years constitutes "an arbitrary deprivation of their liberty."[27] In addition, arbitrary detentions include indefinite detention of individuals who protested against torture,[28] as well as detentions "based on grounds of ethnic origin alone."[29] The African Commission has also held that a law allowing the government to detain people without any charges for up to three months violates the right not to be arbitrarily detained.[30]

## Europe

Article 5 of the European Convention on Human Rights[31] states that "everyone has the right to liberty and security of the person." An exception to this right to liberty is lawful pretrial detention. Article 5(1)(c) states that a person's arrest or detention may be "effected for the purpose of bringing him before the competent legal authority on reasonable suspicion of having committed an offence or when it is reasonably considered necessary to prevent his committing an offence or fleeing after having done so."

Article 5(3) contains a protection for pretrial detainees, stating that anyone detained in accordance with Article 5(1)(c) must be "brought promptly before a judge or other officer authorised by law to exercise judicial power." Moreover, a pretrial detainee "shall be entitled to trial within a reasonable time or to release pending trial. Release may be conditioned by guarantees to appear for trial."

Additionally, anyone deprived of liberty under the exceptions set out in Article 5 "shall be entitled to take proceedings by which the lawfulness of his detention shall be decided speedily by a court and his release ordered if the detention is not lawful" (Article 5(4)).

The European Court of Human Rights has emphasized the "fundamental importance" of the guarantees included in Article 5, which contains "a corpus of substantive rights intended to ensure that the act of deprivation of liberty is amenable to independent judicial scrutiny and secures the accountability of the authorities for that measure."[32]

The European Court's jurisprudence on Article 5 and pretrial detention sets out the following general principles:[33]

> There must be a presumption in favor of pretrial release, and the burden is on the state to show why release pending trial cannot be granted.[34]

> Reasons must be given for refusing pretrial release and the judicial authority must consider alternatives to pretrial detention that would address any concerns it had regarding the defendant's release.[35]

> Pretrial detention cannot be imposed:

- purely because the defendant is suspected of committing an offense (no matter how serious or how strong the evidence against him);[36]
- on the grounds that the defendant represents a flight risk where the only reason for this decision is the absence of a fixed residence, or on the grounds that the defendant faces a long prison term if convicted at trial;[37]
- on the basis that the defendant will reoffend if released, unless there is evidence of a definite risk of a particular offense.[38]

› If financial bail is a condition of pretrial release, the amount set by the court must take into account the defendant's individual means.[39]

› Continued pretrial detention must be subject to regular review.

› The decision on pretrial detention must be taken expeditiously and reasons must be given for the need for continued detention (i.e., previous decisions should not simply be reproduced).[40]

The European Court has found that "by reason of their particular gravity and public reaction to them, certain offences may give rise to public disquiet capable of justifying pre-trial detention… provided that it is based on facts capable of showing that the accused's release would actually prejudice public order."[41] The Council of Europe's Committee of Ministers also includes as a possible criteria for pretrial detention the situation where there are substantial reasons for believing that a defendant, if released pretrial, poses a serious threat to public order.[42]

However, the Office of the UN High Commissioner for Human Rights has challenged the idea that posing a serious threat to public order can be a legitimate criterion for ordering pretrial detention: "The question arises, however, whether, in a democratic society governed by the rule of law, pre-trial detention, however brief, can be legally justified on the basis of a legal notion so easily abused as that of public order."[43]

## Americas

In the Inter-American human rights system, the rights of defendants and pretrial detainees are protected in the American Convention on Human Rights[44] and the American Declaration of the Rights and Duties of Man.[45]

According to the American Declaration, "Every individual who has been deprived of his liberty has the right to have the legality of his detention ascertained without delay by a court, and the right to be tried without undue delay or, otherwise, to be released," (Article XXV) and "every accused person is presumed to be innocent until proved guilty" (Article XXVI).

The American Convention holds that every person accused of a criminal offense has the right to be presumed innocent (Article 8(2)). Moreover, any person detained shall be brought promptly before a judicial officer and shall be entitled to trial within a reasonable time or to be released without prejudice to the continuation of the proceedings. A defendant's release may be subject to guarantees to assure his appearance for trial (Article 7(5)). Anyone who is deprived of his liberty is entitled to recourse to a competent court, in order that the court may decide without delay on the lawfulness of his arrest or pretrial detention and order his release if the arrest or detention is unlawful (Article 7(6)).

The above rights and protections for pretrial detainees were reiterated by the Inter-American Commission on Human Rights in 2008 through a set of Principles and Best Practices on the Protection of Persons Deprived of Liberty in the Americas.[46] According to the Principles and Best Practices:

> - Every person has the right to personal liberty and to be protected against any illegal or arbitrary deprivation of liberty, and, as a general rule, the deprivation of liberty of persons shall be applied for the minimum necessary period (Principle III(1)).
> - Pretrial detention should be used "as an exception, in accordance with international human rights instruments" (Principle III(2)).
> - In order to justify pretrial detention, there must be sufficient evidence that connect the defendant with the facts of the case. This is an essential prerequisite for imposing pretrial detention, but after a certain lapse of time it no longer suffices (Principle III(2)).
> - Pretrial detention is a precautionary measure, not a punitive one, which shall additionally comply with the principles of legality, the presumption of innocence, need, and proportionality, to the extent strictly necessary in a democratic society. It shall only be applied within the strictly necessary limits to ensure that the person will not impede the efficient development of the investigations nor will evade justice, provided that the competent authority examines the facts and demonstrates that the aforesaid requirements have been met in the concrete case (Principle III(2)).

The Inter-American Court of Human Rights has held that in order to detain a defendant pretrial, the state must prove that: (i) there is sufficient evidence to allow a reasonable supposition that the person committed to trial has taken part in the offense under investigation; and (ii) that pretrial detention is based upon the legitimate purpose of ensuring the defendant does not impede the investigation or elude justice.[47]

### The Right to Legal Assistance

According to the International Covenant on Civil and Political Rights (ICCPR), in the determination of any criminal charge against them, persons are entitled to defend themselves in person or through legal assistance of their own choosing. Moreover, they have the right to be informed, if they do not have legal assistance, of the right to legal assistance; and to have legal assistance assigned to them, in any case where the interests of justice so require, and without payment if they do not have sufficient means to pay for it.[48]

The right to legal assistance set out in the ICCPR and other regional and international conventions is reiterated in the United Nations Basic Principles on the Role of Lawyers, which provide that:[49]

> All persons are entitled to call upon the assistance of a lawyer of their choice to protect and establish their rights and to defend them in *all stages* of criminal proceedings.

> Governments shall ensure that efficient procedures for effective and equal access to lawyers are provided for all persons within their territory and subject to their jurisdiction.

> Governments shall ensure the provision of sufficient funding and other resources for legal services to the poor and, as necessary, to other disadvantaged persons.

International standards provide for the right to legal assistance once formal criminal proceedings have commenced, including court hearings concerning pretrial detention. It remains unclear whether the right to legal assistance applies at the pretrial, investigative stage—and particularly while a person is detained at a police station.[50]

It is increasingly recognized that the investigative stage is an integral part of criminal proceedings. The European Committee for the Prevention of Torture has described access to a lawyer for those detained by the police as one of the "three fundamental safeguards against the ill-treatment of detained persons which should apply as from the very outset of deprivation of liberty."[51] The UN Basic Principles on the Role of Lawyers provides that governments must "ensure that all persons arrested or detained, with or without criminal charge, shall have prompt access to a lawyer, and in any case not later than forty-eight hours from the time of arrest or detention."[52]

The European Court of Human Rights has taken the view that the right to legal assistance arises immediately on arrest, and has decided that it applies as soon as a person is made aware by the authorities that he is suspected of having committed a criminal offense, which could be even before an arrest takes place. Access to a lawyer may only be restricted in exceptional circumstances where there are compelling reasons to do so.[53] Moreover, the European Court has determined that a suspect has a right to legal assistance during police interrogation, and that failure to permit this may irretrievably affect his right to fair trial.[54] The European Union is planning to introduce a right to legal assistance during police interrogation as part of its "roadmap" of procedural rights.[55]

# Bibliography

- Books
- Journal articles
- Government reports
- UN documents
- NGO documents
- Miscellaneous

## BOOKS

Baradaran, Shima. "The State of Pretrial Detention," in *The State of Criminal Justice 2011*, Washington: American Bar Association (2011).

Bartlett, Mike. "World Correctional Population Trends and Issues," in *Corrections Criminology*, Sydney: Hawkins Press (2005).

Braman, Donald. "Families and Incarceration," in *Invisible Punishment. The Collateral Consequences of Mass Imprisonment*, New York: The New Press, New York (2002).

del Frate, Anna Alvazzi. "Crime and criminal justice statistics challenges," in *International Statistics on Crime and Justice*, Helsinki: European Institute for Crime Prevention and Control (2010).

Desmond, Chris, Karen Michael, and Jeff Gow. *The Hidden Battle: HIV/AIDS in the Family and Community*. Durban: Health Economics & HIV/AIDS Research Division (HEARD) (2000).

Elveris, Idil, G. Jahic, and S. Kalem. *Alone in the Courtroom: Accessibility and Impact of Criminal Legal Aid*. Istanbul: Istanbul Bilgi University Publications (2007).

Hairston, Creasie Finney. "Prisoners and Their Families: Parenting Issues during Incarceration," in *Prisoners Once Removed. The Impact of Incarceration and Reentry on Children, Families and Communities*, Washington: The Urban Institute Press (2003).

Herman-Stahl, Mindy, Marni L. Kan, and Tasseli McKay. *Incarceration and the Family: A Review of Research and Promising Approaches for Serving Fathers and Families*. Washington: RTI International for the U.S. Department of Health and Human Services (2008).

Holman, Barry, and Jason Ziedenberg. *The Dangers of Detention: The Impact of*

*Incarcerating Youth in Detention and Other Secure Facilities*. Washington: Justice Policy Institute (2006).

Hounmenou, Charles. *Standards for Monitoring Human Rights of People in Police Lockups*. Jane Addams Center for Social Policy and Research, University of Illinois at Chicago (July 2010).

King, Michael. *Bail or Custody*. London: Cobden Trust (1973).

Liebling, Alison. *Suicides in Prison*, London: Routledge (1993).

Loucks, Nancy. *Prisoners with learning difficulties and learning disabilities—Review of prevalence and associated needs*. London: Prison Reform Trust (2007).

McDermott, Kathleen, and Roy D. King. "Prison Rule 102: Stand by your man," in *Prisoners' Children: What Are the Issues?* London: Routledge Publishing (1992).

Murray, Joseph. "The effect of imprisonment on families and children of prisoners," in *The Effects of Imprisonment*, Willan Publishing (2005).

New Economics Foundation. *Unlocking value: How we all benefit from investing in alternatives to prison for women offenders*. London: New Economics Foundation (2008).

Schönteich, Martin. "Pretrial detention and human rights in Africa." in Sarkin, Jeremy (ed.), *Human Rights in African Prisons*, Cape Town: HSRC Press (2008).

Stern, Vivien (ed.). *Sentenced to die? The problem of TB in prisons in Eastern Europe and Central Asia*, London: International Centre for Prison Studies (1999).

Vagg, Jon, and Frieder Dünkel. "Conclusion," in *Waiting for Trial: International Perspectives on the Use of Pre-Trial Detention and the Rights and Living Conditions of Prisoners Waiting for Trial*. Freiburg: Max Planck Institute (1994).

van Kalmthout, Anton M., Marije M. Knapen, and Christine Morgenstern (eds.). *Pre-trial Detention in the European Union. An Analysis of Minimum Standards in Pre-Trial Detention and the grounds for Regular Review in the Member States of the EU*. Nijmegen: Wolf Legal Publishers (2009).

Wilsher, Daniel. *Immigration Detention. Law, History, Politics*. New York: Cambridge University Press (2011).

## JOURNAL ARTICLES

Alexander, J. "Death and disease in Zimbabwe's prisons." *The Lancet*, vol. 373, no. 9668 (March 2009).

Anderson, Hillery. "Justice Delayed in Malawi's Criminal Justice System: Paralegals vs. Lawyers," *International Journal of Criminal Justice Sciences*, vol. 1, no. 1 (2006).

Baradaran, Shima. "The presumption of innocence and pretrial detention in Malawi," *Malawi Law Journal*, vol. 4, no. 1 (2010).

Baussano, Iacopo, et al. "Tuberculosis incidence in prisons: a systematic review," *PLoS Medicine*, Vol. 7, Issue 12 (December, 21, 2010).

Birmingham, Luke, Debbie Mason, and Don Grubin. "Prevalence of Mental Disorder in Remand Prisoners: Consecutive Case Study," *British Medical Journal*, vol. 313, no. 7071 (December 1996).

Bobrik, Alexey, et al. "Prison Health in Russia: The Larger Picture," *Journal of Public Health Policy*, vol. 26, no. 1 (2005).

Bukstel, Lee H., and Peter R Kilmann. "Psychological effects of imprisonment on confined individuals," *Psychological Bulletin*, vol. 88, no. 2 (1980).

Chisholm, John. "Benefit-Cost Analysis and Crime Prevention," Australian Institute of Criminology, *Trends & Issues in Crime and Criminal Justice*, No. 147 (February 2000). http://www.aic.gov.au/documents/9/D/4/%7B9D4E07CA-74FF-4F35-9C31-71504330BD00%7Dti147.pdf

Clements, Carl B. "Crowded Prisons: A Review of Psychological and Environmental Effects," *Law and Human Behavior*, vol. 3, no. 3 (1979).

Coninx, Rudi, et al. "Tuberculosis in prisons in countries with high prevalence," *British Medical Journal*, vol. 320 (12 February 2000).

Dahle, Klaus-Peter, Johannes C. Lohner, and Norbert Konrad. "Suicide Prevention in Penal Institutions: Validation and Optimization of a Screening Tool for Early Identification of High-Risk Inmates in Pretrial Detention," *International Journal of Forensic Mental Health*, vol. 4, no. 1 (2005).

Daniels, Thomas E. "Gideon's Hollow Promise—How Appointed Counsel Are Prevented from Fulfilling Their Role in the Criminal Justice System," *Michigan Bar Journal* (February 1992).

Deltenre, Samuel, and Eric Maes. "Pre-trial detention and the overcrowding of prisons in Belgium. Results from a simulation study into the possible effects of limiting the length of pre-trial detention," *European Journal of Crime, Criminal Law and Criminal Justice*, vol. 12, no. 4 (2004).

Devilly, G.J., et al. "Prison-based peer-education schemes," *Aggression and Violent Behavior*, vol. 10 (2005).

Dolan, K., M. Bijl, and B. White. "HIV education in a Siberian prison colony for drug dependent males." *International Journal for Equity in Health*, vol. 3 (2004).

Gegia, Medea, et al. "Developing a human rights-based program for tuberculosis control in Georgian prisons," *Health and Human Rights*, vol. 13, no. 2 (2011). http://www.hhrjournal.org/index.php/hhr/article/view/429/715

Grogger, Jeffrey. "The Effect of Arrests on the Employment and Earnings of Young Men," *The Quarterly Journal of Economics*, vol. 110, no. 1 (February 1995).

Hatch, Deborah R. "Pre-sentence custody," *LawNow* (2010). http://findarticles.com/p/articles/mi_m0OJX/is_3_34/ai_n47564461/

Himsell, Scott D. "Preventive Detention: A Constitutional but Ineffective Means of Fighting Crime," *The Journal of Criminal Law & Criminology*, vol. 77, no. 2 (1986).

Jaman, Dorothy R., Robert M. Dickover, and Lawrence A. Bennett. "Parole outcome as a function of time served," *British Journal of Criminology*, vol. 12, no. 1 (January 1972).

Jones, Stephen. "Guilty until Proven Innocent?" The Diminished Status of Suspects at the Point of Remand and as Unconvicted Prisoners," *Common Law World Review*, vol. 32, no. 4 (December 2003).

Kellough, Gail, and Scot Wortley. "Remand for Plea. Bail Decisions and Plea Bargaining as Commensurate Decisions," *British Journal of Criminology*, vol. 42, no. 1 (2002).

King, Sue, David Bamford, and Rick Sarre. "Discretionary Decision-Making in a Dynamic Context: The Influences on Remand Decision-Makers in Two Australian Jurisdictions," *Current Issues in Criminal Justice*, vol. 21, no. 1 (2009).

Krieg, Anthea S. "Aboriginal Incarceration: Health and Social Impacts," *Medical Journal of Australia*, vol. 184, no. 10 (2006).

Lee, Sonia Y. "OC's PD's Feeling the Squeeze—the Right to Counsel: In Light of Budget Cuts, can the Orange County Office of the Public Defender Provide Effective Assistance of Counsel?" *Loyola of Los Angeles Law Review*, vol. 29 (1995).

Louw, Antoinette, Eric Pelser, and Sipho Ntuli. "Poor Safety: Crime and Policing in South Africa's rural areas," *ISS Monograph Series*, no. 47 (May 2000).

Morgenstern, Christine. "Pre-trial / remand detention in Europe: Facts and figures and the need for common minimum standards," *ERA-Forum*, vol. 9, no. 4 (2009).

Myers, Barbara J., et al. "Children of Incarcerated Mothers," *Journal of Child and Family Studies*, vol. 8, no. 1 (1999).

Nicholls, Tonia L., et al. "Women Inmates' Mental Health Needs: Evidence of the Validity of the Jail Sentencing Screening Tool (JSAT)," *International Journal of Forensic Mental Health*, vol. 3, no. 2 (2004).

Octigan, Mike. "Pre-Trial Services: Someone Else's Agenda?" *Probation Journal*, vol. 49, no. 1 (March 2002).

Ogletree, Charles J. "An Essay on the New Public Defender for the 21st Century," *Law and Contemporary Problems*, vol. 58, no. 1 (1995).

Parton, Felicity, Andrew Day, and Jack White. "An Empirical Study on the Relationship between Intellectual Ability and an Understanding of the Legal Process in Male Remand Prisoners," *Psychiatry, Psychology and Law*, vol. 11, no. (1) (2004).

Porter, Lindsay, and Donna Calverley. "Trends in the Use of Remand in Canadam," *Juristat* no. 85-002-X, Ottawa: Statistics Canada (May 2011).

Reyes, Hernan. "Pitfalls of TB management in prisons, revisited," *International Journal of Prisoner Health*, vol. 3, no. 1 (2007).

Sarang, Anya, et al. "Drug injecting and syringes use in the HIV risk environment of Russian penitentiary institutions: qualitative study," *Addiction*, vol. 101, no. 12 (December 2006).

Sarre, Rick, Sue King, and David Bamford. "Remand in custody: Critical factors and key issues," *Trends & Issues in Criminal Justice*, no. 310, Australian Institute of Criminology (May 2006).

Senok, Abiola C., and Giuseppe A. Botta. "Human immunodeficiency virus and hepatitis virus infection in correctional institutions in Africa: Is this the neglected source of an epidemic?" *Journal of Medical Microbiology*, vol. 55, no. 5 (2006).

Shukshin, Andrei. "Tough measures in Russian prisons slow spread of TB," *Bulletin of the World Health Organisation*, vol. 84, no. 4 (April 2006). http://www.who.int/bulletin/volumes/84/4/news30406/en/index.html

Snowball, Lucy, Lenny Roth, and Don Weatherburn. "Bail Presumptions and Risk of Bail Refusal: An Analysis of the New Bail Act," *Crime and Justice Statistics— Bureau Brief*, no. 49, NSW Bureau of Crime Statistics and Research (July 2010).

Thomas, James C., and Elizabeth Torrone. "Incarceration as Forced Migration: Effects on Selected Community Health Outcomes," *American Journal of Public Health*, vol. 96, no. 10 (October 2006).

Todrys. Katherine W., and Joseph J Amon. "Criminal Justice Reform as HIV and TB Prevention in African Prisons, *PLoS Medicine*," vol. 9, no. 5 (May 2012). http://www.plosmedicine.org/article/info%3Adoi%2F10.1371%2Fjournal.pmed.1001215

Waller, Irvin, and Daniel Sansfaçon. "Investing Wisely in Crime Prevention. International Experiences," *Bureau of Justice Assistance Monograph*, Crime Prevention Series no. 1 (September 2000).

White, Paul, David Chant, and Harvey Whiteford. "A Comparison of Australian Men with Psychotic Disorders Remanded for Criminal Offences and a Community Group of Psychotic Men Who Have Not Offended," *Australian and New Zealand Journal of Psychiatry*, vol. 40, no. 3 (2006).

## GOVERNMENT REPORTS

Australian Office of Police Integrity. *Conditions for persons in custody. Report of Ombudsman Victoria and Office of Police Integrity* (July 2006).

Australian Parliament's House of Representatives Standing Committee on Aboriginal and Torres Strait Islander Affairs. *Doing Time—Time for Doing: Indigenous Youth in the Criminal Justice System*. Canberra (June 2011).

Bangladesh Ministry of Home Affairs and Prison Directorate. *Improvement of the*

*Real Situation of Overcrowding in Prisons in Bangladesh: GTZ in Bangladesh.*

Beck, Allen J., and Paige M. Harrison. *Special Report: Sexual Victimization in State and Federal Prisons Reported by Inmates*, 2007. U.S. Department of Justice, Bureau of Justice Statistics (19 March 2008). http://bjs.ojp.usdoj.gov/content/pub/pdf/svsfpri07.pdf

Dutch WODC. *European Sourcebook of Crime and Criminal Justice Statistics—2010*, 4th Ed. http://www.europeansourcebook.org/ob285_full.pdf

Farole, Jr., Donald J., and Lynn Langton. *County-based and Local Public Defender Offices*, 2007. U.S. Department of Justice, Bureau of Justice Statistics (September 2010).

Gendreau, Paul, Claire Goggin, and Francis T. Cullen. *The Effects of Prison Sentences on Recidivism.* Ottawa: Solicitor General Canada (1999). http://www.prisonpolicy.org/scans/e199912.htm

Harlow, Caroline Wolf. *Special Report: Defense Counsel in Criminal Cases.* U.S. Department of State, Bureau of Justice Statistics (29 November 2000). http://bjs.ojp.usdoj.gov/index.cfm?ty=pbdetail&iid=772

Harlow, Caroline Wolf. *Special Report: Education and Correctional Populations.* U.S. Department of State, Bureau of Justice Statistics (1 January 2003). http://bjs.ojp.usdoj.gov/index.cfm?ty=pbdetail&iid=814

Her Majesty's Inspectorate of Prisons for England and Wales. *Suicide is Everyone's Concern, A Thematic Review* (1999).

Her Majesty's Inspectorate of Prisons for England and Wales. *Unjust Deserts: A Thematic Review by HM Chief Inspector of Prisons of the Treatment and Conditions for Unsentenced Prisoners in England and Wales* (2000).

Holland, Shasta, et al. "Intellectual Disability in the Victorian Prison System: Characteristics of Prisoners with an Intellectual Disability Released from Prison in 2003-2006," *Corrections Research Paper Series* no. 2, Victoria: Department of Justice (2007).

Indian National Crime Records Bureau, Ministry of Home Affairs. "Arrests and Trials," in *Crime In India: 2010 Statistics*, http://ncrb.nic.in/CII2010/cii-2010/Chapter%2012.pdf

Minton, Todd D. *Jail Inmates at Midyear 2009 – Statistical Tables.* U.S. Department of Justice, Bureau of Justice Assistance (June 2010). http://bjs.ojp.usdoj.gov/content/pub/pdf/jim09st.pdf

Minton, Todd D. *Jail Inmates at Midyear 2011 – Statistical Tables.* U.S. Department of Justice, Bureau of Justice Assistance (April 2012). http://www.bjs.gov/content/pub/pdf/jim11st.pdf

Mumola, Christopher J. *Suicide and Homicide in State Prisons and Local Jails.* Washington: U.S. State Department, Bureau of Justice Statistics (August 2005) http://www.bjs.gov/content/pub/pdf/shsplj.pdf

New York Council of State Governments. *Fact Sheet: Mental Illness and Jails.* http://www.co.larimer.co.us/tencounty/conference/2009/mental_illness.pdf

Office of Program Policy Analysis & Government Accountability (Florida). *Pretrial Release Programs Vary Across the State; New Reporting Requirements Pose Challenges*, Report No. 08-75 (December 2008).

Scottish Prison Commission. *Scotland's Choice* (July 2008). http://www.scotland.gov.uk/Resource/Doc/230180/0062359.pdf

Scottish Prison Service. *Punishment First Verdict Later: A Review of Conditions for remand Prisoners in Scotland at the End of the 20th Century* (2000).

Shankardass, Rani Dhavan. *Exploration towards accessible and equitable justice in the South Asian region; problems and paradoxes of reform.* London: Penal Reform and Justice Association and Penal Reform International (2001).

Singleton, Nicola, Howard Meltzer and Rebecca Gatward. *Psychiatric Morbidity among Prisoners in England and Wales.* London: Home Office, Office for National Statistics (1998).

South African Judicial Inspectorate For Correctional Services. *Annual Report for the period 1 April 2010 to 31 March 2011* (2011). http://judicialinsp.pwv.gov.za/Annualreports/JUDICIAL_INSPECTORATE_ANNUAL%20%20REPORT_2010-2011.pdf

South African Judicial Inspectorate of Prisons. *Annual Report for the period 1 April 2005 to 31 March 2006.* Cape Town (2006).

South African National Treasury. *Estimates of National Expenditure 2012* (Abridged version) (2012). http://www.treasury.gov.za/documents/national%20budget/2012/ene/FullENE.pdf

South African Police Service. *Annual Report 2010/2011* (2011). http://www.saps.gov.za/saps_profile/strategic_framework/annual_report/2010_2011/4_prg2_vispol.pdf

Spier, Philip, and Barb Lash. *Conviction and Sentencing of Offenders in New Zealand: 1994 to 2003.* Wellington: New Zealand Ministry of Justice (2004).

Thompson, Barbara. "Remand Inmates in NSW: Some Statistics," *Research Bulletin* No. 20, Sydney: NSW Department of Correctional Services (June 2001).

U.S. Department of Justice, Criminal Justice Information Services Division. *Crime in the United States: Arrests.* http://www2.fbi.gov/ucr/cius2009/arrests/index.html

U.S. Department of State, Bureau of Justice Statistics. *Compendium of Federal Justice Statistics, 2004* (December 2006). http://bjs.ojp.usdoj.gov/content/pub/pdf/cfjs04.pdf

U.S. Department of State. *2009 Human Rights Report: Japan* (11 March 2010). http://www.state.gov/g/drl/rls/hrrpt/2009/eap/135993.htm

U.S. Department of State. *2009 Human Rights Report: Sri Lanka* (11 March 2010).

http://www.state.gov/g/drl/rls/hrrpt/2009/sca/136093.htm

U.S. Department of State. *2010 Human Rights Report: Peru* (8 April 2011). http://www.state.gov/g/drl/rls/hrrpt/2010/wha/154516.htm

## UN DOCUMENTS

Alston, Philip. *Report of the Special Rapporteur on extrajudicial, summary or arbitrary executions, Mission to Brazil.* UN doc A/HRC/11/2/Add.2 future (28 August 2008).

Atabay, Tomris, and Paul English. *Afghanistan: Implementing Alternatives to Imprisonment, in line with International Standards and National Legislation.* Vienna: UN Office of Drugs and Crime (2008).

Carmona, Magdalena Sepúlveda. *Extreme poverty and human rights: Report of the Special Rapporteur on extreme poverty and human rights.* UN Doc A/66/265 (4 August 2011). http://www.ohchr.org/Documents/Issues/Poverty/A.66.265.pdf

Committee against Torture, *Report on Brazil produced by the Committee under article 20 of the Convention and reply from the Government of Brazil.* UN Doc CAT/C/39/2, advance unedited version of 23 November 2007 made public by decision of the Committee against Torture (22 November 2008).

Committee against Torture. *Consideration of Reports Submitted by States Parties under Article 19 of the Convention: Concluding observations of the Committee against Torture, Kenya.* UN Doc CAT/C/KEN/CO/1 (19 January 2009).

Committee against Torture. *Consideration of reports submitted by States parties under article 19 of the Convention: Concluding Observations of the Committee against Torture, Cameroon.* UN Doc CAT/C/CMR/CO/4 (19 May 2010).

Committee against Torture. *Consideration of reports submitted by States parties under article 19 of the Convention. Concluding observations of the Committee against Torture: Slovakia.* UN Doc CAT/C/SVL/CO/2 (17 December 2009).

Committee against Torture. *Consideration of reports submitted by States parties under article 19 of the Convention. Concluding observations of the Committee against Torture: El Salvador.* UN Doc CAT/C/SLV/CO/2 (9 December 2009). http://www.bayefsky.com/pdf/elsalvador_t4_cat_43.pdf

Committee against Torture. *Consideration Of Reports Submitted By States Parties Under Article 19 Of The Convention. Concluding observations of the Committee Against Torture.* UN Doc CAT/C/TCD/C/1 (4 June 2009).

McIntosh, Steven. *Education and Employment in OECD Countries.* Paris: UNESCO (2008).

Nowak, Manfred. *Mission to Georgia. Report of the Special Rapporteur on torture and other cruel, inhuman or degrading treatment or punishment, 2006.* UN doc. E/CN.4/2006/6/Add.3.

Nowak, Manfred. *Mission to Moldova. Report of the Special Rapporteur on torture and* other cruel, inhuman or degrading treatment or punishment, 2009. UN doc. A/HRC/10/44/Add.3.

Nowak, Manfred. "Fact-Finding on Torture and Ill-Treatment and Conditions of Detention," *Journal of Human Rights Practice*, vol. 1, no. 1 (2009). http://jhrp.oxfordjournals.org/content/1/1/101.full

Nowak, Manfred. *Interim report of the Special Rapporteur on torture and other cruel, inhuman or degrading treatment or punishment.* UN Doc A/64/215 (3 August 2009). http://www.unhcr.org/refworld/category,REFERENCE,UNGA,,,4aae4 eeb0,0.html

Nowak, Manfred. *Mission to Indonesia. Report of the Special Rapporteur on torture and other cruel, inhuman or degrading treatment or punishment, Addendum (10-23 November 2007).* UN Doc A/HRC/7/3/Add.7.

Nowak, Manfred. *Mission to Nigeria. Report of the Special Rapporteur on torture and other cruel, inhuman or degrading treatment or punishment (4 to 10 March 2007).* UN Doc A/HRC/7/3/Add.4 (22 November 2007).

Nowak, Manfred. *Mission to Togo. Report of the Special Rapporteur on torture and other cruel, inhuman or degrading treatment or punishment (11-17 April 2007).* UN Doc A/HRC/7/3/Add.5 (6 January 2008).

Nowak, Manfred. *Mission to Uruguay. Report of the Special Rapporteur on torture and other cruel, inhuman or degrading treatment or punishment (21-27 March 2009).* UN Doc A/HRC/13/39/Add.2 (21 December 2009).

Nowak, Manfred. *Report of the Special Rapporteur on Torture and other Cruel, Inhuman or Degrading Treatment or Punishment. Addendum: Study on the phenomena of torture, cruel, inhuman or degrading treatment or punishment in the world, including an assessment of conditions of detention, 2010.* UN Doc A/HRC/13/39/Add.5.

Nowak, Manfred. *Report of the Special Rapporteur on Torture and other Cruel, Inhuman or Degrading Treatment or Punishment, Mission to Nigeria, (4 to 10 March 2007).* UN Doc A/HRC/7/3/Add.4 (2007).

Nowak, Manfred. *Report of the Special Rapporteur on torture and other cruel, inhuman or degrading treatment or punishment, Addendum, Mission to Uruguay.* UN doc. A/HRC/13/39/Add.2 (21 December 2009). http://www2.ohchr.org/english/bodies/hrcouncil/docs/13session/A-HRC-13-39-Add2.pdf

Nowak, Manfred. *Report of the Special Rapporteur on torture and other cruel, inhuman or degrading treatment or punishment, Manfred Nowak, Addendum: Study on the phenomena of torture, cruel, inhuman or degrading treatment or punishment in the world, including an assessment of conditions of detention.* UN Doc A/HRC/13/39/Add.5 (5 February 2010).

Nowak, Manfred. *Report submitted by the Special Rapporteur on torture and other cruel, inhuman or degrading treatment or punishment: Mission to Greece.* Advance unedited version, UN Doc A/HRC/16/52/Add.4 (4 March 2011).

Pinheiro, P.S. (Independent Expert for the UN Secretary-General). *World report on violence against children.* New York: United Nations (2006). http://www.unicef.org/violencestudy/index.html

Rodley, Nigel S. *Mission to Azerbaijan. Report of the Special Rapporteur on torture and other cruel, inhuman or degrading treatment or punishment, 2000.* UN Doc E/CN.4/2001/66/Add.1.

Rodley, Nigel S. *Mission to the Russian Federation. Report of the Special Rapporteur on torture and other cruel, inhuman or degrading treatment or punishment (addendum), 1994.* UN Doc. E/CN.4/1995/34/Add.1.

Rodley, Nigel S. Mission to Kenya. *Report of the Special Rapporteur on torture and other cruel, inhuman or degrading treatment or punishment (addendum), 2000.* UN doc. E/CN.4/2000/9/Add.4.

U.N. Office on Drugs and Crime, UN AIDS, and World Bank. "HIV and Prisons in sub-Saharan Africa: Opportunities for Action." http://www.unodc.org/documents/hiv-aids/Africa%20HIV_Prison_Paper_Oct-23-07-en.pdf

U.N. Office on Drugs and Crime. *Access to Legal Aid in Criminal Justice Systems in Africa (2011).* http://www.unodc.org/pdf/criminal_justice/Survey_Report_on_Access_to_Legal_Aid_in_Africa.pdf

U.N. Office on Drugs and Crime. *Assessment of Justice System Integrity and Capacity in three Nigerian States.* Technical research report, final draft, Vienna (May 2004), http://www.unodc.org/pdf/crime/corruption/Justice_Sector_Assessment_2004.pdf

U.N. Office on Drugs and Crime. *Draft project idea: Strengthening judicial integrity & capacity,* Phase II. http://www.unodc.org/pdf/crime/corruption/corruption_project_nigeria_judicial_integrity_draft.pdf

U.N. Office on Drugs and Crime. *HIV in Prisons: Situation and Needs Assessment Tool Kit.* http://www.unodc.org/documents/hiv-aids/publications/HIV_in_prisons_situation_and_needs_assessment_document.pdf

U.N. Subcommittee on Prevention of Torture. *Report on the Visit of the Subcommittee on Prevention of Torture and Other Cruel, Inhuman, or Degrading Treatment or Punishment to Honduras.* UN Doc. CAT/OP/HND/1 (10 February 2010).

van Boven, T. *Report of the Special Rapporteur on torture, mission to Uzbekistan (addendum), 2003.* UN doc. E/CN.4/2003/68/Add.2.

Working Group on Arbitrary Detention. *Report of a mission to Angola (addendum), 2008.* UN doc. A/HRC/7/4/Add.4.

Working Group on Arbitrary Detention. *Report of a mission to Belarus (addendum), 2004.* UN doc. E/CN.4/2005/6/Add.3.

Working Group on Arbitrary Detention. *Report of a mission to Ecuador (addendum), 2006.* UN doc. A/HRC/4/40/Add.2.

Working Group on Arbitrary Detention. *Report of a mission to Equatorial Guinea (addendum), 2008.* UN doc. A/HRC/7/4/Add.3.

Working Group on Arbitrary Detention. *Report of a mission to South Africa (addendum)*, 2005. UN doc. E/CN.4/2006/7/Add.3.

Working Group on Arbitrary Detention. *Report of a mission to Ukraine (addendum)*, 2009. UN doc. A/HRC/10/21/Add.4.

# NGO DOCUMENTS

Advocacy Forum, Nepal. *Recent Trends and Patterns of Torture in Nepal: Briefing July to December 2010* (2010).

Advocacy Forum, Nepal. *Torture of Women in Detention: Nepal's Failure to Prevent and Protect* (2011). http://www.advocacyforum.org/downloads/pdf/publications/torture-of-women-in-detention-english-26-june-2011.pdf

Agbakoba, Olisa and Stanley Ibe, *Travesty of Justice. An Advocacy Manual Against The Holding Charge*, Lagos: The Human Rights Law Service (2004).

Aguilar, Ana and Javier Carrasco. *Servicios Previos Al Juicio. Manual de implementación*. Monterrey: Instituto de Justicia Procesal Penal (2011).

Allen, Rob. *Reducing the use of imprisonment. What can we learn from Europe?* London: Criminal Justice Alliance (May 2012).

Altus Global Alliance. *Police Station Visitors Week Global Report 2010* (2011). http://www.altus.org/index.php?option=com_content&view=article&id=17&Itemid=51&lang=en#

Amnesty International. *Lebanon: Torture and ill-treatment of women in pre-trial detention: a culture of acquiescence* (August 2001). http://www.amnesty.org/en/library/asset/MDE18/009/2001/en/71a91f76-d921-11dd-ad8c-f3d4445c118e/mde180092001en.pdf

Amnesty International. *Moldova: Briefing to the Committee Against Torture* (October 2009) http://www2.ohchr.org/english/bodies/cat/docs/ngos/AI_Moldova43.doc

Asian Human Rights Commission. "Disconnected Policing and the Justice Trade in Bangladesh," *Article 2: Special Edition: Use of Police Powers for Profit*, Vol. 8, No. 1 (12 March 2009).

Bane, Janis, and David A Jones. *Harris County Pre-Trial Services: Policies and Practices*. Houston: Houston Ministers Against Crime (2011).

Browne, Deborah C. *Research On Prisoners' Families—Building An Evidence Base For Best Policy And Practice (Addendum)*. London: Action for Prisoners' Families (March 2007). http://www.prisonersfamilies.org.uk/uploadedFiles/Information_and_research/Research%20on%20Prisoners%20Families%20Update.PDF

Buromensky, M.V., O.V. Serduk, and V.I. Tocheny, *Assessment of Social and Economic Costs of Pretrial detention Applications*. Analytical Report, Kiev: Institute of Applied Humanitarian Research (2008).

Campaign for Youth Justice. *Jailing Juveniles: The Dangers of Incarcerating Youth in Adult Jails in America* (November 2007). http://www.campaignforyouthjustice.org/Downloads/NationalReportsArticles/CFYJ-Jailing_Juveniles_Report_2007-11-15.pdf

Canadian HIV/AIDS Legal Network. "HIV Transmission in Prison," *HIV/AIDS in Prisons 2004/2005* (2004).

Canadian HIV/AIDS Legal Network. "HIV/AIDS and Hepatitis C in Prisons: The Facts," *HIV/AIDS in Prisons 2004/2005* (2004).

Cape, Ed, Zaza Namoradze, Roger Smith and Taru Spronken. *Effective Criminal Defence in Europe.* Antwerp: Intersentia (2010). http://www.soros.org/initiatives/justice/focus/criminal_justice/articles_publications/publications/criminal-defence-europe-20100623

Carrasco, Javier. *RENACE: Un modelo mexicano de supervisión de fianzas.* Monterrey: Renace (2005).

Center for Human Rights and Global Justice and Human Rights Watch. *Caste Discrimination Against Dalits or so-called Untouchables in India. Information for the consideration of the Committee on the Elimination of Racial Discrimination in Reviewing India's Fifteenth to Nineteenth Periodic Reports. Presented at the Seventieth Session of the Committee on the Elimination of Racial Discrimination.* (February 2007). http://www2.ohchr.org/english/bodies/cerd/docs/ngos/chrgj-hrw.pdf

Center for Social-Legal Studies. *Justice Sector Reform and Human Rights in Nigeria.* Abuja (2009).

Centro de Estudios de Justicia de las Américas, Report on Pre-Trial Criminal Justice in Brazil (unpublished).

Csete, Joanne, and Dirk van Zyl Smit. *Pretrial Detention and Health: Unintended Consequences, Deadly Results. Literature Review and Recommendations for Health Professionals.* New York: Open Society Justice Initiative (2011).

Danish Institute for Human Rights. *Access to Justice and Legal Aid in East Africa: A comparison of the legal aid schemes used in the region and the level of cooperation and coordination between the various actors* (December 2011). http://www.humanrights.dk/files/images/Publikationer/Legal_Aid_East_Africa_Dec_2011_DIHR_Study_Final.pdf

Defensoría del Pueblo. *El Sistema Penitenciario: componente clave de la seguridad ciudadana y la Política Criminal. Problemas, retos y perspectivas.* Lima (2011), http://www.defensoria.gob.pe/modules/Downloads/documentos/resumen-informe-154.pdf

Derdoy, Malena, et al. *The Economic and Social Costs of Preventive Detention in Argentina.* Buenos Aires: Centre for the Implementation of Public Policies Promoting Equity and Growth (2009).

Dünkel, Frieder, and Jon Vagg (eds.). *Waiting for Trial. International Perspectives on the Use of Pre-Trial Detention and the Rights and Living Conditions of Prisoners*

*Waiting for Trial*. Freiburg: Max Planck Institute (1994).

Ehlers, Louise. "Frustrated Potential: The Short and Long Term Impact of Pretrial Services in South Africa," in *Justice Initiatives: Pretrial Detention*. New York: Open Society Institute (Spring 2008).

Ericson, Matthew, and Tony Vinson. *Young People on Remand in Victoria: Balancing Individual and Community Interests*. Richmond: Jesuit Social Services (2010).

Foglesong, Todd, and Christopher E. Stone. "Prison Exit Samples as a Source for Indicators of Pretrial Detention," *Indicators in Development, Safety and Justice*. Cambridge: Harvard Kennedy School (April 2011). http://www.hks.harvard.edu/var/ezp_site/storage/fckeditor/file/pdfs/centers-programs/programs/criminal-justice/Indicators-PrisonExitSamples.pdf

Frigerio, Francisco. Prisoners' Rights Project Report: Buea Central Prison. Global Conscience Initiative's Prisoners' Rights Project 13 (2009).

Gear, Sasha. *Fear, Violence and Sexual Violence in a Gauteng Juvenile Correctional Centre for Males*, Centre for the Study of Violence and Reconciliation (2007).

Geraghty, Sarah, and Miriam Gohara. *Assembly Line Justice: Mississippi's Indigent Defense Crisis*. New York: NAACP Legal Defense and Educational Fund, Inc. (2003).

Global Fund to fight AIDS, Tuberculosis and Malaria. *The Global Fund Annual Report 2009* (May 2010). http://www.theglobalfund.org/en/library/publications/annualreports/

Griggs, Richard. *Evaluation of PASI's Access to Justice Project 01 October 2009—30 September 2010. The Paralegal Advisory Service Institute's pilot programme for adult pre-trial detainees originating at Kanengo and Mangochi police stations in Malawi*. Unpublished document, Open Society Justice Initiative (January 2011).

Hamilton, Carolyn, Kirsten Anderson, Ruth Barnes, and Kamena Dorling, *Administrative Detention of Children: A Global Report*, Essex: Children's Legal Centre, University of Essex, Essex (March 2011) http://www.unicef.org/protection/files/Administrative_detention_discussion_paper_April2011.pdf

Hands, Tatum L., Victoria Williams, and Danielle Davies. *Aboriginal Customary Laws: The Interaction of Western Australian Law with Aboriginal Law and Culture*. Perth: Law Reform Commission of Western Australia (September 2006).

Henrichson, Christian, and Ruth Delaney. *The Price of Prisons. What Incarceration Costs Taxpayers*. New York: Vera Institute of Justice (January 2012) http://www.vera.org/download?file=3495/the-price-of-prisons-updated.pdf

Henry, D. Alan. "Pathway to Justice: Juvenile Detention Reform in the United States," in *Justice Initiatives: Pretrial Detention*. New York: Open Society Institute (Spring 2008).

Human Rights Watch Prison Project. *Excessive Pretrial Detention*.

Human Rights Watch Prison Project. *Prisons in Europe and Central Asia*.

Human Rights Watch, AIDS and Rights Alliance for Southern Africa, and Prison Care and Counseling Association. *Unjust and unhealthy: HIV, TB and abuse in Zambian prisons* (27 April 2010). http://www.hrw.org/en/node/89819/

Human Rights Watch. "'Prison Is Not For Me': Arbitrary Detention in South Sudan" (21 June 2012). http://www.hrw.org/reports/2012/06/21/prison-not-me

Human Rights Watch. *"And it was Hell all over Again...": Torture in Uzbekistan*. Vol. 12, no. 12 (D) (December 2000).

Human Rights Watch. *Behind Bars in Brazil* (December 1998). http://www.hrw.org/sites/default/files/related_material/BRAZL98D.pdf

Human Rights Watch. *Confessions at Any Cost: Police Torture in Russia* (November 1999).

Human Rights Watch. *Fanning The Flames. How Human Rights Abuses are Fuelling the Aids Epidemic in Kazakhstan*. vol.15, no. 4(D) (30 June 2003). http://www.hrw.org/en/reports/2003/06/29/fanning-flames-0

Human Rights Watch. *Global Report on Prisons* (1992).

Human Rights Watch. *Ill-Equipped: U.S. Prisons and Offenders with Mental Illness* (22 October 2003). http://www.hrw.org/reports/2003/usa1003/

Human Rights Watch. *Making their own rules: Police beatings, rape and torture of children in Papua New Guinea* (31 August 2005). http://www.hrw.org/en/node/11626/

Human Rights Watch. *Paying the price: Violations of the rights of children in detention in Burundi*. Vol. 19, no. 4(A) (March 2007). http://www.hrw.org/sites/default/files/reports/burundi0307webwcover.pdf

Human Rights Watch. *Rhetoric and risk: Human rights abuses impeding Ukraine's fight against HIV/AIDS* (2 March 2006). http://www.hrw.org/en/node/11464/

Human Rights Watch. *The Price of Freedom. Bail and Pretrial Detention of Low Income Nonfelony Defendants in New York City* (December 2010). http://www.hrw.org/sites/default/files/reports/us1210webwcover_0.pdf

Human rights Watch. *Unjust and Unhealthy. HIV, TB, and Abuse in Zambian Prisons* (2010). http://arasa.info/sites/default/files/Zambia%20Prisons%20Report_zambia0410webwcover.pdf

Integrated Regional Information Networks. "Swaziland: Children still share jail cells with adults" (14 July 2010). http://www.unhcr.org/refworld/publisher,IRIN,,SWZ,4c4019bf1a,0.html

Inter-American Commission on Human Rights. *Report on the Human Rights of Persons Deprived of Liberty in the Americas* (2011) http://www.oas.org/en/iachr/pdl/docs/pdf/PPL2011eng.pdf

International Centre for Prison Studies. *World Prison Brief*. http://www.prisonstudies.org/info/worldbrief/

International Crisis Group (ICG). *Central Asia: The Politics of Police Reform*. Osh/Brussels (10 December 2002).

International Crisis Group. *Kyrgyzstan's Prison System Nightmare*. Asia Report no. 118 (16 August 2006). http://www.crisisgroup.org/~/media/Files/asia/central-asia/kyrgyzstan/118_kyrgyzstans_prison_system_nightmare.pdf

International Crisis Group. *Reforming Pakistan's Criminal Justice System*, Asia Report no. 196 (December 2010).

Jolofani, D., and J. DeGabriele. *HIV AIDS in Malawi Prisons - Study of HIV transmission and the care of prisoners with HIV / AIDS in Zomba, Blantyre and Lilongwe Prisons*. Paris: Penal Reform International (1999).

Justiça Global, National Movement of Street Boys and Girls, and the World Organisation Against Torture. T*he Criminalization Of Poverty: A Report on the Economic, Social and Cultural Root Causes of Torture and Other Forms of Violence in Brazil*. http://www2.ohchr.org/english/bodies/cescr/docs/info-ngos/JB_OMCT_MNMMR_Brazil42.pdf

Justice Policy Institute. *System Overload: The Costs of Under-Resourcing Public Defense*. Washington, D.C. (July 2011). http://www.justicepolicy.org/uploads/justicepolicy/documents/system_overload_final.pdf

Justice Policy Institute. *The Costs of Confinement: Why Good Juvenile Justice Policies Make Good Fiscal Sense*. Washington, D.C. (May 2009). http://www.justicepolicy.org/images/upload/09_05_REP_CostsofConfinement_JJ_PS.pdf

Justice Studies Center of the Americas. *Pretrial Detention and Criminal Procedure Code Reform in Latin America: Evaluation and Perspectives* (Country Report on Mexico) (August 2009).

Karth, Vanja. *Between a Rock and a Hard Place. Bail Decisions in Three South African Courts*. Cape Town: Open Society Foundation for South Africa (2008).

Klahr, Marco L. *No más "pagadores". Guía de periodismo sobre presunción de inocencia y reforma del sistema de justicia penal*. Mexico City: Instituto de Justicia Procesal Penal (2011).

La Rota, Miguel. *El uso de la Prisión Preventiva en Nueva León: Estudio Cuantitativo*. New York: Open Society Justice Initiative & Renace (2009).

Markina, Anna, and Jon Spencer. "Reducing the Prison Population: Challenges and Threats," in *Penal Reform and Prison Overcrowding*, Vienna: UNICRI 22 (16 April 2009). http://www.unicri.it/news/2009/0904-4_penalreform/penal_reform2009.pdf

Mehta, Swati. *Maharashtra's Abandoned Prisons. A Study of Sub-Jails*. New Delhi: Commonwealth Human Rights Initiative (2010).

Msiska, Clifford. "On the Front Lines: Insights from Malawi's Paralegal Advisory Service," in *Justice Initiatives: Pretrial Detention*. New York: Open Society Institute (Spring 2008).

National Prison Rape Elimination Commission. *Executive Summary: Report and Standards* (June 2009). http://cybercemetery.unt.edu/archive/nprec/20090820154829/http://www.nprec.us/

Nigerian Federal Ministry of Justice. *Report of the National Working Group on Prison Reforms and Decongestion* (2005).

Nwapa, Anthony. "Building and Sustaining Change: Pretrial Detention Reform in Nigeria," in *Justice Initiatives: Pretrial Detention*. New York: Open Society Institute (Spring 2008).

Open Society Institute. *Detention as Treatment. Detention of Methamphetamine Users in Cambodia, Laos, and Thailand* (March 2010).

Open Society Initiative for Southern Africa. *Pre-trial detention in Malawi: Understanding caseflow management and conditions of incarceration* (2011). http://ppja.org/countries/malawi/Pre-trial%20detention%20in%20Malawi.pdf

Open Society Initiative for Southern Africa. *Pre-trial detention in Zambia: Understanding caseflow management and conditions of incarceration* (2011). http://www.osisa.org/sites/default/files/sup_files/open_learning_-_pre-trial_detention_in_zambia.pdf

Open Society Justice Initiative. *Pretrial Detention and Health: Unintended Consequences, Deadly Results* (2011).

Open Society Justice Initiative. *Pretrial Detention and Torture: Why Pretrial Detainees Face the Greatest Risk* (2011).

Open Society Justice Initiative. *The Socioeconomic Impact of Pretrial Detention* (2011).

Open Society Justice Initiative. *Improving Pretrial Justice: The Roles of Lawyers and Paralegals* (2012).

Open Society Justice Initiative and United Nations Development Programme. "Pretrial detainee surveys on the socioeconomic impact of pretrial detention, 2011" (publication forthcoming).

Open Society Justice Initiative. *Criminal Force: Torture, Abuse, and Extrajudicial Killings by the Nigeria Police Force* (2010). http://www.soros.org/sites/default/files/criminal-force-20100519.pdf

Partners In Health, Zanmi Lasante, Institute for Justice & Democracy in Haiti, Bureau des Avocats Internationaux, François-Xavier Bagnoud Center, for Health & Human Rights. *Health and Human Rights Prison Project: Medical-Legal Advocacy in Haiti: Initial Data Report* (September 2009).

Peillard, Ana María Morales, et al. *Caracterización de la Población en Prisión Preventiva en Chile*, Santiago: Fundacion Paz Ciudadana (March 2011).

Penal Reform International. *Evaluation of PRI and SDC Project: Support to Penitentiary Reform in Ukraine 2009-2012*. London (August 2011).

Penal Reform International. *Pre-trial Detention*. http://www.penalreform.org/themes/pre-trial-detention

Penal Reform International. *Prison Conditions in Africa*. London: PRI and African Centre for Democracy and Human Rights (1993).

Penal Reform International. *Statement to the 20th Session of the UN Commission on Crime Prevention and Criminal Justice* (April 2011). http://www.penalreform.org/files/PRI%20statement%20to%20Crime%20Commission.doc

Philips, Mary T. *Pretrial Detention and Case Outcomes, Part 1: Nonfelony Cases*. New York City Criminal Justice Agency (November 2007).

Prison Reform Trust. *Bromley Briefings Prison Factfile* (June 2009). www.prisonreformtrust.org.uk/uploads/documents/june2009factfile.pdf

Prison Reform Trust. *Innocent Until Proven Guilty. Tackling the Overuse of Custodial Remand* (October 2011). http://www.prisonreformtrust.org.uk/Portals/0/Documents/Remand%20Briefing%20FINAL.PDF

Puzzanchera, Charles, et al. *Juvenile Court Statistics 2006-2007*. National Center for Juvenile Justice (March 2010). http://www.ncjj.org/PDF/jcsreports/jcs2007.pdf

Renner, Michael, and James Paul. "UN Funding Increases, But Falls Short of Global Tasks," *Vital Signs*, Worldwatch Institute (29 February 2012). http://vitalsigns.worldwatch.org/vs-trend/un-funding-increases-falls-short-global-tasks

Resource Center for Human Rights et al. *Alternative Report to the 2nd Report of the Republic of Moldova on the Stage of Implementation of the United Nations Convention against Torture* (2009).

Robertson, Oliver. *The impact of parental imprisonment on children*. Geneva: Quaker United Nations Office (2007).

Rosenberg, Jennifer. *Children Need Dads Too: Children with Fathers in Prison*. Geneva: Quaker United Nations Office (2009).

Ruppel, Oliver C., and Angelique L. Groenewaldt. *Conditions of Police Cells in Namibia*. Human Rights and Documentation Centre, University of Namibia (2008).

Sandefur, Justin, Bilal Siddiqi, and Alaina Varvaloucas. *Timap Criminal Justice Pilot: Baseline Report*. Oxford: Centre for the Study of African Economies (April 2011).

Schönteich, Martin. "The Scale and Consequences of Pretrial detention around the World" in *Justice Initiatives: Pretrial Detention*. New York: Open Society Institute (Spring 2008).

Schönteich, Martin and Denise Tomasini-Joshi. *Programas de medidas cautalares. Experiencias para equilibrar presunción de inocencia y seguridad ciududuna*. New York: Open Society Justice Initiative (2010).

Social and Cultural Planning Office. *Public Sector Performance. An international comparison of education, health care, law and order and public administration*. The Hague (September 2004).

Stern, Vivien. *Alternatives to prison in developing countries*. London: International Centre for Prison Studies and Penal Reform International (1999).

Sullivan, Mercer L. *Getting Paid: Youth Crime and Work in the Inner City*. Ithaca: Cornell University Press (1989).

Talbot, Jenny. *Prisoners' Voices. Experiences of the criminal justice system by prisoners with learning disabilities and difficulties.* London: Prison Reform Trust (2008).

Townhead, Laurel. "Pre-Trial Detention of Women and Its Impact on Their Children," *Women in Prison and Children of Imprisoned Mothers Series*, Geneva: Quaker United Nations Office (2007).

Transtec. *Final Report: Needs Assessment of Investigation and Forensic Capability of the Nigeria Police* (November 2007).

UNICEF. "Juvenile Justice," *Innocenti Digest* (January 1998). http://www.unicef-irc.org/publications/pdf/digest3e.pdf

Varenik, Robert O. "Mixing Politics, Data, and Detention: Reflections on Reform Efforts," in *Justice Initiatives: Pretrial Detention*. New York: Open Society Institute (Spring 2008).

van Zyl Smit, Dirk. "Report of the Rapporteur General," *Prison Conditions in Africa: Report of a Pan-African Seminar*, Kampala, Paris: Penal Reform International, Paris 1997 (19-21 September 1996).

Volz, Anna. *Stop the Violence!: The overuse of pre-trial detention, or the need to reform juvenile justice. Review of the evidence.* Geneva: Defence for Children International (July 2010).

Watts, Harold, and Demetra Smith Nightingale. *Adding It Up: The Economic Impact of Incarceration on Individuals, Families, and Communities.* Washington D.C.: The Urban Institute (1996). http://www.doc.state.ok.us/offenders/ocjrc/96/Adding%20It%20Up.pdf

World Bank. *Gross domestic product 2010, World Development Indicators database* (17 April 2012). http://databank.worldbank.org/databank/download/GDP.pdf

World Bank. *How we Classify Countries.* http://data.worldbank.org/about/country-classifications

World Health Organization and International Committee of the Red Cross. *Mental Health and Prisons: Information Sheet.* http://www.who.int/mental_health/policy/mh_in_prison.pdf

World Health Organization Regional Office for Europe. *Prison health – HIV, drugs and tuberculosis (fact sheet)* (October 2009). http://www.euro.who.int/__data/assets/pdf_file/0009/98973/92295E_FS_Prison.pdf

World Health Organization Regional Office for South-East Asia. *HIV prevention, care and treatment in prisons in the South-East Asia region.* New Delhi (2007). http://www.searo.who.int/LinkFiles/Publications_TreatmentinPrisons.pdf

World Health Organization, *Tuberculosis in Prison.* http://www.who.int/tb/challenges/prisons/story_1/en/

World Health Organization. *Medium-term Strategic Plan 2008–2013 and Proposed Programme budget 2012–2013.* Sixty-Fourth World Health Assembly A64/7 (4 April 2011). http://apps.who.int/gb/ebwha/pdf_files/WHA64/A64_7-en.pdf

World Health Organization. *Preventing Suicide: A Resource for Prison Officers.* Geneva, WHO/MNH/MBD/00.5 (2000).

World Health Organization: Europe. *Status Paper on Prisons, Drugs and Harm Reduction.* EUR/05/5049062 (May 2005).

Zepeda, Guillermo. Myths of Pretrial Detention in Mexico. New York: Open Society Justice Initiative (2005).

Zepeda, Guillermo. *Costly Confinement: The Direct and Indirect Costs of Pretrial Detention in Mexico* (English-language summary). New York: Open Society Institute (2009).

## MISCELLANEOUS

Aebi, Marcelo F. *Council of Europe Annual Penal Statistics* (SPACE I), Survey 2004. Strasbourg: Council of Europe (7 November 2005).

Aebi, Marcelo F., and Natalia Delgrande. *Council of Europe Annual Penal Statistics* (SPACE I), Survey 2010, Strasbourg: Council of Europe (23 March 2012). http://www3.unil.ch/wpmu/space/files/2011/02/SPACE-1_2010_English.pdf

American Bar Association: Criminal Justice Section. "ABA Urges Pre-Trial Release Reform to Save States Money, Reduce Recidivism and Protect the Public." http://www2.americanbar.org/sections/criminaljustice/CR203800/PublicDocuments/pretrialdetention.pdf

Ashenfelter, Orley. "How Convincing is the Evidence Linking Education and Income?" presented as The George Seltzer Distinguished Lecture, University of Minnesota (1991).

Australian Institute of Health and Welfare. "Juvenile Justice in Australia 2007-08," *Juvenile Justice Series,* no. 5 (November 2009).

Barreto, Fabiana Costa Oliveira. *Flagrante e Prisao Provisoria em casos de furto, da presuncao de inocencia a antecipacao de pena.* São Paulo: Instituto Brasileiro de Ciencias Criminais, Brasília, (2007).

Chirwa, Vera Mlangazuwa. *Prisons in Malawi.* Report on a visit 17-28 June 2001 by the Special Rapporteur on Prisons and Conditions of Detention in Africa, African Commission on Human and Peoples' Rights, series IV, no. 9.

Contrôleur general des lieux de privation de liberté. *Rapport d'activité 2011* (2012). http://www.cglpl.fr/wp-content/uploads/2012/02/CGLPL_rapport-2011_texte.pdf

Dankwa, E.V.O. *Prisons in Benin.* Report on a visit 23-31 August 1999 by the Special Rapporteur on Prisons and Conditions of Detention in Africa, African Commission on Human and Peoples' Rights, series IV, no. 6.

Dankwa, E.V.O. *Prisons in the Central African Republic.* Report on a visit June 19-29, 2000 by the Special Rapporteur on Prisons and Conditions of Detention in Africa, African Commission on Human and Peoples' Rights, series IV, no. 7.

European Committee for the Prevention of Torture and Inhuman or Degrading Treatment or Punishment. *The CPT standards.* Strasbourg: Council of Europe, doc. no. CPT/Inf/E (2006), http://www.cpt.coe.int/en/documents/eng-standards.pdf

Gupta, Promita. "Improvement of the Real Situation of Overcrowding in Prisons in Bangladesh, presented at a Conference on Penal Reform in Developing Countries, Dhaka, Bangladesh (6 October 2010).

Haney, Craig. "Prison Overcrowding: Harmful Consequences and Dysfunctional Reactions." Expert Testimony to the Commission on Safety and Abuse in America's Prisons, Newark, (19 July 2005). http://www.prisoncommission.org/public_hearing_2_witness_haney.asp

Hassett, Patricia. "An Expert System for Improving the Pretrial Release/Detention Decision," presented at the 6th BILETA Conference (1991).

Hoffman, Morris B., Paul H. Rubin, and Joanna M. Shepherd. "An Empirical Study of Public Defender Effectiveness: Self-Selection by the 'Marginally Indigent,'" *Bepress Legal Services*, paper 391 (2004).

Ibe, Stanley. "Improving Pretrial Practice: Lessons from Nigeria," presented at a Conference on Access to Justice for Indigent Persons in West Africa, organized by Commonwealth Human Rights Initiative, Accra, Ghana (22-23 March 2011).

International Bar Association. *One in five: The crisis in Brazil's prisons and criminal justice system.* São Paulo (February 2010).

Makhanya, Edward M. *Demographic dynamics and sustainable rural development in South Africa.* Durban: University of Natal.

Matibini, Patrick. *Access to Justice and the Rule of Law.* An issue paper presented for the Commission on Legal Empowerment of the Poor.

Olong, Adefi Matthew. *The Administration of Criminal Justice in Nigeria: A Case for Reform*, A Thesis in the Faculty of Law, Submitted to the School of Postgraduate Studies, University of Jos, in partial fulfilment of the requirements for the award of the Degree of Doctor of Philosophy in Law of the University of Jos (November 2010).

Prison Reform International. *Freedom Inside the Walls* (documentary film) (2005).

Reza, Enrique Ochoa. *La Transparencia y el Ministerio Público. Derecho a Saber: Balance y Perspectivas Cívicas* [Transparency and the Office of the Public Prosecutor. The Right to Know: An Assessment and Public Perspectives] (2007).

# Endnotes

## INTRODUCTION

1.  Mike Octigan, "Pre-Trial Services: Someone Else's Agenda?," *Probation Journal*, Vol. 49, No. 1, March 2002, p. 19.

2.  That is, persons in pretrial detention have not been convicted of the crime(s) that they are alleged to have committed and which led to their arrest and detention. Some pretrial detainees may, however, have been convicted of a crime or crimes on a previous occasion.

3.  In some jurisdictions—notably in countries with a civil law tradition—these numbers may include pretrial detainees who have been convicted by a court of first instance but who have appealed their conviction and/or sentence. However, this is a very small portion of the world's pretrial detainee population.

## THE SCOPE OF PRETRIAL DETENTION AROUND THE WORLD: ITS EXTENT AND COST

1.  International Center for Prison Studies, *World Prison Brief*, available at http://www.prisonstudies.org/info/worldbrief/ (accessed Oct. 30, 2013).

2.  See: *Access to Legal Aid in Criminal Justice Systems in Africa Survey Report*, UNODC, Vienna, 2011, p. 35, available at http://www.unodc.org/pdf/criminal_justice/Survey_Report_on_Access_to_Legal_Aid_in_Africa.pdf (accessed Oct. 7, 2013); Bromley Briefings Prison Factfile, Prison Reform Trust, London, June 2011, p. 18; Philip Spier and Barb Lash, *Conviction and Sentencing of Offenders in New Zealand: 1994 to 2003*, New Zealand Ministry of Justice, Wellington, 2004, p. 110; Ana María Morales Peillard, Pablo Pérez Ahumada, and Gherman Welsch Chahuán, *Caracterización de la Población en Prisión Preventiva en Chile*, Fundacion Paz Ciudadana, Chile, March 2011, p. 18.

3.  *The Price of Freedom: Bail and Pretrial Detention of Low Income Nonfelony Defendants in New York City*, Human Rights Watch, New York, 2010, p. 29; *Bromley Briefings Prison Factfile*, Prison Reform Trust, London, June 2011, p. 18; Vanja Karth, *Between a Rock and a Hard Place. Bail Decisions in Three South African Courts*, Open Society Foundation for South Africa, Cape Town, 2008, pp. 17-18.

4.  Marcelo F. Aebi and Natalia Delgrande, *Council of Europe Annual Penal Statistics* (SPACE I), Survey 2011, Council of Europe, Strasbourg, May 3, 2013, pp. 142-143, available at http://www3.unil.ch/wpmu/space/2013/04/space-i-space-ii-2011-available-online-under-embargo-until-10-00-am-central-european-time-3-may-2013/ (accessed Nov. 12, 2013).

5.  The World Bank, "GDP Ranking by Country," available at http://data.worldbank.org/country (accessed Nov. 1, 2013).

6.  International human rights treaties distinguish between people who have been found guilty—that is, convicted by a court of law and sentenced to prison—and those who have not. Prisoners awaiting trial or the outcome of their trial are regarded differently because the law sees them as innocent until found guilty. While various international instruments make a distinction between unsentenced and sentenced prisoners, the line is typically drawn at the point of conviction rather than sentence. The International Declaration of Human Rights states that all "unconvicted" people in custody "... shall, save in exceptional circumstances, be segregated from convicted persons and shall be subject to

separate treatment appropriate to their status as unconvicted persons" (Article 10 of the Covenant). European Prison Rule 11(3) makes a distinction among untried, convicted, and sentenced prisoners. It also states that "in principle, untried prisoners shall be detained separately." According to Penal Reform International, "prisoners in pre-trial detention, or on remand, are those who have been detained without a sentence and are awaiting legal proceedings. They are also known as untried or unconvicted prisoners." See, *Pre-trial Detention*, Penal Reform International, http://www.penalreform. org/themes/pre-trial-detention (accessed June 12, 2012).

7. The Council of Europe classifies prisoners other than those who have received a "final sentence" into three sub-categories: (i) untried prisoners in respect of whom no court decision has been reached; (ii) prisoners convicted but not sentenced; and (iii) sentenced prisoners who have appealed against their sentence or who are within the statutory time limit for doing so. See, Marcelo F. Aebi, *Council of Europe Annual Penal Statistics* (SPACE I), Survey 2004, Strasburg, November 7, 2005, p 30.

8. See also, Samuel Deltenre and Eric Maes, "Pre-trial detention and the overcrowding of prisons in Belgium. Results from a simulation study into the possible effects of limiting the length of pre-trial detention," *European Journal of Crime, Criminal Law and Criminal Justice*, Vol. 12, Issue 4, 2004, p. 8. Deltenre and Maes define pretrial detention as the time before a "definitive conviction... the time before a judgment against which appeal is no longer possible."

9. According to Recommendation (2006)2 of the Council of Europe's *Committee of Ministers to member states on the European Prison Rules* (adopted by the Committee of Ministers on January 11, 2006 at the 952nd meeting of the Ministers' Deputies), the status of "untried prisoner" is defined in Section 94 as follows: "For the purposes of these rules, untried prisoners are prisoners who have been remanded in custody by a judicial authority prior to trial, conviction or sentence. A state may elect to regard prisoners who have been convicted and sentenced as untried prisoners if their appeals have not been disposed of finally." According to the Recommendation, national jurisdictions can decide who should be classified as a pretrial detainee or untried prisoner. The measure of national or jurisdictional discretion the Recommendation allows is problematic when undertaking cross-national comparisons of pretrial detention numbers. For a discussion of this point, see Christine Morgenstern, "Pre-trial / remand detention in Europe: Facts and figures and the need for common minimum standards," *ERA-Forum*, Vol. 9, No. 4, 2009, pp. 531-532.

10. While the period between arrest and the first court appearance should be short—usually 24 to 72 hours—in some countries the period may be lengthy and extend for days, weeks, and even months. Indications of a problematic practice of arrest and "police detention" in many European countries are given by the reports of the *Committee for the Prevention of Torture and Inhuman or Degrading Punishment* of the Council of Europe published since 1990. See also: Jon Vagg and Frieder Dünkel, "Conclusion," in Frieder Dünkel and Jon Vagg (eds.), *Waiting for Trial. International Perspectives on the Use of Pre-Trial Detention and the Rights and Living Conditions of Prisoners Waiting for Trial*, Max Planck Institute, Freiburg, 1994, pp. 919-926.

11. For a discussion of the administrative detention of persons who use drugs, see: *Detention as Treatment: Detention of Methamphetamine Users in Cambodia, Laos, and Thailand*, Open Society Institute, March 2010.

12. See, for example, Daniel Wilsher, *Immigration Detention: Law, History, Politics*, Cambridge University Press, New York, 2011.

13. Carolyn Hamilton, Kirsten Anderson, Ruth Barnes, and Kamena Dorling, *Administrative Detention of Children: A Global Report*, Children's Legal Centre, University of Essex, Essex, March 2011, p. 2, available at http://www.unicef.org/protection/files/Administrative_detention_discussion paper_April2011.pdf (accessed Oct. 3, 2013).

14. Louis Joinet, Rapporteur of the Sub-Commission on the Fight against Discriminatory Measures and Protection of Minorities, Report on the Practice of Administrative Detention, U.N. Doc. E/CN.4/sub.2/1989/27.

15. *Memorandum on the International Legal Framework on Administrative Detention and Counter-Terrorism*, International Commission of Jurists, Geneva, March 2006, p. 3, available at http://www.mafhoum. com/press9/278S25.pdf (accessed Oct. 3, 2013). Some international organs for the protection of human rights, including the UN Human Rights Committee, for example, have used the phrase "preventive detention" (*détention préventive, detención preventiva*) to refer to administrative detention. As the International Commission of Jurists points out, the use of the expression "preventive detention" may be misleading, notably because it is synonymous, in many national systems, with "detention in custody pending trial," "policy custody," "pre-trial detention," "garde-à-vue," "custodia policial," and "detención preventive."

16. *Human Rights and Pre-Trial Detention*, Centre for Human Rights - Crime Prevention and Criminal Justice Branch, Professional Training Series No. 3, UN Publication, Geneva, 1994, p. 42.

17. For a general discussion of the challenges associated with obtaining criminal justice statistics at the international level see: Anna Alvazzi del Frate, "Crime and criminal justice statistics challenges," pp. 167-175, in Stefan Harrendorf, Markku Heiskanen, and Steven Malby (eds.), *International Statistics on Crime and Justice*, European Institute for Crime Prevention and Control, Helsinki, 2010.

18. International Centre for Prison Studies, World Prison Brief, available at http://www.prisonstudies.org/info/worldbrief/ (accessed Oct. 3, 2013).

19. Given China's high absolute number of prisoners (2,300,000 in 2012), efforts were made to obtain an informed approximation of the number of pretrial detainees in the country. Otherwise, China's omission from the count of pretrial detainees could significantly undercount the global figure. Based on discussions with Chinese lawyers and human rights specialists, it is estimated that China had a pretrial detention population of 940,000 in 2012—approximately 41 percent of the total prison population. This is the figure which is used for calculating regional Asian and global pretrial detention figures in this report. See also Piet Hein van Kempen, "Pre-Trial Detention in National and International Law and Practice: A Comparative Synthesis and Analyses," p. 18, in Piet Hein van Kempen (ed.), *Pre-Trial Detention. Human Rights, Criminal Procedural Law and Penitentiary Law*, Comparative Law, Intersentia, Oxford, 2012, which provides a figure of 941,091 pretrial detainees in China in 2009.

20. Belgian data for persons who are appealing their conviction or sentence from Marcelo F. Aebi and Natalia Delgrande, *Council of Europe Annual Penal Statistics* (SPACE I), Survey 2011, Council of Europe, Strasbourg, May 3, 2013, p. 87, available at http://www3.unil.ch/wpmu/space/2013/04/space-i-space-ii-2011-available-online-under-embargo-until-10-00-am-central-european-time-3-may-2013/ (accessed Nov. 12, 2013). See also, Christine Morgenstern, "Pre-trial / Remand Detention in Europe: Facts and Figures and the Need for Common Minimum Standards," *ERA-Forum*, Vol. 9, No. 4, 2009, p. 533.

21. *The Criminalization of Poverty: A Report on the Economic, Social and Cultural Root Causes of Torture and Other Forms of Violence in Brazil: An Alternative Report to the Committee on Economic, Social and Cultural Rights*, Justiça Global, National Movement of Street Boys and Girls, and the World Organisation Against Torture, (undated), p. 24, available at http://www.omct.org/escr/reports-and-publications/brazil/2010/10/d20938/ (accessed Oct. 3, 2013).

22. IACHR, Press Release 64/10, "IACHR Rapporteurship Confirms Grave Detention Conditions in Buenos Aires Province," Washington, D.C., June 21, 2010, available at http://www.cidh.oas.org/Comunicados/English/2010/64-10eng.htm (accessed Oct. 3, 2013).

23. Section 1 of Recommendation 13 (2006) of the Council of Europe's *Committee of Ministers to Member States on the use of remand in custody, the conditions in which it takes place and the provision of safeguards against abuse*, provides: "(1) 'Remand in custody'... does not include the initial deprivation of liberty by a police or law enforcement officer (or by anyone else so authorized to act) for the purposes of questioning." (Adopted by the Committee of Ministers on 27 September 2006 at the 974th meeting of the Ministers' Deputies, available at https://wcd.coe.int/ViewDoc.jsp?id=1041281&Site=CM) (accessed Oct. 3, 2013).

24. For example, in Christie v. Leachinsky (1947) 1 All ER 567 of 587, 1947 AC 573, Lord Simmons stated emphatically that arrest is the beginning of imprisonment.

25. *Crime in the United States: Arrests*, U.S. Department of Justice, Criminal Justice Information Services Division, available at http://www2.fbi.gov/ucr/cius2009/arrests/index.html (accessed Oct. 3, 2013).

26. The number of people in pretrial detention at any point in time—both for the U.S. and the other countries whose arrest data are cited in this paragraph—are sourced from the International Centre for Prison Studies' World Prison Brief website, http://www.prisonstudies.org/info/worldbrief/.

27. *Police Powers and Procedures England and Wales 2010/11*, The Home Office, London, available at http://www.homeoffice.gov.uk/publications/science-research-statistics/research-statistics/police-research/police-powers-procedures-201011/?view=Standard&pubID=1019491 (accessed Oct. 3, 2013).

28. *Rapport d'activité 2011*, Le Contrôleur general des lieux de privation de liberté, 2012, p. 312, available at http://www.cglpl.fr/wp-content/uploads/2013/02/CGLPL_Rapport-2012_version-WEB.pdf (accessed Oct. 3, 2013).

29. *European Sourcebook of Crime and Criminal Justice Statistics—2010*, 4th Ed., Dutch WODC, p. 144,

available at http://www.europeansourcebook.org/ob285_full.pdf (accessed Oct. 3, 2013). The table reports persons in police custody, but a footnote on p. 145 clarifies that the Portugal figure is the "Number of suspected offenders arrested by the police."

30. *Annual Report 2010/2011*, South African Police Service, Pretoria, 2011, pp. 65-66, available at http://www.saps.gov.za/saps_profile/strategic_framework/annual_report/2010_2011/4_prg2_vispol.pdf (accessed Oct. 3, 2013).

31. *Crime in India: 2010 Statistics*, National Crime Records Bureau: Ministry of Home Affairs, Chapter 12: Arrests and Trials, available at http://ncrb.nic.in/CII2010/cii-2010/Chapter%2012.pdf (accessed Oct. 3, 2013).

32. The data used in this section (unless otherwise indicated as coming from a non-ICPS source) were drawn from the ICPS' World Prison Brief database in late 2013. In some cases the data reflect national pretrial detention numbers from 2013, in most cases from 2012, and in a few cases from 2011 or even earlier. Given that the bulk of the data are from 2012, this is the year which is used in this section unless indicated otherwise.

33. Excluded from this list are countries with a small population—generally around a million or less. Their small population size easily distorts the number of pretrial detainees as a proportion of all prisoners as the absolute numbers of both tend to be small. For example, in Malta (population 408,000), the number of pretrial detainees as a proportion of all prisoners was 64 percent in 2010. The proportion was based on a pretrial detention population of 373 persons and 210 sentenced prisoners. Should the number of pretrial detainees decrease by, for example, 70 people, then the proportion of pretrial detainees would drop from 64 to 52 percent.

34. *Country and Lending Groups*, The World Bank, available at http://data.worldbank.org/about/country-classifications/country-and-lending-groups (accessed Nov. 12, 2013). The World Bank divides economies according to 2012 Gross National Income (GNI) per capita. The groups are: low-income, $1,035 or less; lower-middle income, $1,036 - $4,085; upper-middle income, $4,086 - $12,615; and high income, $12,616 or more. See: *How we Classify Countries*, The World Bank, available at http://data.worldbank.org/about/country-classifications (accessed Oct. 3, 2013).

35. Excluded from this list are countries with a small population—generally around a million or less. Their small population size easily distorts the number of pretrial detainees as a proportion of all prisoners as the absolute numbers of both tend to be small. For example, in Tonga, an archipelago in the South Pacific, the number of pretrial detainees as a proportion of all prisoners was 0.6 percent in 2010 (the lowest of all the jurisdictions on the ICPS database). The proportion was based on a pretrial detention population of one person and a sentenced prisoner population of 159. Should the number of pretrial detainees increase by, for example, a dozen people, then the proportion of pretrial detainees would jump from 0.6 to 8.2 percent.

36. *Country and Lending Groups*, The World Bank, http://data.worldbank.org/about/country-classifications/country-and-lending-groups (accessed on Nov. 12, 2013). The World Bank divides economies according to 2012 Gross National Income (GNI) per capita. The groups are: low-income, $1,035 or less; lower-middle income, $1,036 - $4,085; upper-middle income, $4,086 - $12,615; and high income, $12,616 or more. See: *How we Classify Countries*, The World Bank, http://data.worldbank.org/about/country-classifications (accessed Oct. 3, 2013).

37. Excluded from this list are countries with a population of around one million people or less. Their small population size easily distorts the rate of pretrial detainees. For example, in Saint Kitts and Nevis the pretrial detention rate was 252 in 2010 (the highest of all the jurisdictions on the ICPS database). The rate was based on a small pretrial detention population of 127 people as the islands have a population of just over 50,000 people. Thus, for every 10 additional people in pretrial detention, the islands' rate of pretrial detainees per 100,000 people of the general population increases by about 20.

38. *Country and Lending Groups*, The World Bank, available at http://data.worldbank.org/about/country-classifications/country-and-lending-groups (accessed Nov. 12, 2013). The World Bank divides economies according to 2012 Gross National Income (GNI) per capita. The groups are: low-income, $1,035 or less; lower-middle income, $1,036 - $4,085; upper-middle income, $4,086 - $12,615; and high income, $12,616 or more. See: *How we Classify Countries*, The World Bank, available at http://data.worldbank.org/about/country-classifications (accessed Oct. 3, 2013).

39. *World Prison Brief Online*, International Centre for Prison Studies, available at http://www.prisonstudies.org/info/worldbrief/, (accessed Oct. 4, 2013).

40. *List of countries by population*, http://en.wikipedia.org/wiki/List_of_countries_by_population, (accessed Oct. 4, 2013).

41. Based on the rough calculation that the average length of outstretched arms is 1.8 meters, or 6 feet.

42. The number of persons in pretrial detention on, say, September 1, 2013, is a *stock* variable which is measured at one specific time, and represents a quantity existing at that point in time. The number of pretrial admissions is a *flow* variable which is measured over an interval or unit of time (a year in the present case).

43. Marcelo F. Aebi and Natalia Delgrande, *Council of Europe Annual Penal Statistics* (SPACE I), Survey 2011, Council of Europe, Strasbourg, May 3, 2013, p. 87, available at http://www3.unil.ch/wpmu/space/2013/04/space-i-space-ii-2011-available-online-under-embargo-until-10-00-am-central-european-time-3-may-2013/ (accessed Nov. 12, 2013).

44. Marcelo F. Aebi and Natalia Delgrande, *Council of Europe Annual Penal Statistics* (SPACE I), Survey 2011, Council of Europe, Strasbourg, May 3, 2013, pp. 114-115, available at http://www3.unil.ch/wpmu/space/2013/04/space-i-space-ii-2011-available-online-under-embargo-until-10-00-am-central-european-time-3-may-2013/ (accessed Nov. 12, 2013).

45. *Annual Report for the Period 1 April 2006 to 31 March 2007*, Judicial Inspectorate of Prisons, Cape Town, 2006, p. 37, available at http://judicialinsp.pwv.gov.za/Annualreports/ANNUAL%20REPORT%202007.pdf (accessed Oct. 3, 2013).

46. In the U.S., the vast majority of pretrial detainees are held in local jails. During the 12 months ending on June 30, 2011, 16 times as many persons were admitted to such jails as were incarcerated therein at midyear 2011 (respectively, 11.8 million and 735,601). It should be noted that in 2011, 60.6 percent of local jail inmates in the U.S. were pretrial detainees; the remainder were sentenced prisoners, mentally ill persons pending their movement to mental health facilities, sentenced juveniles pending transfer to juvenile facilities, etc. The 1:16 ratio applies to all jail inmates, and may be somewhat different if it were available for pretrial detainees only. See: Todd D. Minton, *Jail Inmates at Midyear 2011 – Statistical Tables*, Bureau of Justice Assistance, Department of Justice, April 2012, p. 3, available at http://www.bjs.gov/content/pub/pdf/jim11st.pdf (accessed Sept. 30, 2013).

47. The annual admission figures do not relate to the number of individuals, but to the number of admissions or entries. That is, the same individual may, for example, enter a pretrial detention center more than once in the same year for different cases. It is probable, however, that over a one year period the vast majority of admissions are comprised of distinct individuals. For a detailed explanation of what counts as an admission see Marcelo F. Aebi, *Council of Europe Annual Penal Statistics* (SPACE I), Survey 2003, Strasburg, September 29, 2004, p. 5.

48. Based on the rough calculation that the average length of outstretched arms is 1.8 meters, or 6 feet.

49. Marcelo F Aebi and Natalia Delgrande, *Council of Europe Annual Penal Statistics* (SPACE I), Survey 2011, Council of Europe, Strasbourg, May 3, 2013, p. 127, available at http://www3.unil.ch/wpmu/space/2013/04/space-i-space-ii-2011-available-online-under-embargo-until-10-00-am-central-european-time-3-may-2013/ (accessed Nov. 12, 2013).

50. *Innocent Until Proven Guilty: Tackling the Overuse of Custodial Remand*, Prison Reform Trust, October 2011, London, p. 2, available at http://www.prisonreformtrust.org.uk/Portals/0/Documents/Remand%20Briefing%20FINAL.PDF (accessed June 12, 2012).

51. *Evaluation of PRI and SDC Project: Support to Penitentiary Reform in Ukraine 2009-2012*, Penal Reform International, London, August 2011, p. 4.

52. *Compendium of Federal Justice Statistics, 2004*, Bureau of Justice Statistics, U.S. Department of Justice, December 2006, p. 55, available at http://bjs.ojp.usdoj.gov/content/pub/pdf/cfjs04.pdf (accessed Sept. 30, 2013). (Other jurisdictions' data do not generally distinguish between defendants who were explicitly not released awaiting trial and those who were granted conditional release.)

53. *Estimates of National Expenditure 2012* (abridged version), National Treasury (South Africa), Pretoria, 2012, p. 461, available at http://www.treasury.gov.za/documents/national%20budget/2012/ene/FullENE.pdf (accessed Oct. 3, 2013).

54. Anthony Nwapa, "Building and Sustaining Change: Pretrial Detention Reform in Nigeria," in *Justice Initiatives: Pretrial Detention*, Open Society Foundations, New York, 2008, p. 86. Evidence from Lagos State tends to indicate that the 3.7 years average figure may be too high. See Todd Foglesong and

Christopher E. Stone, "Prison Exit Samples as a Source for Indicators of Pretrial Detention," *Indicators in Development, Safety and Justice*, April 2011, Harvard Kennedy School, Cambridge MA, available at http://www.hks.harvard.edu/var/ezp_site/storage/fckeditor/file/pdfs/centers-programs/programs/criminal-justice/Indicators-PrisonExitSamples.pdf (accessed Oct. 3, 2013).

55. Olawale Fapohunda, "Nigeria: Fayemi's Victory, Justice Administration's Low Point," *This Day*, Oct. 19, 2010, available at http://allafrica.com/stories/printable/201010190813.html (accessed April 21, 2011).

56. Davidson Iriekpen, "Nigeria: Saving Pre-Trial Detainees," *This Day*, July 26, 2010, available at http://allafrica.com/stories/201007270184.html (accessed April 21, 2011).

57. *Prisons in Benin*. Report on a visit 23-31 August 1999, by Prof. E.V.O. Dankwa, Special Rapporteur on Prisons and Conditions of Detention in Africa, African Commission on Human and Peoples' Rights, Series IV, No. 6, pp. 14, 31.

58. *Prisons in Malawi*. Report on a visit 17-28 June 2001, by Dr. Vera Mlangazuwa Chirwa, Special Rapporteur on Prisons and Conditions of Detention in Africa, African Commission on Human and Peoples' Rights, Series IV, No. 9, p. 7.

59. *Health and Human Rights Prison Project: Medical-Legal Advocacy in Haiti: Initial Data Report*, September 2009. Partners In Health, Zanmi Lasante, Institute for Justice & Democracy in Haiti, Bureau des Avocats Internationaux, François-Xavier Bagnoud Center, for Health & Human Rights, p. 15.

60. Adnan Aziz, "Penal Reform," *The News*, May 7, 2011, available at http://www.thenews.com.pk/TodaysPrintDetail.aspx?ID=45633&Cat=9 (accessed Oct. 3, 2013).

61. *Excessive Pretrial Detention*, Human Rights Watch Prison Project, available at http://hrw.org/advocacy/prisons/pretrial.htm, (accessed Feb. 12, 2007).

62. Vaibhav Vats, "1,36,217 prisoners, in for petty crime, have been set free in a drive that ends in a few days. Will freedom reform them, or will they come right back to jail?" *Tehelka Magazine*, Vol. 7, Issue 30, July 31, 2010, available at http://www.tehelka.com/story_main46.asp?filename=Ne310710undertrial.asp (accessed Oct. 3, 2013).

63. Sankarshan Thakur, "Justice Under Trial," *Tehelka Magazine*, February 16, 2006, available at http://www.tehelka.com/story_main16.asp?filename=Ne021806Justice.asp (accessed Oct. 3, 2013).

64. Calculated on the assumption that the pyramid builders worked an average of eight hours a day. See Stuart Wier, "Recent Pyramid Calculations: Manpower Estimates for Khufu's Pyramid," August 1998, available at http://www.unexplained-mysteries.com/forum/index.php?showtopic=97834 (accessed Oct. 3, 2013).

65. *Empire State Building Official Internet Site*, http://www.esbnyc.com/esb_story_historical_timeline.asp, (accessed Oct. 3, 2013).

66. See John Chisholm, "Benefit-Cost Analysis and Crime Prevention," *Trends & Issues in Crime and Criminal Justice*, No. 147, February 2000, Australian Institute of Criminology, available at http://www.aic.gov.au/documents/9/D/4/%7B9D4E07CA-74FF-4F35-9C31-71504330BD00%7Dtii147.pdf (accessed Oct. 3, 2013); and Irvin Waller and Daniel Sansfaçon, "Investing Wisely in Crime Prevention: International Experiences," *Bureau of Justice Assistance Monograph*, Crime Prevention Series No. 1, September 2000.

67. *Estimates of National Expenditure 2012* (abridged version), National Treasury (South Africa), Pretoria, 2012, pp. x-xi, available at http://www.treasury.gov.za/documents/national%20budget/2012/ene/FullENE.pdf (accessed Oct. 3, 2013).

68. *Judicial Inspectorate for Correctional Services Annual Report for the Period 1 April 2010 to 31 March 2011*, Cape Town, 2011, p. 15, available at http://judicialinsp.pwv.gov.za/Annualreports/JUDICIAL_INSPECTORATE_ANNUAL%20%20REPORT_2010-2011.pdf (accessed Oct. 3, 2013).

69. "ABA Urges Pre-Trial Release Reform to Save States Money, Reduce Recidivism and Protect the Public," American Bar Association Criminal Justice Section, (undated), available at http://www2.americanbar.org/sections/criminaljustice/CR203800/PublicDocuments/pretrialdetention.pdf (accessed Oct. 2, 2013).

70. Shima Baradaran, "The State of Pretrial Detention," in *The State of Criminal Justice 2011*, American Bar Association, Washington DC, 2011, p. 190. See also "Cost of Pre-Trial Detention in City Jails Takes Bite Out of Big Apple's Budget," http://www.ibo.nyc.ny.us/newsfax/nws56pretrialdetention.html (accessed

Oct. 3, 2013). A survey of expenditure among 40 U.S. states, representing more than 1.2 million prisoners (of 1.4 million total people incarcerated in all 50 state prison systems), the total 2010 fiscal year annual per-inmate cost averaged $31,307 and ranged from $14,603 in Kentucky to $60,076 in New York. See Christian Henrichson and Ruth Delaney, *The Price of Prisons. What Incarceration Costs Taxpayers*, Vera Institute of Justice, New York, January 2012, p. 9, available at http://www.vera.org/pubs/special/price-prisons-what-incarceration-costs-taxpayers (accessed Oct. 3, 2013).

71. *The Costs of Confinement: Why Good Juvenile Justice Policies Make Good Fiscal Sense*, Justice Policy Institute, Washington DC, May 2009, p. 1, available at http://www.justicepolicy.org/images/upload/09_05_REP_CostsofConfinement_JJ_PS.pdf (accessed Oct. 3, 2013).

72. Matthew Ericson and Tony Vinson, *Young People on Remand in Victoria: Balancing Individual and Community Interest*, Jesuit Social Services, Richmond, Victoria, 2010, p. 25.

73. Marcelo F. Aebi and Natalia Delgrande, *Council of Europe Annual Penal Statistics* (SPACE I), Survey 2011, Council of Europe, Strasbourg, May 3, 2013, pp. 142-143, available at http://www3.unil.ch/wpmu/space/2013/04/space-i-space-ii-2011-available-online-under-embargo-until-10-00-am-central-european-time-3-may-2013/ (accessed Nov. 12, 2013).

74. Pretrial detainee numbers for Council of Europe Member States come from the International Centre for Prison Studies' World Prison Brief.

75. "Gross domestic product 2010," World Development Indicators database, World Bank, April 17, 2012, available at http://databank.worldbank.org/databank/download/GDP.pdf (accessed June 11, 2012).

76. The U.N. core "regular" budget (US$ 2.5bn in 2009) funded by mandatory national assessments, covers many different costs, including meeting expenses, staff salaries, building maintenance, travel, security, conflict mediation, development initiatives, and human rights activities. Beyond the core U.N. budget is the much larger peacekeeping budget which rises and falls according to the number and size of missions mandated by the Security Council. See Michael Renner and James Paul, "UN Funding Increases, But Falls Short of Global Tasks," *Vital Signs*, February 29, 2012, Worldwatch Institute, available at http://vitalsigns.worldwatch.org/vs-trend/un-funding-increases-falls-short-global-tasks (accessed Oct. 3, 2013).

77. *The Global Fund Annual Report 2009*, The Global Fund to fight AIDS, Tuberculosis and Malaria, Geneva, 2010, p. 8, available at http://www.theglobalfund.org/en/library/publications/annualreports/ (accessed Oct. 2, 2013). The Global Fund's disbursements amounted to US$ 2.7bn in 2009.

78. *Medium-term Strategic Plan 2008–2013 and Proposed Programme budget 2012–2013*, Sixty-Fourth World Health Assembly A64/7, April 4, 2011, World Health Organization, p. 2, available at http://apps.who.int/gb/ebwha/pdf_files/WHA64/A64_7-en.pdf (accessed Oct. 3, 2013).

79. "More than a million children in Southern Somalia in need of lifesaving assistance," July 29, 2011, available at http://www.unicefusa.org/news/releases/more-than-a-million-children-need-immediate-aid-somalia.html (accessed Oct. 3, 2013). See also, Lutheran World Relief, "How Much Does It Take to Feed $5,000 in the Horn of Africa? Not as Much as You Think," http://lwr.org/atf/cf/%7B3F934D1F-3443-49CB-95AC-954E18EF5D03%7D/OW_WWD_E_E_Africa_Bulletin_K.pdf (accessed Oct. 3, 2013).

80. "Gov't spending P64K/year per prisoner," ABS-CBN News, May 26, 2011, available at http://www.abs-cbnnews.com/nation/05/26/11/govt-spending-p64kyear-prisoner (accessed Oct. 2, 2013).

81. Daniel Nemukuyu, "Prisoners gobble US$1,7m monthly," *The Herald Online*, September 1, 2011, available at http://www.herald.co.zw/index.php?option=com_content&view=article&id=20019:prisoners-gobble-us17m-monthly&catid=37:top-stories&Itemid=130 (accessed Oct. 2, 2013).

82. Victoria Ojeme, "FG spends N2.36bn to feed prison inmates annually," *Vanguard*, August 1, 2011, available at http://www.vanguardngr.com/2011/08/fg-spends-n2-36bn-to-feed-prison-inmates-annually/ (accessed Oct. 3, 2013).

83. "List of countries by percentage of population living in poverty," available at http://en.wikipedia.org/wiki/List_of_countries_by_percentage_of_population_living_in_poverty (accessed Oct. 3, 2013).

84. Guillermo Zepeda (with contributions by Miguel La Rota), *La prisión preventiva en México: Dimensiones, características, costos, alternativas*, Open Society Foundations, New York, 2009.

85. Hans-Jörg Albrecht, "Prison Overcrowding: Finding Effective Solutions: Strategies and Best Practices against Overcrowding in Correctional Facilities," in *Report of the Workshop: Strategies and Best Practices Against Overcrowding in Correctional Facilities: Twelfth United Nations Congress on Crime Prevention and*

*Criminal Justice. Salvador, Brazil, 12-19 April 2010.* United Nations Asia and Far East Institute for the Prevention of Crime and the Treatment of Offenders (UNAFEI), Tokyo, 2011, p. 85, available at http://www.unafei.or.jp/english/pdf/Congress_2010/13Hans-Jorg_Albrecht.pdf (accessed Oct. 3, 2013).

86. In South Africa, for example, the country's 239 prisons had an average occupancy level of 139 percent in 2009-2010. In 19 prisons, the occupancy rate was 200 percent or higher. At the time, pretrial detainees comprised some 30 percent of South Africa's prisoner population, but 52 percent of inmates in the 19 critically overcrowded prisons. See Deon Hurter van Zyl, *Annual Report for the Period 1 April 2009 to 31 March 2010*, Judicial Inspectorate for Correctional Services, Cape Town, 2010, pp. 11-13.

87. See, for example "Chile Plan to Build New Prisons and Grant Pardons to Ease Overcrowding," *Hispanically Speaking News*, March 14, 2011, available at http://www.hispanicallyspeakingnews.com/notitas-de-noticias/details/is-your-prison-full-follow-chiles-lead-grant-limited-pardons-and-let-p/6072/ (accessed Oct. 3, 2013); "2600 to be pardoned by Vesak," *The Daily Mirror*, May 16, 2011, available at http://www.highbeam.com/doc/1P3-2347634971.html (accessed Oct. 3, 2013); "President to pardon 300 convicts on the occasion of Independence Day," *Haveeru Daily*, July 26, 2011, available at http://www.haveeru.com.mv/english/details/36857 (accessed Oct. 3, 2013); "Venezuela plans 'to release 40% of prisoners," *BBC News*, July 31, 2011, available at http://www.bbc.co.uk/news/world-latin-america-14361079 (accessed Oct. 3, 2013); "Tajik parliament to consider amnesty bill for independence anniversary," *Trend*, August 19, 2011, available at http://pda.trend.az/en/1920348.html (accessed Oct. 3, 2013); "Ashgabat Frees 3,700 inmates," *The Moscow Times*, August 29, 2011, available at http://www.themoscowtimes.com/news/article/ashgabat-frees-3700-inmates/442803.html (accessed Oct. 3, 2013); "Vietnam Releasing 10,000 Prisoners in Annual Amnesty," *VOA News*, August 29, 2011, available at http://www.voanews.com/content/vietnam-releasing-10000-prisoners-in-annual-amnesty----128598328/167948.html (accessed Oct. 3, 2013); Dmitry Solovyov, "Kazakhstan to amnesty 16,000 for independence holiday," *Arab News*, October 26, 2011, available at http://www.arabnews.com/node/396110 (accessed Oct. 3, 2013); "Egypt releases inmates on revolt anniversary," January 25, 2012, *Al Jazeera*, available at http://www.aljazeera.com/news/middleeast/2012/01/2012125132412573594.html (accessed Oct. 3, 2013); "Burundi president pardons 'several thousand' prisoners," *AFP*, June 27, 2012, available at http://www.google.com/hostednews/afp/article/ALeqM5i-7wQ702HX9ksfJfo6K4At7yZYcw?hl=en (accessed Oct. 3, 2013); "Sata releases 2,314 prisoners and calls for fight against corruption," *Lusaka Times*, May 25, 2012, available at http://www.lusakatimes.com/2012/05/25/sata-releases-2314-prisoners-calls-fight-corruption/ (accessed Oct. 3, 2013); "Burundi president pardons 'several thousand' prisoners," *Radio Netherlands Worldwide*, June 27, 2012, available at http://www.rnw.nl/africa/bulletin/burundi-president-pardons-several-thousand-prisoners (accessed Oct. 3, 2013); Green Muheya, "JB pardons 377 prisoners to celebrate Malawi independence," *Nyasa Times*, July 6, 2012, available at http://www.nyasatimes.com/malawi/2012/07/06/jb-pardons-377-prisoners-to-celebrate-malawi-independence/ (accessed Oct. 3, 2013).

88. For example, "Govt grants remission to 55,234 prisoners nationwide," *The Jakarta Post*, August 17, 2011, available at http://www.thejakartapost.com/news/2011/08/17/govt-grants-remissions-55234-prisoners-nationwide.html (accessed Oct. 3, 2013); "President grants special remission in prisoners sentences," *Pakistan Observer*, November 1, 2011, available at http://pakobserver.net/detailnews.asp?id=145816 (accessed Oct. 3, 2013); Conor Lally, "Early release considered to deal with prison crisis," *Irish Times*, August 8, 2011, available at http://www.politics.ie/forum/justice/167279-early-release-considered-deal-prison-crisis.html (accessed Oct. 3, 2013); "S. Africa reduces prison sentences of over 35,000 inmates," *CNTV News*, May 1, 2012, available at http://english.cntv.cn/program/africalive/20120501/105788.shtml (accessed Oct. 3, 2013).

89. See, for example Lee Rondganger, "Freed cons will soon be back: Nicro," *Daily News*, June 13, 2012, available at http://www.iol.co.za/dailynews/news/freed-cons-will-soon-be-back-nicro-1.1317880#.T-hjaBePlGQ (accessed Oct. 3, 2013).

## WHO ARE THE WORLD'S PRETRIAL DETAINEES?

1. Working Group on Arbitrary Detention, *Report of the Working Group on Arbitrary Detention*, 2006, (E/CN.4/2006/7), para. 66.

2. *Unjust Deserts: A Thematic Review by HM Chief Inspector of Prisons of the Treatment and Conditions for Unsentenced Prisoners in England and Wales*, Her Majesty's Inspectorate of Prisons for England and Wales, London, 2000.

3. *Bromley Briefings Prison Factfile*, Prison Reform Trust, June 2009, p. 46, available at www.prisonreformtrust.org.uk/uploads/documents/june2009factfile.pdf ( accessed Oct. 7, 2013).

4. Matthew Ericson and Tony Vinson, *Young People on Remand in Victoria: Balancing Individual and Community Interests*, Jesuit Social Services, Richmond, 2010, p. 54.

5. *Scotland's Choice: Report of the Scottish Prison Commission*, Edinburgh, July 2008, p. 15.

6. Orley Ashenfelter, "How Convincing Is the Evidence Linking Education and Income?" The George Seltzer Distinguished Lecture, University of Minnesota, 1991. See also, Steven McIntosh, *Education and Employment in OECD Countries*, UNESCO, Paris, 2008, pp. 19-24.

7. Penal Reform International, *Prison Conditions in Africa*, PRI and African Centre for Democracy and Human Rights, London, 1993.

8. *Report of the National Working Group on Prison Reforms and Decongestion*, Federal Ministry of Justice, Abuja, 2005, cited in Stanley Ibe, "Improving Pretrial Practice: Lessons from Nigeria," paper presented at a Conference on Access to Justice for Indigent Persons in West Africa organized by Commonwealth Human Rights Initiative, Accra, Ghana, March, 22-23, 2011, p. 7.

9. Rani Dhavan Shankardass, *Exploration towards accessible and equitable justice in the South Asian region; problems and paradoxes of reform*, Penal Reform and Justice Association and Penal Reform International, London, 2001.

10. Caroline Wolf Harlow, *Special Report: Education and Correctional Populations*, Bureau of Justice Statistics, January 2003 (NCJ 195670), p. 2, available at http://bjs.ojp.usdoj.gov/index.cfm?ty=pbdetail&iid=814 (accessed Sept. 17, 2013).

11. See also, *Bromley Briefings Prison Factfile*, Prison Reform Trust, June 2009, p. 46, available at www.prisonreformtrust.org.uk/uploads/documents/june2009factfile.pdf (accessed Oct. 7, 2013).

12. Shima Baradaran, "The presumption of innocence and pretrial detention in Malawi," *Malawi Law Journal*, Vol. 4, Issue 1, 2010, p. 128.

13. Prison Fellowship International, *Freeing Prisoners in Sri Lanka*, 2008, available at http://www.pfi.org/cjr/human-rights/newsitems/freeing-prisoners-in-sri-lanka (accessed Oct. 7, 2013).

14. Harshi C. Perera, "Kumari's Story; Separation of Prisoners," *Sri Lanka Guardian*, Oct. 20, 2010 available at http://www.srilankaguardian.org/2010/10/kumaris-story-separation-of-prisoners.html (accessed Oct. 7, 2013).

15. Miguel La Rota, *El uso de la Prisón Preventiva en Nuevo León: Estudio Cuantitativo*, Open Society Justice Initiative, New York, 2010, pp. 100-101.

16. *Prisons in Malawi*. Report on a visit 17-28 June 2001, by Dr. Vera Mlangazuwa Chirwa, Special Rapporteur on Prisons and Conditions of Detention in Africa, African Commission on Human and Peoples' Rights, Series IV, No. 9, p. 34.

17. Open Society Justice Initiative, *The Socioeconomic Impact of Pretrial Detention in Sierra Leone*, Open Society Foundations, New York, 2013, p. 41.

18. Gideon Morris, Director: Judicial Inspectorate of Prisons, personal communication, January 18, 2006.

19. Vaibhav Vats, "1,36,217 prisoners, in for petty crime, have been set free in a drive that ends in a few days. Will freedom reform them, or will they come right back to jail?," *Tehelka Magazine*, Vol. 7, Issue 30, July 31, 2010, available at: http://www.tehelka.com/story_main46.asp?filename=Ne310710undertrial.asp (accessed Oct. 7, 2013).

20. Vaibhav Vats, "1,36,217 prisoners, in for petty crime, have been set free in a drive that ends in a few days. Will freedom reform them, or will they come right back to jail?," *Tehelka Magazine*, Vol. 7, Issue 30, July 31, 2010, available at: http://www.tehelka.com/story_main46.asp?filename=Ne310710undertrial.asp (accessed Oct. 7, 2013).

21. Vaibhav Vats, "1,36,217 prisoners, in for petty crime, have been set free in a drive that ends in a few days. Will freedom reform them, or will they come right back to jail?," *Tehelka Magazine*, Vol. 7, Issue 30, July 31, 2010, available at: http://www.tehelka.com/story_main46.asp?filename=Ne310710undertrial.asp (accessed Oct. 7, 2013).

22. Carline Wolf Harlow, *Special Report: Defense Counsel in Criminal Cases*, Bureau of Justice Statistics, November 2000 (NCJ 179023), p. 5, available at http://bjs.ojp.usdoj.gov/index.cfm?ty=pbdetail&iid=772 (accessed Sept. 17, 2013).

23. *The Price of Freedom. Bail and Pretrial Detention of Low Income Nonfelony Defendants in New York City*, Human Rights Watch, New York, 2010, p. 2.

24. Sarah Geraghty and Miriam Gohara, *Assembly Line Justice: Mississippi's Indigent Defense Crisis*, NAACP Legal Defense and Educational Fund, New York, 2003, p. 8.

25. *The Price of Freedom. Bail and Pretrial Detention of Low Income Nonfelony Defendants in New York City*, Human Rights Watch, New York, 2010, p. 31.

26. Antoinette Louw, Eric Pelser, and Sipho Ntuli, "Poor Safety: Crime and Policing in South Africa's Rural Areas," *ISS Monograph Series*, No. 47, May 2000.

27. *Access to Justice and Legal Aid in East Africa: A comparison of the legal aid schemes used in the region and the level of cooperation and coordination between the various actors*, The Danish Institute for Human Rights, Copenhagen, December 2011, p. 29.

28. Magdalena Sepúlveda Carmona, *Extreme poverty and human rights*: Report of the Special Rapporteur on extreme poverty and human rights, August 4, 2011, A/66/265, paragraph 66, available at http://www.ohchr.org/Documents/Issues/Poverty/A.66.265.pdf (accessed Oct. 7, 2013).

29. *Access to Legal Aid in Criminal Justice Systems in Africa*. Survey Report, UNODC, Vienna, 2011, pp. 9-10.

30. Patrick Matibini, *Access to Justice and the Rule of Law*. An issue paper presented for the Commission on Legal Empowerment of the Poor, (undated), p. 16.

31. Hillery Anderson, "Justice Delayed in Malawi's Criminal Justice System: Paralegals vs. Lawyers," *International Journal of Criminal Justice Sciences*, Vol. 1, Issue 1, 2006.

32. *Access to Legal Aid in Criminal Justice Systems in Africa*. Survey Report, UNODC, Vienna, 2011.

33. *Access to Legal Aid in Criminal Justice Systems in Africa*. Survey Report, UNODC, Vienna, 2011, p. 12. The real figure may be even higher. The Nigerian Bar Association estimates the number of lawyers in Nigeria at around 70,000 at the time of writing (and a membership of 55,000 in 2010).

34. Davidson Iriekpen, "Nigeria: Saving Pre-Trial Detainees," This Day, July 26, 2010 available at http://allafrica.com/stories/201007270184.html (accessed Oct. 13, 2013).

35. *Improvement of the Real Situation of Overcrowding in Prisons in Bangladesh*, GTZ – Dhaka (undated), p. 1.

36. Personal communication, Heidi Cerneka, Deputy National Coordinator, Pastoral Carceraria Nacional – Brazil, March 9, 2011.

37. Idil Elveris, G Jahic, and S Kalem, *Alone in the Courtroom: Accessibility and Impact of Criminal Legal Aid*, Istanbul Bilgi University Publications, Istanbul, 2007, p. 182.

38. In *Scott v. Illinois*, 440 U.S. 367 (1979), the U.S. Supreme Court held that the Sixth and Fourteenth Amendments to the Constitution require that no indigent criminal defendant be sentenced to a term of imprisonment unless the state has afforded him the right to assistance of appointed counsel in his defense (but did not require a state trial court to appoint counsel for a criminal defendant who is charged with a statutory offense for which imprisonment upon conviction is authorized but not imposed.) See http://caselaw.lp.findlaw.com/scripts/getcase.pl?court=us&vol=440&invol=367 (accessed Oct. 7, 2013).

39. Carline Wolf Harlow, *Special Report: Defense Counsel in Criminal Cases*, Bureau of Justice Statistics, November 2000 (NCJ 179023), p. 1, available at http://bjs.ojp.usdoj.gov/index.cfm?ty=pbdetail&iid=772 (accessed Sept. 7, 2013).

40. "Pretrial Release Programs Vary Across the State; New Reporting Requirements Pose Challenges," Office of Program Policy Analysis & Government Accountability (Florida), December 2008, Report No. 08-75, p. 5.

41. *System Overload: The Costs of Under-Resourcing Public Defense*, Factsheet, Justice Policy Institute, Washington D.C., July 2011, p. 18, available at http://www.justicepolicy.org/uploads/justicepolicy/documents/system_overload_final.pdf (accessed Oct. 7, 2013).

42. Carline Wolf Harlow, *Special Report: Defense Counsel in Criminal Cases*, Bureau of Justice Statistics, November 2000 (NCJ 179023), p. 5, available at http://bjs.ojp.usdoj.gov/index.cfm?ty=pbdetail&iid=772 (accessed Sept. 17, 2013).

43. Carline Wolf Harlow, *Special Report: Defense Counsel in Criminal Cases*, Bureau of Justice Statistics, November 2000 (NCJ 179023), p. 7, available at http://bjs.ojp.usdoj.gov/index.cfm?ty=pbdetail&iid=772 (accessed Sept. 17, 2013). See also, Thomas E. Daniels, "Gideon's Hollow Promise – How Appointed Counsel Are Prevented from Fulfilling their Role in the Criminal Justice System," *Michigan Bar Journal*, February 1992, pp. 136-141; Morris B. Hoffman, Paul H. Rubin, and Joanna M. Shepherd, "An Empirical Study of Public Defender Effectiveness: Self-Selection by the 'Marginally Indigent,'" *Bepress Legal Services*, Paper 391, 2004; Sonia Y. Lee, "OC's PD's Feeling the Squeeze – the Right to Counsel: In Light of Budget Cuts, Can the Orange County Office of the Public Defender Provide Effective Assistance of Counsel?," *Loyola of Los Angeles Law Review*, 1995, Vol. 29, pp. 1895-1928; Charles J. Ogletree, "An Essay on the New Public Defender for the 21st Century," *Law and Contemporary Problems*, Vol. 58, No. 1, pp. 85-88.

44. Carline Wolf Harlow, Special Report: Defense Counsel in Criminal Cases, Bureau of Justice Statistics, November 2000 (NCJ 179023), p. 1, available at http://bjs.ojp.usdoj.gov/index.cfm?ty=pbdetail&iid=772 (accessed Sept. 17, 2013).

45. *System Overload: The Costs of Under-Resourcing Public Defense*, Factsheet, Justice Policy Institute, Washington D.C., July 2011, p. 1, available at http://www.justicepolicy.org/uploads/justicepolicy/documents/system_overload_factsheet_final.pdf (accessed Sept. 17, 2013).

46. Donald J. Farole Jr. and Lynn Langton, *County-based and Local Public Defender Offices*, 2007, Bureau of Justice Statistics Special Report, U.S. Department of Justice, September 2010, NCJ231175, pp. 8-10.

47. *System Overload: The Costs of Under-Resourcing Public Defense*, Factsheet, Justice Policy Institute, Washington D.C., July 2011, p. 10, available at http://www.justicepolicy.org/uploads/justicepolicy/documents/system_overload_final.pdf (accessed Sept. 17, 2013).

48. *System Overload: The Costs of Under-Resourcing Public Defense*, Factsheet, Justice Policy Institute, Washington D.C., July 2011, p. 19, available at http://www.justicepolicy.org/uploads/justicepolicy/documents/system_overload_final.pdf (accessed Sept. 17, 2013).

49. Ed Cape, Zaza Namoradze, Roger Smith, and Taru Spronken, *Effective Criminal Defence in Europe. Executive Summary and Recommendations*, Intersentia, Antwerp, 2010, p. 9, available at http://www.soros.org/initiatives/justice/focus/criminal_justice/articles_publications/publications/criminal-defence-europe-20100623 (accessed Sept. 17, 2013).

50. Ed Cape, Zaza Namoradze, Roger Smith, and Taru Spronken, *Effective Criminal Defence in Europe. Executive Summary and Recommendations*, Intersentia, Antwerp, 2010, p. 7, available at http://www.soros.org/initiatives/justice/focus/criminal_justice/articles_publications/publications/criminal-defence-europe-20100623 (accessed Sept. 17, 2013).

51. Author interview with Nur-A-Alam Nobi, Bogra, Bangladesh, October 5, 2010.

52. "Disconnected Policing and the Justice Trade in Bangladesh," *Article 2: Special Edition: Use of Police Powers for Profit*, Vol. 8 (1), March 2009.

53. *Assessment of Justice System Integrity and Capacity in Three Nigerian States*, United Nations Office on Drugs and Crime, Vienna, May 2004, pp. 112-116, available at http://www.unodc.org/pdf/crime/corruption/Justice_Sector_Assessment_2004.pdf (accessed Oct. 7, 2013).

54. *Draft project idea: Strengthening judicial integrity & capacity*, Phase II, United Nations Office on Drugs and Crime, Vienna (undated), available at http://www.unodc.org/pdf/crime/corruption/corruption_project_nigeria_judicial_integrity_draft.pdf (accessed Oct. 7, 2013).

55. *Criminal Force: Torture, Abuse, and Extrajudicial Killings by the Nigeria Police Force*, Open Society Justice Initiative, New York, 2010, pp. 82-83.

56. *Criminal Force. Torture, Abuse, and Extrajudicial Killings by the Nigeria Police Force*, Open Society Justice Initiative, New York, 2010, pp. 82-83.

57. *Prisons in the Central African Republic*. Report on a visit June 19-29, 2000, by Prof. E.V.O. Dankwa, Special Rapporteur on Prisons and Conditions of Detention in Africa, African Commission on Human and Peoples' Rights, Series IV, No. 7, p. 7.

58. *Prisons in Malawi*. Report on a visit 17-28 June 2001, by Dr. Vera Mlangazuwa Chirwa, Special Rapporteur on Prisons and Conditions of Detention in Africa, African Commission on Human and Peoples' Rights, Series IV, No. 9, p. 39.

59. *Prisons in Benin*. Report on a visit 23-31 August 1999, by Prof. E.V.O. Dankwa, Special Rapporteur on Prisons and Conditions of Detention in Africa, African Commission on Human and Peoples' Rights, Series IV, No. 6, p. 20.

60. *The Socioeconomic Impact of Pretrial Detention in Ghana*, Open Society Foundations, New York, 2013, p. 31.

61. "Bones Picked by Legal Vultures," *The Age*, February 23, 2008.

62. "Bones Picked by Legal Vultures," *The Age*, February 23, 2008.

63. Sarah Geraghty and Miriam Gohara, *Assembly Line Justice: Mississippi's Indigent Defense Crisis*, NAACP Legal Defense and Educational Fund, New York, 2003, p. 15.

64. Sarah Geraghty and Miriam Gohara, *Assembly Line Justice: Mississippi's Indigent Defense Crisis*, NAACP Legal Defense and Educational Fund, New York, 2003, p. 13.

65. *Pretrial Detention and Criminal Procedure Code Reform in Latin America: Evaluation and Perspectives*, (Country Report on Mexico), Justice Studies Center of the Americas, August 2009.

66. Enrique Ochoa Reza, *La Transparencia y el Ministerio Público. Derecho a Saber: Balance y Perspectivas Cívicas*, 2007, p. 135.

67. This is not to suggest that systems of state governance should be reformed through empowering the poor and marginalized to gain access to political benefactors to facilitate their pretrial release independently of the reasons for their detention.

68. International Crisis Group, *Reforming Pakistan's Criminal justice System*, Asia Report No. 196, December 2010, p. 12.

69. Promita Gupta, "Improvement of the Real Situation of Overcrowding in Prisons in Bangladesh," presentation at the Conference on Penal Reform in Developing Countries, Dhaka, Bangladesh, October 6, 2010.

70. Ananias Ndlovu, "100 times in court and case continued," *Sowetan LIVE*, March 22, 2011.

71. Adefi Matthew Olong, *The Administration of Criminal Justice in Nigeria: A Case for Reform*, A Thesis in the Faculty of Law, Submitted to the School of Postgraduate Studies, University of Jos, November 2010, pp. 148-149.

72. Vivien Stern, *Alternatives to prison in developing countries*, International Centre for Prison Studies and Penal Reform International, London, 1999, p. 87.

73. Denise Tomasini-Joshi, "Children, Torture, and Pretrial Detention," April 15, 2010, available at http://blog.soros.org/2010/04/children-torture-and-pretrial-detention/ (accessed Oct. 13, 20130).

74. Magdalena Sepúlveda Carmona, *Extreme poverty and human rights,* Report of the Special Rapporteur on Extreme Poverty and Human Rights, August 4, 2011, A/66/265, paragraphs 33-34, available at http://www.ohchr.org/Documents/Issues/Poverty/A.66.265.pdf (accessed Oct. 7, 2013).

75. Interview conducted by Justice Initiative researcher, Bishkek, October, 2010.

76. *Fanning the Flames: How Human Rights Abuses Are Fueling the Aids Epidemic in Kazakhstan*, Human Rights Watch, New York June 2003, Vol.15, No. 4 (D), pp. 18-19. See also, information on police quotas in the Russian Federation, *Confessions at Any Cost: Police Torture in Russia*, Human Rights Watch, New York, November, 1999, pp. 122-123; and in Uzbekistan, in Human Rights Watch, *"And it was Hell all over Again...": Torture in Uzbekistan*, Human Rights Watch, New York, December 2000, Vol. 12, No. 12 (D), p. 5; International Crisis Group, *Central Asia: The Politics of Police Reform* ICG, Osh/Brussels, December 10, 2002, pp. 16, 24.

77. Katherine Wilkinson, "Knysna police ordered to meet arrest quotas," *West Cape News*, May 17, 2010, available at http://westcapenews.com/?p=1454 (accessed Oct. 7, 2013).

78. "Russian police detain 'YouTube cop,'" *European Forum for Democracy and Solidarity*, January 25, 2010, available at http://www.europeanforum.net/news/814/russian_police_detain_youtube_cop (accessed Oct. 7, 2013).

79. Rocco Parascandola, "NYPD Lt. Janice Williams pushes for more busts, but brass say there's no quotas," *Daily News*, March 3, 2011, available at http://articles.nydailynews.com/2011-03-03/local/28666735_1_officer-adrian-schoolcraft-illegal-quotas-nypd, (accessed Oct. 7, 2013); Rocco Parascandola, "Ex-Bronx cop Venessa Hicks suing city, says quotas led to axing," *Daily News*, May 2, 2011, available at http://articles.nydailynews.com/2011-05-02/local/29518522_1_illegal-quotas-cop-claims-42nd-precinct (accessed Oct. 7, 2013); Graham Rayman, "The NYPD Tapes Confirmed," *The Village Voice*, March 7, 2012, available at http://www.villagevoice.com/2012-03-07/news/the-nypd-tapes-confirmed/all/ (accessed Oct. 7, 2013).

80. Interview conducted by Justice Initiative researcher, Kharkov, Ukraine, November, 2010.

81. Advocacy Forum-Nepal, personal communication with Paul English, January 2010.

82. *Torture of Women in Detention: Nepal's Failure to Prevent and Protect*, Advocacy Forum – Nepal, Kathmandu, 2011, p. 8.

83. *Recent Trends and Patterns of Torture in Nepal: Briefing July to December 2010*, Advocacy Forum – Nepal, Kathmandu, 2010, p. 10.

84. *Caste Discrimination against Dalits or so-called Untouchables in India: Information for the consideration of the Committee on the Elimination of Racial Discrimination in Reviewing India's Fifteenth to Nineteenth Periodic Reports, Presented at the Seventieth Session of the Committee on the Elimination of Racial Discrimination.* Prepared by the Center for Human Rights and Global Justice and Human Rights Watch. February 2007, p. 21, available at http://www2.ohchr.org/english/bodies/cerd/docs/ngos/chrgj-hrw.pdf (accessed Oct. 7, 2013).

85. Mike Bartlett, "World Correctional Population Trends and Issues," in Sean O' Toole and Simon Eyland (eds.), *Corrections Criminology*, Hawkins Press, Leichhardt, pp. 8-16.

86. Lindsay Porter and Donna Calverley, *Trends in the Use of Remand in Canada*, Juristat (Catalogue no. 85-002-X), Statistics Canada, Ottawa, May 2011, p. 14.

87. *Juvenile Justice in Australia 2007-08*, Juvenile Justice Series, Number 5, Australian Institute of Health and Welfare, Canberra, November 2009, p. 62.

88. Lucy Snowball, Lenny Roth, and Don Weatherburn, "Bail Presumptions and Risk of Bail Refusal: An Analysis of the New Bail Act," *Crime and Justice Statistics – Bureau Brief*, No. 49, July 2010, NSW Bureau of Crime Statistics and Research, p. 5.

89. *Aboriginal Customary Laws: The Interaction of Western Australian Law with Aboriginal Law and Culture*, Law Reform Commission of Western Australia, Final Report, Project 94, Perth, September 2006, p. 159.

90. Anthea S. Krieg, "Aboriginal Incarceration: Health and Social Impacts," *Medical Journal of Australia*, 184(10).

91. Charles Puzzanchera et al., *Juvenile Court Statistics 2006-2007*, National Center for Juvenile Justice 33 (March 2010).

92. Todd D. Minton, *Jail Inmates at Midyear 2009 – Statistical Tables*, Bureau of Justice Statistics, U.S. Department of Justice, June 2010, NCJ 230122, available at http://bjs.ojp.usdoj.gov/index.cfm?ty=pbdetail&iid=2195, (accessed Sept. 17, 2013). Data on jail inmates who are pretrial detainees versus those who are not do not appear to be disaggregated by race or ethnicity. (U.S. jails also typically accommodate persons serving a prison sentence of one year or less and some other categories of inmates who are not pretrial detainees, such as probation and parole violators.)

93. *The Price of Freedom: Bail and Pretrial Detention of Low Income Nonfelony Defendants in New York City*, Human Rights Watch, New York, 2010, p. 48.

94. Janis Bane and David A. Jones, *Harris County Pre-Trial Services: Policies and Practices*, Houston Ministers Against Crime, Houston, 2011, p. 3.

95. Janis Bane and David A. Jones, *Harris County Pre-Trial Services: Policies and Practices*, Houston Ministers Against Crime, Houston, 2011, p. 1.

96. UN Special Rapporteur on Torture, Nigel Rodley, A/55/290, para. 35.

97. UN Special Rapporteur on Torture, Manfred Nowak, A/HRC/10/44, para. 55, as observed in Indonesia.

98. UN Special Rapporteur on Torture, Nigel Rodley, A/56/156, paras. 17-25.

99. A.M. van Kalmthout, M.M. Knapen, and C. Morgenstern (eds.), *Pre-trial Detention in the European Union: An Analysis of Minimum Standards in Pre-Trial Detention and the Grounds for Regular Review in the Member States of the EU*, Wolf Legal Publishers, Nijmegen, 2009, p. 45.

100. Data on the number of foreigners in pretrial detention in Denmark, France, Hungary, and Latvia are not available.

101. International Centre for Prison Studies, World Prison Brief, available at http://www.prisonstudies.org/info/worldbrief/ (accessed Oct. 7, 2013).

102. Matthew Ericson and Tony Vinson, *Young People on Remand in Victoria: Balancing Individual and Community Interests*, Jesuit Social Services, Richmond, 2010, p. 21. See also, Paul White, David Chant, and Harvey Whiteford, "A Comparison of Australian Men with Psychotic Disorders Remanded for Criminal Offences and a Community Group of Psychotic Men Who Have Not Offended," *Australian and New Zealand Journal of Psychiatry* 40(3), 2006, pp. 260-265.

103. Matthew Ericson and Tony Vinson, *Young People on Remand in Victoria: Balancing Individual and Community Interests*, Jesuit Social Services, Richmond, 2010, p. 21.

104. Sue King, David Bamford, and Rick Sarre, "Discretionary Decision-Making in a Dynamic Context: The Influences on Remand Decision-Makers in Two Australian Jurisdictions," *Current Issues in Criminal Justice* 21(1), 2009, p. 33.

105. Luke Birmingham, Debbie Mason, and Don Grubin, "Prevalence of Mental Disorder in Remand Prisoners: Consecutive Case Study," *British Medical Journal*, Vol. 313, No. 7071, December 1996, pp. 1521-1524.

106. Nicola Singleton, Howard Meltzer, and Rebecca Gatward, *Psychiatric Morbidity among Prisoners in England and Wales*, Home Office: Office for National Statistics, London, 1998.

107. *Fact Sheet: Mental Illness and Jails*, Council of State Governments, New York, Undated.

108. Felicity Parton, Andrew Day, and Jack White, "An Empirical Study on the Relationship between Intellectual Ability and an Understanding of the Legal Process in Male Remand Prisoners," *Psychiatry, Psychology and Law* 11(1), 2004, pp. 96-109.

109. Matthew Ericson and Tony Vinson, *Young People on Remand in Victoria: Balancing Individual and Community Interests*, Jesuit Social Services, Richmond, 2010, p. 22.

110. Shasta Holland, Peter Persson, Megan McClelland, and Robyn Berends, "Intellectual Disability in the Victorian Prison System: Characteristics of Prisoners with an Intellectual Disability Released from Prison in 2003-2006," *Corrections Research Paper Series* No 2, Department of Justice – Victoria, Melbourne, 2007.

111. Nancy Loucks, *Prisoners with learning difficulties and learning disabilities – Review of prevalence and associated needs*, London, Prison Reform Trust, 2007.

112. Jenny Talbot, *Prisoners' Voices: Experiences of the criminal justice system by prisoners with learning disabilities and difficulties*, Prison Reform Trust, London, 2008, p. 60.

113. Jenny Talbot, *Prisoners' Voices: Experiences of the criminal justice system by prisoners with learning disabilities and difficulties*, Prison Reform Trust, London, 2008, p. 62.

114. Patricia Hassett, "An Expert System for Improving the Pretrial Release/Detention Decision," Paper delivered at the 6th BILETA Conference, 1991, p. 5.

115. Miguel La Rota, *El uso de la prisión preventiva en Nuevo León. Estudio cuantitativo*, Open Society Justice Initiative, Monterrey, 2010, available at http://presunciondeinocencia.insyde.org.mx/index.php?option=com_content&view=article&id=126, (accessed Oct. 7, 2013).

116. *Access to Legal Aid in Criminal Justice Systems in Africa: Survey Report*, UNODC, Vienna, 2011, p. 35, available at http://www.unodc.org/pdf/criminal_justice/Survey_Report_on_Access_to_Legal_Aid_in_Africa.pdf ( accessed Oct. 7, 2013).

117. Fabiana Costa Oliveira Barreto, *Flagrante e Prisao Provisoria em casos de furto, da presuncao de inocencia a antecipacao de pena*, Instituto Brasileiro de Ciencias Criminais, Brasília, 2007.

118. Scott Henson, "Bail blunders boost bulging Harris jail population," August 13, 2005, available at http://gritsforbreakfast.blogspot.com/2005/08/bail-blunders-boost-bulging-harris.html, (accessed Oct. 7, 2013).

119. Jordan Flaherty, "The Incarceration Capital of the US: A struggle over the size of New Orleans' jail could define the city's future," *Infoshop News*, November 15, 2010, available at http://news.infoshop.org/article.php?story=20101110014650348 (accessed Oct. 7, 2013).

120. Interview with Justice Initiative researcher, Bucharest, December, 2010.

121. *Bromley Briefings Prison Factfile*, Prison Reform Trust, London, June 2011, p. 18.

122. *Bromley Briefings Prison Factfile*, Prison Reform Trust, London, June 2009, p. 13.

123. Mike Octigan, "Pre-Trial Services: Someone Else's Agenda?," *Probation Journal*, 2002, Volume 49, pp. 19-26.

124. *Scotland's Choice: Report of the Scottish Prison Commission*, Edinburgh, July 2008, p. 29.

125. Philip Spier and Barb Lash, *Conviction and Sentencing of Offenders in New Zealand: 1994 to 2003*, New Zealand Ministry of Justice, Wellington, 2004, p. 110.

126. Barbara Thompson, "Remand Inmates in NSW: Some Statistics," Research Bulletin No. 20, NSW Department of Correctional Services, Sydney, June 2001, p. 6.

127. *Doing Time – Time for Doing: Indigenous Youth in the Criminal Justice System*. Report by the Australian Parliament's House of Representatives Standing Committee on Aboriginal and Torres Strait Islander Affairs, Canberra, June 2011, paragraph 7.99, p. 219. See also, Joel Gibson, "Juvenile detainees at greater risk of assault," *The Sydney Morning Herald*, August 9, 2010, available at http://www.smh.com.au/nsw/juvenile-detainees-at-greater-risk-of-assault-20100808-11qao.html (accessed Oct. 7, 2013).

128. Rick Sarre, Sue King, and David Bamford, "Remand in custody: Critical factors and key issues," *Trends & Issues in Criminal Justice*, No. 310, May 2006, Australian Institute of Criminology, p. 5.

129. Ana María Morales Peillard, Pablo Pérez Ahumada, and Gherman Welsch Chahuán, *Caracterización de la Población en Prisión Preventiva en Chile*, Fundacion Paz Ciudadana, Chile, March 2011, p. 18.

130. A.M. van Kalmthout, M.M. Knapen, and C. Morgenstern (eds.), *Pre-trial Detention in the European Union. An Analysis of Minimum Standards in Pre-Trial Detention and the Grounds for Regular Review in the Member States of the EU*, Wolf Legal Publishers, Nijmegen, 2009, p. 415.

131. Jon Vagg and Frieder Dünkel, "Conclusion," in Frieder Dünkel and Jon Vagg (eds.), *Waiting for Trial: International Perspectives on the Use of Pre-Trial Detention and the Rights and Living Conditions of Prisoners Waiting for Trial*, Max Planck Institute, Freiburg, 1994, p. 927.

132. Mary T. Philips, *Pretrial Detention and Case Outcomes, Part 1: Nonfelony Cases*, New York City Criminal Justice Agency, November 2007, New York, p. 59.

133. *The Price of Freedom: Bail and Pretrial Detention of Low Income Nonfelony Defendants in New York City*, Human Rights Watch, New York, 2010, p. 29.

134. *Bromley Briefings Prison Factfile*, Prison Reform Trust, London, June 2011, p. 18.

135. Philip Spier and Barb Lash, *Conviction and Sentencing of Offenders in New Zealand: 1994 to 2003*, New Zealand Ministry of Justice, Wellington, 2004, p. 110.

136. Vanja Karth, *Between a Rock and a Hard Place: Bail Decisions in Three South African Courts*, Open Society Foundation for South Africa, Cape Town, 2008, pp. 17-18.

137. Working Group on Arbitrary Detention, *Report of the Working Group on Arbitrary Detention*, Geneva, UN Commission on Human Rights, E/CN.4/2006/7,2006, para. 66.

# CIRCUMSTANCES OF DETENTION AND IMPACT ON DETAINEES AND THEIR COMMUNITIES

1. Mike Octigan, "Pre-Trial Services: Someone Else's Agenda?," *Probation Journal*, Vol. 49, No. 1, March 2002, p. 19.

2. That is, persons in pretrial detention have not been convicted of the crime(s) that they are alleged to have committed and which led to their arrest and detention. Some pretrial detainees may, however, have been convicted of a crime or crimes on a previous occasion.

3. *Innocenti Digest: Juvenile Justice*, UNICEF, Florence, January 1998, p. 9, available at http://www.unicef-irc.org/publications/pdf/digest3e.pdf (accessed Oct. 30, 2013).

4. *Justice Sector Reform and Human Rights in Nigeria*, Centre for Social-Legal Studies, Abuja, 2009, p. 307.

5. N.S. Rodley, *Report of the Special Rapporteur on Torture, Mission to Kenya* (addendum), 2000. UN doc. E/CN.4/2000/9/Add.4.

6. Human Rights Watch, AIDS and Rights Alliance for Southern Africa, and Prison Care and Counseling Association. *Unjust and Unhealthy: HIV, TB, and Abuse in Zambian Prisons*, Human Rights Watch, New York, 2010, p. 35, available at http://www.hrw.org/sites/default/files/reports/zambia0410webwcover.pdf (accessed Oct. 30, 2013).

7. Penal Reform International, "Statement to the 20th Session of the UN Commission on Crime Prevention and Criminal Justice," April 2011, available at http://www.penalreform.org/files/PRI%20statement%20to%20Crime%20Commission.doc (accessed July 12, 2011).

8. Working Group on Arbitrary Detention, *Report of a Mission to South Africa* (addendum), 2005, UN doc. E/CN.4/2006/7/Add.3.

9. Stephen Jones, "Guilty until Proven Innocent? The Diminished Status of Suspects at the Point of Remand and as Unconvicted Prisoners," *Common Law World Review*, Vol. 32, Issue 4, December 2003, p. 408.

10. Stephen Jones, "Guilty until Proven Innocent? The Diminished Status of Suspects at the Point of Remand and as Unconvicted Prisoners," *Common Law World Review*, Vol. 32, Issue 4, December 2003, p. 409.

11. *Punishment First Verdict Later: A Review of Conditions for Remand Prisoners in Scotland at the End of the 20th Century*, Scottish Prison Service, Edinburgh, 2000, Annexure 5, para. 21, available at http://www.scotland.gov.uk/hmip/docs/pfvl-00.asp, (accessed January 8, 2010).

12. Human Rights Watch, AIDS and Rights Alliance for Southern Africa, and Prison Care and Counseling Association. *Unjust and Unhealthy: HIV, TB, and Abuse in Zambian Prisons*, Human Rights Watch, New York, 2010, p. 105, available at http://www.hrw.org/sites/default/files/reports/zambia0410webwcover.pdf (accessed Oct. 30, 2013).

13. International Crisis Group, "Reforming Pakistan's Criminal justice System," Asia Report No. 196, December 2010, p. 8.

14. According to paragraph 89 of the Standard Minimum Rules for the Treatment of Prisoners, "An untried prisoner shall always be offered opportunity to work, but shall not be required to work. If he chooses to work, he shall be paid for it."

15. Manfred Nowak, *Mission to Nigeria. Report of the Special Rapporteur on torture and other cruel, inhuman or degrading treatment or punishment* (4 to 10 March 2007), November 22, 2007, A/HRC/7/3/Add.4, p. 16.

16. Stephen Jones, "Guilty until Proven Innocent? The Diminished Status of Suspects at the Point of Remand and as Unconvicted Prisoners," *Common Law World Review*, Vol. 32, Issue 4, December 2003, p. 413.

17. *Innocenti Digest: Juvenile Justice*, UNICEF, Florence, January 1998, p. 9, available at http://www.unicef-irc.org/publications/pdf/digest3e.pdf (accessed Oct. 30, 2013).

18. Transtec, Final Report: Needs Assessment of Investigation and Forensic Capability of the Nigeria Police, November 2007, p. 13.

19. Frieder Dünkel and Jon Vagg (eds.), *Waiting for Trial: International Perspectives on the Use of Pre-Trial Detention and the Rights and Living Conditions of Prisoners Waiting for Trial*, Max Planck Institute, Freiburg, 1994, p. XIV.

20. Gail Kellough and Scot Wortley, "Remand for Plea: Bail Decisions and Plea Bargaining as Commensurate Decisions," *British Journal of Criminology*, Vol. 42, Issue 1, 2002, p. 186.

21. In relation to France and Hungary, see Ed Cape, Zaza Namoradze, Roger Smith, and Taru Spronken, *Effective Criminal Defence in Europe*, Intersentia, Antwerp, 2010, p. 604.

22. Working Group on Arbitrary Detention, *Report of a mission to Belarus* (addendum), 2004. UN doc. E/CN.4/2005/6/Add.3. M. Nowak, *Report of the Special Rapporteur on Torture, mission to Moldova*, 2009. UN doc. A/HRC/10/44/Add.3.

23. N.S. Rodley, *Report of the Special Rapporteur on Torture, mission to the Russian Federation* (addendum), 1994. UN doc. E/CN.4/1995/34/Add.1.

24. Working Group on Arbitrary Detention, *Report of a mission to Belarus* (addendum), 2004. UN doc. E/CN.4/2005/6/Add.3.

25. Human Rights Watch, *The Human Rights Watch Global Report on Prisons*, Human Rights Watch, New York, 1992, p. 3.

26. Oliver C. Ruppel and Angelique L. Groenewaldt, *Conditions of Police Cells in Namibia*, Human Rights and Documentation Centre, University of Namibia, 2008, p. 11.

27. Charles Hounmenou, *Standards for Monitoring Human Rights of People in Police Lockups*, Jane Addams Center for Social Policy and Research, University of Illinois at Chicago, July 2010, p. 1.

28. Human Rights Watch, *The Human Rights Watch Global Report on Prisons*, Human Rights Watch, New York, 1992, p. 3.

29. Charles Hounmenou, *Standards for Monitoring Human Rights of People in Police Lockups*, Jane Addams Center for Social Policy and Research, University of Illinois at Chicago, July 2010, p. 1.

30. *Conditions for persons in custody. Report of Ombudsman Victoria and Office of Police Integrity*, Office of Police Integrity – Victoria, July 2006, p. 16.

31. Human Rights Council, 13th Session, *Report of the Special Rapporteur on torture and other cruel, inhuman or degrading treatment or punishment, Manfred Nowak, Addendum: Study on the phenomena of torture, cruel, inhuman or degrading treatment or punishment in the world, including an assessment of conditions of detention*, UN Doc A/HRC/13/39/Add.5, 5 February 2010, para. 232.

32. *Prisons in the Central African Republic*, Report on a visit June 19-29, 2000, by Prof. E.V.O. Dankwa, Special Rapporteur on Prisons and Conditions of Detention in Africa, African Commission on Human and Peoples' Rights, Series IV, No. 7, p. 7.

33. *Prisons in Malawi*, Report on a visit 17-28 June 2001, by Dr. Vera Mlangazuwa Chirwa, Special Rapporteur on Prisons and Conditions of Detention in Africa, African Commission on Human and Peoples' Rights, Series IV, No. 9, p. 27.

34. Working Group on Arbitrary Detention, *Report of a mission to Equatorial Guinea* (addendum), 2008, UN doc. A/HRC/7/4/Add.3.

35. *Conditions for persons in custody: Report of Ombudsman Victoria and Office of Police Integrity*, Office of Police Integrity – Victoria, July 2006, p. 17.

36. Justin Sandefur, Bilal Siddiqi, and Alaina Varvaloucas, *Timap Criminal Justice Pilot: Baseline Report*, Centre for the Study of African Economies, April 2011, p. 21.

37. *Prisons in the Central African Republic*, Report on a visit June 19-29, 2000, by Prof. E.V.O. Dankwa, Special Rapporteur on Prisons and Conditions of Detention in Africa, African Commission on Human and Peoples' Rights, Series IV, No. 7, p. 7.

38. M. Nowak, *Report of the Special Rapporteur on Torture and Other Cruel, Inhuman, or Degrading Treatment or Punishment, Mission to Togo*, UN Doc A/HRC/7/3/Add.5 para 43 (2008).

39. Human Rights Council, 13th Session, *Report of the Special Rapporteur on torture and other cruel, inhuman or degrading treatment or punishment, Manfred Nowak, Addendum: Study on the phenomena*

*of torture, cruel, inhuman or degrading treatment or punishment in the world, including an assessment of conditions of detention*, UN Doc A/HRC/13/39/Add.5, 5 February 2010, para. 233. A similar situation has been found to exist in Cameroon. See Committee against Torture, *Consideration of reports submitted by States parties under article 19 of the Convention: Concluding Observations of the Committee against Torture, Cameroon*, UN Doc CAT/C/CMR/CO/4, 19 May 2010, [54].

40. *"Prison Is Not For Me": Arbitrary Detention in South Sudan*, Human Rights Watch, New York, 2012, p. 24, available at http://www.hrw.org/reports/2012/06/21/prison-not-me (accessed Oct. 30, 2013).

41. US Department of State, Bureau of Democracy, Human Rights, and Labor, *2009 Human Rights Report: Sri Lanka*, available at http://www.state.gov/g/drl/rls/hrrpt/2009/sca/136093.htm (accessed Oct. 30, 2013). See also "South Africa: Overcrowding fuels TB in prisons," *IRIN News*, June 19, 2012, available at http://www.irinnews.org/Report/95684/SOUTH-AFRICA-Overcrowding-fuels-TB-in-prisons (accessed Oct. 30, 2013).

42. Craig Haney, "Prison Overcrowding: Harmful Consequences and Dysfunctional Reactions," Expert Testimony to the Commission on Safety and Abuse in America's Prisons, July 19, 2005, Newark, New Jersey, p. 4, available at http://www.prisoncommission.org/public_hearing_2_witness_haney.asp (accessed Oct. 20, 2010).

43. World Prison Brief, International Centre for Prison Studies, available at http://www.prisonstudies.org/info/worldbrief/ (accessed Oct. 30, 2013).

44. *Report on the Human Rights of Persons Deprived of Liberty in the Americas*, Inter-American Commission on Human Rights, 2011, paragraph 470, available at http://www.oas.org/en/iachr/pdl/docs/pdf/PPL2011eng.pdf (accessed Oct. 30, 2013).

45. Human Rights Watch, AIDS and Rights Alliance for Southern Africa, and Prison Care and Counseling Association. *Unjust and Unhealthy: HIV, TB, and Abuse in Zambian Prisons*, Human Rights Watch, New York, 2010, p. 29, available at: http://www.hrw.org/sites/default/files/reports/zambia0410webwcover.pdf (accessed Oct. 30, 2013).

46. Human Rights Watch, AIDS and Rights Alliance for Southern Africa, and Prison Care and Counseling Association. *Unjust and Unhealthy: HIV, TB, and Abuse in Zambian Prisons*, Human Rights Watch, New York, 2010, p. 31, available at http://www.hrw.org/sites/default/files/reports/zambia0410webwcover.pdf (accessed Oct. 30, 2013).

47. Manfred Nowak, *Mission to Nigeria. Report of the Special Rapporteur on torture and other cruel, inhuman or degrading treatment or punishment (4 to 10 March 2007)*, November 22, 2007, A/HRC/7/3/Add.4, p. 16.

48. "845 Inmates Await Trial In Onitsha Prisons – Official," *Leadership*, February 14, 2012, available at http://leadership.ng/nga/articles/16366/2012/02/14/845_inmates_await_trial_onitsha_prisons_%E2%80%93_official.html (accessed February 16, 2012).

49. *Improvement of the Real Situation of Overcrowding in Prisons in Bangladesh: GTZ in Bangladesh*, GTZ – Office Dhaka (undated), p. 1.

50. *Improvement of the Real Situation of Overcrowding in Prisons in Bangladesh: GTZ in Bangladesh*, GTZ – Office Dhaka (undated), p. 1.

51. N.S. Rodley, Report of the Special Rapporteur on Torture, mission to the Russian Federation (addendum), 1994. UN doc. E/CN.4/1995/34/Add.1.

52. A. Bobrik, K. Danishevski, K. Eroshina, and M. McKee, "Prison health in Russia: the larger picture," *Journal of Public Health Policy*, 2005, 26(1), pp. 30-59.

53. "Report: Most Honduras Fire Inmates Awaited Trial," *New York Times*, February 15, 2012, available at http://www.nytimes.com/aponline/2012/02/15/world/americas/AP-LT-Honduras-Prison-Fire.html?_r=2&smid=tw-nytimes&seid=auto (accessed February 16, 2012).

54. Laura Smith-Spark, "Nasty, harsh, overcrowded: Life in a Honduran prison," *CNN*, February 16, 2012, available at http://edition.cnn.com/2012/02/15/world/americas/honduras-prison-conditions/index.html?iref=allsearch (accessed Oct. 30, 2013).

55. *Report on the Human Rights of Persons Deprived of Liberty in the Americas*, Inter-American Commission on Human Rights, 2011, paragraph 287, available at http://www.oas.org/en/iachr/pdl/docs/pdf/PPL2011eng.pdf (accessed Oct. 30, 2013).

56. "Overcrowding in prisons poses global water and sanitation challenges," *ICRC Feature*, March 17, 2008, available at: http://www.icrc.org/web/eng/siteeng0.nsf/html/water-detention-feature-170308 (accessed Oct. 30, 2013).

57. *Prisons in Benin*. Report on a visit 23-31 August 1999, by Prof. E.V.O. Dankwa, Special Rapporteur on Prisons and Conditions of Detention in Africa, African Commission on Human and Peoples' Rights, Series IV, No. 6, p. 43.

58. *Directory of Prisons in Africa*, Penal Reform International (undated), available at http://www.penalreform.org/download/ouaga/index_engl.pdf.

59. *Public Sector Performance: An international comparison of education, health care, law and order and public administration* (The Hague: Social and Cultural Planning Office, September 2004), pp. 219-220.

60. M. Nowak, Mission to Togo. *Report of the Special Rapporteur on torture and other cruel, inhuman or degrading treatment or punishment (11-17 April 2007)*, January 6, 2008, A/HRC/7/3/Add.5, p. 20.

61. *Prisons in Benin*. Report on a visit 23-31 August 1999, by Prof. E.V.O. Dankwa, Special Rapporteur on Prisons and Conditions of Detention in Africa, African Commission on Human and Peoples' Rights, Series IV, No. 6, pp. 20-21.

62. Henry Chilobwe, "Sex slavery at Zomba Prison," October 22, 2006, available at http://groups.yahoo.com/group/MALAWIANA/message/11349 (accessed Oct. 30, 2013).

63. D. Jolofani and J. DeGabriele, *HIV AIDS in Malawi Prisons - Study of HIV transmission and the care of prisoners with HIV / AIDS in Zomba, Blantyre and Lilongwe Prisons*, Penal Reform International, Paris, 1999.

64. David Agren, "Self-rule on the rise in Mexico's prisons," USA Today, May 1, 2011, available at http://www.usatoday.com/news/world/2011-04-28-zeta-prison-self-rule_n.htm (accessed Oct. 30, 2013).

65. As cited in *Report on the Human Rights of Persons Deprived of Liberty in the Americas*, Inter-American Commission on Human Rights, 2011, paragraph 85, available at http://www.oas.org/en/iachr/pdl/docs/pdf/PPL2011eng.pdf (accessed Oct. 30, 2013).

66. Jeanna Cullinan, "Violence in Venezuela Prisons Claims Over 400 Lives in 2011," *InSight*, November 10, 2011, available at http://insightcrime.org/insight-latest-news/item/1828-violence-in-venezuelas-prisons-claims-over-400-lives-in-2011 (accessed Oct. 30, 2013).

67. *Report on the Human Rights of Persons Deprived of Liberty in the Americas*, Inter-American Commission on Human Rights, 2011, paragraph 275, available at http://www.oas.org/en/iachr/pdl/docs/pdf/PPL2011eng.pdf (accessed Oct. 30, 2013).

68. Girish Gupta, "Venezuela inmates wield machineguns, smoke cannabis," Reuters, September 23, 2011, available at http://www.reuters.com/article/2011/09/23/us-venezuela-prisons-idUSTRE78M3LD20110923 (accessed Oct. 30, 2013).

69. N.S. Rodley, *Report of the Special Rapporteur on Torture, mission to the Russian Federation* (addendum), 1994. UN doc. E/CN.4/1995/34/Add.1; Nowak, M. *Report of the Special Rapporteur on Torture, mission to Moldova*, 2009. UN doc. A/HRC/10/44/Add.3.

70. Graham Rayman, "Rikers Violence: Out Of Control," *Village Voice*, May 9, 2012, available at http://www.villagevoice.com/2012-05-09/news/rikers-violence-out-of-control/ (accessed Oct. 30, 2013); Isolde Raftery, "6-Year Sentence for Guard in Rikers Island Beatings," *New York Times*, August 6, 2010, available at http://www.nytimes.com/2010/08/07/nyregion/07guard.html (accessed Oct. 30, 2013).

71. P.S. Pinheiro, *World report on violence against children*, UNICEF, New York, 2006, p. 199, available at http://www.unicef.org/violencestudy/index.html (accessed Oct. 30, 2013).

72. M. Nowak, *Interim report of the Special Rapporteur on torture and other cruel, inhuman or degrading treatment or punishment*, August 3, 2009, A/64/215, para. 76, available at http://www.juvenilejusticepanel.org/resource/items/A/_/A_64_215%20eng.pdf (accessed Oct. 30, 2013).

73. Working Group on Arbitrary Detention, *Report of a mission to Belarus* (addendum), 2004. UN doc. E/CN.4/2005/6/Add.3; Working Group on Arbitrary Detention, *Report of a mission to Equatorial Guinea* (addendum), 2008. UN doc. A/HRC/7/4/Add.3; Working Group on Arbitrary Detention, *Report of a mission to Ukraine* (addendum), 2009. UN doc. A/HRC/10/21/Add.4; M. Nowak, *Report of the Special Rapporteur on Torture, mission to Nigeria*, 2007. UN doc. A/HRC/7/3/Add.4.0; Human Rights Watch,

*Paying the price: Violations of the rights of children in detention in Burundi*, Human Rights Watch, New York, 2007, available at http://www.hrw.org/reports/2007/burundi0307/ (accessed Oct. 30, 2013); Human Rights Watch, "Nepal: End torture of children in police custody," (press statement), Human Rights Watch, New York, 2008, available at www.hrw.org/en/news/2008/11/18/ (accessed Oct. 30, 2013); Adnan Aziz, "Penal reform," *The News*, May 7, 2011, available at http://www.thenews.com.pk/TodaysPrintDetail.aspx?ID=45633&Cat=9 (accessed Oct. 30, 2013).

74. Working Group on Arbitrary Detention, *Report of a mission to South Africa* (addendum), 2005. UN doc. E/CN.4/2006/7/Add.3; Human Rights Watch, *Making their own rules: Police beatings, rape and torture of children in Papua New Guinea*, Human Rights Watch, New York, 2005, available at http://www.hrw.org/en/node/11626/section/7 (accessed Oct. 30, 2013).

75. Working Group on Arbitrary Detention, *Report of a mission to Angola* (addendum), 2008. UN doc. A/HRC/7/4/Add.4.

76. *Consideration of reports submitted by States parties under article 19 of the Convention. Concluding observations of the Committee against Torture: Slovakia.* UN Doc.: CAT/C/SVL/CO/2. December 17, 2009, para. 8.

77. Manfred Nowak, *Mission to Nigeria. Report of the Special Rapporteur on torture and other cruel, inhuman or degrading treatment or punishment (4 to 10 March 2007)*, November 22, 2007, A/HRC/7/3/Add.4, p. 16.

78. Isaac Wolf, "Youths do time in adult facilities," *Ventura County Star*, November 19, 2011, available at http://m.vcstar.com/news/2011/nov/19/youths-do-time-in-adult-facilities/ (accessed Oct. 30, 2013).

79. *Jailing Juveniles: The Dangers of Incarcerating Youth in Adult Jails in America*, A Campaign for Youth Justice Report, November 2007, p. 10, available at http://www.campaignforyouthjustice.org/Downloads/NationalReportsArticles/CFYJ-Jailing_Juveniles_Report_2007-11-15.pdf (accessed Oct. 31, 2013).

80. Isaac Wolf, "Youths do time in adult facilities," *Ventura County Star*, November 19, 2011, available at http://m.vcstar.com/news/2011/nov/19/youths-do-time-in-adult-facilities/ (accessed Oct. 30, 2013).

81. Francisco Frigerio, *Prisoners' Rights Project Report: Buea Central Prison*, Global Conscience Initiative's Prisoners' Rights Project 13 (2009).

82. Human Rights Watch, AIDS and Rights Alliance for Southern Africa, and Prison Care and Counseling Association. *Unjust and Unhealthy: HIV, TB, and Abuse in Zambian Prisons*, Human Rights Watch, New York, 2010, pp. 29-31, available at http://www.hrw.org/sites/default/files/reports/zambia0410webwcover.pdf (accessed Oct. 30, 2013).

83. Swati Mehta, *Maharashtra's Abandoned Prisons: A Study of Sub-Jails*, Commonwealth Human Rights Initiative, New Delhi, 2010, p. 21.

84. Manfred Nowak, *Report of the Special Rapporteur on torture and other cruel, inhuman or degrading treatment or punishment: Addendum, Mission to Uruguay.* UN Doc.: A/HRC/13/39/Add.2, 21 December 2009, para. 50, available at http://www2.ohchr.org/english/bodies/hrcouncil/docs/13session/A-HRC-13-39-Add2.pdf (accessed Oct. 30, 2013).

85. *Consideration of reports submitted by States parties under article 19 of the Convention: Concluding observations of the Committee against Torture: El Salvador.* UN Doc.: CAT/C/SLV/CO/2, December 9, 2009, para. 5, available at http://www.bayefsky.com/pdf/elsalvador_t4_cat_43.pdf (accessed Oct. 30, 2013).

86. Hemanth Kashyap, "Young prisoners used as sex slaves in the central jail," *BangaloreMirror.com*, November 28, 2010, available at http://www.bangaloremirror.com/bangalore/cover-story/Young-prisoners-used-as-sex-slaves-in-the-central-jail/articleshow/21738424.cms?, (accessed Oct. 30, 2013).

87. The United Nations Convention against Torture and Other Cruel, Inhuman or Degrading Treatment or Punishment defines torture as: "Any act by which severe pain or suffering, whether physical or mental, is intentionally inflicted on a person for such purposes as obtaining from him or a third person, information or a confession, punishing him for an act he or a third person has committed or is suspected of having committed... when such pain or suffering is inflicted by or at the instigation of or with the consent or acquiescence of a public official or other person acting in an official capacity." See article 1.1, United Nations Convention against Torture and Other Cruel, Inhuman or Degrading Treatment or Punishment, available at http://www1.umn.edu/humanrts/instree/h2catoc.

htm (accessed Oct. 30, 2013). Actions which fall short of torture may still constitute cruel, inhuman or degrading treatment in terms of the Convention.

88. *Report on the Human Rights of Persons Deprived of Liberty in the Americas*, Inter-American Commission on Human Rights, 2011, paragraph 356, available at http://www.oas.org/en/iachr/pdl/docs/pdf/PPL2011eng.pdf (accessed Oct. 30, 2013).

89. Open Society Justice Initiative, "Fact Sheet: El Masri and CIA 'Capture Shock,'" December, 2012, available at http://www.opensocietyfoundations.org/fact-sheets/el-masri-and-cia-capture-shock (accessed Nov. 1, 2013).

90. Manfred Nowak, *Report of the Special Rapporteur on torture and other cruel, inhuman or degrading treatment or punishment: Mission to Nigeria. (4 to 10 March 2007)*, November 22, 2007, A/HRC/7/3/Add.4, p 13.

91. Open Society Justice Initiative, *Criminal Force: Torture, Abuse, and Extrajudicial Killings by the Nigeria Police Force*, Open Society Foundations, New York, 2010, p. 68.

92. Open Society Justice Initiative, *"We're Tired of Taking You to the Court": Human Rights Abuses by Kenya's Anti-Terrorism Police Unit*, Open Society Foundations, New York, 2013, p. 19.

93. Manfred Nowak, *Report of the Special Rapporteur on torture and other cruel, inhuman or degrading treatment or punishment: Mission to Indonesia. Addendum, 10-23 November 2007*, A/HRC/7/3/Add.7, pp. 47, 53.

94. Manfred Nowak, *Report of the Special Rapporteur on Torture: Mission to Georgia*, 2006. UN doc. E/CN.4/2006/6/Add.3; Manfred Nowak, *Report of the Special Rapporteur on Torture: Mission to Indonesia*, 2008. UN doc. A/HRC/7/3/Add.7; N.S. Rodley, *Report of the Special Rapporteur on Torture, mission to Azerbaijan*, 2000. UN doc. E/CN.4/2001/66/Add.1; Working Group on Arbitrary Detention. *Report of a mission to South Africa* (addendum), 2005. UN doc. E/CN.4/2006/7/Add.3; Working Group on Arbitrary Detention, *Report of a mission to Ecuador* (addendum), 2006. UN doc. A/HRC/4/40/Add.2; Working Group on Arbitrary Detention, *Report of a mission to Equatorial Guinea* (addendum), 2008b. UN doc. A/HRC/7/4/Add.3; T. van Boven, *Report of the Special Rapporteur on torture: Mission to Uzbekistan* (addendum), 2003. UN doc. E/CN.4/2003/68/Add.2.

95. Denise Tomasini-Joshi, "Children, Torture, and Pretrial Detention," April 15, 2010, available at http://blog.soros.org/2010/04/children-torture-and-pretrial-detention/.

96. Manfred Novak, *Fact-Finding on Torture and Ill-Treatment and Conditions of Detention*, 1 J. Human Rights Practice 101 (2009), available at http://jhrp.oxfordjournals.org/content/1/1/101.full#sec-4 (accessed Oct. 30, 2013).

97. Amnesty International, *Lebanon: Torture and ill-treatment of women in pre-trial detention: a culture of acquiescence* (2001), available at http://www.amnesty.org/en/library/asset/MDE18/009/2001/en/71a91f76-d921-11dd-ad8c-f3d4445c118e/mde180092001en.pdf (accessed Oct. 30, 2013).

98. Open Society Justice Initiative, *"We're Tired of Taking You to the Court": Human Rights Abuses by Kenya's Anti-Terrorism Police Unit*, Open Society Foundations, New York, 2013, p. 17.

99. *Izoliatory vremennogo soderzhaniia* (IVS), is where suspects are confined until a prosecutor determines whether to pursue the case. Officially, the maximum time a suspect can spend in an IVS is ten days after being formally charged.

100. International Crisis Group, *Kyrgyzstan's Prison System Nightmare*, Asia Report N°118 –August 16, 2006, pp. 14-15, available at http://www.crisisgroup.org/~/media/Files/asia/central-asia/kyrgyzstan/118_kyrgyzstans_prison_system_nightmare.pdf (accessed Oct. 30, 2013).

101. International Crisis Group, *Kyrgyzstan's Prison System Nightmare*, Asia Report N°118 –August 16, 2006, p. 14, available at http://www.crisisgroup.org/~/media/Files/asia/central-asia/kyrgyzstan/118_kyrgyzstans_prison_system_nightmare.pdf (accessed Oct. 30, 2013).

102. Centro de Estudios de Justicia de las Américas, *Report on Pre-Trial Criminal Justice in Brazil*, p. 13.

103. Centro de Estudios de Justicia de las Américas, *Report on Pre-Trial Criminal Justice in Brazil*, p. 36.

104. Amnesty International, *Moldova: Briefing to the Committee Against Torture*, October 2009, p. 2, available at http://www.amnesty.org/en/library/info/EUR59/007/2009/en (accessed Oct. 30, 2013).

105. Resource Center for Human Rights et al., *Alternative Report to the 2nd Report of the Republic of Moldova on the Stage of Implementation of the United Nations Convention against Torture,* 2009, pp. 12-13.

106. Manfred Nowak, *Report of the Special Rapporteur on Torture and Other Cruel, Inhuman, or Degrading Treatment or Punishment, Mission to Togo,* UN Doc A/HRC/7/3/Add.5 Appx I, Para 63, Jan. 6, 2008.

107. Human Rights Watch, *Behind Bars in Brazil,* New York, December 1998, pp. 2-4.

108. Norimitsu Onishi, "Coerced Confessions: Justice Derailed in Japan," *The New York Times,* May 7, 2007, available at http://www.nytimes.com/2007/05/07/world/asia/07iht-japan.1.5596308.html (accessed Oct. 30, 2013).

109. US Department of State, Bureau of Democracy, Human Rights, and Labor, *2009 Human Rights Report: Japan,* March 11, 2010, available at http://www.state.gov/g/drl/rls/hrrpt/2009/eap/135993.htm (accessed Oct. 30, 2013).

110. Manfred Nowak, *Report of the Special Rapporteur on Torture and other Cruel, Inhuman or Degrading Treatment or Punishment. Addendum: Study on the phenomena of torture, cruel, inhuman or degrading treatment or punishment in the world, including an assessment of conditions of detention,* 2010. UN doc. A / HRC/13/39/Add.5, p. 21.

111. Manfred Nowak, *Report of the Special Rapporteur on torture and other cruel, inhuman or degrading treatment or punishment: Mission to Togo, (11-17 April 2007),* January 6, 2008, A/HRC/7/3/Add.5, p. 15.

112. Manfred Nowak, *Civil and Political Rights, Including the Question of Torture and Detention: Report of the Special Rapporteur on torture and other cruel, inhuman or degrading treatment or punishment: Mission to China,* (20 Nov. – 5 Dec., 2005), March 10, 2006, E/CN.4/2006/6/Add.6, p. 19.

113. Manfred Nowak, *Report of the Special Rapporteur on torture and other cruel, inhuman or degrading treatment or punishment: Mission to Togo, (11-17 April 2007),* January 6, 2008, A/HRC/7/3/Add.5, p. 30.

114. Manfred Nowak, *Report of the Special Rapporteur on torture and other cruel, inhuman or degrading treatment or punishment: Mission to Nigeria, (4 to 10 March 2007),* November 22, 2007, A/HRC/7/3/Add.4, p. 35.

115. Manfred Nowak, *Report of the Special Rapporteur on torture and other cruel, inhuman or degrading treatment or punishment: Mission to Indonesia, Addendum, 10-23 November 2007,* A/HRC/7/3/Add.7, p. 12.

116. Manfred Nowak, *Report of the Special Rapporteur on torture and other cruel, inhuman or degrading treatment or punishment: Mission to Togo, (11-17 April 2007),* January 6, 2008, A/HRC/7/3/Add.5, p. 14.

117. Manfred Nowak, *Report of the Special Rapporteur on torture and other cruel, inhuman, or degrading treatment or punishment, addendum: mission to indonesia,* UN Doc A/HRC/7/3/Add.7 Appendix I, para 121, March 10, 2008.

118. Deborah R. Hatch, "Pre-sentence custody," *LawNow,* 2010, available at http://www.thefreelibrary.com/Pre-sentence+custody.-a0216180758 (accessed Oct. 30, 2013). See also, Human Rights Watch, *The Price of Freedom. Bail and Pretrial Detention of Low Income Nonfelony Defendants in New York City,* New York, 2010, p 33.

119. P.S. Pinheiro, *World Report on Violence against Children,* United Nations, New York, 2006, p. 196, available at http://www.unicef.org/violencestudy/index.html (accessed Oct. 30, 2013).

120. Manfred Nowak, *Report of the Special Rapporteur on Torture, Mission to Moldova,* 2009. UN doc. A/HRC/10/44/Add.3.

121. P.S. Pinheiro, *World Report on Violence against Children,* United Nations, New York, 2006, p. 197, available at http://www.unicef.org/violencestudy/index.html (accessed Oct. 30, 2013).

122. For a detailed discussion of the impact and consequences of pretrial detention on detainees' health and public health more generally see: Joan Csete and Dirk van Zyl Smit, *Pretrial Detention and Health: Unintended Consequences, Deadly Results. Literature Review and Recommendations for Health Professionals,* Open Society Justice Initiative, New York, 2011.

123. Open Society Justice Initiative / United Nations Development Programme pretrial detainee surveys on the socioeconomic impact of pretrial detention, publication forthcoming.

124. UN Office on Drugs and Crime, "HIV in Prisons: Situation and Needs Assessment Tool Kit," p. 11, available at http://www.unodc.org/documents/hivaids/publications/HIV_in_prisons_situation_and_needs_assessment_document.pdf.

125. *Status Paper on Prisons, Drugs and Harm Reduction*, World Health Organization: Europe, EUR/05/5049062, May 2005, p. 3.

126. UN Office on Drugs and Crime, "HIV in Prisons: Situation and Needs Assessment Tool Kit," p. 11, available at http://www.unodc.org/documents/hivaids/publications/HIV_in_prisons_situation_and_needs_assessment_document.pdf (noting that "The groups most vulnerable to HIV are those at increased risk for incarceration," such as injecting drug users); see also United Nations Office on Drugs and Crime, "HIV and Prisons in Sub-Saharan Africa: Opportunities for Action,"p. 15, available at http://www.unodc.org/documents/hiv-aids/Africa%20HIV_Prison_Paper_Oct-23-07-en.pdf (noting that HIV rates of prison populations in surveyed countries were 6 (USA) to 50 (Mauritius) times the rate in the population at large); World Health Organization Regional Office for Southeast Asia, "HIV Prevention, Care and Treatment in South-east Asia," p. 24 (2007). (Surveys place Indian prison infection rate at 1.7 percent overall (nearly five times the national rate), 9.5 percent for women. In Indonesia, 12 percent overall prison infection rate (75 times the national rate) rising to 21 percent in some prisons. One survey showed 25 percent of prisoners in a Thai prison were HIV positive.

127. UN Office on Drugs and Crime, "HIV in Prisons: Situation and Needs Assessment Tool Kit," p. 9, available at http://www.unodc.org/documents/hivaids/publications/HIV_in_prisons_situation_and_needs_assessment_document.pdf.

128. Katherine W. Todrys and Joseph J. Amon, "Criminal Justice Reform as HIV and TB Prevention in African Prisons," *PLoS Medicine*, Vol. 9, Issue 5, May 2012, p. 1, available at http://www.plosmedicine.org/article/info%3Adoi%2F10.1371%2Fjournal.pmed.1001215 (accessed Oct. 30, 2013); Iacopo Baussano, Brian G. Williams, Paul Nunn, Marta Beggiato, Ugo Fedeli, and Fabio Scano, "Tuberculosis incidence in prisons: a systematic review," *PLoS Medicine*, Vol. 7, Issue 12, available at http://www.plosmedicine.org/article/info%3Adoi%2F10.1371%2Fjournal.pmed.1000381 (accessed Oct. 30, 2013).

129. A.C. Senok, and G.A. Botta, "Human immunodeficiency virus and hepatitis virus infection in correctional institutions in Africa: Is this the neglected source of an epidemic?" *Journal of Medical Microbiology*, 55(5), 2006, pp. 481-82.

130. World Health Organization Regional Office for Southeast Asia, "HIV Prevention, Care and Treatment in South-east Asia," p. 15 (2007), available at: http://www.searo.who.int/LinkFiles/Publications_TreatmentinPrisons.pdf.

131. Canadian HIV/AIDS Legal Network, "HIV/AIDS and Hepatitis C in Prisons: The Facts," *HIV/AIDS in Prisons 2004/2005*, 2004, p. 2.

132. Canadian HIV/AIDS Legal Network, "HIV/AIDS and Hepatitis C in Prisons: The Facts," *HIV/AIDS in Prisons 2004/2005*, 2004, p. 1.

133. World Health Organization, *Tuberculosis in Prison*, available at http://www.who.int/tb/challenges/prisons/story_1/en/ (accessed Oct. 30, 2013).

134. World Health Organization, *Tuberculosis in Prison*, available at http://www.who.int/tb/challenges/prisons/story_1/en/ (accessed Oct. 30, 2013). See also, World Health Organization Regional Office for South-east Asia, "HIV prevention, care and treatment in prisons in the South-East Asia region," New Delhi, 2007, available at http://www.searo.who.int/LinkFiles/Publications_TreatmentinPrisons.pdf.

135. Andrei Shukshin, "Tough measures in Russian prisons slow spread of TB," *Bulletin of the World Health Organization*, Vol. 84, No. 4, April 2006, available at http://www.who.int/bulletin/volumes/84/4/news30406/en/index.html (accessed Oct. 30, 2013). See also: Vivien Stern (ed.), *Sentenced to die? The problem of TB in prisons in Eastern Europe and Central Asia*, International Centre for Prison Studies, London, 1999.

136. Medea Gegia, Iagor Kalandadze, Mikheil Madzgharashvili, and Jennifer Furin, "Developing a human rights-based program for tuberculosis control in Georgian prisons," *Health and Human Rights*, Vol. 13, No. 2, 2011, available at http://www.hhrjournal.org/index.php/hhr/article/view/429/715.

137. World Health Organization Regional Office for Europe. Prison health (fact sheet), undated, available at http://www.euro.who.int/Document/HIPP/HIP_Factsheet.pdf.

138. Anna Markina and Jon Spencer, "Reducing the Prison Population: Challenges and Threats," *Penal Reform and Prison Overcrowding*, UNICRI, April 2009,.p. 22.

139. N.S. Rodley, *Report of the Special Rapporteur on Torture, Mission to Azerbaijan*, 2000, UN doc. E/CN.4/2001/66/Add.1.

140. See, World Health Organization, *Mental Health and Prisons: Information Sheet*, Geneva, undated, available at http://www.who.int/mental_health/policy/mh_in_prison.pdf, (accessed Oct. 30, 2013).

141. Human Rights Watch, *Ill-Equipped: U.S. Prisons and Offenders with Mental Illness*, New York, 1999, pp. 17-19, available at http://www.hrw.org/reports/2003/usa1003/usa1003.pdf, (accessed Oct. 30, 2013); World Health Organization, Mental Health and Prisons: Information Sheet, Geneva, undated, available at http://www.who.int/mental_health/policy/mh_in_prison.pdf, (accessed Oct. 30, 2013).

142. Alison Liebling, *Suicides in Prison*, Routledge, London, 1993, p. 59.

143. Marcelo F. Aebi, *Council of Europe Annual Penal Statistics* (SPACE I), Survey 2004, Strasburg, November 7, 2005, p. 52. It is likely that the number of prison fatalities outside of the Council of Europe area is higher but less well recorded. For example, in 1996, 2,531 prisoners died in Kazakhstan, roughly half of them from tuberculosis. At the time Kazakhstan had approximately 85,000 prisoners. The high death rate prompted a government official to defend his country's death penalty on the grounds that prison conditions were so atrocious that few prisoners would survive a long sentence anyway. See, Human Rights Watch Prison Project, *Prisons in Europe and Central Asia*, February 15, 2007.

144. *Preventing Suicide. A Resource for Prison Officers*, WHO/MNH/MBD/00.5, World Health Organization, Geneva, 2000, p. 6.

145. Emma Kasprzak, "'Shocking' toll of prison remand deaths," *BBC News*, February 10, 2012, available at http://www.bbc.co.uk/news/uk-england-16980452 (accessed Oct. 30, 2013).

146. In England and Wales, for example, the highest risk for suicide among pretrial detainees is within the first month of their confinement. See, *Suicide Is Everyone's Concern: A Thematic Review*. Her Majesty's Inspectorate of Prisons for England and Wales, Home Office, London, 1999.

147. *Punishment First Verdict Later: A Review of Conditions for Remand Prisoners in Scotland at the End of the 20th Century*, Scottish Prison Service, Edinburgh, 2000, Annexure 5, para. 17.

148. *Jailing Juveniles: The Dangers of Incarcerating Youth in Adult Jails in America*, A Campaign for Youth Justice Report, November 2007, p. 10, available at http://www.campaignforyouthjustice.org/Downloads/NationalReportsArticles/CFYJ-Jailing_Juveniles_Report_2007-11-15.pdf (accessed Oct. 30, 2013).

149. Christopher J. Mumola, *Suicide and Homicide in State Prisons and Local Jails*, U.S. Department of Justice, Office of Justice Programs, Bureau of Justice Statistics, Washington D.C., August 2005, p. 8, available at http://www.bjs.gov/content/pub/pdf/shsplj.pdf (accessed Oct. 30, 2013).

150. See, for example, *Unjust Deserts. A Thematic Review by HM Chief Inspector of Prisons of the Treatment and Conditions for Unsentenced Prisoners in England and Wales*, HM Inspectorate of Prisons, London, December 2000.

151. Carl B. Clements, "Crowded Prisons: A Review of Psychological and Environmental Effects," *Law and Human Behavior*, Vol. 3, No. 3, 1979, p. 222.

152. *Punishment First Verdict Later: A Review of Conditions for Remand Prisoners in Scotland at the End of the 20th Century*, Scottish Prison Service, Edinburgh, 2000, para. 5.4.

153. Human Rights Watch, AIDS and Rights Alliance for Southern Africa, and Prison Care and Counseling Association. *Unjust and Unhealthy: HIV, TB, and Abuse in Zambian Prisons*, Human Rights Watch, New York, 2010, p. 105, available at http://www.hrw.org/sites/default/files/reports/zambia0410webwcover.pdf (accessed Oct. 30, 2013).

154. *El Sistema Penitenciario: componente clave de la seguridad ciudadana y la Política Criminal. Problemas, retos y perspectivas*, Defensoría del Pueblo, Lima, 2011, pp. 7-8, available at http://www.defensoria.gob.pe/modules/Downloads/documentos/resumen-informe-154.pdf (accessed Oct. 30, 2013).

155. R. Coninx, D. Maher, H. Reyes, and M. Grzemska, "Tuberculosis in prisons in countries with high prevalence," *British Medical Journal*, 2000, Vol. 3, No.20, pp. 440-442.

156. H. Reyes, "Pitfalls of TB management in prisons, revisited," *International Journal of Prisoner Health* 2007, Vol. 3, No. 1, pp. 43-67.

157. K. Dolan, M. Bijl, B. White, "HIV education in a Siberian prison colony for drug dependent males," *International Journal for Equity in Health*, 2004, 3, pp. 7-12; G.J. Devilly, L. Sorbello, L. Eccleston, and T. Ward, "Prison-based peer-education schemes," Aggression and Violent Behavior, 2005, 10, pp. 219-40.

158. H. Reyes, "Pitfalls of TB management in prisons, revisited," *International Journal of Prisoner Health* 2007, Vol. 3, No. 1, p. 54.

159. Open Society Justice Initiative, *Criminal Force: Torture, Abuse, and Extrajudicial Killings by the Nigeria Police Force*, Open Society Foundations, New York, 2010, p. 68.

160. Human Rights Watch, Fanning the flames: *How human rights abuses are fueling the AIDS epidemic in Kazakhstan*, Human Rights Watch, New York, 2003, available at http://www.hrw.org/en/reports/2003/06/29/fanning-flames-0 (accessed Oct. 30, 2013); Human Rights Watch, *Rhetoric and risk: Human rights abuses impeding Ukraine's fight against HIV/AIDS*, Human Rights Watch, New York, 2006, available at http://www.hrw.org/en/node/11464/section/1 (accessed Oct. 30, 2013).

161. Manfred Nowak, *Report of the Special Rapporteur on Torture, Mission to Moldova*, 2009, UN doc. A/HRC/10/44/Add.3.

162. Human Rights Watch, AIDS and Rights Alliance for Southern Africa, and Prison Care and Counseling Association. *Unjust and Unhealthy: HIV, TB, and Abuse in Zambian Prisons*, Human Rights Watch, New York, 2010, p. 74, available at http://www.hrw.org/sites/default/files/reports/zambia0410webwcover.pdf (accessed Oct. 30, 2013).

163. Human Rights Watch, AIDS and Rights Alliance for Southern Africa, and Prison Care and Counseling Association. *Unjust and Unhealthy: HIV, TB, and Abuse in Zambian Prisons*, Human Rights Watch, New York, 2010, p. 74, available at http://www.hrw.org/sites/default/files/reports/zambia0410webwcover.pdf (accessed Oct. 30, 2013).

164. Open Society Justice Initiative, *Pretrial Detention and Health: Unintended Consequences, Deadly Results*, Open Society Foundations, New York, 2011, pp. 53-54.

165. TalkingDrugs.org, "UN to tackle HIV related Deaths in Prison," July 27, 2010, available at http://www.talkingdrugs.org/un-to-tackle-hiv-related-deaths-in-prison (quoting UN Special Rapporteur on Torture Manfred Novak as referring to prisons as "HIV incubators").

166. Anya Sarang, Tim Rhodes, Lucy Playy, Valentina Kirzhanova, Olga Shelkovnikova, Venyamin Volnov, Dmitri Blagovo, and Andrei Rylkov, "Drug injecting and syringes use in the HIV risk environment of Russian penitentiary institutions: qualitative study," *Addiction*, Vol. 101, Issue 12, December 2006, p. 1787.

167. *Annual Report for the period 1 April 2005 to 31 March 2006*, Judicial Inspectorate of Prisons, Cape Town, 2006, p. 13.

168. Médecins Sans Frontières, "Peru's Lurigancho prison project: Five years working with people forgotten before they were dead," March 22, 2006, available at http://www.msf.org/article/perus-lurigancho-prison-project-five-years-working-people-forgotten-they-were-dead (accessed Oct. 13, 2013).

169. Niko Kyriakou, "Latin America's In-Prison Diseases Spilling into General Population," *OneWorld*, September 15, 2006, available at http://uk.oneworld.net/article/view/139448/1/5847 (accessed Oct. 13, 2013).

170. James C. Thomas and Elizabeth Torrone, "Incarceration as Forced Migration: Effects on Selected Community Health Outcomes," *American Journal of Public Health*, Vol. 96, No. 10, October 2006, p. 1762.

171. James C. Thomas and Elizabeth Torrone, "Incarceration as Forced Migration: Effects on Selected Community Health Outcomes," *American Journal of Public Health*, Vol. 96, No. 10, October 2006, p. 1765.

172. Merrill Goozner, "Prisons in Post-Soviet Russia Incubate a Plague," *Scientific American*, August 25, 2008, available at http://www.scientificamerican.com/article.cfm?id=prison-plague-post-soviet-russia (accessed Oct. 30, 2013).

173. Merrill Goozner, "Prisons in Post-Soviet Russia Incubate a Plague," *Scientific American*, August 25, 2008, available at http://www.scientificamerican.com/article.cfm?id=prison-plague-post-soviet-russia (accessed Oct. 30, 2013).

174. Alexey Bobrik, Kirill Danishevski, Ksenia Eroshina, and Martin McKee, "Prison Health in Russia: The Larger Picture," *Journal of Public Health Policy*, Volume 26, 2005, p. 31.

175. Andrei Shukshin, "Tough measures in Russian prisons slow spread of TB," *Bulletin of the World Health*

*Organisation*, Vol. 84, No. 4, April 2006, available at http://www.who.int/bulletin/volumes/84/4/news30406/en/index.html (accessed Oct. 30, 2013).

176. Vivien Stern, *Alternatives to prison in developing countries*, International Centre for Prison Studies and Penal Reform International, London, 1999, p. 10.

177. Magdalena Sepúlveda Carmona, *Extreme poverty and human rights*: Report of the Special Rapporteur on extreme poverty and human rights, August 4, 2011, A/66/265, paragraphs 68-71, available at http://www.ohchr.org/Documents/Issues/Poverty/A.66.265.pdf (accessed Oct. 30, 2013).

178. *Unjust Deserts: A Thematic Review by HM Chief Inspector of Prisons of the Treatment and Conditions for Unsentenced Prisoners in England and Wales*, HM Inspectorate of Prisons for England and Wales, London, 2000.

179. Guillermo Zepeda, *Costly Confinement: The Direct and Indirect Costs of Pretrial Detention in Mexico* (English-language summary), Open Society Foundations, New York, 2009.

180. Malena Derdoy, Mariano Fernández Valle, Diego Freedman, Laura Malajovich, Laura Roth, and Raúl Salinas, *The Economic and Social Costs of Preventive Detention in Argentina*, Centre for the Implementation of Public Policies Promoting Equity and Growth, Buenos Aires, 2009, p. 22. See also M. V. Buromensky, O. V. Serduk, and V. I. Tocheny, *Assessment of Social and Economic Costs of Pretrial Detention Applications: Analytical Report*, Institute of Applied Humanitarian Research, Kiev, 2008.

181. Jeffrey Grogger, "The Effect of Arrests on the Employment and Earnings of Young Men," *The Quarterly Journal of Economics*, Vol. 110, Issue 1, February 1995, pp. 51-71.

182. Guillermo Zepeda, *Costly Confinement: The Direct and Indirect Costs of Pretrial Detention in Mexico* (English-language summary), Open Society Foundations, New York, 2009.

183. *Freedom Inside the Walls* (documentary film), Prison Reform International, 2005, available at http://www.youtube.com/watch?v=R_8DHLlWSbc (accessed Oct. 30, 2013).

184. Open Society Justice Initiative / United Nations Development Programme pretrial detainee surveys on the socioeconomic impact of pretrial detention, publication forthcoming.

185. Open Society Justice Initiative / United Nations Development Programme pretrial detainee surveys on the socioeconomic impact of pretrial detention, publication forthcoming.

186. Tomris Atabay and Paul English, *Afghanistan: Implementing Alternatives to Imprisonment, in line with International Standards and National Legislation*, UNODC, Vienna, 2008, p. xiii.

187. Interview conducted by Justice Initiative researcher, Krakow, October, 2010.

188. Oliver Robertson, *The impact of parental imprisonment on children*, Quaker United Nations Office, Geneva, 2007, p. 7.

189. Barbara J. Myers, Tina M. Smarsh, Kristine Amlund-Hagen and Suzanne Kennon, "Children of Incarcerated Mothers," *Journal of Child and Family Studies*, Vol. 8, No. 1, 1999, p. 11.

190. Jennifer Rosenberg, *Children Need Dads Too: Children with Fathers in Prison*, Quaker United Nations Office, Geneva, 2009, p. 14.

191. Herman-Stahl, Kan & McKay, *Incarceration and the Family: A Review of Research and Promising Approaches for Serving Fathers and Families*, RTI International for the US Department of Health and Human Services, Washington, DC, 2008, pp. 1-3.

192. Herman-Stahl, Kan & McKay, *Incarceration and the Family: A Review of Research and Promising Approaches for Serving Fathers and Families*, RTI International for the US Department of Health and Human Services, Washington, DC, 2008, p. 2.

193. Herman-Stahl, Kan & McKay, *Incarceration and the Family: A Review of Research and Promising Approaches for Serving Fathers and Families*, RTI International for the US Department of Health and Human Services, Washington, DC, 2008, p. 9.

194. Guillermo Zepeda, *Costly Confinement: The Direct and Indirect Costs of Pretrial Detention in Mexico* (English-language summary), Open Society Foundations, New York, 2009.

195. Malena Derdoy, Mariano Fernández Valle, Diego Freedman, Laura Malajovich, Laura Roth, and Raúl Salinas, *The Economic and Social Costs of Preventive Detention in Argentina*, Centre for the

Implementation of Public Policies Promoting Equity and Growth, Buenos Aires, 2009, p. 22.

196. "True Hell on Earth: Simon Mann faces imprisonment in the cruellest jail on the planet," *Daily Mail*, May 18, 2007, available at http://www.dailymail.co.uk/news/article-455635/True-hell-earth-Simon-Mann-faces-imprisonment-cruellest-jail-planet.html (accessed Oct. 13, 2013).

197. Manfred Nowak, *Report of the Special Rapporteur on Torture and Other Cruel, Inhuman, or Degrading Treatment or Punishment, Addendum: Mission to Indonesia*, UN Doc A/HRC/7/3/Add.7 Appendix I, para 22, March 10, 2008.

198. Manfred Nowak, *Report of the Special Rapporteur on Torture and other Cruel, Inhuman or Degrading Treatment or Punishment, Mission to Nigeria, 4 to 10 March 2007*, UN Human Rights Council, Geneva, A/HRC/7/3/Add.4, 2007, para. 51.

199. *The Criminalization of Poverty. A Report on the Economic, Social and Cultural Root Causes of Torture and Other Forms of Violence in Brazil*, Justiça Global, the National Movement of Street Boys and Girls, and the World Organisation Against Torture, p. 26, available at http://www2.ohchr.org/english/bodies/cescr/docs/info-ngos/JB_OMCT_MNMMR_Brazil42.pdf (accessed Oct. 30, 2013).

200. *Pre-trial detention in Malawi: Understanding caseflow management and conditions of incarceration*, Open Society Institute for Southern Africa, Johannesburg, 2011, p. 57. The only exception is Mzimba police station where maize meal is provided for breakfast and detainees prepare their own food.

201. *Pre-trial detention in Malawi: Understanding caseflow management and conditions of incarceration*, Open Society Institute for Southern Africa, Johannesburg, 2011, p. 57.

202. *Pre-trial detention in Malawi: Understanding caseflow management and conditions of incarceration*, Open Society Institute for Southern Africa, Johannesburg, 2011, p. 57.

203. *Pre-trial detention in Malawi: Understanding caseflow management and conditions of incarceration*, Open Society Institute for Southern Africa, Johannesburg, 2011, p. 61. Soap is provided at one police station only, namely Mzimba police station.

204. Richard Griggs, *Evaluation of PASI's Access to Justice Project 01 October 2009 – 30 September 2010. The Paralegal Advisory Service Institute's pilot programme for adult pre-trial detainees originating at Kanengo and Mangochi police stations in Malawi*, Open Society Justice Initiative, January 2011 (unpublished).

205. For a review of the literature, see Paul Gendreau, Claire Goggin, and Francis T. Cullen, *The Effects of Prison Sentences on Recidivism*, Solicitor General Canada, Ottawa, 1999, available at http://www.prisonpolicy.org/scans/e199912.htm, (accessed Oct. 30, 2013). See also, Dorothy R. Jaman, Robert M. Dickover, and Lawrence A. Bennett, "Parole outcome as a function of time served," *British Journal of Criminology*, Vol. 12, No. 1, January 1972, p. 7.

206. Lee H. Bukstel and Peter R. Kilmann,"Psychological effects of imprisonment on confined individuals," *Psychological Bulletin*, Vol. 88, Issue 2, 1980, p. 472.

207. Barry Holman and Jason Ziedenberg, *The Dangers of Detention: The Impact of Incarcerating Youth in Detention and Other Secure Facilities*, Justice Policy Institute, Washington, DC, 2006, p. 3.

208. Barry Holman and Jason Ziedenberg, *The Dangers of Detention: The Impact of Incarcerating Youth in Detention and Other Secure Facilities*, Justice Policy Institute, Washington, DC, 2006, p. 9.

209. Philip Alston, *Report of the Special Rapporteur on extrajudicial, summary or arbitrary executions: Mission to Brazil*, A/HRC/11/2/Add.2 future, August 28, 2008, para. 41.

210. Philip Alston, *Report of the Special Rapporteur on extrajudicial, summary or arbitrary executions: Mission to Brazil*, A/HRC/11/2/Add.2 future, 28 August 2008, paras. 45-46.

211. Her Majesty's Inspectorate of Prisons for England and Wales, *Unjust Deserts: A Thematic Review by HM Chief Inspector of Prisons of the Treatment Conditions for Unsentenced Prisoners in England and Wales*, Home Office, London, December 2000, para. 3.04.

212. Her Majesty's Inspectorate of Prisons for England and Wales, *Unjust Deserts: A Thematic Review by HM Chief Inspector of Prisons of the Treatment Conditions for Unsentenced Prisoners in England and Wales*, Home Office, London, December 2000, para. 3.06.

213. Donald Braman, "Families and Incarceration," in Marc Mauer and Meda Chesney-Lind (eds.), *Invisible Punishment. The Collateral Consequences of Mass Imprisonment*, The New Press, New York, 2002, p. 118.

214. James C. Thomas and Elizabeth Torrone, "Incarceration as Forced Migration: Effects on Selected Community Health Outcomes," *American Journal of Public Health*, Vol. 96, No. 10, October 2006, p. 1762.

215. Jennifer Rosenberg, *Children Need Dads Too: Children with Fathers in Prison*, Quaker United Nations Office, Geneva, 2009, p. 14.

216. James C. Thomas and Elizabeth Torrone, "Incarceration as Forced Migration: Effects on Selected Community Health Outcomes," *American Journal of Public Health*, Vol. 96, No. 10, October 2006, p. 1765.

217. Herman-Stahl, Kan, and McKay, *Incarceration and the Family: A Review of Research and Promising Approaches for Serving Fathers and Families*, RTI International for the US Department of Health and Human Services, Washington, 2008, pp. 1-3.

218. Michael King, *Bail or Custody*, Cobden Trust, London, 1973, p

# THE CAUSES OF ARBITRARY & EXCESSIVE USE OF PRETRIAL DETENTION

1. *Eighth United Nations Congress on the Prevention of Crime and the Treatment of Offenders*, Havana, August 27–September 7, 1990, chapter 1, section C, paragraph 2(b).

2. Rule 6, *United Nations Standard Minimum Rules for Non-custodial Measures (The Tokyo Rules)*, Adopted by the General Assembly on December 14, 1990.

3. *Morais v. Angola*, Communication No. 1128/2002, U.N. Doc. CCPR/C/83/D/1128/2002 (2005) (para. 6.1), available at http://www1.umn.edu/humanrts/undocs/1128-2002.html (accessed November 22, 2013).

4. *Morais v. Angola*, Communication No. 1128/2002, U.N. Doc. CCPR/C/83/D/1128/2002 (2005) (para. 6.1), available at http://www1.umn.edu/humanrts/undocs/1128-2002.html (accessed November 22, 2013).

5. See Martin Schönteich, "The Scale and Consequences of Pretrial Detention Around the World," *Justice Initiatives: Pretrial Detention*, Open Society Justice Initiative, New York, Spring 2008, pp. 26–28.

6. Lonneke Stevens, "Pre-Trial Detention: The Presumption of Innocence and Article 5 of the European Convention on Human Rights Cannot and Does Not Limit Its Increasing Use," *European Journal of Crime, Criminal Law and Criminal Justice*, Vol. 17, Issue 2, 2009, p. 168.

7. Lonneke Stevens, "Pre-Trial Detention: The Presumption of Innocence and Article 5 of the European Convention on Human Rights Cannot and Does Not Limit Its Increasing Use," *European Journal of Crime, Criminal Law and Criminal Justice*, Vol. 17, Issue 2, 2009, pp. 170–171.

8. See also David Garland, *The Culture of Control: Crime and Social Order in Contemporary Society*, University of Chicago Press, Chicago, 2001. Garland analyzes the social, economic, and political forces that gave rise to the contemporary culture of crime control in the United States and United Kingdom. He seeks to explain the radical changes that have occurred in the fields of crime control and criminal justice since the 1970s, especially the rise of punitiveness in Western countries. Garland argues that "penal welfarism" (which he sees as distinguished by a commitment to community based solutions to the crime problem, rehabilitating offenders, and creating individualized solutions for offenders) characterized criminal justice practice from the 1890s to the 1970s but has been progressively dismantled since. He suggests that the new politics of crime control have become increasingly more expressive and instrumental, and that contemporary justice policy stresses coercive control of offenders. According to Garland, this trend emerged when high crime rates became normal, the rehabilitative ideal fell out of favor, and the penal welfare complex failed to protect the public from the risks associated with crime. Garland argues that in contrast to penal welfarism, contemporary crime control policy can be distinguished by the (re)emergence of punitive sanctions and expressive justice, an emphasis on victims of crime, the politicization of crime issues and, relatedly, a focus on protecting the public from crime and criminals. This latter change notably departs from previous concerns about the need for protection from the state towards a preference for protection by the state. Public concern has become focused on developing protection from crime as opposed to the abuse of powers that

have been invested in the state and its agencies. Moreover, the discussion on crime control policies has shifted away from the experts and has increasingly become a part of the political process. Experts in the field have been increasingly excluded from the policy making process, and the public has become a new source of support for these policies. Crime initiatives are now a major part of the electoral process, and as a result crime policy is developed based on public approval of the measures. For an accessible summary of Garland's book, see Mathieu Deflem and Chicoine Stephen, "A Summary of *The Culture of Control* by David Garland (2010)," online paper available at http://deflem.blogspot.com/2010/04/garland.html (accessed November 22, 2013).

9. Mauricio J. Duce, Claudio M. Fuentes, and Cristián R. Riego, "La Reforma Procesal Penal en América Latina y su Impacto en el Uso de la Prisón Preventiva," in Cristián R. Riego and Mauricio J. Duce (eds.), *Prisón Preventiva y Reforma Procesal Penal en América Latina. Evaluación y Perspectivas*, Centro de Estudios de Justicia de las Américas, Santiago, 2008, p. 30.

10. Laurence H. Tribe, "An Ounce of Detention: Preventive Justice in the World of John Mitchell," *Virginia Law Review*, Vol. 56, No. 3, April 1970, p. 375.

11. Mark Kelly, *Limiting the Use of Pre-Trial Detention*, discussion paper presented to COLPI, September 10, 2001 (unpublished).

12. For example, Article 9(3) of the International Covenant on Civil and Political Rights stipulates that "it shall not be the general rule that persons awaiting trial shall be detained in custody." It is not clear what percentage of arrested people can be sent to pretrial detention under this principle.

13. Ed Cape and Adam Stapleton, *Improving Pretrial Justice: The Role of Lawyers and Paralegals*, Open Society Justice Initiative, New York, 2012, available at http://www.opensocietyfoundations.org/sites/default/files/improving-pretrial-justice-20120416.pdf (accessed November 19, 2013).

14. See, M. J. Doherty and R. East, "Bail Decisions in Magistrates' Courts," *British Journal of Criminology*, Vol. 25, No. 3, July 1985, p. 262, for examples from Welsh magistrates' courts.

15. Michael R. Gottfredson and Don M. Gottfredson, *Decision-Making in Criminal Justice: Toward the Rational Exercise of Discretion*, Plenum Press, New York, 1988.

16. Mandeep K. Dhami, "From Discretion to Disagreement: Disparities in Judges' Pretrial Decisions," *Behavioral Sciences and the Law*, Vol. 23, 2005, p. 368.

17. Stevens H. Clarke and Susan T. Kurtz, "The Importance of Interim Decisions to Felony Trial Court Dispositions," *The Journal of Criminal Law and Criminology*, Vol. 74, No. 2, 1983, pp. 475–518. The first systematic investigation of the effects of bail, the Vera Institute's Manhattan Bail Project, found that arrestees in New York City who had been detained pending trial were more likely to receive a custodial sentence—and given longer sentences—than those who were released awaiting trial. (See Charles Ares, Anne Rankin, and Herbert Sturz, "The Manhattan Bail Project: An Interim Report on the Use of Pretrial Parole," *New York University Law Review*, Vol. 38, January 1963, pp. 67–92; Anne Rankin, "The Effect of Pretrial Detention," *New York University Law Review*, Vol. 39, 1964, pp. 641–65.) Two subsequent studies support the Manhattan Bail Project findings, where pretrial detention was used as a control variable (along with other legal and extralegal variables) in an assessment of the effect of counsel on case outcomes. Both studies found that pretrial detention was a significant predictor of a custodial sentence: detained defendants were more likely to be incarcerated than defendants who were released prior to trial. (See Jean G. Taylor, Thomas P. Stanley, Barbara J. DeFlorio, and Lynne N. Seekamp, "An Analysis of Defense Counsel in the Processing of Felony Defendants in San Diego, California," *Denver Law Journal*, Vol. 49, 1972, pp. 233–275; Robert Hermann, Eric Single, and John Boston, *Counsel for the Poor: Criminal Defense in Urban America*, Lexington Books, Lexington, MA, 1977.) A separate study found that, although pretrial detention did not affect guilty verdicts, detainees were more likely to be sentenced to prison. (See John S. Goldkamp, "The Effects of Detention on Judicial Decisions: A Closer Look," *Justice System Journal*, Vol. 5, Spring 1980, pp. 234–257.) A further study found that pretrial detention was a strong, significant predictor of both the likelihood of an arrestee's receiving a custodial sentence and the length of sentence. (See Marian R. Williams, "The Effect of Pretrial Detention on Imprisonment Decisions," *Criminal Justice Review*, Vol. 28, No. 2, Autumn 2003, pp. 299–316.)

18. Gary T. Trotter, *The Law of Bail in Canada*, Carswell, Toronto, 1992, pp. 31-32; Craig Ethan Allen, "Pretrial Detention and the Loss of Innocence: United States v. Salerno," *Hamline Law Review*, Vol. 11, 1988, pp. 344–345; Sam J. Ervin, Jr., "Preventive Detention: An Empirical Analysis," *Harvard Civil Rights-Civil Liberties Law Review*, Vol. 6, 1971, pp. 357–358; Charles Patrick Ewing, "Schall v. Martin: Preventive Detention and Dangerousness Through the Looking Glass," *Buffalo Law Review*, Vol. 34, 1985, p. 173.

19. Jack F. Williams, "Process and Detention: A Return to a Fuzzy Model of Pretrial Detention," *Minnesota Law Review*, Vol. 79, 1994, pp. 343–344.

20. Rinat Kitai-Sangero, "The Limits of Preventive Detention," *McGeorge Law Review*, Vol. 40, 2009, p. 910.

21. Article 5(3), European Convention on Human Rights.

22. Anton M. van Kalmthout, Marije M. Knapen, and Christine Morgenstern (eds.), *Pre-trial Detention in the European Union: An Analysis of Minimum Standards in Pre-trial Detention and the Grounds for Regular Review in the Member States of the EU*, Wolf Legal Publishers, Nijmegen, 2009, pp. 81–82.

23. *Detained Without Trial: Fair Trial Internationals' Response to the European Commission's Green Paper on Detention*, Fair Trials International, London, October 2011, p. 21, available at http://ec.europa.eu/justice/newsroom/criminal/opinion/files/110510/fti_pre-trial_detention_report_en.pdf (accessed November 22, 2013).

24. Interview conducted by Justice Initiative researcher, San Pedro, March 2011.

25. Anton M. van Kalmthout, Marije M. Knapen, and Christine Morgenstern (eds.), *Pre-trial Detention in the European Union: An Analysis of Minimum Standards in Pre-trial Detention and the Grounds for Regular Review in the Member States of the EU*, Wolf Legal Publishers, Nijmegen, 2009, pp. 95–96.

26. Anton M. van Kalmthout, Marije M. Knapen, and Christine Morgenstern (eds.), *Pre-trial Detention in the European Union: An Analysis of Minimum Standards in Pre-trial Detention and the Grounds for Regular Review in the Member States of the EU*, Wolf Legal Publishers, Nijmegen, 2009, p. 592.

27. Ed Cape, Zaza Namoradze, Roger Smith, and Taru Spronken, *Effective Criminal Defense in Europe*, Intersentia, Antwerp, 2010, p. 345.

28. For Mexico, see Benjamin Naimark-Rowse, Martin Schönteich, Mykola Sorochinsky, and Denise Tomasini-Joshi, "Studies in Reform: Pretrial Detention Investments in Mexico, Ukraine, and Latvia," *Justice Initiatives: Pretrial Detention*, Open Society Justice Initiative, New York, Spring 2008, p. 153. For Nepal, see R. Cohen, *Fair Trials in Nepal: A Critical Study*, Advocacy Forum, 2010, p. 9.

29. Anton M. van Kalmthout, Marije M. Knapen, and Christine Morgenstern (eds.), *Pre-trial Detention in the European Union: An Analysis of Minimum Standards in Pre-trial Detention and the Grounds for Regular Review in the Member States of the EU*, Wolf Legal Publishers, Nijmegen, 2009, p. 64.

30. See Martin Schönteich, "The Story of a Good Law, Its Bad Application, and the Ugly Results: An Analysis of the South African Bail Law, and Its Inadequate Application Due to an Ineffective Criminal Justice System," *Spotlight 1/97*, South African Institute of Race Relations, Johannesburg, July 1997.

31. Paragraph 3142, *Bail Reform Act of 1984*.

32. *United States v. Salerno*, 481 U.S. 739 (1987).

33. UN Economic and Social Council, Commission on Human Rights, *Civil and Political Rights, Including the Questions of Torture and Detention: Torture and Other Cruel, Inhuman or Degrading Treatment or Punishment, Report of the Special Rapporteur, Theo van Boven*, U.N. Doc E/CN.4/2004/56, December 23, 2003, para. 34.

34. UN Committee Against Torture, 40th Session, *Consideration of Reports Submitted by States Parties Under Article 19 of the Convention: Concluding Observations of the Committee Against Torture, Algeria*, U.N. Doc CAT/C/DZA/CO/3, May 26, 2008, para. 5.

35. UN Committee Against Torture, *Consideration of Reports by States Parties Under Article 19 of the Convention: Concluding Observations of the Committee Against Torture, Chad*, U.N. Doc CAT/C/TCD/CO/1, June 4, 2009, para. 25.

36. UN Committee Against Torture, *Consideration of Reports Submitted by States Parties Under Article 19 of the Convention: Concluding Observations of the Committee Against Torture, Cameroon*, U.N. Doc CAT/C/CMR/CO/4, May 19, 2010, para. 11; Committee Against Torture, 35th session, *Consideration of Reports by States Parties Under Article 19 of the Convention: Concluding Observations of the Committee Against Torture, Burundi*, U.N. Doc CAT/C/BDI/CO/1, February 15, 2007, para. 9; see, e.g., United Nations Human Rights Council, *Report of the Working Group on Arbitrary Detention: Mission to Senegal*, U.N. Doc A/HRC/13/30/Add.3, March 23, 2010, para. 39; U.N. Human Rights Council, 7th Session, *Report of the Special Rapporteur on Torture and Other Cruel, Inhuman or Degrading Treatment or Punishment*,

Manfred Nowak, *Mission to Togo*, U.N. Doc A/HRC/7/3/Add.5, January 6, 2008, para. 15.

37. UN Human Rights Council, *Report of the Working Group on Arbitrary Detention (Addendum): Mission to Mauritania*, U.N. Doc A/HRC/10/21/Add.2, November 21, 2008, para. 89; UN Human Rights Council, *Report of the Working Group on Arbitrary Detention: Mission to Angola, Addendum*, U.N. Doc A/HRC/7/4/Add.3, February 29, 2008, p. 3.

38. UN Human Rights Council, 13th Session, *Report of the Special Rapporteur on Torture and Other Cruel, Inhuman or Degrading Treatment or Punishment, Manfred Nowak, Addendum: Study on the Phenomena of Torture, Cruel, Inhuman or Degrading Treatment or Punishment in the World, Including an Assessment of Conditions of Detention*, U.N. Doc A/HRC/13/39/Add.5, February 5, 2010, para. 81.

39. UN Economic and Social Council, Commission on Human Rights, 56th Session, *Report of the Special Rapporteur, Sir Nigel Rodley, Submitted Pursuant to Commission on Human Rights Resolution 1999/32, Addendum, Visit of the Special Rapporteur to Kenya*, U.N. Doc E/CN.4/2009/9/Add.4, March 9, 2000, paras. 59–60.

40. UN Human Rights Council, *Report of the Working Group on Arbitrary Detention: Mission to Equatorial Guinea, Addendum*, U.N. Doc A/HRC/7/4/Add., February 18, 2008, para. 62.

41. Section 42(2) Malawi Constitution. Minor exceptions are made in cases where the 48 hours expire outside ordinary court hours or on a day which is not a court day. In such cases, the arrestee must be brought before a court on the first court date after such expiry.

42. *Pre-trial Detention in Malawi: Understanding Caseflow Management and Conditions of Incarceration*, Open Society Initiative for Southern Africa, Johannesburg, 2011, p. 55.

43. R. Cohen et al., *Fair Trials in Nepal: A Critical Study*, Advocacy Forum, 2010, p. 8.

44. See *People (Attorney General) v. Callaghan* [1966] IR 501, confirmed by the court in *Ryan v. Director of Public Prosecutions* [1989] IR 399.

45. *People (Attorney General) v. Callaghan* [1966] IR 501 at 516–517. Stephen Jones, "Guilty until Proven Innocent? The Diminished Status of Suspects at the Point of Remand and as Unconvicted Prisoners," *Common Law World Review*, Vol. 32, Issue 4, December 2003, p. 405.

46. Stephen Jones, "Guilty until Proven Innocent? The Diminished Status of Suspects at the Point of Remand and as Unconvicted Prisoners," *Common Law World Review*, Vol. 32, Issue 4, December 2003, p. 405.

47. Mauricio J. Duce, Claudio M. Fuentes, and Cristián R. Riego, "La Reforma Procesal Penal en América Latina y su Impacto en el Uso de la Prisón Preventiva," in Cristián R. Riego and Mauricio J. Duce (eds.), *Prisón Preventiva y Reforma Procesal Penal en América Latina: Evaluación y Perspectivas*, Centro de Estudios de Justicia de las Américas, Santiago, 2008, p. 55.

48. Mauricio J. Duce, Claudio M. Fuentes, and Cristián R. Riego, "La Reforma Procesal Penal en América Latina y su Impacto en el Uso de la Prisón Preventiva," in Cristián R. Riego and Mauricio J. Duce (eds.), *Prisón Preventiva y Reforma Procesal Penal en América Latina: Evaluación y Perspectivas*, Centro de Estudios de Justicia de las Américas, Santiago, 2008, p. 57–58.

49. Rick Sarre, Sue King, and David Bamford, "Remand in Custody: Critical Factors and Key Issues," *Trends & Issues in Criminal Justice*, No. 310, May 2006, pp. 2–3.

50. *Evaluation of PRI and SDC Project: Support to Penitentiary Reform in Ukraine 2009–2012*, Penal Reform International, London, August 2011, p. 5.

51. Wieger van der Heide, Frank van Tulder, and Caspar Wiebrens, Strafrechter en strafketen: de gang van de zaken, 1995-2006, Rechtstreeks, No. 3, 2007, p. 59, as cited in Lonneke Stevens, "Pre-Trial Detention: The Presumption of Innocence and Article 5 of the European Convention on Human Rights Cannot and Does Not Limit its Increasing Use," *European Journal of Crime, Criminal Law and Criminal Justice*, Vol. 17, Issue 2, 2009, p. 166.

52. For example, UN Human Rights Council, *Report of the Working Group on Arbitrary Detention: Mission to Equatorial Guinea*, Addendum, U.N. Doc A/HRC/7/4/Add., February 18, 2008, para. 28.

53. Morgan Whitaker, "The Legacy of the Willie Horton Ad Lives on, 25 Years Later," MSNBC.com, Oct. 21, 2013, available at http://www.msnbc.com/msnbc/the-legacy-the-willie-horton-ad-lives (accessed Nov. 29, 2013).

54. *Report of the All India Committee on Jail Reforms, 1980-1983*, Ministry of Home Affairs, Government of India, New Delhi, 1983.

55. Swati Mehta, *Maharashtra's Abandoned Prisons: A Study of Sub-Jails*, Commonwealth Human Rights Initiative, New Delhi, 2010, p. 9.

56. *Prisons and Human Rights*. (Report based on the proceedings of the workshops on "Prisons and Human Rights" organized by the Commonwealth Human Rights Initiative in Collaboration with the Madhya Pradesh Human Rights Commission, April 25–26, 1998). Commonwealth Human Rights Initiative, New Delhi, 1998, pp. 1–2.

57. Mohammed Tipu Sultan, "Rights of Prisoners," in Hameeda Hossain and Sara Hossain (eds.), *Human Rights in Bangladesh 2006*, Ain o Salish Kendra, Dhaka, 2006, available at http://www.askbd.org/web/?page_id=504 (accessed November 22, 2013).

58. See, Emeka E. Obioha, "Challenges and Reforms in the Nigerian Prison System," *Journal of Social Sciences*, Vol. 27, No. 2, 2011, pp. 100–101, available at http://www.krepublishers.com/02-Journals/JSS/JSS-27-0-000-11-Web/JSS-27-2-000-11-Abst-PDF/JSS-27-2-095-11-1116-Obioha-E-E/JSS-27-2-095-11-1116-Obioha-E-E-Tt.pdf (accessed November 22, 2013).

59. Chinwuba Iyizoba, "Nigeria's Citadel of Injustice," Mercator Net, August 13, 2009, available at http://www.mercatornet.com/articles/view/nigerias_citadel_of_injustice (accessed November 22, 2013).

60. "Prison Reform: Panel's recommendations will be implemented – Obasanjo," *New Nigerian*, November 15, 2006, as cited in Nigeria: Prisoners' Rights Systematically Flouted, Amnesty International, London, February 2008 (AFR 44/001/2008), p. 3.

61. *World Prison Brief*, International Centre for Prison Studies, available at http://www.prisonstudies.org/world-prison-brief (accessed February 21, 2014). See also various annual editions of Roy Walmsley, World Prison Population List, International Centre for Prison Studies.

62. Stephen Jones, "Guilty until Proven Innocent? The Diminished Status of Suspects at the Point of Remand and as Unconvicted Prisoners," *Common Law World Review*, Vol. 32, Issue 4, December 2003, p. 404.

63. Douglas J. Klein, "The Pretrial Detention 'Crisis': The Causes and the Cure," *Journal of Urban and Contemporary Law*, Vol. 52, 1997, p. 290.

64. Mary Phillips, "Bail, Detention, and Nonfelony Case Outcomes," CJA Research Brief 14, May 2007, New York Criminal Justice Agency, New York, p. 5.

65. See Lisa Ritchie, *A Report on the Bail Process in the Criminal Justice System*, Honors Thesis Submitted In Partial Fulfillment of the Requirements for the Bachelor of Arts Degree, University of Waterloo, Waterloo ON, 2005, pp. 36–37. Jeffrey Manns, "Liberty Takings: A Framework For Compensating Pretrial Detainees," *Cardoza Law Review*, Vol. 26, No. 5, April 2005, pp. 1947–2022.

66. Gail Kellough and Scot Wortley, "Remand For Plea: Bail Decisions and Plea Bargaining as Commensurate Decisions," *British Journal of Criminology*, Vol. 42, Issue 1, 2002, pp. 186–210.

67. Gail Kellough and Scot Wortley, "Remand For Plea: Bail Decisions and Plea Bargaining as Commensurate Decisions," *British Journal of Criminology*, Vol. 42, Issue 1, 2002, pp. 198–199.

68. Anthony N. Doob and Carla Cesaroni, *Responding to Youth Crime in Canada*, University of Toronto Press, Toronto, 2004, p. 169.

69. Jeffrey Manns, "Liberty Takings: A Framework For Compensating Pretrial Detainees," *Cardoza Law Review*, Vol. 26, No. 5, April 2005, pp. 1947–2022.

70. Gail Kellough and Scot Wortley, "Remand For Plea: Bail Decisions and Plea Bargaining as Commensurate Decisions," *British Journal of Criminology*, Vol. 42, Issue 1, 2002, p. 199.

71. Interview conducted by Justice Initiative researcher, Bishkek, October, 2010.

72. Li Jiao, *Comparative Study of Bail*, LL.M. dissertation, Central European University, Budapest, November 2009, p. 20.

73. See, An Raes and Sonja Snacken, "The Future of Remand Custody and its Alternatives in Belgium," *Howard Journal of Criminal Justice*, Vol. 43, No. 5, December 2004, pp. 506–517.

74. Ed Cape, Zaza Namoradze, Roger Smith, and Taru Spronken, *Effective Criminal Defense in Europe*, Intersentia, Antwerp, 2010, p. 604.

75. Todd Foglesong, "Encouraging Trends in Pretrial Detention in Russia," *Research in Brief: Safety and Justice*, Harvard Kennedy School, June 2011, p. 2.

76. *Submission to the 103rd Session of the Human Rights Committee, October 2011, Country Report Task Force on ARMENIA*, September 2, 2011, Penal Reform International, p. 6. Email communication with Tamuna Kaldani, Progamme Manager, Open Society Georgia Foundation, June 24, 2011. See also Supreme Court of Georgia, The Judiciary in Georgia – Statistical Data for the Year 2010, Part III, Criminal Cases, available at http://www.supremecourt.ge/eng/statistical-data-for-the-year-2010/ (accessed November 22, 2013). Ed Cape and Zaza Namoradze, *Effective Criminal Defence in Eastern Europe*, Legal Aid Reformers' Network, Moldova, 2012, p. 432, available at http://www.legalaidreform.org/news/item/383-effective-criminal-defence-in-eastern-europe (accessed November 22, 2013).

77. Stephen Jones, "Guilty until Proven Innocent? The Diminished Status of Suspects at the Point of Remand and as Unconvicted Prisoners," *Common Law World Review*, Vol. 32, Issue 4, December 2003, p. 404.

78. Anthea Hucklesby, "Bail or Jail? The Practical Operation of the Bail Act 1976," *Journal of Law and Society*, Vol. 23, No. 2, June 1996, p. 217.

79. Anthea Hucklesby, "Bail or Jail? The Practical Operation of the Bail Act 1976," *Journal of Law and Society*, Vol. 23, No. 2, June 1996, pp. 217, 230.

80. Stephen Jones, "Guilty until Proven Innocent? The Diminished Status of Suspects at the Point of Remand and as Unconvicted Prisoners," *Common Law World Review*, Vol. 32, Issue 4, December 2003, p. 404.

81. See, *Pretrial Detention and Corruption: Unable to Pay Bribes, Millions Languish in Detention*, Open Society Justice Initiative, New York, 2010, available at http://www.opensocietyfoundations.org/publications/pretrial-detention-and-corruption-unable-pay-bribes-millions-languish-detention (accessed November 22, 2013); and *The Socioeconomic Impact of Pretrial Detention*, Open Society Justice Initiative, New York, 2011, available at http://www.opensocietyfoundations.org/reports/socioeconomic-impact-pretrial-detention (accessed November 22, 2013).

82. See, for example, R. K. Saxena, "Catalyst for Change: The Effect of Prison Visits on Pretrial Detention in India," *Justice Initiatives: Pretrial Detention*, Open Society Justice Initiative, New York, Spring 2008, p. 60. Justin Sandefur, Billal Siddiqi, and Alaina Varvaloucas, *Timap Criminal Justice Pilot: Baseline Report*, Centre for the Study of African Economies, Oxford, 2011 (unpublished).

83. See, in relation to England and Wales, Andrew Sanders, Richard Young, and Mandy Burton, Criminal Justice, Oxford University Press, Oxford, 2010, p. 463; in relation to Nigeria, see *Criminal Force: Torture, Abuse, and Extrajudicial Killings by the Nigeria Police Force*, Open Society Justice Initiative, New York, 2010.

84. See, *Global Corruption Report 2007: Corruption in Judicial Systems*, Cambridge University Press, New York, 2007.

85. *Global Corruption Barometer 2013*, Transparency International, Berlin, 2013, p. 13, available at http://issuu.com/transparencyinternational/docs/2013_globalcorruptionbarometer_en/5?e=2496456/3903358 (accessed November 20, 2013).

86. *Pretrial Detention and Corruption: Unable to Pay Bribes, Millions Languish in Detention*, Open Society Justice Initiative, New York, 2010, available at http://www.opensocietyfoundations.org/publications/pretrial-detention-and-corruption-unable-pay-bribes-millions-languish-detention (accessed November 22, 2013).

87. Open Society Justice Initiative / United Nations Development Programme pretrial detainee surveys on the socioeconomic impact of pretrial detention, publication forthcoming.

88. See *Pretrial Detention and Corruption: Unable to Pay Bribes, Millions Languish in Detention*, Open Society Justice Initiative, New York, 2010, available at http://www.opensocietyfoundations.org/publications/pretrial-detention-and-corruption-unable-pay-bribes-millions-languish-detention (accessed November 22, 2013).

89. *Snap-shot of the Use and Conditions of Pre-Trial Detention in Police Cells in Africa*, The African Policing

and Civilian Oversight Forum, Cape Town, 2011, p. 12. See also, UN Committee Against Torture, *Consideration of Reports Submitted by States Parties Under Article 19 of the Convention: Concluding Observations of the Committee Against Torture, Cameroon*, U.N. Doc CAT/C/CMR/CO/4, May 19, 2010, para. 11; UN Human Rights Council, 7th Session, *Report of the Special Rapporteur on Torture and other Cruel, Inhuman or Degrading Treatment or Punishment, Manfred Nowak, Mission to Nigeria (4 to 10 March 2007)*, U.N. Doc A/HRC/7/3/Add.4, November 22, 2007, para. 39; UN Human Rights Council, 7th Session, *Report of the Special Rapporteur on Torture and Other Cruel, Inhuman or Degrading Treatment or Punishment, Manfred Nowak, Mission to Togo*, U.N. Doc A/HRC/7/3/Add.5, January 6, 2008, para. 79; UN Committee Against Torture, *Consideration of Reports by States Parties Under Article 19 of the Convention: Concluding Observations of the Committee against Torture, Chad*, U.N. Doc CAT/C/TCD/CO/1, June 4, 2009, para. 17.

90. United Nations Human Rights Council, *Report of the Working Group on Arbitrary Detention: Mission to Senegal*, U.N. Doc A/HRC/13/30/Add.3, 23 March 2010, para. 78.

91. *Snap-shot of the Use and Conditions of Pre-trial Detention in Police Cells in Africa*, The African Policing and Civilian Oversight Forum, Cape Town, 2011, p. 11.

92. U.N. Economic and Social Council, Commission on Human Rights, 56th session, *Report of the Special Rapporteur, Sir Nigel Rodley, Submitted Pursuant to Commission on Human Rights Resolution 1999/32, Addendum, Visit of the Special Rapporteur to Kenya*, U.N. Doc E/CN.4/2009/9/Add.4, March 9, 2000, para. 17.

93. *Criminal Force: Torture, Abuse, and Extrajudicial Killings by the Nigeria Police Force*, Open Society Justice Initiative, New York, 2010, pp. 78-79.

94. *One in Five: The Crisis in Brazil's Prisons and Criminal Justice System*, International Bar Association, Sao Paulo, February 2010, p. 9.

95. Shamim Bano, "The Injustice of Justice," *The International News*, August 22, 2011, available at http://www.thenews.com.pk/Todays-News-4-63949-The-injustice-of-justice (accessed November 22, 2013).

96. See M. Doherty and R. East, "Bail Decisions in Magistrates' Courts," *British Journal of Criminology*, Vol. 25, Issue 3, 1985.

97. Michael Zander, "Operation of the Bail Act in London Magistrates' Courts," *New Law Journal*, 1979.

98. Rick Sarre, Sue King, and David Bamford, "Remand in Custody: Critical Factors and Key Issues," *Trends & Issues in Criminal Justice*, No. 310, May 2006, Australian Institute of Criminology, p. 4.

99. Study of Cook County Video Bond Court conducted by clinical law students in the Bluhm Legal Clinic, Northwestern University, Chicago, Autumn 2007, as cited in Ed Cape and Adam Stapleton, *Improving Pretrial Justice: The Role of Lawyers and Paralegals*, Open Society Justice Initiative, New York, 2012, available at http://www.opensocietyfoundations.org/sites/default/files/improving-pretrial-justice-20120416.pdf (accessed November 19, 2013).

100. Kimmett Edgar, *Lacking Conviction: The Rise of the Women's Remand Population*, Prison Reform Trust, London, 2004, p. 4.

101. Article 5(4), European Convention on Human Rights.

102. *Bezicheri vs. Italy*, Judgment of October 25, 1989, Series A, No. 164.

103. Namely, Czech Republic, Greece, Italy, Poland, Romania, Slovakia, Spain, and Sweden. See, *Detained Without Trial: Fair Trial Internationals' Response to the European Commission's Green Paper on Detention* (draft report), Fair Trials International, London, October 2011, p. 21, available at http://ec.europa.eu/justice/newsroom/criminal/opinion/files/110510/fti_pre-trial_detention_report_en.pdf (accessed November 22, 2013).

104. *Submission to the Public Consultation on the "European Commission Green Paper on the Application of EU Criminal Justice Legislation in the Field of Detention,"* by the Czech Helsinki Committee and others, November 25, 2011, Brussels, p. 8.

105. Ed Cape and Adam Stapleton, *Improving Pretrial Justice: The Role of Lawyers and Paralegals*, Open Society Justice Initiative, New York, 2012, available at http://www.opensocietyfoundations.org/sites/default/files/improving-pretrial-justice-20120416.pdf (accessed November 19, 2013).

106. R. K. Saxena, "Catalyst for Change: The Effect of Prison Visits on Pretrial Detention in India,"

*Justice Initiatives: Pretrial Detention*, Open Society Justice Initiative, Spring 2008, New York, p. 60; J Baguenard et al., Activating the Justice System in Bangladesh: A Report by the Justice Identification Mission, European Commission, 2005.

107. *Reform of the Holding Charge Practice in Nigeria*, Nigerian Bar Association, May 2008. See also Stanley Ibe, *Travesty of Justice: An Advocacy Manual against the Holding Charge*, Human Rights Law Service, Lagos, 2004.

108. *Reform of the Holding Charge Practice in Nigeria*, Nigerian Bar Association, May 2008.

109. *Nigeria: Prisoners' Rights Systematically Flouted*, Amnesty International, London, February 2008 (AFR 44/001/2008], pp. 3, 50.

110. *Reform of the Holding Charge Practice in Nigeria*, Nigerian Bar Association, May 2008. See also Adefi Matthew Olong, *The Administration of Criminal Justice in Nigeria: A Case for Reform*, A Thesis in the Faculty of Law, Submitted to the School of Postgraduate Studies, University of Jos, in Partial Fulfillment of the Requirements for the Award of the Degree of Doctor of Philosophy in Law of the University of Jos, November 2010, pp. 79–80.

111. *Snap-shot of the Use and Conditions of Pre-trial Detention in Police Cells in Africa*, The African Policing and Civilian Oversight Forum, Cape Town, 2011, p. 20. See also, UN Economic and Social Council, Commission on Human Rights, 61st Session, *Report of the Working Group on Arbitrary Detention*, U.N. Doc E/CN.4/2005/6, December 1, 2004, para. 63.

112. UN Committee against Torture, *Consideration of Reports Submitted by States Parties under article 19 of the Convention: Concluding Observations of the Committee Against Torture, Cameroon*, U.N. Doc CAT/C/CMR/CO/4, May 19, 2010, para. 13.

113. UN Economic and Social Council, Commission on Human Rights, 56th session, *Report of the Special Rapporteur, Sir Nigel Rodley, Submitted Pursuant to Commission on Human Rights Resolution 1999/32, Addendum, Visit of the Special Rapporteur to Kenya*, U.N. Doc E/CN.4/2009/9/Add.4, March 9, 2000, paras. 59–60; UN Human Rights Council, *Report of the Working Group on Arbitrary Detention: Mission to Angola, Addendum*, U.N. Doc A/HRC/7/4/Add.3, February 29, 2008, p. 2.

114. Justin Sandefur, Billal Siddiqi, and Alaina Varvaloucas, *Timap Criminal Justice Pilot: Baseline Report*, Centre for the Study of African Economies, Oxford, 2011 (unpublished).

115. R. K. Saxena, "Catalyst for Change: The Effect of Prison Visits on Pretrial Detention in India," *Justice Initiatives: Pretrial Detention*, Open Society Justice Initiative, Spring 2008, New York, p. 61; Anthony Nwapa, "Building and Sustaining Change: Pretrial Detention Reform in Nigeria," *Justice Initiatives: Pretrial Detention*, Open Society Justice Initiative, Spring 2008, New York, p. 89.

116. Anthony Nwapa, "Building and Sustaining Change: Pretrial Detention Reform in Nigeria," *Justice Initiatives: Pretrial Detention*, Open Society Justice Initiative, Spring 2008, New York, p. 89.

117. Adefi Matthew Olong, *The Administration of Criminal Justice in Nigeria: A Case for Reform*, A Thesis in the Faculty of Law, Submitted to the School of Postgraduate Studies, University of Jos, in partial fulfillment of the requirements for the award of the Degree of Doctor of Philosophy in Law of the University of Jos, November 2010, p. 145.

118. *Report of the Presidential Working Group on Prison Reforms and Decongestion*, Abuja, February 2005, pp. 6–7, 73.

119. *Pre-trial Detention in Malawi: Understanding Caseflow Management and Conditions of Incarceration*, Open Society Initiative for Southern Africa, Johannesburg, 2011, p. 24.

120. The pretrial detention crisis came about in the late 1980s as the number of pretrial detainees in the federal U.S. criminal justice system swelled to unmanageable proportions. As a result, federal pretrial detainees were frequently housed in detention centers far removed from their places of trial. This resulted in delayed trials and created practical problems of access to detainees by defense lawyers and pretrial services. See *Report of the Judicial Conference Committee on Criminal Law and Probation Administration*, January 1990, p. 8.

121. Daniel B. Ryan, "The Federal Detention Crisis: Causes and Effects," *Federal Probation*, Vol. 57, No. 1, 1993, p. 61.

122. *Access to Legal Aid in Criminal Justice Systems in Africa: Survey Report*, United Nations Office on Drugs and Crime, Vienna, 2011, p. 35, available at http://www.unodc.org/pdf/criminal_justice/Survey_Report_on_Access_to_Legal_Aid_in_Africa.pdf (accessed November 22, 2013).

123. *Federal Republic of Nigeria, Presidential Committee on the Reform of the Nigeria Police Force*, Main Report, Vol. 1, April 2008, p. 145.

124. *Federal Republic of Nigeria, Presidential Committee on the Reform of the Nigeria Police Force: Main Report*, Vol. 1, April 2008, p. 145.

125. *Snap-shot of the Use and Conditions of Pre-Trial Detention in Police Cells In Africa*, The African Policing and Civilian Oversight Forum, Cape Town, 2011, p. 10.

126. Shima Baradaran, "The Presumption of Innocence and Pretrial Detention in Malawi," *Malawi Law Journal*, Vol. 4, Issue 1, 2010, p. 128.

127. See, e.g., Adefi Matthew Olong, *The Administration of Criminal Justice in Nigeria: A Case for Reform*, A Thesis in the Faculty of Law, Submitted to the School of Postgraduate Studies, University of Jos, in Partial Fulfillment of the Requirements for the Award of the Degree of Doctor of Philosophy in Law of the University of Jos, November 2010, pp. 146–147.

128. Ademola Adegbamigbe, "Impotent Force: Here Are the Reasons the Nigeria Police Is Helpless in the Face of Rising Crimes," The News, February 4, 2008. For a more detailed discussion of the resource constraints faced by the Nigeria Police Force, see *Criminal Force. Torture, Abuse, and Extrajudicial Killings by the Nigeria Police Force*, Open Society Justice Initiative, New York, 2010, pp. 31–37.

129. Clifford Msiska, Director of the Paralegal Advisory Service Institute (Malawi), January 17 2012, personal communication with the author.

130. "No Joy for Chitungwiza Remand Prisoners," Newsday, October 24, 2011. For South Africa, see "No cars for cops," *The Witness*, April 26, 2010, available at http://www.witness.co.za/index.php?showcontent&global[_id]=39511 (accessed November 22, 2013). Mncedi Mkokeli, "South Africa: Police Investigators Hitch Hike Due to Vehicle Shortages," *East Cape News*, November 17, 2000, available at http://allafrica.com/stories/200011170433.html (accessed November 22, 2013).

131. *Kyrgyzstan's Prison System Nightmare*, Asia Report No.118, August 16, 2006, International Crisis Group, p. 15, available at http://www.crisisgroup.org/~/media/Files/asia/central-asia/kyrgyzstan/118_kyrgyzstans_prison_system_nightmare.pdf (accessed November 22, 2013).

132. *Pre-trial Detention in Zambia: Understanding Caseflow Management And Conditions Of Incarceration*, Open Society Initiative for Southern Africa, Johannesburg, 2011, p. 28.

133. Rick Sarre, Sue King, and David Bamford, "Remand in Custody: Critical Factors and Key Issues," *Trends & Issues in Criminal Justice*, No. 310, May 2006, Australian Institute of Criminology, p. 5.

134. Douglas J. Klein, "The Pretrial Detention 'Crisis': The Causes and the Cure," *Journal of Urban and Contemporary Law*, Vol. 52, 1997, pp. 289–290.

135. Adefi Matthew Olong, *The Administration of Criminal Justice in Nigeria: A Case for Reform*, A Thesis in the Faculty of Law, Submitted to the School of Postgraduate Studies, University of Jos, in Partial Fulfillment of the Requirements for the Award of the Degree of Doctor of Philosophy in Law of the University of Jos, November 2010, pp. 135¬136.

136. Ed Cape and Adam Stapleton, *Improving Pretrial Justice: The Role of Lawyers and Paralegals*, Open Society Justice Initiative, New York, 2012, available at http://www.opensocietyfoundations.org/sites/default/files/improving-pretrial-justice-20120416.pdf (accessed November 19, 2013).

137. Anthony Nwapa, "Building and Sustaining Change: Pretrial Detention Reform in Nigeria," *Justice Initiatives: Pretrial Detention*, Open Society Justice Initiative, Spring 2008, New York, pp. 97–98.

138. Clifford Msiska, "On the Front Lines: Insights from Malawi's Paralegal Service," *Justice Initiatives: Pretrial Detention*, Open Society Justice Initiative, Spring 2008, New York, pp. 70–85. See also, *Pre-Trial Detention and Legal Aid in Malawi*, available at http://www.humanrights.ie/index.php/2011/08/04/pre-trial-detention-legal-aid-in-malawi/ (accessed November 22, 2013).

139. Douglas L. Colbert, Ray Paternoster, and Shawn Bushway, "Do Attorneys Really Matter? The Empirical and Legal Case for the Right of Counsel at Bail," *Cardozo Law Review* Vol. 23, No. 5, 2002, p. 1720.

140. Douglas L. Colbert, Ray Paternoster, and Shawn Bushway, "Do Attorneys Really Matter? The Empirical and Legal Case for the Right of Counsel at Bail," *Cardozo Law Review* Vol. 23, No. 5, 2002, pp. 1747–1748.

141. *Gideon's Broken Promise: America's Continuing Quest For Equal Justice*, A Report on the American Bar Association's Hearings on the Right to Counsel in Criminal Proceedings, American Bar Association, Chicago, 2004, p. 23, available at http://www.americanbar.org/groups/legal_aid_indigent_defendants/initiatives/indigent_defense_systems_improvement/gideons_broken_promise.html (accessed November 22, 2013).

142. Ed Cape, Zaza Namoradze, Roger Smith, and Taru Spronken, *Effective Criminal Defense in Europe*, Intersentia, Antwerp, 2010, pp. 605–606.

143. Ed Cape and Adam Stapleton, *Improving Pretrial Justice: The Role of Lawyers and Paralegals*, Open Society Justice Initiative, New York, 2012, available at http://www.opensocietyfoundations.org/sites/default/files/improving-pretrial-justice-20120416.pdf (accessed November 19, 2013).

144. Douglas L. Colbert, "Prosecution Without Representation," *Buffalo Law Review* Vol. 59, No. 2, April 2011, p. 389.

145. Douglas L. Colbert, Ray Paternoster, and Shawn Bushway, "Do Attorneys Really Matter? The Empirical and Legal Case for the Right of Counsel at Bail," *Cardozo Law Review* Vol. 23, No. 5, 2002, pp. 1723-1724.

146. Daniel B. Ryan, "The Federal Detention Crisis: Causes and Effects," *Federal Probation*, Vol. 57, No. 1, 1993, p. 54.

147. *Decisoes Judiciais Nos Crimes de Roubo em Sao Paulo*, Instituto de Defesa do Direito de Defesa e Instituto Brasileiro de Ciências Criminais (undated).

148. *Access to Legal Aid in Criminal Justice Systems in Africa: Survey Report*, United Nations Office on Drugs and Crime, New York, 2011, available at http://www.unodc.org/pdf/criminal_justice/Survey_Report_on_Access_to_Legal_Aid_in_Africa.pdf (accessed November 22, 2013), pp. 18, 21. According to the report (p. 19), annual per capita spending on legal aid varies from a high of $38 in the United Kingdom, to 3 cents per capita in Ghana and Kenya, 1.5 cents in Malawi, and 1 cent in Nigeria. See also, *Handbook on Improving Access to Legal Aid in Africa*, United Nations Office on Drugs and Crime, New York, 2011, p. 100. See also, *Access to Justice and Legal Aid in East Africa: A Comparison of the Legal Aid Schemes Used in the Region and the Level of Cooperation and Coordination Between the Various Actors*, The Danish Institute for Human Rights, Copenhagen, December 2011.

# IMPLICATIONS FOR THE RULE OF LAW

1. Clifford Msiska, "On the Front Lines: Insights from Malawi's Paralegal Advisory Service," *Justice Initiatives: Pretrial Detention*, Open Society Foundations, New York, 2008, p. 72.

2. Asiff Hussein, "Whither prison reforms," *Sunday Observer Magazine*, August 11, 2002, available at: http://www.sundayobserver.lk/2002/08/11/fea19.html (accessed October 15, 2013).

3. Human Rights Watch, *Unjust and Unhealthy: HIV, TB, and Abuse in Zambian Prisons*, Human Rights Watch, New York, 2010, pp. 109-110, available at: http://www.hrw.org/sites/default/files/reports/zambia0410webwcover.pdf (accessed Oct. 15, 2013).

4. Human Rights Watch, *Unjust and Unhealthy: HIV, TB, and Abuse in Zambian Prisons*, Human Rights Watch, New York, 2010, pp. 109-110, available at: http://www.hrw.org/sites/default/files/reports/zambia0410webwcover.pdf (accessed Oct. 15, 2013).

5. "In Mexico, justice means catch and release," *Americas on msnbc.com*, July 27, 2010, available at http://www.msnbc.msn.com/id/38432505/ns/world_news-americas/t/mexico-justice-means-catch-release/#.TokmeXJdCo8 (accessed Oct. 15, 2013).

6. "In Mexico, justice means catch and release," *Americas on msnbc.com*, July 27, 2010, available at http://www.msnbc.msn.com/id/38432505/ns/world_news-americas/t/mexico-justice-means-catch-release/#.TokmeXJdCo8 (accessed Oct. 15, 2013).

7. Human Rights Watch, *Neither Rights Nor Security*, Human Rights Watch, New York, 2011, p. 78, available at http://www.hrw.org/node/102793/section/4 (accessed Oct. 15, 2013). Emphasis added.

8. Cámara de Diputados, "*Arraigo judicial: Datos generales, contexto y temas de debate,*" Nov. 2011, p. 9, available at http://www3.diputados.gob.mx/camara/content/download/269265/825108/file/Carpeta13_Arraigo_judicial.pdf (hereafter, "Arraigo judicial").

9. Article 16, Mexican Constitution, available at http://www.diputados.gob.mx/LeyesBiblio/pdf/1.pdf; Article 12, *Ley Federal contra le Delincuencia Organizada*, available at *http://www.diputados.gob.mx/LeyesBiblio/pdf/101.pdf*. Under applicable law, "organized crime" includes three persons organized on an ongoing basis or who come together repeatedly to commit any one of a schedule of criminal offenses. See also, *Ley Federal de Delincuencia Organizada*, Article 2; see Comisión Mexicana de Defensa y Promoción de los Derechos Humanos et al., "*El impacto en México de la figura de arraigo penal en los derechos humanos,*" September 2011, p. 17 (hereafter, "*Impacto de arraigo*").

10. There are substantial discrepancies in the figures from different government sources about the extent of *arraigo*. For example, regarding the period June 2008-April/May 2010, the Federal Prosecutor's Office acknowledged 647 persons detained under *arraigo*, while the Federal Judicial Council had figures that were more than 60% higher. See *Impacto de arraigo*, p.9; Interview with Silvano Cantú of the Comisión Mexicana de Defensa y Promoción de los Derechos Humanos, Mexico City, October 5, 2011; *Arraigo judicial*, pp. 19-20.

11. State level figures are harder to compile, but they are estimated at about 60% of the federal level. *Arraigo judicial*, p. 3.

12. Comisión Mexicana de Defensa y Promoción de los Derechos Humanos, A.C. and Organización Mundial Contra la Tortura, "Arraigo made in Mexico: A violation to human rights," Oct. 2012, p. 4, available at: http://tbinternet.ohchr.org/Treaties/CAT/Shared%20Documents/MEX/INT_CAT_NGO_MEX_12965_E.pdf (accessed March 24, 2014).

13. *Impacto de arraigo*, p. 15 (figures covering June 2008- April 2010). Another three percent of the detentions lasted the maximum renewal period, a total of 80 days. Only three percent were less than 40 days. The figures suggest a routine practice of holding people for the maximum duration, irrespective of the amount of time actually needed to investigate.

14. *El Economista*, "ONU pide a México eliminar figura del arraigo," February 20, 2013, (citing an Interior Ministry official noting that in 96.7 percent of the *arraigo* cases prosecutors never obtained sufficient evidence to justify a proceeding); see also *El Universal*, "*Magistrada critica figura de arraigo,*" November 20, 2012, available at http://www.eluniversal.com.mx/notas/884510.html (accessed Oct. 13, 2013).

15. Comision Mexicana de Defensa y Promoción de los derechos Humanos and Instituto Mexicanos de los Derechos Humanos y la Democracia, "Acceso a la justicia en México: la constante impunidad en casos de violaciones de derechos humanos," available at http://cmdpdh.org/wp- content/uploads/2013/07/Acceso-a-la-Justicia-en-M%C3%A9xico.pdf. Even discounting the vast majority of *arraigo* cases that don't make it to a criminal court case, the rate of successful prosecutions based on *arraigo* is far less than in Mexico's criminal cases generally.

16. Comision Mexicana de Defensa y Promoción de los derechos Humanos and Instituto Mexicanos de los Derechos Humanos y la Democracia, "Acceso a la justicia en México: la constante impunidad en casos de violaciones de derechos humanos," p. 1, available at http://cmdpdh.org/wp- content/uploads/2013/07/Acceso-a-la-Justicia-en-M%C3%A9xico.pdf. A year later an OAS mission to Mexico voiced similar concerns: see "IACHR Wraps Up Mission to Mexico," at http://www.oas.org/en/iachr/media_center/PReleases/2011/105.asp (accessed Oct. 15, 2013).

17. *Report on the visit of the Subcommittee on Prevention of Torture and Other Cruel, Inhuman or Degrading Treatment or Punishment to Mexico*, CAT/OP/MEX/1(May 2010) at 48.

18. *Impacto de arraigo*, p. 28 (quoting the text of Article 12 of the Federal Law on Organized Crime).

19. *Impacto de arraigo*, p. 23.

20. Although the decision had no binding effect outside of the state in question, the rationale was viewed as readily applicable to other statutes, including federal law, and effectively warned the Calderon government that the practice lacked legal foundation. See Gaspar Romero, "Eliminar el Arraigo," available at http://columnaretrospectiva.blogspot.com/2011/07/eliminar-el-arraigo.html (accessed Oct. 15, 2013); Amnesty International, "La Corte Suprema elimina la figura del arraigo," available at http://www.lainsignia.org/2005/septiembre/der_008.htm (accessed Oct. 15, 2013); Saberderecho.com, available at http://www.saberderecho.com/2006/01/suprema-corte-de-justicia-de-mxico-19.html, (accessed Oct. 15, 2013).

21. A February 2014 decision by Mexico's Supreme Court limited the use of *arraigo* at the state level: it struck down *arraigo* provisions in several state procedure codes on the grounds that they infringed on an exclusively federal legislative authority.

22. Most recently, the United Nations' state- to-state peer review process echoed calls to end the practice. See, e.g., *Report of the Working Group on the Universal Periodic Review (Mexico)* A/HRC/25/7 at 17, available at http://www.upr-info.org/IMG/pdf/a_hrc_25_7_mexico_e.pdf; http://mexico.cnn.com/nacional/2013/10/24/a-pesar-de-recomendaciones-mexico-aun-analiza-los-limites-del-arraigo (accessed October 24, 2013). On March 20, 2014, in its official response to the Universal Period Review, Mexico rejected the recommendation that it abolish *arraigo*.

23. *Arraigo judicial*, pp. 51-62.

24. The judgment of the court, denying a challenge to the holding charge by defendants who had been held three months without having other charges brought against them, or having been arraigned, reads in part:

    The fact is there was strong suspicion that the respondent and some others have committed an indictable offence - to wit treason. After their arrest by the police, there was the need to properly and lawfully keep them in custody, and the only way to do tins [sic] was to take them to a Magistrate court who would in turn remand them in custody. They couldn't possibly continue to remain in police custody without the order of a court. Police investigations sometimes take time, and sometimes there is the fear of a likelihood of continued committal of the same or other offences. There is also a likelihood of interference with investigations. What is reasonable time is subjective, and since this is dependent on the completion of investigations; all factors will be taken into consideration.

    On the presumption of innocence as laid down in Section 33 (5) of the supra Constitution, I fail to see anything in the record before us that there was a contrary presumption in respect of the appellant. The appellant and his co-accuseds were taken before the Magistrate Court for the purpose of lawful remand in custody; and that was exactly what the Chief Magistrate did. She did not ask him of whether he was guilty or not, so the issue of his innocence didn't come to play at that stage of the proceedings.

    *Lufadeju v. Bayo Johnson*, S. Ct. Nigeria (2007), available at http://www.nigerialaw.org/Mrs%20E.A%20Lufadeju%20&%20Anor%20v%20Evangelist%20Bayo%20Johnson.htm (accessed Oct. 15, 2013).

25. The detainee under a holding charge is technically not yet even an "accused" person since the entering of a holding charge before a magistrate is not an arraignment proceeding, and no formal charge or plea is formulated.

26. Human Rights Watch, *Unjust and Unhealthy: HIV, TB, and Abuse in Zambian Prisons*, Human Rights Watch, New York, 2010, pp. 114-115, available at http://www.hrw.org/sites/default/files/reports/zambia0410webwcover.pdf (accessed Oct. 15, 2013).

27. Human Rights Watch, *Unjust and Unhealthy: HIV, TB, and Abuse in Zambian Prisons*, Human Rights Watch, New York, 2010, p. 114, available at http://www.hrw.org/sites/default/files/reports/zambia0410webwcover.pdf (accessed Oct. 15, 2013).

28. Human Rights Watch, *Unjust and Unhealthy: HIV, TB, and Abuse in Zambian Prisons*, New York: Human Rights Watch, 2010, p. 115, available at http://www.hrw.org/sites/default/files/reports/zambia0410webwcover.pdf (accessed Oct. 15, 2013).

29. Institute for Reporters' Freedom and Safety et al., *NGO Report on the Implementation of the Convention Against Torture and Other Cruel, Inhuman, or Degrading Treatment or Punishment*, (October 2009), p. 10.

30. Institute for Reporters' Freedom and Safety et al., *NGO Report on the Implementation of the Convention Against Torture and Other Cruel, Inhuman, or Degrading Treatment or Punishment*, (October 2009), p. 16.

31. Organization for Security and Cooperation in Europe, *2009 Trial Monitoring Report: Azerbaijan*, Baku: OSCE, 2009, p. 41, available at http://www.osce.org/baku/73359 (accessed Oct. 15, 2013).

32. See, e.g., *Effective Criminal Defense in Europe*, which found, among other things, that:

    In Belgium, there is no obligation to inform suspects of their procedural rights in writing, including the right to remain silent (p. 3); in Finland: there is no obligation to provide suspects with a letter of rights on arrest (p. 5); in Germany: there is a right to a lawyer but police officers often try to dissuade suspects from exercising the right (p. 7); Hungarian police don't inform suspects of their procedural rights in cases of short term arrests and when suspects are classified as "witnesses" (p. 8); Italian defendants are often unaware that they can qualify for legal aid and exercise a right to a lawyer (p. 10); and in Turkey, there is a statutory right to a lawyer but police often fail to inform suspects and/or try to discourage them from exercising the right (p. 12).

33. Centro de Estudios de Justicia de las Américas, *Report on Pre-Trial Criminal Justice in Brazil*, p.56.

34. Asian Legal Resource Center, *Alternative Report to the United Nations Committee Against Torture: The Situation of Torture in the Philippines*, p. 28 (April 2009).

35. Mexican jurisprudence rationalizes this approach by citing the principle of procedural immediacy (*principio de inmediatez procesal*). But elsewhere in the hemisphere, this principle stands for just the opposite: that the statement by the defendant in open court outweighs that made more remotely in both time and space. See Lawyers Committee for Human Rights (now Human Rights First) and the Centro de Derechos Humanos Miguel Agustin Pro Juarez, *Legalized Injustice*, 2001, pp. 65-66.

36. See e.g., Lawyers Committee for Human Rights (now Human Rights First) and the Centro de Derechos Humanos Miguel Agustin Pro Juarez, *Legalized Injustice*, 2001, p. 2.

37. Mary Phillips, "Bail, Detention, and Nonfelony Case Outcomes," *CJA Research Brief 14*, New York Criminal Justice Agency, New York, May 2007, p. 5. "The hypothesis is impossible to prove because some factor or factors for which data are unavailable – the strength of the evidence, for instance – could be the reason for both higher bail (resulting in detention) and for the conviction. However, we were able to control for a wide range of case and defendant characteristics. None, either singly or in combination, completely explained away the relationship between detention and likelihood of conviction in non-felony cases."

38. Mary Phillips, "Bail, Detention, and Nonfelony Case Outcomes," *CJA Research Brief 14*, New York Criminal Justice Agency, New York, May 2007, p. 7.

39. Open Society Justice Initiative, *El uso de la prisión preventiva en Nuevo León: Estudio cuantitativo*, Open Society Foundations, New York, 2009, pp. 34-35.

40. Interview with Julita Lemgruber of the Center for the Study in Public Security and Citizenship, conducted November 30, 2011; see also Lemgruber and Fernandes, "*Impacto da assistencia jurídica a prsos provisórios,*" *(Assoção pela Reforma Prisional, 2011)*.

41. UN Committee against Torture, *Consideration of reports submitted by States parties under article 19 of the Convention: Concluding Observations of the Committee against Torture, Cameroon*, UN Doc CAT/C/CMR/CO/4, May 19, 2010, para. 11; Committee against Torture, 35th session, *Consideration of reports by states parties under article 19 of the Convention: Concluding observations of the Committee against Torture, Burundi*, UN Doc CAT/C/BDI/CO/1, February 15, 2007, para. 9; See, e.g., United Nations Human Rights Council, *Report of the Working Group on Arbitrary Detention: Mission to Senegal*, UN Doc A/HRC/13/30/Add.3, March 23, 2010, para. 39; UN Human Rights Council, 7th Session, *Report of the Special Rapporteur on torture and other cruel, inhuman or degrading treatment or punishment, Manfred Nowak, Mission to Togo*, UN Doc A/HRC/7/3/Add.5, January 6, 2008, para. 15.

42. UN Human Rights Council, *Report of the Working Group on Arbitrary Detention (Addendum): Mission to Mauritania*, UN Doc A/HRC/10/21/Add.2, November 21, 2008, para. 89; UN Human Rights Council, *Report of the Working Group on Arbitrary Detention: Mission to Angola, Addendum*, UN Doc A/HRC/7/4/Add.3, February 29, 2008, p 3.

43. UN Human Rights Council, 13th Session, *Report of the Special Rapporteur on torture and other cruel, inhuman or degrading treatment or punishment, Manfred Nowak, Addendum: Study on the phenomena of torture, cruel, inhuman or degrading treatment or punishment in the world, including an assessment of conditions of detention*, UN Doc A/HRC/13/39/Add.5, February 5, 2010, para. 81.

44. First in a list of Amnesty International's "most pressing concerns" about human rights in Kazakhstan was torture, "in particular before the formal detention takes place, in the street or during transfer to detention centres ... and in unofficial places of detention," available at http://www2.ohchr.org/english/bodies/hrc/docs/ngos/AI_Kazakhstan99.pdf (accessed Oct. 15, 2013). A group of Kazakh and international NGOs noted in a 2010 submission to the UN Human Rights Council that police "routinely hold people they arrest for more than three days [the legal time limit for holding someone without formally registering the detention], and sometimes even for weeks, in unregistered and

incommunicado detention...," available at http://wwww.soros.org/initiatives/justice/news/kazakhstan-universal-periodic-review-20100212/upr-kazakhstan-20100208.pdf.

45. Open Society Justice Initiative, *"We're Tired of Taking You to the Court": Human Rights Abuses by Kenya's Anti-Terrorism Police Unit*, Open Society Foundations, New York, 2013.

46. National Center for State Courts, *Practice Matters: Mexico City's Criminal Courts*, 2003, on file with authors.

47. Human Rights Watch, *Unjust and Unhealthy: HIV, TB, and Abuse in Zambian Prisons*, Human Rights Watch, New York, 2010, p. 109, available at: http://www.hrw.org/sites/default/files/reports/zambia0410webwcover.pdf (accessed Oct. 15, 2013).

48. For a discussion that questions Nigerian government recordkeeping regarding pretrial detention (and the common belief that it is characterized by very long stays), reviews the results of sampling exit data at a Lagos prison, and suggests a dominant pattern of a majority of short length detentions in the studied facilities, see Todd Fogelsong and Christopher Stone, "Prison Exit Samples as a Source for Indicators of Pretrial Detention," available at http://www.hks.harvard.edu/var/ezp_site/storage/fckeditor/file/pdfs/centers-programs/programs/criminal-justice/Indicators-PrisonExitSamples.pdf (accessed Oct. 15, 2013).

49. Anthony Nwapa, "Building and Sustaining Change: Pretrial Detention Reform in Nigeria," *Justice Initiatives: Pretrial Detention*, Open Society Foundations, New York, Spring 2008, p. 89.

50. Long term pretrial detention cases include those of Machang Lalung, held for 54 years, and as reported in a 2005 article, Khalilur Rehman, 35 years, Anil Kumar Burman, 33 years, and Sonamani Deb, 32 years. Parbati Mallik has been detained in a psychiatric unit for 32 years. See "Inmate's 50 years without trial," BBC News, July 24, 2005, available at http:/news.bbc.co.uk/2/hi/south_asia/4712619.stm (accessed Oct. 15, 2013); "Fifty-four Years in Jail Without Trial," Countercurrents.org, August 26, 2005, available at http://www.countercurrents.org/hr-zora260805.htm (accessed Oct. 15, 2013).

51. Sri Lanka Department of Prisons, Prison Statistics, "Average length of time spent on remand as on 31st December of each year, 2005-2009," available at: http://www.prisons.gov.lk/Statistics/statistic.html (accessed Oct. 15, 2013).

52. Section 42(2) Malawi Constitution. Minor exceptions are made in cases where the 48 hours expire outside ordinary court hours or on a day which is not a court day. In such cases, the arrestee must be brought before a court on the first court date after such expiry.

53. Open Society Initiative of Southern Africa, *Pre-trial detention in Malawi: Understanding caseflow management and conditions of incarceration*, OSISA, Johannesburg, 2011, p. 55.

54. R. Cohen et al., "Fair trials in Nepal: A critical study," Advocacy Forum, 2010, p. 8.

55. Clifford Msiska, "On the Front Lines: Insights from Malawi's Paralegal Advisory Service" *Justice Initiatives: Pretrial Detention*, Open Society Justice Initiative, New York, 2008, p. 74.

56. Kalmthout et al., *Pre-trial Detention in the European Union: An Analysis of Minimum Standards in Pre-trial Detention and the Grounds for Regular Review in the Member States of the EU*, 2009, p. 889.

57. http://www.state.gov/g/drl/rls/hrrpt/2010/eur/154413.htm. Judges appear to make their detention decisions at the instruction of the Prosecutor General's Office.

58. Fair Trials International, "Pre-Trial Detention Comparative Research," available at http://ec.europa.eu/justice/newsroom/criminal/opinion/files/110510/appendix_2_-_comparative_research_en.pdf (accessed Nov. 1, 2013).

59. Amnesty International, "Spain: Briefing to Committee Against Torture," (November 2009).

60. UN Subcommittee on Prevention of Torture, *Report on the Visit of the Subcommittee on Prevention of Torture and Other Cruel, Inhuman, or Degrading Treatment or Punishment to Honduras*, UN Doc. CAT/OP/HND/1 para 142 (2/10/10).

61. UN Subcommittee on Prevention of Torture, *Report on the Visit of the Subcommittee on Prevention of Torture and Other Cruel, Inhuman, or Degrading Treatment or Punishment to Honduras*, UN Doc. CAT/OP/HND/1 para 143 (2/10/10).

62. UN Subcommittee on Prevention of Torture, *Report on the Visit of the Subcommittee on Prevention of*

*Torture and Other Cruel, Inhuman, or Degrading Treatment or Punishment to Honduras*, UN Doc. CAT/OP/HND/1 para 152 (2/10/10).

63. UN Subcommittee on Prevention of Torture, *Report on the Visit of the Subcommittee on Prevention of Torture and Other Cruel, Inhuman, or Degrading Treatment or Punishment to Honduras*, UN Doc. CAT/OP/HND/1 para 153 (2/10/10).

64. Interview with Rupert Skilbeck, Litigation Director, Open Society Justice Initiative, August 27, 2012.

65. Asian Legal Resource Center, *Alternative Report to the United Nations Committee Against Torture: The Situation of Torture in the Philippines*, April 2009, p. 24.

66. See Network on Police Reform in Nigeria and Open Society Justice Initiative, *Criminal Force: Torture, Abuse, and Extrajudicial Killings by the Nigerian Police Force*, Open Society Foundations, 2010, p. 62, for a discussion of acknowledged police killings of "armed robbers" between January 2000 and, respectively, April 2004 and January 2005, by two successive Inspectors General of the Nigeria Police Force (NPF), including an approximately 4,800 disparity in the two officials' reported body counts.

67. Tashikalmah Hallah, "Nigeria: Police Kill 785 Armed Robbers in Three Months," available at http://allafrica.com/stories/200711150425.html (accessed Oct. 15, 2013).

68. Special Rapporteur on Extra Judicial Executions Phillip Alston wrote of his mission to Nigeria in 2006:

> In terms of *governmental accountability*, the Police Service Commission is charged with police discipline, but has opted to refer all complaints of extrajudicial police killings back to the police for investigation. The Commission's mandate is potentially empowering. But despite efforts by one or two excellent commissioners, its performance has been dismal and self-restraining.

E/CN.4/2006/53/Add.4 (January 7, 2006) at para 58.

69. UN Subcommittee on Prevention of Torture, *Report on the Visit of the Subcommittee on Prevention of Torture and Other Cruel, Inhuman, or Degrading Treatment or Punishment to Honduras*, UN Doc. CAT/OP/HND/1 para 157-159 (2/10/10).

70. John Goldkamp, *Restoring Accountability in Pretrial Release: The Philadelphia Pretrial Release Supervision Experiments*, Crime and Justice Research Institute, Philadelphia, 2001, p. 14, available at http://www.ncjrs.gov/pdffiles1/nij/grants/189164.pdf (accessed Oct. 15, 2013).

71. John Goldkamp, *Restoring Accountability in Pretrial Release: The Philadelphia Pretrial Release Supervision Experiments*, Crime and Justice Research Institute, Philadelphia, 2001, pp. 10-11 (available at http://www.ncjrs.gov/pdffiles1/nij/grants/189164.pdf (accessed Oct. 15, 2013). In addition to the direct cost imposed by the need to re-arrest non-appearing defendants, this program of effectively random release meant that individuals who posed a low risk of failure-to-appear in court often remained detained unnecessarily.

72. Bottoms and Tankebe, "Beyond procedural justice: a dialogic approach to legitimacy in criminal justice," *Journal of Criminal Law and Criminology*, 102:1, 2012, p. 123.

73. Tyler, *Why People Obey the Law*, Yale University Press, New Haven, 1990. Some prison research suggests that unlike in public communities, in closed populations where the outcome of most incidents can be widely known, perceived outcome fairness can be an important source of legitimacy for the jailers in the eyes of the jailed. Bottoms and Tankebe, "Beyond procedural justice: a dialogic approach to legitimacy in criminal justice," *Journal of Criminal Law and Criminology*, 102:1 (2012), p. 123.

74. Bottoms and Tankebe, "Beyond procedural justice: a dialogic approach to legitimacy in criminal justice," *Journal of Criminal Law and Criminology*, 102:1, 2012, p. 75.

75. This phrase refers to empirical research done in London in the 1980s which revealed how police whose behavior routinely deviated from the law nonetheless developed narrative techniques to reframe their actions as norm-compliant, or at least diminish the gap between actual practice and the norms. See Smith and Gray, *Police and People in London (The PSI Report)*, Policy Studies Institute, London, 1985.

76. David Smith, "The Foundations of Legitimacy," in Tyler, (ed.), *Legitimacy and Criminal Justice*, New York: Russell Sage Foundation, 2007, pp. 40-41.

77. As Wesley Skogan puts it, police are unique in being "the only local bureaucracy whose annual statistical reports routinely make front-page news." Wesley Skogan, "Citizen Satisfaction with Police Encounters," *Police Quarterly*, Vol. 8, No. 3, Sept. 2005, p. 102.

78. The removed and inaccessible quality of custodial environments is conducive to wide discretion and its abuse by custodians. Then UN Special Rapporteur on Torture, Nigel Rodley, urged in one of his reports:

> [T]here needs to be a radical transformation of assumptions in international society about the nature of deprivation of liberty. The basic paradigm, taken for granted over at least a century, is that prisons, police stations and the like are closed and secret places, with activities inside hidden from public view. The international standards referred to are conceived of as often unwelcome exceptions to the general norm of opacity, merely the occasional ray of light piercing the pervasive darkness. What is needed is to replace the paradigm of opacity by one of transparency. The assumption should be one of open access to all places of deprivation of liberty. Of course, there will have to be regulations to safeguard the security of the institution and individuals within it, and measures to safeguard their privacy and dignity. But those regulations and measures will be the exception, having to be justified as such; the rule will be openness.

*Report of the Special Rapporteur on the question of torture and other cruel, inhuman or degrading treatment or punishment,* UN Doc A/56/156, (2001), para 35. Anticipating the misgivings of law enforcement officials to the proposal, Rodley goes on to argue for a virtuous cycle of increased transparency, diminished discretion and official malfeasance, greater legitimacy, and ultimately support for the budgetary resources which would in turn improve custodial conditions and help professionalize the conduct of corrections officers.

79. Statement of Senator Maurice Cummings (Fine Gael), November 11, 2010, available at http://www.kildarestreet.com/sendebates/?id=2010-11-11.149.0 (accessed Oct. 15, 2013).

80. "Former Mountjoy governor calls for research into prison violence," *The Irish Times*, September 17, 2012.

81. Some political scientists have pointed out that those operating in corrupt environments might see it as beneficial. Well placed or timed payments can speed or favorably tilt transactions or adjudication, for instance. Even if this salutary view of petty corruption were widely shared among a population, it would not diminish the damage done by prevalent corruption to a belief in the rule of law as a governing principle. In this view, the law is insufficient for the wheels of government or business to turn effectively.

# REDUCING THE ARBITRARY AND EXCESSIVE USE OF PRETRIAL DETENTION

1. Anton M. van Kalmthout, Marije M. Knapen, and Christine Morgenstern (eds.), *Pre-trial Detention in the European Union: An Analysis of Minimum Standards in Pre-trial Detention and the Grounds for Regular Review in the Member States of the EU*, Wolf Legal Publishers, Nijmegen, 2009, p. 328.

2. Tapio Lappi-Seppälä, "Controlling Prisoner Rates: Experiences From Finland," *135th International Senior Seminar Visiting Experts' Papers, Resource Material Series No.74*, The United Nations Asia and Far East Institute for the Prevention of Crime and the Treatment of Offenders, Tokyo, 2008, p. 9, available at http://www.unafei.or.jp/english/pdf/RS_No74/No74_05VE_Seppala1.pdf (accessed November 18, 2013).

3. Anton M. van Kalmthout, Marije M. Knapen, and Christine Morgenstern (eds.), *Pre-trial Detention in the European Union: An Analysis of Minimum Standards in Pre-trial Detention and the Grounds for Regular Review in the Member States of the EU*, Wolf Legal Publishers, Nijmegen, 2009, p. 339. Tapio Lappi-Seppälä, "Controlling Prisoner Rates: Experiences From Finland," *135th International Senior Seminar Visiting Experts' Papers, Resource Material Series No.74*, The United Nations Asia and Far East Institute for the Prevention of Crime and the Treatment of Offenders, Tokyo, 2008, p. 9, available at http://www.unafei.or.jp/english/pdf/RS_No74/No74_05VE_Seppala1.pdf (accessed November 18, 2013).

4. Peter Joo Hee Ng, "Offender Rehabilitation, Community Engagement, and Preventing Re-Offending in Singapore," *142nd International Training Course Visiting Experts' Papers, Resource Material Series No. 80*, The United Nations Asia and Far East Institute for the Prevention of Crime and the Treatment of Offenders, Tokyo, March 2010.

5. Mauricio J. Duce, Claudio M. Fuentes, and Cristián R. Riego, La reforma procesal penal en América Latina y su impacto en el uso de la prisón preventiva, in Cristián R. Riego and Mauricio J. Duce (eds.), *Prisón Preventiva y Reforma Procesal Penal en América Latina. Evaluación y Perspectivas, Centro de Estudios de Justicia de las Américas*, Santiago, 2008, p. 57.

6. Mauricio J. Duce, Claudio M. Fuentes, and Cristián R. Riego, La reforma procesal penal en América Latina y su impacto en el uso de la prisón preventiva, in Cristián R. Riego and Mauricio J. Duce (eds.), *Prisón Preventiva y Reforma Procesal Penal en América Latina. Evaluación y Perspectivas, Centro de Estudios de Justicia de las Américas*, Santiago, 2008, pp. 57-58.

7. *Catálogo de delitos graves en la República Mexicana*, Asistencia Legal por los Derechos Humanos, Mexico City, 2012, (unpublished document).

8. *2010 Country Reports on Human Rights Practices – Ecuador*, United States Department of State, Washington, April 2011, available at http://www.refworld.org/cgi-bin/texis/vtx/rwmain?page=country&category=&publisher=USDOS&type=&coi=ECU&rid=&docid=4da56dce9b&skip=0 (accessed November 18, 2013).

9. Anton M. van Kalmthout, Marije M. Knapen, and Christine Morgenstern (eds.), *Pre-trial Detention in the European Union: An Analysis of Minimum Standards in Pre-trial Detention and the Grounds for Regular Review in the Member States of the EU*, Wolf Legal Publishers, Nijmegen, 2009, p. 64.

10. The Penal Code Act of Zambia, available at http://www.parliament.gov.zm/downloads/VOLUME%207.pdf (accessed Oct. 13, 2013).

11. Republic of South Africa, Department of Correctional Services, *White Paper on Remand Detention Management in South Africa*, 2012, available at http://ppja.org/countries/south-africa/Draft%20White%20Paper2012.pdf/at_download/file (accessed Oct. 11, 2013).

12. Article 18, Constitution of Mexico (1917), available at http://www.oas.org/juridico/mla/en/mex/en_mex-int-text-const.pdf (accessed November 18, 2013).

13. Mauricio J. Duce and Cristián R. Riego, "La prisón preventive en Chile: El impacto de la reforma procesal penal y de sus cambios posteriors," in Cristián R. Riego and Mauricio J. Duce (eds.), *Prisón Preventiva y Reforma Procesal Penal en América Latina. Evaluación y Perspectivas, Centro de Estudios de Justicia de las Américas*, Santiago, 2008, pp. 170–171.

14. Personal communication with Javier Carrasco, Director, Instituto de Justicia Procesal Penal, Mexico City, May 2, 2012.

15. Eduardo Soares, "Brazil: Provisions of Code of Criminal Procedure on Preventive Detention, Amended," available at http://www.loc.gov/lawweb/servlet/lloc_news?disp3_l205402738_text (accessed November 18, 2013).

16. *2010 Country Reports on Human Rights Practices – Ecuador*, United States Department of State, Washington, April 2011, available at http://www.refworld.org/cgi-bin/texis/vtx/rwmain?page=country&category=&publisher=USDOS&type=&coi=ECU&rid=&docid=4da56dce9b&skip=0 (accessed November 18, 2013).

17. *Detained Without Trial: Fair Trials International's Response to the European Commission's Green Paper on Detention*, Fair Trials International, London, October 2011, p. 52, available at http://www.fairtrials.net/documents/DetentionWithoutTrialFullReport.pdf (accessed November 18, 2013).

18. Anton M. van Kalmthout, Marije M. Knapen, and Christine Morgenstern (eds.), *Pre-trial Detention in the European Union: An Analysis of Minimum Standards in Pre-trial Detention and the Grounds for Regular Review in the Member States of the EU*, Wolf Legal Publishers, Nijmegen, 2009, p. 277.

19. *Detained Without Trial: Fair Trials International's Response to the European Commission's Green Paper on Detention*, Fair Trials International, London, October 2011, p. 58, available at http://www.fairtrials.net/documents/DetentionWithoutTrialFullReport.pdf (accessed November 18, 2013).

20. *Detained Without Trial: Fair Trials International's Response to the European Commission's Green Paper on Detention*, Fair Trials International, London, October 2011, p. 59, available at http://www.fairtrials.net/documents/DetentionWithoutTrialFullReport.pdf (accessed November 18, 2013).

21. Anton M. van Kalmthout, Marije M. Knapen, and Christine Morgenstern (eds.), *Pre-trial Detention in the European Union: An Analysis of Minimum Standards in Pre-trial Detention and the Grounds for Regular Review in the Member States of the EU*, Wolf Legal Publishers, Nijmegen, 2009, p. 704.

22. *Detained Without Trial: Fair Trials International's Response to the European Commission's Green Paper on Detention*, Fair Trials International, London, October 2011, p. 72, available at http://www.fairtrials.net/documents/DetentionWithoutTrialFullReport.pdf (accessed November 18, 2013).

23. Section 2, *Prosecution of Offences Act 1985* as amended, available at http://www.legislation.gov.uk/ukpga/1985/23/section/22/enacted (accessed June 27, 2012). Prosecution of Offences (Custody Time Limits) Regulations 1987 as amended. See also Jean Redpath, *Custody Time Limits: Exploring Implementation Mechanisms*, Open Society Initiative for Southern Africa, Johannesburg (forthcoming).

24. *Making Law and Policy that Work: A Handbook for Law and Policy Makers on Reforming Criminal Justice and Penal Legislation, Policy and Practice*, Penal Reform International, London, 2010, p. 44.

25. Anthea Hucklesby, "Police bail and the use of conditions," *Criminal Justice* Vol. 1, No. 4, 2001, pp. 441–463.

26. George Mair, "Community Penalties: probation, punishment and 'what works,'" in Mike Maguire, Rodney Morgan, and Robert Reiner (eds.) *The Oxford Handbook of Criminology*, Oxford University Press, Oxford, 2002.

27. *Better Bail Decisions: A Project to Improve the Quality and Consistency of Bail Decision Making by Courts in England and Wales, Spain and the Czech Republic*, The Law Society of England and Wales, London (undated), p. 9, http://www.cak.cz/files/255/bb040701.pdf (November 18, 2013).

28. Anton M. van Kalmthout, Marije M. Knapen, and Christine Morgenstern (eds.), *Pre-trial Detention in the European Union: An Analysis of Minimum Standards in Pre-trial Detention and the Grounds for Regular Review in the Member States of the EU*, Wolf Legal Publishers, Nijmegen, 2009, pp. 95–96.

29. *Handbook of Basic Principles and Promising Practices on Alternatives to Imprisonment*, Criminal Justice Handbook Series, United Nations Office on Drugs and Crime, New York, 2007, p. 13, available at http://www.unodc.org/pdf/criminal_justice/07-80478_ebook.pdf (accessed November 18, 2013).

30. South African Parliament, *Report of the Portfolio Committee on Correctional Services on Factors Contributing to Overcrowding in Correctional Centres*, September 14, 2011, available at http://www.pmg.org.za/docs/2011/comreports/110920pccorrectreport.htm (accessed November 18, 2013).

31. South African Parliament, *Report of the Portfolio Committee on Correctional Services on Factors Contributing to Overcrowding in Correctional Centres*, September 14, 2011, available at http://www.pmg.org.za/docs/2011/comreports/110920pccorrectreport.htm (accessed November 18, 2013).

32. South African Parliament, *Report of the Portfolio Committee on Correctional Services on Factors Contributing to Overcrowding in Correctional Centres*, September 14, 2011, available at http://www.pmg.org.za/docs/2011/comreports/110920pccorrectreport.htm (accessed November 18, 2013).

33. South African Parliament, *Report of the Portfolio Committee on Correctional Services on Factors Contributing to Overcrowding in Correctional Centres*, September 14, 2011, available at http://www.pmg.org.za/docs/2011/comreports/110920pccorrectreport.htm (accessed November 18, 2013).

34. *Making Law and Policy that Work: A Handbook for Law and Policy Makers on Reforming Criminal Justice and Penal Legislation, Policy and Practice*, Penal Reform International, London, 2010, pp. 44-45.

35. Marcelo F Aebi and Natalia Delgrande, *Council of Europe Annual Penal Statistics* (SPACE I), Survey 2011, Council of Europe, Strasbourg, May 3, 2013, p. 127, available at http://www3.unil.ch/wpmu/space/2013/04/space-i-space-ii-2011-available-online-under-embargo-until-10-00-am-central-european-time-3-may-2013/ (accessed Nov. 12, 2013).

36. Clare Ballard, *Research Report on Remand Detention in South Africa: An Overview of the Current Law and Proposals for Reform*, Civil Society Prison Reform Initiative, Cape Town, 2011, p. 21, available at http://cspri.org.za/publications/research-reports/Remand%20detention%20in%20South%20Africa.pdf (accessed November 18, 2013).

37. Hans-Jörg Albrecht, "Prison Overcrowding: Finding Effective Solutions. Strategies and Best Practices Against Overcrowding in Correctional Facilities," in: *Report of the Workshop: Strategies and Best Practices Against Overcrowding in Correctional Facilities, Twelfth United Nations Congress on Crime Prevention and Criminal Justice, Salvador, Brazil, 12–19 April 2010*, United Nations Asia and Far East Institute for the Prevention of Crime and the Treatment of Offenders, Tokyo, 2011, p 94, http://www.unafei.or.jp/english/pdf/Congress_2010/13Hans-Jorg_Albrecht.pdf (November 18, 2013).

38. Hans-Jörg Albrecht, "Prison Overcrowding: Finding Effective Solutions. Strategies and Best Practices

Against Overcrowding in Correctional Facilities," in: *Report of the Workshop: Strategies and Best Practices Against Overcrowding in Correctional Facilities, Twelfth United Nations Congress on Crime Prevention and Criminal Justice, Salvador, Brazil, 12–19 April 2010*, United Nations Asia and Far East Institute for the Prevention of Crime and the Treatment of Offenders, Tokyo, 2011, p 94, http://www.unafei.or.jp/english/pdf/Congress_2010/13Hans-Jorg_Albrecht.pdf (November 18, 2013).

39. Hans-Jörg Albrecht, "Prison Overcrowding: Finding Effective Solutions. Strategies and Best Practices Against Overcrowding in Correctional Facilities," in: *Report of the Workshop: Strategies and Best Practices Against Overcrowding in Correctional Facilities, Twelfth United Nations Congress on Crime Prevention and Criminal Justice, Salvador, Brazil, 12–19 April 2010*, United Nations Asia and Far East Institute for the Prevention of Crime and the Treatment of Offenders, Tokyo, 2011, p 94, http://www.unafei.or.jp/english/pdf/Congress_2010/13Hans-Jorg_Albrecht.pdf (November 18, 2013).

40. Hans-Jörg Albrecht, "Prison Overcrowding: Finding Effective Solutions. Strategies and Best Practices Against Overcrowding in Correctional Facilities," in *Report of the Workshop: Strategies and Best Practices Against Overcrowding in Correctional Facilities, Twelfth United Nations Congress on Crime Prevention and Criminal Justice, Salvador, Brazil, 12–19 April 2010*, United Nations Asia and Far East Institute for the Prevention of Crime and the Treatment of Offenders, Tokyo, 2011, p. 94, available at http://www.unafei.or.jp/english/pdf/Congress_2010/13Hans-Jorg_Albrecht.pdf (accessed November 18, 2013).

41. "Handbook on Prisoner File Management," *Criminal Justice Handbook Series*, United Nations Office on Drugs and Crime, New York, 2008, p. 2, available at http://www.unodc.org/documents/justice-and-prison-reform/Prison_management_handbook.pdf (accessed November 18, 2013). See also Curt Taylor Griffiths and Danielle J. Murdoch, *Strategies and Best Practices Against Overcrowding in Correctional Institutions*, The International Centre for Criminal Law Reform and Criminal Justice Policy, Vancouver, February 2009, pp. 37–39, available at http://dspace.cigilibrary.org/jspui/bitstream/123456789/25467/1/Strategies%20and%20Best%20Practices%20Against%20Overcrowding%20in%20Correctional%20Institutions.pdf?1 (accessed November 18, 2013).

42. Mandeep K. Dhami, "Conditional Bail Decision Making on the Magistrates' Court," *The Howard Journal*, Vol. 43, No. 1, February 2004, p. 42.

43. *One in Five: The Crisis in Brazil's Prisons and Criminal Justice System*, International Bar Association, Sao Paulo, February 2010, p. 8.

44. *One in Five: The Crisis in Brazil's Prisons and Criminal Justice System*, International Bar Association, Sao Paulo, February 2010, p. 8. Personal communication with Helena Romanach, Criminal Justice Coordinator, Instituto Sou da Paz, Sao Paulo, May 2, 2012.

45. *Cero Presos Sin Sentencia*, Ecuadorian Public Criminal Defence Service, 2011 (unpublished document). See also Committee Against Torture Considers Report of Ecuador, November 9, 2010, available at http://www.ohchr.org/en/NewsEvents/Pages/DisplayNews.aspx?NewsID=10516&LangID=E (accessed November 18, 2013).

46. *Index of Good Practices in Reducing Pre-Trial Detention*, Penal Reform International, London, October 2005, p. 8.

47. Clifford Msiska, "On the front lines: Insights from Malawi's Paralegal Advisory Service," *Justice Initiatives: Pretrial Detention*, Open Society Foundations, New York, Spring 2008, p. 72.

48. Rick Sarre, Sue King, and David Bamford, "Remand in custody: Critical factors and key issues," *Trends & Issues in Criminal Justice*, No. 310, May 2006, Australian Institute of Criminology, p. 4.

49. Rick Sarre, Sue King, and David Bamford, "Remand in custody: Critical factors and key issues," *Trends & Issues in Criminal Justice*, No. 310, May 2006, Australian Institute of Criminology, p. 5.

50. The Nizhny Novgorod Project on Justice Assistance was managed by the Center for Justice Assistance in Moscow with support from the Vera Institute of Justice's international programs department.

51. Final Report to the Open Society Institute on Reducing Pretrial Detention in Russia, September 2004, Vera Institute of Justice (unpublished narrative report).

52. Todd Foglesong and Christopher E. Stone, "Prison Exit Samples as a Source for Indicators of Pretrial Detention," *Indicators in Development, Safety and Justice*, April 2011, Harvard Kennedy School, Cambridge MA, available at http://www.hks.harvard.edu/var/ezp_site/storage/fckeditor/file/pdfs/centers-programs/programs/criminal-justice/Indicators-PrisonExitSamples.pdf (accessed November 18, 2013).

53. Todd Foglesong and Christopher E. Stone, "Prison Exit Samples as a Source for Indicators of Pretrial Detention," *Indicators in Development, Safety and Justice*, April 2011, Harvard Kennedy School, Cambridge MA, p. 10, available at http://www.hks.harvard.edu/var/ezp_site/storage/fckeditor/file/pdfs/centers-programs/programs/criminal-justice/Indicators-PrisonExitSamples.pdf (accessed November 18, 2013).

54. *Report of the Twelfth United Nations Congress on Crime Prevention and Criminal Justice, Salvador, Brazil, 12–19 April 2010*, available at https://www.unodc.org/documents/crime-congress/12th-Crime-Congress/Documents/A_CONF.213_18/V1053828e.pdf (accessed November 13, 2013).

55. *Index of Good Practices in Reducing Pre-Trial Detention*, Penal Reform International, London, October 2005, p. 9.

56. *Safety, Security and Accessible Justice: Putting Policy into Practice*, Department for International Development, London, July 2002, p. 58, available at http://www.gsdrc.org/docs/open/SSAJ23.pdf (accessed November 18, 2013).

57. "Handbook on Improving access to Legal Aid in Africa," *Criminal Justice Handbook Series*, United Nations Office on Drugs and Crime, New York, 2011, p. 66, available at http://www.unodc.org/documents/justice-and-prison-reform/Webbook_Legal_Aid_in_Africa_lr.pdf (accessed November 18, 2013).

58. *Index of Good Practices in Reducing Pre-Trial Detention*, Penal Reform International, London, October 2005, p. 12.

59. *P.A.S.I. Newsletter* No. 15, January 2012, pp. 9–10.

60. *Criminal Justice Reform in Post-Conflict States: A Guide for Practitioners*, United Nations Office for Drugs and Crime, New York, 2011, p. 87, available at http://www.unodc.org/documents/justice-and-prison-reform/11-83015_Ebook.pdf (accessed November 18, 2013).

61. *Criminal Justice Reform in Post-Conflict States: A Guide for Practitioners*, United Nations Office for Drugs and Crime, New York, 2011, p. 88, available at http://www.unodc.org/documents/justice-and-prison-reform/11-83015_Ebook.pdf (accessed November 18, 2013).

62. D.C.J. Burger, et al., *Summary report of the Integrated Justice System*, November 17, 1998, p. 3. The same objective is also contained in I.J.S. Project: Executive Summary, September 20, 1999, p. 3, which is attached to the Business Against Crime business plan submission to Business Trust on the Integrated Justice System, September 27, 1999.

63. For a discussion of case attrition in the criminal justice process, see Paul Smit and Stefan Harrendorf, "Responses of the criminal justice system," in Stefan Harrendorf, Markku Heiskanen, and Steven Malby (eds.), *International Statistics on Crime and Justice*, European Institute for Crime Prevention and Control, Affiliated with the United Nations and the United Nations Office on Drugs and Crime, Helsinki, 2010, pp. 91–94.

64. *Crime in the United States: Arrests*, U.S. Department of Justice, Criminal Justice Information Services Division, available at http://www2.fbi.gov/ucr/cius2009/arrests/index.html (accessed November 18, 2013).

65. William J. Sabol, Heather C. West, and Matthew Cooper, *Prisoners in 2008*, Bureau of Justice Statistics Bulletin, U.S. Department of Justice, December 2009, N.C.J. 228417, available at http://bjs.ojp.usdoj.gov/content/pub/pdf/p08.pdf (accessed November 18, 2013).

66. *Crime Prevention and Community Safety: Trends and Perspectives 2010*, International Center for the Prevention of Crime, Montreal, 2010, p. ix, available at http://www.crime-prevention-intl.org/fileadmin/user_upload/Publications/Crime_Prevention_and_Community_Safety_ANG.pdf (accessed November 18, 2013).

67. *Crime Prevention and Community Safety: Trends and Perspectives 2010*, International Center for the Prevention of Crime, Montreal, 2010, pp. ix-x, available at http://www.crime-prevention-intl.org/fileadmin/user_upload/Publications/Crime_Prevention_and_Community_Safety_ANG.pdf (accessed November 18, 2013).

68. Brandon C. Welsh and David P. Farrington, *Effects of Improved Street Lighting on Crime*, Campbell Collaboration, Oslo, 2008, available at www.campbellcollaboration.org/lib/download/223/ (accessed November 18, 2013).

69. *Crime Prevention and Community Safety: Trends and Perspectives 2010*, International Center for the Prevention of Crime, Montreal, 2010, pp. 108-109, available at http://www.crime-prevention-intl.org/fileadmin/user_upload/Publications/Crime_Prevention_and_Community_Safety_ANG.pdf, (accessed March 15, 2012).

70. *Crime Prevention and Community Safety: Trends and Perspectives 2010*, International Center for the Prevention of Crime, Montreal, 2010, pp. 108-109, available at http://www.crime-prevention-intl.org/fileadmin/user_upload/Publications/Crime_Prevention_and_Community_Safety_ANG.pdf, (accessed March 15, 2012).

71. *Handbook of Basic Principles and Promising Practices on Alternatives to Imprisonment*, Criminal Justice Handbook Series, United Nations Office on Drugs and Crime, New York, 2007, p. 13, available at http://www.unodc.org/pdf/criminal_justice/07-80478_ebook.pdf (accessed November 18, 2013).

72. *Index of Good Practices in Reducing Pre-Trial Detention*, Penal Reform International, London, October 2005, p. 31.

73. *Crime in the United States 2010: F.B.I. Uniform Crime Report*, U.S. Department of Justice, Washington D.C., September 2011, Table 29, available at http://www.fbi.gov/about-us/cjis/ucr/crime-in-the-u.s/2010/crime-in-the-u.s.-2010/tables/10tbl29.xls (accessed November 18, 2013). *Arrests for Drug Abuse Violations*, available at http://www.fbi.gov/about-us/cjis/ucr/crime-in-the-u.s/2010/crime-in-the-u.s.-2010/persons-arrested (accessed November 18, 2013). Alice Speri, "2010 Marijuana Arrests Top 1978–96 Total," *New York Times*, February 11, 2011, available at http://cityroom.blogs.nytimes.com/2011/02/11/marijuana-arrests-increase-in-new-york-city/ (accessed November 18, 2013).

74. Rebecca Webber, "A New Kind of Criminal Justice," *Parade*, October 25, 2009, available at http://www.parade.com/news/intelligence-report/archive/091025-a-new-kind-of-criminal-justice.html (accessed November 18, 2013).

75. Marty Price, "Personalizing Crime: Mediation Produces Restorative Justice for Victims and Offenders," *Dispute Resolution Magazine*, Fall 2001, available at http://www.vorp.com/articles/justice.html (accessed November 18, 2013).

76. *Between Law and Society: Paralegals and the Provision of Primary Justice Services in Sierra Leone*, Open Society Justice Initiative, New York, 2010, available at http://timapforjustice.org/ (accessed November 18, 2013).

77. Janine Ubink, "Customary Justice Sector Reform," Research and Policy Note, International Development Law Organization, Rome, 2011, p. 1, available at http://www.isn.ethz.ch/Digital-Library/Publications/Detail/?lng=en&id=139416 (accessed November 18, 2013).

78. *Safety, Security and Accessible Justice: Putting Policy into Practice*, Department for International Development, London, July 2002, p. 58, available at http://www.gsdrc.org/docs/open/SSAJ23.pdf (accessed November 18, 2013).

79. Bilal Siddiqi, *Law Without Lawyers: Assessing a Community-Based Mobile Paralegal Program in Liberia*, International Development Law Organization, Rome, 2012, pp. 23–24.

80. Noah Coburn and John Dempsey, *Informal Dispute Resolution in Afghanistan*, United States Institute of Peace, Special Report 247, August 2010, Washington D.C., available at http://www.usip.org/files/resources/sr247_0.pdf (accessed November 18, 2013).

81. *Handbook of Basic Principles and Promising Practices on Alternatives to Imprisonment*, Criminal Justice Handbook Series, United Nations Office on Drugs and Crime, New York, 2007, p. 14, available at http://www.unodc.org/pdf/criminal_justice/07-80478_ebook.pdf (accessed November 18, 2013). For an example of prosecutorial guidelines on the use of diversion, see *Diversion Project: A Guideline for Prosecutors*, Directorate of Public Prosecutions, Lilongwe, 2012.

82. *Promising Practices in Pretrial Diversion*, National Association of Pretrial Services Agencies, Washington D.C., 2010, pp. 11–12.

83. Kittipong Kittayarak, "Community-Based Alternatives to Incarceration in Thailand: Current Trends and Future Prospects," *141st International Senior Seminar Visiting Experts' Papers, Resource Material Series No.79*, The United Nations Asia and Far East Institute for the Prevention of Crime and the Treatment of Offenders, Tokyo, 2009, available at http://www.unafei.or.jp/english/pdf/RS_No79/No79_25VE_Kittayarak.pdf (accessed November 18, 2013).

84. *UNICEF Toolkit on Diversion and Alternatives to Detention 2009*, the United Nations Children's Fund, available at www.unicef.org/tdad/projectexamplesummtable(2).doc (accessed November 18, 2013).

85. *The long road toward juvenile justice in Papua New Guinea*, the United Nations Children's Fund, available at http://www.unicef.org/infobycountry/papuang_30356.html (accessed November 18, 2013).

86. Community Peace Programme, available at http://www.ideaswork.org/ (accessed March 28, 2012). The Community Peace Programme model has been adopted in Argentina, Australia, Brazil, Canada, and Uganda.

87. Charmain Badenhorst, *Overview of the Implementation of the Child Justice Act, 2008* (Act 75 of 2008), Open Society Foundation for South Africa, Pinelands, 2011.

88. Lukas Muntingh and Clare Ballard, *Report on Children in Prison in South Africa*, Civil Society Prison Reform Initiative, Cape Town, 2012, p. 19, available at http://cspri.org.za/publications/research-reports/report-on-children-in-prison-in-south-africa (accessed November 18, 2013).

89. *The Lilongwe Declaration on Accessing Legal Aid in the Criminal Justice System in Africa.*

90. Much of the material in this section is drawn from *Improving Pretrial Justice: The Roles of Lawyers and Paralegals*, Open Society Justice Initiative, New York, 2012.

91. Barry Walsh, *In Search of Success: Case Studies in Justice Sector Development in Sub-Saharan Africa*, The World Bank, Washington DC, June 2010, p. 26, available at http://www-wds.worldbank.org/external/default/WDSContentServer/WDSP/IB/2010/10/22/000334955_20101022003638/Rendered/PDF/574450ESW0P112in0Africa010June02010.pdf (accessed November 18, 2013).

92. Lee Bridges and Satnam Choongh, *Improving Police Station Legal Advice*, Law Society, London, 1998.

93. *The Lilongwe Declaration on Accessing Legal Aid in the Criminal Justice System in Africa, and Lilongwe Plan of Action for Accessing Legal Aid in the Criminal Justice System in Africa* (2004), available at http://www.penalreform.org/publications/lilongwe-declaration-accessing-legal-aid-criminal-justice-system-africa (accessed November 18, 2013).

94. *Dhaka Declaration on Reducing Overcrowding in Prisons in South Asia (2010)*, available at http://www.penalreform.org/resource/dhaka-declaration-reducing-overcrowding-prisons-south-asia/ (accessed November 18, 2013).

95. Guideline 14, *United Nations Principles and Guidelines on Access to Legal Aid in Criminal Justice Systems*, Commission on Crime Prevention and Criminal Justice, Twenty-first session, Vienna, 23–27 April 2012, E/CN.15/2012/L.14/Rev.1.

96. Sonkita Conteh and Lotta Teale, *New Legal Aid Law in Sierra Leone Embraces the Role of Paralegals*, Open Society Justice Initiative, available at http://www.soros.org/voices/new-legal-aid-law-sierra-leone-embraces-role-paralegals (accessed November 18, 2013).

97. "Locked Up and Forgotten?," Conference on Penal Reform in Developing Countries, October 6-7, 2010, available at http://www.penalreform.org/wp-content/uploads/2013/05/Dhaka-Declaration-FINAL-version-October-7_0.pdf (accessed November 18, 2013). See also, *Improvement of the Real Situation of Overcrowding in Prisons*, Deutsche Gesellschaft für Internationale Zusammenarbeit, Dakar, April 2012 (informational brochure).

98. Clifford Msiska, "On the Front Lines: Insights from Malawi's Paralegal Advisory Service," *Justice Initiatives: Pretrial Detention*, Open Society Justice Initiative, New York, Spring 2008, p. 76.

99. *Sierra Leone: Justice Sector Development Programme, Annual Report 2010*, U.K. Department for International Development, London, 2010.

100. *Paralegals in Rwanda: A Case Study by Penal Reform International*, Penal Reform International, London, January 2012, p. 6, available at http://www.penalreform.org/publications/paralegals-rwanda-case-study (accessed November 18, 2013).

101. Adam Stapleton, "Empowering the Poor to Access Criminal Justice – A Grass-Roots Perspective," *Legal Empowerment Working Papers* No. 2, International Development Law Organization, Rome, 2009, p. 23.

102. *Evaluation: Uganda Paralegal Advisory Services 2007–2010*, The Law & Development Partnership, London, December 2010 (unpublished document), pp. 26–27.

103. *Evaluation: Uganda Paralegal Advisory Services 2007–2010*, The Law & Development Partnership, London, December 2010 (unpublished document), p. 27. Figures as of October 2007.

104. In Malawi many communities generally do not trust the formal courts and sometimes take the law into their own hands when a defendant is released awaiting trial. See Shima Baradaran, "The Presumption of Innocence and Pretrial Detention in Malawi," *Malawi Law Journal*, Vol. 4, Issue 1, 2010, p. 128.

105. *Access to Justice in Africa and Beyond: Making the Rule of Law a Reality*, Penal Reform International and Bluhm Legal Clinic of the Northwestern University School of Law, Chicago, 2007, pp. 67–68.

106. Ed Cape, *Defending Suspects at Police Stations*, 5th edition, Legal Action Group, London, 2006.

107. International Renaissance Foundation, *Public Defender Offices Report 2009*, IRF, Kyiv, 2010.

108. *Rights Enforcement and Public Law Centre (REPLACE) Final Narrative Report: Reporting period: July 2008 to July 2009*, unpublished document. See also Anthony Nwapa, "Building and Sustaining Change: Pretrial Detention Reform in Nigeria," in Justice Initiatives: Pretrial Detention, Open Society Foundations, New York, 2008.

109. Timap for Justice website, available at www.timapforjustice.org/ (accessed November 18, 2013).

110. *Final Report on the Criminal Justice Pilot Supported by OSJI*, Timap for Justice, Freetown, 2012 (unpublished document). Personal communication with Timap staff, April 2012. See also *Between Law and Society: Paralegals and the Provision of Primary Justice Services in Sierra Leone*, Open Society Justice Initiative, New York, 2006.

111. Douglas L. Colbert, Ray Paternoster, and Shawn Bushway, "Do Attorneys Really Matter? The Empirical and Legal Case for the Right of Counsel at Bail," *Cardozo Law Review* Vol. 23, 2002, pp. 1719–1793.

112. Heinz Schöch, *Der Einfluß der Strafverteidigung auf den Verlauf der Untersuchungshaft: Erfahrungsbericht über ein Projekt der Hessischen Landesregierung zur "Entschädigung von Anwälten für die Rechtsberatung von Untersuchungsgefangenen,"* Nomos Verlag, Baden-Baden, 1997.

113. *Access to Justice in Africa and Beyond: Making the Rule of Law a Reality*, Penal Reform International and Bluhm Legal Clinic of the Northwestern University School of Law, Chicago, 2007, p. 68.

114. *Handbook on Improving Access to Legal Aid in Africa, Criminal Justice Handbook Series*, United Nations Office on Drugs and Crime, New York, 2011, p. 35, available at http://www.unodc.org/documents/justice-and-prison-reform/Webbook_Legal_Aid_in_Africa_lr.pdf (accessed November 18, 2013).

115. *P.A.S.I. Newsletter* No. 15, January 2012, p. 9.

116. *Improvement of the Real Situation of Overcrowding in Prisons*, Deutsche Gesellschaft für Internationale Zusammenarbeit, Dakar, April 2012 (informational brochure). Personal communication, Syed Ziaul Hasan, National Programme Coordinator, Improvement of the Real Situation of Overcrowding in Prisons, Deutsche Gesellschaft für Internationale Zusammenarbeit, Dakar, May 2, 2012.

117. See: *Rational and Transparent Bail Decision Making: Moving from a Cash-Based to a Risk-Based Process*, Pretrial Justice Institute, Washington D.C., March 2012, pp. 29–20, available at http://www.pretrial.org/Featured%20Resources%20Documents/Rational%20and%20Transparent%20Bail%20Decision%20Making.pdf (accessed November 18, 2013).

118. *A.B.A. Standards for Criminal Justice: Pretrial Release*, American Bar Association, Washington D.C., 2007, Third Edition, Standard 10-2.1, available at http://www.americanbar.org/publications/criminal_justice_section_archive/crimjust_standards_pretrialrelease_toc.html (accessed November 18, 2013).

119. *Better Bail Decisions: A Project to Improve the Quality and Consistency of Bail Decision Making by Courts in England and Wales, Spain and the Czech Republic*, The Law Society of England and Wales, London (undated), pp. 53–55, available at http://www.cak.cz/files/255/bb040701.pdf (accessed April 26, 2012).

120. *Better Bail Decisions: A Project to Improve the Quality and Consistency of Bail Decision Making by Courts in England and Wales, Spain and the Czech Republic*, The Law Society of England and Wales, London (undated), p. 61, available at http://www.cak.cz/files/255/bb040701.pdf (accessed November 18, 2013).

121. Clare Ballard, *Research Report on Remand Detention in South Africa: An Overview of the Current Law and Proposals for Reform*, Civil Society Prison Reform Initiative, Cape Town, 2011, p. 21, available at http://cspri.org.za/publications/research-reports/Remand%20detention%20in%20South%20Africa.pdf (accessed November 18, 2013).

122. *UNODC Criminal Justice Assessment Toolkit, Access to Justice: The Prosecution Service*, United Nations Office on Drugs and Crime, New York, 2006, pp. 8–9, available at http://www.unodc.org/documents/justice-and-prison-reform/cjat_eng/3_Prosecution_Service.pdf (accessed November 18, 2013).

123. *Guidelines on the Role of Prosecutors*, Guideline 17, Adopted by the Eighth United Nations Congress on the Prevention of Crime and the Treatment of Offenders, Havana, Cuba, August 27 to September 7 1990, available at http://www.ohchr.org/EN/ProfessionalInterest/Pages/RoleOfProsecutors.aspx (accessed November 18, 2013).

124. See *Handbook on Strategies to Reduce Overcrowding in Prisons*, United Nations Office on Drugs and Crime, (forthcoming).

125. *Guidelines on the Role of Prosecutors*, Adopted by the Eighth United Nations Congress on the Prevention of Crime and the Treatment of Offenders, Havana, Cuba, August 27 to September 7, 1990, available at http://www.ohchr.org/EN/ProfessionalInterest/Pages/RoleOfProsecutors.aspx (accessed November 18, 2013).

126. Todd Foglesong, "Encouraging Trends in Pretrial Detention in Russia," *Research in Brief: Safety and Justice*, Harvard Kennedy School, Cambridge MA, June 2011, p. 1.

127. *Rational and Transparent Bail Decision Making: Moving From a Cash-Based to a Risk-Based Process*, Pretrial Justice Institute, Washington DC, March 2012, pp. 24–25, available at http://www.pretrial.org/Featured%20Resources%20Documents/Rational%20and%20Transparent%20Bail%20Decision%20Making.pdf (accessed May 8, 2012).

128. Thomas H. Cohen and Tracey Kyckelhahn, *Felony Defendants in Large Urban Counties, 2006*, Bureau of Justice Statistics, Washington D.C., May 2010, p. 1, available at http://bjs.ojp.usdoj.gov/content/pub/pdf/fdluc06.pdf (accessed May 9, 2012).

129. *National Prosecution Standards*, Third Edition, National District Attorneys Association, Alexandria VA, 2009, paragraphs 4-1.1 to 4-1.3, available at http://www.ndaa.org/pdf/NDAA%20NPS%203rd%20Ed.%20w%20Revised%20Commentary.pdf (accessed November 18, 2013).

130. *Philadelphia's Less Crowded, Less Costly Jails: Taking Stock of a Year of Change and the Challenges that Remain*, Pew Charitable Trust: Philadelphia Research Initiative, July 2011, p. 9, available at http://www.pewtrusts.org/uploadedFiles/wwwpewtrustsorg/Reports/Philadelphia_Research_Initiative/Philadelphia-Jail-Population.pdf (accessed November 18, 2013).

131. *Philadelphia's Less Crowded, Less Costly Jails: Taking Stock of a Year of Change and the Challenges that Remain*, Pew Charitable Trust: Philadelphia Research Initiative, July 2011, p. 9, available at http://www.pewtrusts.org/uploadedFiles/wwwpewtrustsorg/Reports/Philadelphia_Research_Initiative/Philadelphia-Jail-Population.pdf (accessed November 18, 2013).

132. *Philadelphia's Less Crowded, Less Costly Jails: Taking Stock of a Year of Change and the Challenges that Remain*, Pew Charitable Trust: Philadelphia Research Initiative, July 2011, p. 13, available at http://www.pewtrusts.org/uploadedFiles/wwwpewtrustsorg/Reports/Philadelphia_Research_Initiative/Philadelphia-Jail-Population.pdf (accessed November 18, 2013).

133. *Philadelphia's Less Crowded, Less Costly Jails: Taking Stock of a Year of Change and the Challenges that Remain*, Pew Charitable Trust: Philadelphia Research Initiative, July 2011, pp. 13–14, available at http://www.pewtrusts.org/uploadedFiles/wwwpewtrustsorg/Reports/Philadelphia_Research_Initiative/Philadelphia-Jail-Population.pdf (accessed November 18, 2013).

134. *Philadelphia's Less Crowded, Less Costly Jails: Taking Stock of a Year of Change and the Challenges that Remain*, Pew Charitable Trust: Philadelphia Research Initiative, July 2011, p. 14, available at http://www.pewtrusts.org/uploadedFiles/wwwpewtrustsorg/Reports/Philadelphia_Research_Initiative/Philadelphia-Jail-Population.pdf (accessed November 18, 2013). In any scheme such as S.M.A.R.T., it is important that sufficient care is taken not to push defendants—especially those not represented by counsel—into pleading guilty on charges they did not commit or for which they should not be convicted. For a discussion of the dangers and benefits of plea bargaining, see Oren Gazal-Ayal, "Partial Ban on Plea Bargains," *Cardozo Law Review*, Vol. 27, No. 5, March 2006, pp. 2295–2351.

135. *Ethics: A Practical Guide to the Ethical Code of Conduct for Members of the National Prosecuting Authority*, National Prosecuting Authority, Pretoria, March 2004, sections 3.3.3 and 3.3.8, available at http://www.npa.gov.za/UploadedFiles/Ethics%20%28Final%29.pdf (accessed November 18, 2013).

136. *Awaiting Trial Detainee Guidelines*, National Prosecuting Authority, Pretoria (undated), available at http://www.npa.gov.za/UploadedFiles/ATD%20Guidelines%20%283c%29%20doc%20final.pdf (accessed November 18, 2013).

137. *Custody Time Limits: National Standard for the Effective Management of Prosecution Cases Involving Custody Time Limits*, Crown Prosecution Service, London, August 2011, available at http://www.cps.gov.uk/legal/assets/uploads/files/National%20Standard%20-%20Custody%20Time%20Limits.doc (accessed November 18, 2013).

138. *International Experience in Reform of Penal Management Systems: A Report by the International Centre for Prison Studies*. International Centre For Prison Studies, London, 2008, No. 78, paragraphs 5, 14, and 15, available at http://www.prisonstudies.org/images/downloads/International_Experience.pdf (accessed November 18, 2013).

139. *International Experience in Reform of Penal Management Systems: A Report by the International Centre for Prison Studies,* International Centre For Prison Studies, London, 2008, No. 78, paragraphs 14 and 15, available at http://www.prisonstudies.org/images/downloads/International_Experience.pdf (accessed November 18, 2013). This has also been recognized in the European Prison Rules. Rule 71 states that "Prisons shall be the responsibility of public authorities separate from military, police or criminal investigation services." See *Council of Europe Committee of Ministers Recommendation Rec(2006)2, of the Committee of Ministers to member states on the European Prison Rules,* Adopted by the Committee of Ministers on 11 January 2006 at the 952nd meeting of the Ministers' Deputies, available at https://wcd.coe.int/ViewDoc.jsp?id=955747 (accessed November 18, 2013).

140. See Olga Schwartz, "Ebb Tide: The Russian Reforms of 2001 and Their Reversal," *Justice Initiatives: Pretrial Detention*, Open Society Justice Initiative, New York, Spring 2008, pp. 103–120.

141. Anthea Hucklesby, "Keeping the Lid on the Prison Remand Population: The Experience in England and Wales," *Current Issues in Criminal Justice*, Vol. 21, No. 1, July 2009, p. 19.

142. Pretrial Evaluation and Supervision services exist in various guises in the United States (where they are known as Pretrial Services), the United Kingdom (Bail Information and Supervision Service), Australia (Bail Assessment Program), Ireland (Bail Support and Supervision Schemes), Argentina (Oficinas de Medidas Alternativas y Sustitutivas), Chile (Servicios Previos al Juicio), Mexico (Unidad de Medidas Cautelares para Adolescentes), and Peru (Servicios Previos al Juicio). In the late 1990s and early 2000s, a number of South Africa courts experimented with such services (Pretrial Services).

143. John Clark and D. Alan Henry, *The Pretrial Release Decision Making Process: Goals, Current Practices, and Challenges,* November 1996.

144. *A Second Look at Alleviating Jail Overcrowding: A Systems Perspective,* Bureau of Justice Assistance, U.S. Department of Justice, Washington D.C., October 2000, p. 46; Barry Mahoney et al., *Pretrial Services Programs: Responsibilities and Potential,* U.S. Department of Justice, National Institute of Justice, Washington D.C., March 2001, pp. 22–34.

145. Charles Lloyd, *Bail Information Schemes: Practice and Effect*, Research and Planning Unit, Paper No. 69, Home Office, London, 1992; David Godson and Christopher Mitchell, *Bail Information Schemes in English Magistrates' Courts: A Review of the Data*, Inner London Probation Service, London, 1991. See also Patricia M Morgan and Paul F Henderson, *Remand Decisions and Offending on Bail: Evaluation of the Bail Process Project,* Home Office Research Study 184, Home Office, London, 1998, available at http://www.nationalarchives.gov.uk/erorecords/ho/421/2/rds/pdfs/hors184.pdf (accessed April 30, 2012).

146. Mandeep K. Dhami, "Do Bail Information Schemes Really Affect Bail Decisions?," *The Howard Journal,* Vol. 41 No. 3, July 2002, p. 247.

147. *Bail Information Schemes Probation Circular* 19/2005, National Probation Service for England and Wales, Home Office, London, March 2005, available at http://www.scribd.com/doc/1429884/UK-Home-Office-PC19202005 (accessed April 30, 2012).

148. This list is slightly adapted from a list found in the American Bar Association Pretrial Release Standards (2nd Edition, February 2002). These standards list factors that can be considered as indicative of non-appearance or danger to the community when deciding whether to release a defendant on his own recognizance: http://www.americanbar.org/publications/criminal_justice_section_archive/crimjust_standards_pretrialrelease_toc.html.

149. *Bail Reform Act 1981–2: Hearings Before The Subcomm. on Courts, Civil Liberties, and the Administration of Justice of the House Comm. on the Judiciary*, 97th Cong., 1st and 2d Sess., pp. 85–86 (Testimony of Guy Willets, Administrative Office of the U.S. Courts).

150. Gabrielle Denning-Cotter, *Bail Support in Australia*, Indigenous Justice Clearinghouse, April 2008, p. 1, available at http://www.indigenousjustice.gov.au/briefs/brief002.pdf (accessed November 18, 2013).

151. See, *Bail Bond Supervision in Three Counties: Report on Intensive Pretrial Supervision in Nassau, Bronx, and Essex Counties*, Vera Institute of Justice, New York, August 1995.

152. Gabrielle Denning-Cotter, *Bail Support in Australia*, Indigenous Justice Clearinghouse, April 2008, p. 1, available at http://www.indigenousjustice.gov.au/briefs/brief002.pdf (accessed November 18, 2013).

153. "The D.C. Pretrial Services Agency: Lessons from Five Decades of Innovation and Growth," *Case Studies*, Vol. 2, No. 1, Pretrial Justice Institute, Washington D.C. (undated), p. 2.

154. Ana Aguilar García and Javier Carrasco Solís, *Servicios Previos al Juicio. Manual de implementación*, Instituto de Justicia Procesal Penal, Mexico City, 2011, pp. 13–15. Personal communication with Javier Carrasco, Director, Instituto de Justicia Procesal Penal, Mexico City, March 23, 2012.

155. Sue Thomas, Nacro Cymru, and Anthea Hucklesby, *Remand Management*, Youth Justice Board, London (undated), p. 40, available at http://www.yjbstandards.org/bexley/resources/documents/Ref%2039%20KEEP%20RemandManagementSource.pdf (accessed November 18, 2013).

156. Sinead Freeman, "The Experience of Young People Remanded in Custody: A Case for Bail Support and Supervision Schemes," *Irish Probation Journal*, Vol. 5, September 2008, p. 100.

157. Sue Thomas, *National Evaluation of the Bail Supervision and Support Scheme Funded by the Youth Justice Board for England and Wales from April 1999 to March 2002*, Youth Justice Board for England and Wales, London, 2005, p. 144, available at http://yjbpublications.justice.gov.uk/en-gb/Resources/Downloads/National%20Evaluation%20of%20the%20Bail%20Supervision%20and%20Support%20Schemes.pdf (accessed November 18, 2013).

158. Ewen McCaig and Jeremy Hardin, *Evaluation of Experimental Bail Supervision Schemes*, Scottish Executive Central Research Unit, Edinburgh, 1999, available at http://www.scotland.gov.uk/Publications/1999/10/86695596-53f5-44df-8392-824beb221090 (accessed November 18, 2013).

159. See: *Rational and Transparent Bail Decision Making: Moving from a Cash-Based to a Risk-Based Process*, Pretrial Justice Institute, Washington D.C., March 2012, pp. 29–20, available at http://www.pretrial.org/Featured%20Resources%20Documents/Rational%20and%20Transparent%20Bail%20Decision%20Making.pdf (accessed November 18, 2013).

160. Marie VanNostrand, "Alternatives to Pretrial Detention: Southern District of Iowa," *Federal Probation*, Vol. 74, No. 3, December 2010, available at http://www.uscourts.gov/viewer.aspx?doc=/uscourts/FederalCourts/PPS/Fedprob/2010-12/index.html (accessed November 18, 2013).

161. James Austin, Barry Krisberg, and Paul Litsky, "The Effectiveness of Supervised Pretrial Release," *Crime & Delinquency*, Vol. 31, No. 4, October 1985, pp. 147–155.

162. *Bail Bond Supervision in Three Counties: Report on Intensive Pretrial Supervision in Nassau, Bronx, and Essex Counties*, Vera Institute of Justice, New York, August 1995, pp. 15–16, available at http://www.vera.org/pubs/bail-bond-supervision-three-counties-report-intensive-pretrial-supervision-nassau-bronx-and (accessed November 18, 2013).

163. *Bail Bond Supervision in Three Counties: Report on Intensive Pretrial Supervision in Nassau, Bronx, and Essex Counties*, Vera Institute of Justice, New York, August 1995, pp. 15–16, available at http://www.vera.org/pubs/bail-bond-supervision-three-counties-report-intensive-pretrial-supervision-nassau-bronx-and (accessed November 18, 2013).

164. Personal communication with Clifford Msiska, Director, Paralegal Advisory Service Institute, Lilongwe, Malawi, April 2012.

165. Murali Karnam, *Conditions of Detention in the Prisons of Karnataka*, Commonwealth Human Rights Initiative, New Delhi, 2010, p. 20, available at http://www.humanrightsinitiative.org/publications/prisons/conditions_of_detention_in_the_prisons_of_karnataka.pdf (accessed November 18, 2013). See also Kundan Pandey, "Cops Crunch Hits Escorting Prisoners," *The Times of India*, March 23, 2012, available at http://articles.timesofindia.indiatimes.com/2012-03-23/indore/31229627_1_inmates-superintendent-cops (accessed November 18, 2013).

166. *Pre-Trial Detention Taskforce: Sub-Committee Action Proposal*, Ministry of Justice and the Supreme Court of Liberia, Monrovia, June 2011, p. 5 (unpublished document). See also Boima Yates, "Justice Releases 1500 Inmates...As Pre-Trial Program Gains Momentum," *The Media Watch*, April 16, 2012, available at http://themediawatchlib.blogspot.com/2012/04/justice-releases-1500-inmates.html (accessed November 18, 2013).

167. "Mimiko Commissions Africa's First Court in Prison," *Nigerian Tribune*, April 3, 2012.

168. See also "Seven acquitted in 'Jail Adalat,'" *One India News*, January 27, 2011; "32 Prisoners Released at Jail Adalat," *The Hindu*, May 29, 2011.

169. Priti Bharadwaj, *Liberty at the Cost of Innocence: A Report on Jail Adalats in India*, Commonwealth Human Rights Initiative, New Delhi, 2009, pp. 33-35, available at http://www.humanrightsinitiative.org/publications/prisons/liberty_at_the_cost_of_innocence.pdf (accessed November 18, 2013).

170. Priti Bharadwaj, *Liberty at the Cost of Innocence: A Report on Jail Adalats in India*, Commonwealth Human Rights Initiative, New Delhi, 2009, p. 15, available at http://www.humanrightsinitiative.org/publications/prisons/liberty_at_the_cost_of_innocence.pdf (accessed November 18, 2013).

171. Anthea Hucklesby, "Keeping the Lid on the Prison Remand Population: The Experience in England and Wales," *Current Issues in Criminal Justice*, Vol. 21, No. 1, July 2009, pp. 13–14.

172. *Innocent Until Proven Guilty: Tackling the Overuse of Custodial Remand*, Prison Reform Trust, London, October 2011, p. 2, available at http://www.prisonreformtrust.org.uk/Portals/0/Documents/Remand%20Briefing%20FINAL.PDF (accessed November 18, 2013).

173. See: *Handbook on Strategies to Reduce Overcrowding in Prisons*, United Nations Office on Drugs and Crime (forthcoming).

174. See: *Handbook on Strategies to Reduce Overcrowding in Prisons*, United Nations Office on Drugs and Crime (forthcoming).

175. See also Tapio Lappi-Seppälä, "Enhancing the Community Alternatives – Getting the Measures Accepted and Implemented," Resource Material Series No. 61, 2003, United Nations Asia and Far East Institute for the Prevention of Crime and the Treatment of Offenders, Tokyo, available at http://www.unafei.or.jp/english/pdf/RS_No61/No61_11VE_Seppala3.pdf (accessed November 18, 2013).

176. For example: Thomas Carothers, *Aiding Democracy Abroad: The Learning Curve*, Carnegie Endowment for International Peace, Washington, D.C., 1999; David M. Trubek, "The 'Rule of Law' in Development Assistance: Past, Present, and Future," in David M. Trubek and Alvaro Santos (eds.), *The New Law and Economic Development*, Cambridge University Press, Cambridge, 2006; Carol V. Rose, "The 'New' Law and Development Movement in the Post-Cold War Era: A Vietnam Case Study," Law and Society Review, Vol. 32, 1998; David M. Trubek and Marc Galanter, "Scholars in Self-Estrangement: Some Reflections on the Crisis in Law and Development Studies in the United States," *Wisconsin Law Review*, Issue 4, 1974, pp. 1062–1102; James Gardner, *Legal Imperialism: American Lawyers and Foreign Aid in Latin America*, University of Wisconsin Press, Madison, 1980; José E Alvarez, "Promoting the 'Rule of Law' in Latin America: Problems and Prospects," *George Washington Journal of International Law and Economics*, Vol. 25, No. 2, 1991; Wade Channell, "Lessons Not Learned about Legal Reform," in Thomas Carothers (ed.), Promoting the *Rule of Law Abroad: In Search of Knowledge*, Carnegie Endowment for International Peace, Washington, D.C., 2006; Henrik Alffram, Equal Access to Justice. *A Mapping of Experiences*, Sida, 2011; Eric Scheye, *Some thoughts on law and justice: What to do about the crisis of "confidence"?*, AusAID, August 2011.

177. Jonathan L. Hafetz, *Pretrial Detention, Human Rights, and Judicial Reform in Latin America*, Fordham International Law Journal, Volume 26, Issue 6, p. 1772.

# APPENDIX: INTERNATIONAL AND REGIONAL STANDARDS, NORMS, AND JURISPRUDENCE

1. For information on international standards, norms, and jurisprudence about conditions of pretrial detention see: *United Nations Standard Minimum Rules for the Treatment of Prisoners*, 1955 and 1977, Articles 8, 84-93, available at http://www2.ohchr.org/english/law/treatmentprisoners.htm (accessed July 12, 2012); *International Covenant on Civil and Political Rights*, 1966, Article 10, available at

http://www2.ohchr.org/english/law/ccpr.htm (accessed July 10, 2012); *Convention Against Torture and Other Cruel, Inhuman or Degrading Treatment of Punishment*, 1987, http://www2.ohchr.org/english/law/cat.htm (12 July 2012); Body of Principles for the Protection of all Persons Under Any Form of Detention or Imprisonment, 1988, principles 8, 19-27, available at http://www.un.org/documents/ga/res/43/a43r173.htm (accessed July 12, 2012); *Human Rights and Pre-Trial Detention. A Handbook of International Standards relating to Pre-trial Detention*, Centre for Human Rights: Crime Prevention and Criminal Justice Branch, United Nations, New York, 1994, pp. 93-98, 126-150; Jeremy McBride, *Pre-Trial Detention in the OSCE area*, ODIHR Background Paper 1999/2, Organization for Security and Co-operation in Europe, 1999, pp 27-32, available at http://www.osce.org/odihr/42851 (accessed July 12, 2012); *Handbook of International Standards on Pretrial Detention Procedure*, American Bar Association, Washington D.C., 2010, pp 24-27, available at http://www.cejamericas.org/manualsaj/%5BABA%5DHandbookofInternationalStandardsonPretrialDetentionProcedure2010.pdf (accessed July 12, 2012).

2. See: Jeremy McBride, *Pre-Trial Detention in the OSCE Area*, ODIHR Background Paper 1999/2, Organization for Security and Co-operation in Europe, 1999, available at http://www.osce.org/odihr/42851 (accessed July 13, 2013); *Handbook of International Standards on Pretrial Detention Procedure*, American Bar Association, Washington D.C., 2010, available at http://www.cejamericas.org/manualsaj/%5BABA%5DHandbookofInternationalStandardsonPretrialDetentionProcedure2010.pdf (accessed July 12, 2012).

3. Universal Declaration of Human Rights, adopted by General Assembly Resolution 217A (III), 10 December 1948, Articles 8 and 9.

4. Universal Declaration of Human Rights, adopted by General Assembly Resolution 217A (III), 10 December 1948, Article 11(1).

5. International Covenant on Civil and Political Rights, Article 9(3), available at http://www2.ohchr.org/english/law/ccpr.htm (accessed July 10, 2012).

6. Body of Principles for the Protection of All Persons under Any Form of Detention or Imprisonment, adopted by General Assembly Resolution A/RES/43/173, 9 December 1988, Principle 39, available at http://www.un.org/documents/ga/res/43/a43r173.htm (July 10, 2012).

7. Rule 6, *United Nations Standard Minimum Rules for Non-custodial Measures* (The Tokyo Rules), adopted by General Assembly resolution 45/110 on 14 December 1990, available at http://www2.ohchr.org/english/law/tokyorules.htm (accessed July 10, 2012).

8. Laurel Townhead, *Pre-Trial Detention of Women and Its Impact on Children*, Quaker United Nations Office, Geneva, February 2007, p 9, available at http://www.quno.org/geneva/pdf/humanrights/women-in-prison/WiP-pretrial-detention200702-English.pdf (accessed July 10, 2012).

9. *Eighth United Nations Congress on the Prevention of Crime and the Treatment of Offenders*, Havana, August 27 –September 7, 1990, chapter 1, section C, paragraph 2(b).

10. The United Nations Human Rights Committee is a body of independent experts that monitors implementation of the International Covenant on Civil and Political Rights by its state parties. All states parties are obliged to submit regular reports to the committee on how the rights are being implemented. The committee examines each report and addresses its concerns and recommendations to the state party in the form of "concluding observations." The First Optional Protocol to the Covenant gives the committee competence to examine individual complaints with regard to alleged violations of the covenant by states parties to the protocol. For those countries, the Human Rights Committee functions as a mechanism for the international redress of human rights abuses.

11. UN Human Rights Committee (HRC), *UN Human Rights Committee: Concluding Observations: Argentina*, November 15, 2000, CCPR/CO/70/ARG, paragraph 10, available at http://www.unhcr.org/refworld/docid/3b39f0977.html (accessed July 10, 2012); UN Human Rights Committee (HRC), *UN Human Rights Committee: Concluding Observations, Italy*, April 24, 2006, CCPR/C/ITA/CO/5, paragraph 14, available at http://www.unhcr.org/refworld/docid/453777852.html (accessed July 10, 2012).

12. *Human Rights and Pre-Trial Detention. A Handbook of International Standards relating to Pre-Trial Detention*, Professional Training Series no. 3, United Nations, New York, 1994, pp 14-15.

13. *Rafael Marques de Morais v. Angola*, Communication No. 1128/2002, U.N. Doc. CCPR/C/83/D/1128/2002 (2005) (paragraph 6.1), available at http://www1.umn.edu/humanrts/undocs/1128-2002.html (accessed July 11, 2012).

14. *Rafael Marques de Morais v. Angola*, Communication No. 1128/2002, U.N. Doc. CCPR/C/83/D/1128/2002 (2005) (paragraph 6.1), available at http://www1.umn.edu/humanrts/undocs/1128-2002.html (accessed July 11, 2012).

15. Laurel Townhead, *Pre-Trial Detention of Women and Its Impact on Children*, Quaker United Nations Office, Geneva, February 2007, p. 9, available at http://www.quno.org/geneva/pdf/humanrights/women-in-prison/WiP-pretrial-detention200702-English.pdf (accessed July 10, 2012).

16. Clare Ballard, *Research Report on Remand Detention in South Africa: An Overview of the Current Law and Proposals for Reform*, Civil Society Prison Reform Initiative, Cape Town, 2011, available at http://www.cspri.org.za/publications/research-reports/Remand%20detention%20in%20South%20Africa.pdf (accessed July 12, 2012).

17. Article 7(1), African Charter on Human and Peoples' Rights, available at http://www1.umn.edu/humanrts/instree/z1afchar.htm (accessed July 10, 2012).

18. Article 7(1)(d), African Charter on Human and Peoples' Rights, available at http://www1.umn.edu/humanrts/instree/z1afchar.htm (accessed July 10, 2012). In *Huri-Laws v. Nigeria*, the African Commission on Human and Peoples' Rights found that detaining two applicants for, respectively, five months and a bit over one month without their being brought before a judge violated the right to be tried within a reasonable time by an independent court or tribunal. (*Huri-Laws v. Nigeria*, African Commission on Human and Peoples' Rights, Comm. No. 225/98 (2000), paragraphs 5, 7, 10 and 46, available at http://www1.umn.edu/humanrts/africa/comcases/225-98.html (accessed July 10, 2012). In another ruling the African Commission held that detaining someone for seven years without a trial "violates the 'reasonable time' standard" under the African Charter (*Alhassan Abubaker v. Ghana*, African Commission on Human and Peoples' Rights, Comm. No. 103/93 (1996), paragraph 12, available at http://www1.umn.edu/humanrts/africa/comcases/103-93.html (accessed July 10, 2012)).

19. Article 6, African Charter on Human and Peoples' Rights, http://www1.umn.edu/humanrts/instree/z1afchar.htm (10 July 2012).

20. The African Commission on Human and Peoples' Rights was established in 1986 by the African Charter on Human and Peoples' Rights. The commission is tasked with promoting and protecting rights and interpreting the African Charter.

21. *Resolution on the Right to Recourse and Fair Trial*, African Commission on Human and Peoples' Rights, Eleventh Ordinary Session, Tunis, Tunisia, March 2-9, 1992, available at http://www.achpr.org/sessions/11th/resolutions/4/ (accessed July 11, 2012).

22. *Huri-Laws v. Nigeria*, African Commission on Human and Peoples' Rights, Comm. No. 225/98 (2000), paragraph 45, available at http://www1.umn.edu/humanrts/africa/comcases/225-98.html (accessed July 10, 2012)

23. *Civil Liberties Organisation, Legal Defence Centre, Legal Defence and Assistance Project v. Nigeria*, African Commission on Human and Peoples' Rights, Comm. No. 218/98 (1998), paragraph 44, available at http://www1.umn.edu/humanrts/africa/comcases/218-98.html (accessed July 10, 2012).

24. *Achutan (on behalf of Banda) and Amnesty International (on behalf of Orton and Vera Chirwa) v. Malawi*, African Commission on Human and Peoples' Rights, Comm. No. 64/92, 68/92, and 78/92 (1995), paragraph 9, available at http://www1.umn.edu/humanrts/africa/comcases/64-92b.html (accessed July 10, 2012). See also Civil Liberties Organization v. Nigeria, African Commission on Human and Peoples' Rights, Comm. No. 129/94 (1995), paragraph 18, available at http://www1.umn.edu/humanrts/africa/comcases/129-94.html (accessed July 10, 2012).

25. *Civil Liberties Organisation, Legal Defence Centre, Legal Defence and Assistance Project v. Nigeria*, African Commission on Human and Peoples' Rights, Comm. No. 218/98 (1998), paragraphs 26 & 44, available at http://www1.umn.edu/humanrts/africa/comcases/218-98.html (accessed July 10, 2012).

26. *Amnesty International and Others v. Sudan*, African Commission on Human and Peoples' Rights, Comm. No. 48/90, 50/91, 52/91, 89/93 (1999), paragraph 68, available at http://www1.umn.edu/humanrts/africa/comcases/48-90_50-91_52-91_89-93.html (accessed July 10, 2012).

27. *Constitutional Rights Project and Civil Liberties Organisation v. Nigeria*, African Commission on Human and Peoples' Rights, Comm. No. 102/93 (1998), paragraph 55, available at http://www1.umn.edu/humanrts/africa/comcases/102-93.html (accessed July 10, 2012).

28. *Free Legal Assistance Group and Others v. Zaire*, African Commission on Human and Peoples' Rights, Comm. No. 25/89, 47/90, 56/91, 100/93 (1995), paragraph 42, available at http://www1.umn.edu/humanrts/africa/comcases/25-89_47-90_56-91_100-93.html (accessed July 10, 2012).

29. *Organisation Mondiale Contre La Torture v. Rwanda*, African Commission on Human and Peoples' Rights, Comm. Nos. 27/89, 46.91, 49/91, 99/93 (1996), paragraph 28, available at http://www1.umn.edu/humanrts/africa/comcases/27-89.html (accessed July 10, 2012).

30. *International Pen and Others v. Nigeria*, African Commission on Human and Peoples' Rights, Comm. Nos. 137/94, 139/94, 154/96 and 161/97 (1998), paragraph 83, available at http://www1.umn.edu/humanrts/africa/comcases/137-94_139-94_154-96_161-97.html (accessed July 10, 2012).

31. *European Convention for the Protection of Human Rights and Fundamental Freedoms*, November 4, 1950, Council of Europe, available at http://www.unhcr.org/refworld/docid/3ae6b3b04.html (accessed July 11, 2012).

32. *Bazorkina v Russia* [2006] ECHR 751, paragraph 146, available at http://hudoc.echr.coe.int/sites/eng/pages/search.aspx#{%22dmdocnumber%22:[%22807138%22],%22itemid%22:[%22001-76493%22]} (accessed July 11, 2012).

33. See: *Detained without trial: Fair Trials International's response to the European Commission's Green Paper on detention*, Fair Trials International, London, October 2011, pp. 7-8.

34. *Ilijkov v. Bulgaria* [2001] ECHR 489.

35. *Wemhoff v. Germany* [1968] ECHR 2.

36. *Tomasi v. France* [1992] ECHR 53; *Caballero v. UK* [2000] ECHR 53.

37. *Sulaoja v. Estonia* [2005] ECHR 104; *Muller v. France* [1997] ECHR 11.

38. *Matznetter v. Austria* [1969] ECHR 1; *Sulaoja v. Estonia* [2005] ECHR 104.

39. *Mangouras v. Spain* [2010] ECHR 1364, paragraph 79.

40. *Yagci and Sargin v. Turkey* [1995] ECHR 20; *Labita v. Italy* [2008] ECHR 50; *Bakhmutskiy v. Russia* (ECHR Application no. 36932/02, June 25, 2009).

41. *Tomasi v. France*, 12850/87 [1992] ECHR 53 (August 27, 1992), paragraph 91, available at www.univie.ac.at/bimtor/dateien/ecthr_1992_tomasi_vs_france.doc (accessed July 10, 2012).

42. Recommendation Rec(2006)13 of the Committee of Ministers of the Council of Europe to member states on the use of remand in custody, the conditions in which it takes place and the provision of safeguards against abuse (adopted September 27, 2006), paragraph 7(b), available at https://wcd.coe.int/ViewDoc.jsp?id=1041281&Site=CM (accessed July 10, 2012).

43. Office of the UN High Commissioner for Human Rights in association with the International Bar Association (2003) *Human Rights and the Administration of Justice: A Manual on Human Rights for Judges, Prosecutors and Lawyers* (United Nations), p. 194, available at http://www.ibanet.org/Document/Default.aspx?DocumentUid=D9B7ADB4-9A67-49E5-92C5-11DC1525D491 (accessed July 10, 2012).

44. The American Convention on Human Rights entered into force in 1978, and is binding for 24 member states of the Organization of American States at the time of writing. See http://www.oas.org/dil/access_to_information_American_Convention_on_Human_Rights.pdf (accessed July 11, 2012).

45. The American Declaration of the Rights and Duties of Man was adopted in 1948 and incorporated into the Charter of the Organization of American States through the Protocol of Buenos Aires, adopted in 1967. See http://www.oas.org/dil/1948%20American%20Declaration%20of%20the%20Rights%20and%20Duties%20of%20Man.pdf (accessed July 11, 2012).

46. *Principles and Best Practices on the Protection of Persons Deprived of Liberty in the Americas*, (Approved by the Commission during its 131st regular period of sessions, held from March 3-14, 2008), Inter-American Commission on Human Rights, available at http://www.cidh.org/basicos/english/Basic21.a.Principles%20and%20Best%20Practices%20PDL.htm (accessed July 11, 2012).

47. *Barreto Leiva v Venezuela*, Inter-American Court of Human Rights, Judgment of November 17, 2009, available at http://www.corteidh.or.cr/docs/casos/articulos/seriec_206_ing.pdf (accessed July 12, 2012).

48. International Covenant on Civil and Political Rights, Article 14(3)(d), available at http://www2.ohchr.org/english/law/ccpr.htm (accessed July 12, 2012).

49. *Basic Principles on the Role of Lawyers*, Adopted by the Eighth United Nations Congress on the Prevention of Crime and the Treatment of Offenders, Havana, Cuba, 27 August to 7 September 1990, principles 1-3, available at http://www2.ohchr.org/english/law/lawyers.htm, (accessed July 12, 2012).

50. *Improving Pretrial Justice: The Roles of Lawyers and Paralegals*, Open Society Justice Initiative, New York, 2012, p. 25, available at http://www.soros.org/reports/improving-pretrial-justice-roles-lawyers-and-paralegals (accessed July 12, 2012).

51. Committee for the Prevention of Torture, *2nd General Report*, CPT/Inf (92) 3, paragraph 36, available at http://www.cpt.coe.int/en/annual/rep-02.htm (accessed July 12, 2012).

52. *Basic Principles on the Role of Lawyers*, Adopted by the Eighth United Nations Congress on the Prevention of Crime and the Treatment of Offenders, Havana, Cuba, 27 August to 7 September 1990, principle 7, available at http://www2.ohchr.org/english/law/lawyers.htm, (accessed July 12, 2012).

53. *John Murray v. The United Kingdom* [1996] ECHR No. 18731/91; *Zaichenko v. Russia* [2010] ECHR No. 39660/02; *Dayanan v. Turkey* [2009] ECHR No. 7377/03; *Salduz v. Turkey* [2008] ECHR No. 36391/02.

54. *Demirkaya v. Turkey*, [2009] ECHR No. 31721/02; and *Brusco v. France*, [2010] ECHR No. 1466/07.

55. Council of the European Union, 12141/09, DROIPEN 69, COPEN 142, Brussels July 23, 2009, and European Commission, *Action Plan for Implementing the Stockholm Programme*, COM (2010) 171 final, Brussels April 20, 2010.

## OPEN SOCIETY JUSTICE INITIATIVE

The Open Society Justice Initiative uses law to protect and empower people around the world. Through litigation, advocacy, research, and technical assistance, the Justice Initiative promotes human rights and builds legal capacity for open societies. Our staff is based in Abuja, Amsterdam, Bishkek, Brussels, Budapest, The Hague, London, Mexico City, New York, Paris, and Washington, D.C.

www.JusticeInitiative.org

The Justice Initiative is a founding partner of the Global Campaign for Pretrial Justice, which is dedicated to reducing the excessive and arbitrary use of pretrial detention and demonstrating how this can be accomplished without undermining public safety. Activities of the campaign include documenting the scale and gravity of arbitrary and excessive pretrial detention and the dearth of effective legal aid and assistance; fostering exchanges among practitioners, researchers, and policy makers as a means of building awareness and capacity around pretrial justice; persuading governments and donors to support pretrial justice efforts; and securing adoption or improvement of international and regional standards on pretrial justice.

The campaign has given rise to regional efforts to draw attention to, and help improve, pretrial justice practices, including the Latin American Network for Pretrial Justice, the Europe-based Justicia Network, and the Promoting Pretrial Justice in Africa initiative.

Related Justice Initiative publications include *Justice Initiatives: Pretrial Detention; The Socioeconomic Impact of Pretrial Detention; Pretrial Detention and Torture: Why Pretrial Detainees Face the Greatest Risk; Pretrial Detention and Health: Unintended Consequences, Deadly Results;* and *Improving Pretrial Justice: The Roles of Lawyers and Paralegals.*

## OPEN SOCIETY FOUNDATIONS

The Open Society Foundations work to build vibrant and tolerant democracies whose governments are accountable to their citizens. Working with local communities in more than 70 countries, the Open Society Foundations support justice and human rights, freedom of expression, and access to public health and education.

www.OpenSocietyFoundations.org